DAILY SPIRITUAL DIET

2nd Quarter
May-August

ELIZABETH DAS

ENGLISH

Copyright © 2023 ELIZABETH DAS.

All rights reserved for audio, eBook (digital), and paper book. No part of this book may be used or reproduced by any means, graphic, electronic, or mechanical, including photocopying, recording, taping, or by any information storage retrieval system without the written permission of the author except in the case of brief quotations embodied in critical articles and reviews. Because of the dynamic nature of the internet, any web address links contained in this book may have changed since publication and may no longer be valid. Any people depicted in stock imagery provided by Thinkstock are models, and such images are beings used for illustrative purposes only. Certain Stock imagery © Thinkstock. Excerpt From: Elizabeth Das: "DAILY SPIRITUAL DIET'

DAILY SPIRITUAL DIET ISBN

ISBN: 978-1-961625-03-7 Paperback
ISBN: 978-1-961625-04-4 EBook-EPub
ISBN: 978-1-961625-05-1 Digital Online

Library of Congress Control Number: 202344250

CONTACT: nimmidas@gmail.com nimmidas1952@gmail.com

YOUTUBE CHANNEL "DAILY SPIRITUAL DIET 'BY ELIZABETH DAS

PREFACE

It was 1st January 2018. I was home alone, resting on the sofa. The voice of my Lord ordered me to write. In spirit, I perceived He meant every day. I said every day, meaning how and what to write every day. And the LORD said I would give you what you need to write. According to His plan, I inclined my ear to hear HIS voice as He shared a message for the day. I wrote, recorded, and put it on YouTube. I did it for 365 days by taking notes from the Lord. Now I have a message for you all who will accept it. Writing under the Instructions of the Holy Spirit, I learned that religion, organizations, denominations, and non-denomination are organized by Satan. It has a powerless system to take you away from following Jesus and put you in a different name-brand building where you learn to know of Jesus but do not learn HIM in His might and power. Long ago, I read an article written by Satanic PROPHETESS saying that if we want the kingdom of Satan, then we must convert the people to the majority, that is, Christians. And how to destroy the Kingdom of Jesus? Use the same old tactics. Target the forbidden. If the Lord Jesus overthrew the table, built a den, and put thieves there. The biggest benefit of labeling a building as a church is that they will never learn that their body is the Church of Jehovah God. Also, poor, hungry, druggy, alcoholic, possessed, and oppressed will never find salvation. Do not allow trained and taught by the Holy Spirit saints, but start a theological college for all our divided conflicting doctrines and train people to teach and preach.

What a plan! Not just wonderful but successful as well. Keep targeting women since she can be our mouthpiece. She still loves window shopping, a good bargain, and a glamorous lifestyle. They have a form of godliness but deny power. These types of doctrinal will satisfy the greed, lust of eyes, lust of the flesh, and pride of life crowd. I learned another thing, living in the boundary of religious territories will not allow people to seek, knock and ask God! The religious authority has literature and books written by false teachers and prophets. It also stops the home meetings from reaching out to our family, neighbors, and friends. That is called total control. Best of all, religion boxes speak WORD, but they do not practice. They ensure you don't do what Jesus asked but do what they say. Word works if you act accordingly without adding or subtracting. We are following everything else except Jesus. I urge you, from today, to study the one you have to follow since Jesus said follow me. Lord said I am the way, the truth, and the Life. The way to reach eternal life is by following Jesus. It was years of searching for the truth to be free from the devil's trap. We have marvelous instructions from the LORD to look for His disciples, so we don't mix up with Satan's counterfeit confounding plan. His disciple will turn the world upside down by doing miracles, healing, and supernatural work in the town. Isn't these fruits we should look out there and not in cages of religion? According to the New Testament, if we repent of all baptized in Jesus's NAME to wash away our sins, then the LORD comes in us to live. We again become Holy Spirit residents, or you may say, the house of Lord Jesus. Now our body is the church. Fellowship home to home and city to city with your brother and sister is necessary, but establishing a building is not. You are called to work. Preaching the Gospel that is good news by opening blind eyes, healing all kinds of sicknesses, healing the broken heart, and casting all sorts of demons out, is your and my job. The Holy Spirit gives the power to do supernatural things. The Spirit within us does all healing, miracles, and deliverance. We JUST need to get out there and work as Jesus did. To learn the ways of the LORD, you need to surrender and yield to His Spirit. If we do, we won't find the oppressed, possessed, sick, brokenhearted, lame, blind, and depressed creation of God. Lord Himself will do all, and you will return home rejoicing. What an excellent plan of God! Not only that, there are many benefits to being His disciples. Provisions, protection, peace, and all labor privileges are extras. You also receive the title of the beautiful mansion in an eternal place in yonder called heaven. It is definite that life's journey will be over soon shortly. May this book help you understand the definite plan of God. I have learned the Bible by doing, and you also can learn by going around and doing as it says. May Lord send you true prophets, evangelists, pastors, teachers, and apostles to train you to work in God's army. Follow Jesus! Amen!

TABLE OF CONTENTS

MAY 1

May 1 2
IT REQUIRES SACRIFICE! 2
May 2 5
BUT BY THY SPIRIT! 5
May 3 8
HOW TO ATTACH A BLESSING! 8
May 4 11
GIVE GOD A GLORY! 11
May 5 14
LEARN BY OBEYING! 14
May 6 18
ENGAGE YOURSELF WITH KINGDOM ACTIVITIES! 18
May 7 22
CHARACTERISTICS OF SPIRITUAL LEADERS! 22
May 8 25
I AM A SPOKESPERSON OF GOD! 25
May 9 28
LOOK FOR THE GREAT GOD! 28
May 10 32
SOMEONE USHERED YOU! 32
May 11 35
YOU CAN'T UNDERSTAND. JUST DO IT! 35
May 12 38
WORD GIVES PLATFORM TO GOD OR ENEMY! 38
May 13 41
YOU ARE MY RESPONSIBILITY, IF! 41
May 14 44
WHAT IS YOUR ROLE IN THE KINGDOM? 44
May 15 48
DIE TO SELF SO CHRIST CAN LIVE! 48
May 16 51
WHY AREN'T YOU USING THE TREASURE? 51
May 17 54

KNOW GOD, BE STRONG, AND DO EXPLOITS! 54

May 18 58

GOD MANAGES THE EARTH WITH EXPECTATION! 58

May 19 62

DETERMINE TO WAIT ON THE LORD! 62

May 20 65

DO NOT LET YOUR HEART FAIL WITH FEAR! 65

May 21 69

PLACE LOANED TO LIVE WITH CONDITION! 69

May 22 73

TAKE IT BACK FROM SATAN! 73

May 23 77

A LITTLE LEAVEN LEAVENETH THE WHOLE LUMP! 77

May 24 80

USE YOUR HELPER, HOLY SPIRIT! 80

May 25 83

CATCH AND LOOSE! 83

May 26 86

GOD WATCHES AND KEEPS AN ACCOUNT! 86

May 27 89

MAKE ROOM FOR GOD! 89

May 28 93

HEALING WILL COME IF YOU CLEAN FROM WITHIN! 93

May 29 97

THE DEVIL IS HIDING BEHIND RELIGIOUS CHURCHES! 97

May 30 101

THE DEVIL IS A LIAR, AND THE HOLY SPIRIT IS TRUE! 101

May 31 104

BUILD YOUR ALTAR AND NEVER LOSE IT! 104

JUNE **107**

June 1 108

FEAR THE JUDGE JESUS! 108

June 2 112

GET EGYPT OUT OF YOU! 112

June 3 115

HOW TO ACTIVATE YOUR MIRACLE!	115
June 4	118
DO WE HAVE A NOBLEMAN?	118
June 5	122
CONTINUE TILL YOU FINISH!	122
June 6	126
THE SPIRIT OF JEALOUSY IS A KILLER!	126
June 7	129
THE DEVIL USES SUMMER AS AN EXCUSE!	129
June 8	132
THE SOLUTION IS TO UPROOT THE CAUSE!	132
June 9	135
LEARN TO GIVE YOURSELF!	135
June 10	139
DIFFERENCE BETWEEN RELIGIOUS AND SPIRITUAL!	139
June 11	142
LEARN TO BATTLE WITH UNSEEN ENEMIES!	142
June 12.	146
WHAT KIND OF EXAMPLES ARE YOU?	146
June 13	150
CONFUSION OF GIFT OF TONGUE AND SPEAKING IN THE TONGUE!	150
June 14	154
GO DEEPER TO FIND THE ROOT OF THE CAUSE!	154
June 15	157
IT WILL NOT WORK!	157
June 16	160
POWER OF CONFESSION!	160
June 17	163
THE FOLLOWER OF JESUS USE HIS AUTHORITY!	163
June 18	167
LEVEL UP YOUR LIFESTYLE TO GOD'S EXPECTATIONS!	167
June 19	171
GOD IS THE SAME ALL THE TIME!	171
June 20	175

LIVE FOR JESUS!	175
June 21	179
TIME TO STAND FOR THE TRUTH!	179
June 22	182
LONG SUFFERING OF GOD!	182
June 23	186
WHEN GOD SAYS NO, DEVIL SAYS YES!	186
June 24	189
MAJOR CHANGES IN END-TIME CHURCHES!	189
June 25	193
DO YOU KNOW GOD OR KNOW OF GOD?!	193
June 26	196
WE ARE THE REPRESENTATIVES OF GOD!	196
June 27	199
ONLY HAPPENS IF GOD GRANTS!	199
June 28	202
YOU OWN NOTHING!	202
June 29	205
DO NOT PREACH, BUT TEACH BY EXAMPLE!	205
June 30	208
AM NOT IMPRESSED WITH THE DEVIL'S IDEA!	208
JULY	**212**
July 1	213
MAY I COME IN?	213
July 2	216
PRAY FOR YOUR RULERS!	216
July 3	220
PREPARATION FOR THE END TIME!	220
July 4	223
CARRY A BURDEN OF NATION!	223
July 5	226
LIVE IN GOD'S BOUNDARY!	226
July 6	229
WORKS OF DEMON!	229
July 7	232

WHY IS CHRISTIANITY BECOME POWERLESS?	232
July 8	235
MAKE IT CONTAGIOUS!	235
July 9	238
WHO IS RESPONSIBLE?	238
July 10	241
THERE IS A RIGHTFUL FIGHT!	241
July 11	244
SUCCESSFULLY DEVIL REMOVED THE BLOOD!	244
July 12	248
LOOK AT THE FRUITS!	248
July 13	251
DO NOT STOP, PRESS THOUGH!	251
July 14	255
I CARRY YOUR BURDEN; YOU CARRY MINE!	255
July 15	259
GET VIOLENT IN THE SPIRIT AND NOT IN THE FLESH!	259
July 16	262
A FALSE WITNESS WILL SUFFER PUNISHMENT!	262
July 17	265
CURSES DO NOT WORK ON BLESSED PEOPLE!	265
July 18	268
GOD WILL TRY YOU EVERY POINT!	268
July 19	272
DREAM NEEDS INTERPRETATION AND KNOWLEDGE!	272
July 20	275
WHAT BRINGS LIGHT OR DARKNESS TO THE WORLD?	275
July 21	278
SIMPLE INSTRUCTION FOR DELIVERANCE!	278
July 22	281
IT NEEDS TOTAL CONSECRATION!	281
July 23	284
IF THE FOUNDATIONS ARE DESTROYED!	284
July 24	287

MAKE UP YOUR MIND! 287
July 25 290
YOU ARE THE DESIGNER OF YOUR LIFE! 290
July 26 293
GOD'S WAY IS EASY AND SUPERNATURAL! 293
July 27 296
WHISPERERS CREATE CHAOS! 296
July 28 299
YOU WILL WANDER IN THE WILDERNESS! 299
July 29 302
WHY DON'T WE SEE SUPERNATURAL? 302
July 30 305
WISDOM IS PEACEABLE! 305
July 31 308
SURRENDER TO JESUS! 308
AUGUST **311**
August 1 312
WHY IS THE WORK OF GOD NOT DONE? 312
August 2 315
POWER OF TRUTH! 315
August 3 318
DOUBLE FOR THE TROUBLE! 318
August 4. 321
MATURE CHRISTIAN! 321
August 5 324
HAVE PASSION TO ACHIEVE A MEDAL! 324
August 6 327
BLESSING AND CURSING RESULTS FROM YOUR ACTIONS! 327
August 7 330
HOW DOES DISPENSATION END? 330
August 8 333
WHAT IS RELIGION, DENOMINATION, AND ORGANIZATIONS? 333
August 9 336
LORD, MAKE ME HUMBLE! 336
August 10 339

REMEMBER, GOD COMES FIRST!	339
August 11	342
FRUIT BEARING WORD!	342
August 12	345
IT IS THAT EASY!	345
August 13	348
FOR YOUR SAKE, DO NOT TOUCH RIGHTEOUS!	348
August 14	351
RESPONSE TO THE WORD OF GOD!	351
August 15	354
SUPPLY COMES WHEN YOU WORK!	354
August 16	357
LIFE PLANNING IS MUST!	357
August 17	360
TOUCH, NOT MY GLORY!	360
August 18	363
JESUS HAS ALL AUTHORITY!	363
August 19	366
WISDOM IS A MUST FOR CHRISTIANS.	366
August 20	369
HAVE YOU RECEIVED THE HOLY SPIRIT?	369
August 21	372
YOUR LEADERS WILL MAKE YOU JUST LIKE THEM!	372
August 22	375
WHAT IS THE BLASPHEME?	375
August 23	378
BEAUTY!	378
August 24	381
MARY PONDERED IN HER HEART!	381
August 25	384
TRUTH REQUIRES SACRIFICE!	384
August 26	387
THE POINT OF TOUCH!	387
August 27	390

CONNECTION WITH THE CREATOR IS A MUST!	390
August 28	393
MAY THE LORD HAVE HIS WAY!	393
August 29	396
YOUR LOVE FOR GOD BRINGS REVELATION!	396
August 30	399
WHAT CHRISTIANS MUST KNOW!	399
August 31	402
WHO BEWITCHED YOU?	402

ELIZABETH DAS

MAY

MAY 1

IT REQUIRES SACRIFICE!

There are times when a sacrifice is necessary for a birth. Wheat needs to die to have more grain, a seed to bury in the ground and die to have more. Jesus had to die to have more of His kind. Peter had to die to have more of Peter's kind. Paul had to die to have more of his type in Europe and Asia. Thomas died in India to have more of his kind. To reproduce more, one must be willing to sacrifice their life. The sacrifice of kingship by Moses in Egypt was the birth of Israel. Through your sacrifice, the mentally unstable find sanity, the incurable find healing, life and death merge, poverty transforms into wealth, and so much more.

By the same token, if you do not sacrifice, you will bring destruction, death, and much more.

God made garments out of animal skin when humans sinned. Someone's sacrifices to clothe your shame of sin. Abraham gave the sacrifice of his only son, Isaac. The birth of Isaac was God's promise, and so a ram was provided by God to rescue him. Instead of Isaac, Ram was the one who was sacrificed.

All humans have to die, but Jehovah God put on flesh to provide the blood sacrifice to give us life. He gave His life at Calvary, and that life is in the blood. By turning to the cross and sacrificing ourselves, humankind can discover life. Giving up our desire for attention, physical pleasure, and arrogance in life.

We are following in Eve's footsteps, repeating the same sin. In order to receive a 100% outcome, we must give a 100% sacrifice and adhere to God's commandments, statutes, laws, and precepts. We need 100% sacrifice to live for God at His command and statutes, laws, and precepts to receive a 100% outcome.

Egypt will come to know God if you take action. Babylon will come to acknowledge the existence of Daniel's God.

Daniel 2:47 The king answered unto Daniel, and said, Of a truth, it is, that your God is a God of gods, and a Lord of kings, and a revealer of secrets, seeing thou couldest reveal this secret.

Despite the passing of the decree, Daniel remained steadfast in his practice of praying three times a day to His God. The consequence of the decree was his execution through lion attacks. He sacrificed life, not prayer. Make sure to prioritize your prayer, fasting, and Christian life.

Daniel 6:16 Then the king commanded, and they brought Daniel and cast him into the lions den. Now the king spake and said unto Daniel, Thy God whom thou servest continually, he will deliver thee. 25 Then king Darius wrote unto all people, nations, and languages, that dwell in all the earth; Peace be multiplied unto you. 26 I make a decree, That in every dominion of my kingdom men tremble and fear before the God of Daniel: for he is the living God, and steadfast forever, and his kingdom that which shall not be destroyed, and his dominion shall be even unto the end. 27 He delivereth and rescueth and worketh signs and wonders in heaven and the earth, who hath delivered Daniel from the power of the lions.

Birth is the result of a life of sacrifice. Obeying God's voice and sacrificing leads to the activation of God's power. He demonstrates his mastery as the creator and sustainer of life. When you live in harmony with God's Word, no one can defeat you. There is nothing above God's Word. Why? The truth resides in His Word. The truth has no boundaries.

Psalms 138:2a or thou hast magnified thy word above all thy name.

Both testing and worship involve making sacrifices. When you fulfill God's requests, you become an acceptable offering. Your reward and achievement are beyond imagination. Jesus triumphed over all through His sacrifice.

Ephesians 1: 20 Which he wrought in Christ when he raised him from the dead and set him at his right hand in the heavenly places, 21 Far above all principality, and power, and might, and dominion, and every name that is named, not only in this world, but also in that which is to come: 22 And hath put all things under his feet, and gave him to be the head over all things to the church, 23 Which is his body, the fulness of him that filleth all in all.

The plan of God is made known through sacrifice. The plan of God is higher than yours. You can chart your life and establish your timetable. But as you divert yourself into the plan of God, you will see the supernatural outcome.

Romans 12: 1 I beseech you therefore, brethren, by the mercies of God, that ye present your bodies a living sacrifice, holy, acceptable unto God, which is your reasonable service. 2 And be not conformed to this world: but be ye transformed by the renewing of your mind, that ye may prove what that good, and acceptable, and perfect, will of God is.

Sacrificial life does not know the result of their action. Only God knows the result. God is concluding the story if you sacrifice what it requires.

Did Moses know what would result from sacrificing the throne?

Exodus 11:3a Moreover, the man Moses was very great in the land of Egypt, in the sight of Pharaoh's servants, and in the sight of the people.

Sacrifice does not have vocabulary like, wait, but, if, oh no, why me, for what, later, hmmm, or oh my Lord!

Isaiah 6:8 Also, I heard the voice of the Lord, saying, Whom shall I send, and who will go for us? Then said I, Here am I; send me.

God tested all who responded and saw the outcome of the power of God. No man can take you where God can. Only if you learn to sacrifice pride, the lust of the flesh, and the lust of eyes.

MAY 1

1 Samuel 3:4 That the LORD called Samuel: and he answered, Here am I.

Samuel was the Priest, well trusted by people and God. Samuel sacrificed his life for the service of Israelis.

1 Samuel 3:19 And Samuel grew, and the LORD was with him and did let none of his words fall to the ground.

What is the meaning of sacrifice? It means surrender, giving up, gift oblation, burnt offering, resignation, etc.

Matthew 19:29 And everyone that hath forsaken houses, or brethren, or sisters, or father, or mother, or wife, or children, or lands, for my name's sake, shall receive a hundredfold and shall inherit everlasting life.

Look, this is the Word of God, the assurance of God. God's plan is to bless you when you sacrifice and surrender to His will. However, if not,

Matthew 10:37 He that loveth father or mother more than me is not worthy of me: and he that loveth son or daughter more than me is not worthy of me. 38 And he that taketh not his cross, and followeth after me, is not worthy of me.

By sacrificing for God's plan, you will experience a transformation from ashes to beauty, mourning to joy, and heaviness to praise. A broken heart will be mended, the sick will be healed, and yoke and chains will be released by God.

It is a profit and blessing to you and many. To witness God's work flourish, sacrifice is required.

LET US PRAY

In the name of Jesus 'Lord, we give the sacrifice of praise. We give if we feel like it or not. We express our gratitude to God through the sacrifice of praise, giving thanks with our lips. Life gets rough, but makes it tough to destroy the resistance coming against us. In water, fire, mountains, and valleys, we acknowledge your existence, Lord. So we give thanks to your name in trouble and trial. We will see the outcome as victory, healing, freedom, and miracles. Lord, we desire a sacrificial life to bring you glory in Jesus 'name. Amen! God bless you!

MAY 2

BUT BY THY SPIRIT!

What is the reason behind the supernatural abilities of Christians, who are followers of Jesus Christ? Because the Holy Ghost or Holy Spirit empowers Christians. Christianity involves supernatural work, such as the miracles performed by Lord Jesus. We can also do the supernatural only if we have His Spirit. If we repent, get baptized in Jesus 'name, and receive the Spirit of God, we can have the Spirit of the almighty within us.

Acts 1:8a But ye shall receive power, after that the Holy Ghost comes upon you:

Zechariah 4:6b Not by might, nor by power, but by my spirit, saith the Lord of hosts.

Why Spirit?

Because the body without the spirit is dead, James 2:26.

The Bible says Spirit quickens us, which means it makes us alive. Use the Word, speak, and obey and see how it works. You can give life to the Word of God by putting it into action.

Roman 8:11 But if the Spirit of him that raised Jesus from the dead dwell in you, he that raised Christ from the dead shall also quicken your mortal bodies by his Spirit that dwelleth in you.

How many spirits?

Ephesians 4:4 says one Spirit. In 1 Corinthians 12:4 Now there are [distinctive] varieties of spiritual gifts

[special abilities given by the grace and extraordinary power of the Holy Spirit operating in believers]. Still, it is the same Spirit [who grants them and empowers believers]. Spirit will provide knowledge that you otherwise wouldn't know. The Spirit offers wisdom; otherwise, you will be clueless. Miracles, healing, prophecy, discernment, and all nine offices are all guided by the SPIRIT of ONE GOD. You will need to be more knowledgeable. Spirit is the sole source of empowerment.

The Holy Spirit has authority over every evil spirit.

MAY 2

Please read Mark 5: Man possessed with an unclean spirit was so powerful to break fetters of iron. Why? He had legions of evil spirits.

Jesus received the anointing of the Spirit of God to break the chains that bind. Evil spirits have bound people with drugs, alcohol, killing, sickness, etc. All demons can be destroyed if His Holy Spirit empowers you.

How many Spirit of truth? One spirit. The Spirit we are referring to is God, who is Spirit. John 4:24.

What is the necessity for having Spirit? Spirit performs supernaturally.

Have you ever cast out demons, opened blind eyes, or healed the sick? If not, then you need the Spirit of God to perform all this supernatural work.

1 Samuel 16:13 Then Samuel took the horn of oil, and anointed him in the midst of his brethren: and the Spirit of the LORD came upon David from that day forward.

Observe the contrast between God's anointing and the anointing of HIS chosen prophets on the people. You will receive the Spirit, and you will do Supernatural through HIS Spirit. Ask the Lord to give you a gift from the Spirit and have different offices within you through His one Spirit.

Do not reject the One same Spirit to enable you to edify God's Kingdom. Why?

Roman 8:9 But ye are not in the flesh, but in the Spirit, if so be that the Spirit of God dwells in you. Now if any man has not the Spirit of Christ, he is none of his.

Who anointed Jesus to perform mighty work?

Acts 10:38 How God anointed Jesus of Nazareth with the Holy Ghost and with power: who went about doing good and healing all that were oppressed of the devil; for God was with him.

Anointing is God's Spirit at work within us. Let us see How you receive His Spiritual gifts?

1 Timothy 4:14 Neglect, not the gift that is in thee, which was given thee by prophecy, with the laying on of the hands of the presbytery.

You receive the Holy Spirit when you baptize in Jesus 'NAME.

Acts 2:38 Then Peter said unto them, Repent, and be baptized every one of you in the name of Jesus Christ for the remission of sins, and ye shall receive the gift of the Holy Ghost.

Acts 8:17 Then laid their hands on them, and they received the Holy Ghost.

Acts 19:6 And when Paul had laid his hands upon them, the Holy Ghost came on them; and they spake with tongues, and prophesied.

When you have the Spirit of God, *1 John 2:20 But ye have an unction from the Holy One, and ye know all things.27As for you, the anointing you received from him remains in you, and you do not need anyone to teach you.*

But as His anointing teaches you, all things and anointing are real, not counterfeit. It is a teacher if you use Him.

When you do not see the supernatural, the Church does not have a different Spirit administering office doing work through the Holy Spirit. Without nine gifts of the Spirit, churches are powerless people. The New Testament Church is embodied in you. Don't associate the building with being a church. In God's administration, you need His Spirit to do the supernatural performance. People who have particular Spirit Gifts within will perform healing, miracles, etc. This is why the Spirit is the same God and becomes Sovereign.

Now you know One God's Spirit was in the temple of Jerusalem. When the Lord Jesus gave His blood, it came out from the temple. Blood has life, and sinless blood gives us life. No building is required for this divine entity. Different religions, organizations, denominations, and non-denominations want to put this God in their name-brand religion. Examples of Covenant Christian Coalition, World Evangelical Alliance, UPC, World Methodist Council, Lutheran World Federation, World Assemblies of God Fellowship, and Baptist World Alliance under many Catholic partitions as well.

You have limitations when it comes to selecting your religion in these boxes. You must follow their agenda, program, and bylaw.

Let the Spirit flow through you as you carry on God's work!

LET US PRAY

Pray you will work for JESUS through His Spirit, work through the leading, teaching, and guiding of His Spirit called the Holy Spirit. It's possible to be filled with spirit, but not to be led or allow spirit to guide you. So Lord, help us yield to your Spirit. Enter Supernatural By allowing His Spirit to work through you! In Jesus 'name. Amen! God bless you.

MAY 3

HOW TO ATTACH A BLESSING!

Ways to connect blessings to your life, children, and future generations. There are both blessings and curses in this world.

What does the term blessings mean? It means protection or favor. My niece's son has always had a fascination with the Revelation and would regularly ask his mom to read it. At an early age, I did not understand Revelation. I wanted to know the reason behind his choice to read or listen to Revelation. He responded to receive blessings. It's unusual for someone at that age to understand what they hear while reading. He will read from Revelation even on this day. I have faith that the kid is blessed.

Revelation 1:3 Blessed is he that readeth, and they that hear the words of this prophecy, and keep those things which are written therein: for the time is at hand.

Individuals strive for wealth, education, or promotion to attain their fullest potential. I can't help but wonder if they ever acknowledge our capacity to decide our destiny. Our time on Earth is limited, so we must prepare for our eternal future. I want to fulfill my desires, but not through deceitful means. Following what the Bible teaches, I put my trust in God and seek His guidance through prayer.

Proverb 10:22 The blessing of the LORD, it maketh rich, and he addeth no sorrow with it.

The Lord has written a book called the Bible. All the knowledge you seek is written by God, Jehovah. Beauty lies in effortlessly receiving all of God's blessings. Many people possess riches but lack peace, and joy, and suffer from trouble, sorrow, sickness, and chaos. To receive God's blessings, learn step by step through His Word.

Psalm 1:1 Blessed is the man that walketh not in the counsel of the ungodly, nor standeth in the way of sinners, nor sitteth in the seat of the scornful.2 But his delight is in the law of the Lord; and in his law doth he meditate day and night.3 And he shall be like a tree planted by the rivers of water, that bringeth forth his fruit in his season; his leaf also shall not wither; and whatsoever doeth shall prosper.

I always like to give my tithes offerings, missions, and extras. We learned this at an early age. I intended to work to give to God. In my younger years, I would give and patiently await the resulting increase. Every time I receive blessings in return, I share my story with others, explaining how I gave my first check to God and began tithing, resulting in God blessing me abundantly. I recently got hired for a new job that pays better than my previous one. I make it a point to seek the way of the Lord so that I can receive blessings. I am amazed by the blessings He has given.

I no longer have a job because God took it from me. I am His laborer. I am acknowledging that my blessings have reached a higher level. God is unbeatable. There is no earthly calculator or method that can explain how He operates. My mindset has shifted, and I no longer seek any reward or compensation for my work in service of God. People constantly reach out to come to my house seeking healing, deliverance, and counseling. All books, audio, CDs, and DVDs are available for free through my services.

Only the Lord is aware of His action, I am not. It's common to hear people complain about money, even if they have a good paying job. Always expressing dissatisfaction about not having money. Are they delivering prophecies about them or what exactly? I find stability and beauty in my work through the promises of the Word of God. With peace and confidence, I stand tall.

Once more, the lady reached out for prayer. Every now and then, she reaches out to me for prayer. People reach out to me when they need help, and once the problem is resolved, they say goodbye.

She asked me; you have not worked for almost twenty years. I said, yes; I haven't. She commented on your ability to keep going and stay alive. God's words have kept me alive, that's why I said yes to the Lord. God instructed me to work for Him, promising to provide for me.

Luke 22:35 And he said unto them, When I sent you without purse, and scrip, and shoes, lacked ye any thing? And they said, Nothing.

Our confidence must be in the Lord. One thing I have never worried about is my finances. Jesus is the source of my financial support through His bank, Bank of Jesus Provisions.

It is common for people to tell me that praying for them will result in blessings from the Lord. I agree that He has and will. They provide funds to thieves as a result of their involvement with established and non-established groups. They teach them to bring money and use a bag that passes along the pews.

Genesis 22:8 And Abraham said, My son, God will provide himself a lamb for a burnt offering: so they went both of them together.13 And Abraham lifted up his eyes, and looked, and behold behind him a ram caught in a thicket by his horns: and Abraham went and took the ram, and offered him up for a burnt offering in the stead of his son.14 And Abraham called the name of that place Jehovahjireh: as it is said to this day, In the mount of the LORD it shall be seen.

Your blessings will become visible to you and those in your presence when you have faith and obey God's commands.

Genesis 12:2 And I will make of thee a great nation, and I will bless thee, and make thy name great; and thou shalt be a blessing:

Your actions, reactions, and works are associated with a unique kind of blessing.

Matthew 5:3 Blessed are the poor in spirit: for theirs is the kingdom of heaven. 4 Blessed are they that mourn: for they shall be comforted. 5 Blessed are the meek: for they shall inherit the earth. 6 Blessed are

MAY 3

they which do hunger and thirst after righteousness: for they shall be filled. 7 Blessed are the merciful: for they shall obtain mercy. 8

How to attach a blessing!

Blessed are the pure in heart: for they shall see God. 9 Blessed are the peacemakers: for they shall be called the children of God. 10 Blessed are they which are persecuted for righteousness sake: for theirs is the kingdom of heaven.11 Blessed are ye, when men shall revile you, and persecute you, and shall say all manner of evil against you falsely, for my sake.

Wow, how many blessings are attached if you are meek, upright, merciful, pure in heart, peacemaker, righteous, persecuted, evil spoken against, and accused falsely? You need to turn on some music and dance, worship, and praise God when you go through trials. Heaven holds the ultimate reward, not this earthly existence.

Giving to someone who cannot repay is a tremendous blessing. There's no greater joy than secretly doing something for someone and not being recognized for it. The deeds we do are always remembered by God in heaven.

Blessings cannot be measured in money or material possessions. Provision and protection in such a way that you do not have to worry ever again.

Psalms 37:25 I have been young, and now am old; yet have I not seen the righteous forsaken, nor his seed begging bread.

God blessed King David, allowing him to pass on the throne to his children. He was a man of great integrity and received eternal blessings.

Their lifestyle shifts when money and wealth start to rise. Increasing greed, focusing solely on myself. It is the waste of wealth, health, and life. Their investment becomes earthly. They transform into alcoholics, ungodly individuals, abandoning their unholy children.

By obeying and achieving the Lord's blessings, you can leave behind children who are blessed, godly, and holy. Discover the art of connecting blessings to your possessions. Blessings can be passed down to future generations.

LET US PRAY

Lord, our precious God, gives us a heavenly direction. We live with high BP, blood diseases, heart problems, or many other illnesses, not doing what you asked us to do. But there is money or effort to live the great blessings of God. Guide us to live and act by your word, ensuring blessings for generations to come. The land, animals, sea creatures, fruits, and veg are things we want to be blessed with. We want to do all that it takes to leave the blessed world behind for the next generation. We are grateful for unlimited favor, four-fold, and hundredfold blessings. Teach us, so we receive an unlimited blessing from you for us and our world, in Jesus 'name. Amen! God bless you!

MAY 4

GIVE GOD A GLORY!

The Bible says Glory goes to the Lord God Jesus alone.

The world has many gods and goddesses, and human hands make them. They cannot see, talk, walk, or speak. The human makes and prays to them. They Make idols in every shape and form of their imagination. But Jehovah, who is Jesus in the flesh, is the only true God. The God who can heal, deliver and set free. We pray in the name of Jesus to cast the demon out. He gives peace and salvation to our souls! All is possible if you follow Jesus and not religion. The creator of all living in the universe! Nothing is hidden from Him. He said I did it all.

Psalm 115:4 Their idols are silver and gold, the work of men's hands. 5 They have mouths, but they speak not: eyes have they, but they see not: 6 They have ears, but they hear not: noses have they, but they smell not: 7 They have hands, but they handle not: feet have them, but they walk not: neither speaks they through their throat. 8 They that make them are like unto them; so is everyone that trusteth in them.

The Bible talks about the clear truth. Anyone can understand who has a sound mind. Creator God would not tolerate His creation to be ignorant. The Bible says you shall know the truth to be free. This truth hides in the Bible. It has the power to set us free. I preach truth to idol worshipers. I work with the true teachers and prophets of Jesus Christ. Whenever I pray over idol worshipers, and they feel peace, healed, or set free, I tell them to thank Jesus, not me. I have the authority to pray for your situation in the name of Jesus. But I have no power or skills to do this on my own. We introduce Jesus to all colors, looks, languages, and nationalities. They can kill you, but Jesus gives life eternal.

When a miracle happens, we say Jesus did it. He alone has the power to do healing and miracles.

Isaiah 42:8 I am the LORD: that is my name: and my glory will I not give to another, neither my praise to graven images.

There was a time Israelites knew the true God, but after shedding their blood for the sin of this world, Jesus involved heathen as well. Thank you, Lord. That is why I am a partaker of salvation.

1 Corinthians 10:31 Whether therefore ye eat, or drink, or whatsoever ye do, do all to the glory of God.

MAY 4

1 Corinthians 4:6 And these things, brethren, I have in a figure transferred to myself and Apollos for your sakes; that ye might learn in us not to think of men above that which is written, that no one of you be puffed up for one against another. 7 For who maketh thee to differ from another? and what hast thou that thou didst not receive? Now if thou didst receive it, why dost thou glory, as if thou hadst not received it?

If you go out to work for God and do not introduce Jesus, it is done in vain. When you pray, first you must say that it is all Jesus who is doing, so forget me but remember Jesus. I never get out of any place without introducing Lord Jesus. I have never preached to them pastors, organizations, or churches. I give glory to Lord Jesus. When things improve, forget me, but give thanks to Jesus. He makes the way, opens the door, and heals the sick. Lord Jesus provides your need and what you think unbearable, unresolvable sicknesses, questions, and diseases. Jesus will take care of it all. The forerunner of Jesus, John the Baptist, cleared the channel between humans and the creator God by baptizing repentance to remit our sins. He made the crooked, broken relationship between humans and God straight. He gave glory by testifying to Majesty on High Jesus Christ.

John 3:30 He must increase, but I must decrease. 31 He that cometh from above is above all: he that is of the earth is earthly, and speaketh of the earth: he that cometh from heaven is above all.32 And what he hath seen and heard, that he testifieth; and no man receiveth his testimony.33 He that hath received his testimony hath set to his seal that God is true.34 For he whom God hath sent speaketh the words of God: for God giveth not the Spirit by measure unto him.

I was delayed when God asked me to write the book until the Lord said it would give me glory. God is using me as the gift of the Spirit. The Lord is doing all work. I am just a vessel providing His Spirit to flow freely. Jesus has entrusted me with much work, and I give Him glory and no one. There will be a time people try to pressure you to give others glory but do not give anyone glory. If you do, then that is the end of your story. It is Lord Jesus, and He alone does all. Do not worry about death; Jesus has conquered it. You will reign with Him in His glory.

If you are smart, rich, intelligent, found favor, beautiful, the best athlete, or whatever, the Lord gave you all.

There was a King who tried to steal the glory from God and destroy it.

Acts 12:21 And upon a set day Herod, arrayed in royal apparel, sat upon his throne, and made an oration unto them. 22 And the people gave a shout, saying, It is the voice of a god, and not of a man. 23 And immediately the angel of the Lord smote him because he gave not God the glory: and he was eaten of worms, and gave up the ghost.

If you are king or ruler of the world, remember the Higher authority is in heaven. His name is Jesus. He has all the wisdom, knowledge, and understanding. He can give and take it away. The most powerful God in the universe is Him. Humans can't look for life on any other planet but the earth.

Psalms 115:16 The heaven, even the heavens, are the LORD'S: but the earth hath he given to the children of men.

I have taken this from Wikipedia, the Beatles, a famous group, stated, "We're more popular than Jesus" This was a remark made by the Beatles, John Lennon during a 1966 interview, in which he argued

Christianity would end before rock music. The Beatles group ended in the 1970s. That brought the end of the Beatles. Never try to come against the Living God; His name is Jesus. They shot Lennon in December 1980, and another died of lung cancer; all separated, but Christianity and Jesus are still going.

Once you go sky high and forget to give God glory, then you will come down quickly. Stay humble, so you do not lose your status. Pride makes you think you are above God. If you forget to give God glory at your pick time will bring calamity and end your fame, power, and position. Reminder, never to touch the glory. It belongs to the Lord Jesus and Him alone. You can say, I am grateful that God used me to do this and that, but never say I did it.

Satan, the Lucifer called the old serpent, was kicked out of heaven. The most beautiful, Cherub, who forgot to give God Glory,

Isaiah 14:12 How art thou fallen from heaven, O Lucifer, son of the morning! How art thou cut down to the ground, which didst weakens the nations!

Lucifer was a Covering Cherub, but the story ended when He tried to touch the Glory of Almighty God.

Revelation 12:7 And there was war in heaven: Michael and his angels fought against the dragon, and the dragon fought and his angels,8 And prevailed not; neither was their place found any more in heaven.9 And the great dragon was cast out, that old serpent, called the Devil, and Satan, which deceiveth the whole world: he was cast out into the earth, and his angels were cast out with him.

Some want to shut down the work of God, kill the pastors, and burn the Bible. The good news is that you cannot shut down the God of heaven. It is your end in the name of Jesus.

LET US PRAY

Lord, we are your creation. Life and death are in your hands. Power, position, and glory belong to you.

Help us stay humble. Never touch your glory; it belongs to you alone. Please use us in this world. Use us in any place to give your name glory. The promotion of perfect gifts comes from you. We thank you for every provision and help. We thank you, you have blessed us, but it is all you and nothing of us. You took away all from righteous Job still; He gave you glory. We realize you blessed Job in the beginning, and the ending was even greater. Let us finish. Let us complete this race by giving Lord Jesus glory. Knowing it is you and you alone, a sovereign God. May our Lord grant us a humble heart In Jesus 'name. Amen! God bless you!

MAY 5

LEARN BY OBEYING!

The Bible says Jesus learned by obeying the word!

I have a memory of God urging me to baptize, but I hesitated to baptize in the name of Jesus. I never realized it had biblical origins. I followed Jesus 'words and had a transformative experience. I exited the water, experiencing a sense of forgiveness. I felt as light as a feather. The mountain of sins on my head was taken away by God. I exclaimed, what a remarkable experience! Jesus followed all of the scriptures without fail. Lord Jesus fulfilled the word. He demonstrated his name and role through his actions. The Bible has shifted from being a manual for life to being treated as a regular book. A lot of church leaders seek to engage in debates, and arguments, and discourage people from accepting and adhering to the truth. The most significant benefit for Satan is to lure a multitude of people to hell.

By obeying, Moses brought liberation to the enslaved Hebrews. The nation of Israel was born as a result of Moses's obedience to the voice of the almighty. The outcome was heard or witnessed by all nations as they became the voice of God and carried it out. It was absolutely mind-blowing, both the scene and the outcome. Eternity is reserved for an obedient bride chosen by the Lord. By offering just a little, the Devil lures you into fulfilling his destructive plan.

1 King 2:3 And keep the charge of the Lord thy God, to walk in his ways, to keep his statutes, and his commandments, and his judgments, and his testimonies, as it is written in the law of Moses, that thou mayest prosper in all that thou doest, and whithersoever thou turnest thyself.

Disobedience leads to destruction.

Joshua 22:20 "Did not Achan the son of Zerah commit a trespass in the accursed thing, and wrath fell on all the congregation of Israel? And that man perished not alone in his iniquity."

If Eve and Adam hadn't disobeyed, the disconnection wouldn't have happened. The curse follows when humans give in to lust and pride through disobedience. By heeding God's words, you'll experience a significance beyond your imagination.

According to the Bible, we are told to place our hands on sick people and anoint them with oil. How many of you are doing this? He already authorized us to go. What is the reason for your delay? You may visit the sick sometimes. You may deliver food, but do you lay your hand on the sick? I make sure to always have anointed oil and prayer clothes with me. I utilize oil in the market, bank, hospital, and convalescent home for prayer over the sick. By adhering to the word of God without deviation, the manifestation will unfold as promised.

The Bible says, Baptize them. How many go around baptizing people? I have a dear sister in the Lord who gives Bible study in jail. She carries in her truck the portable baptistry. As she teaches about repentance and wants their sin to wash away, she fills baptistry with water and baptizes them. In and out of season, you must obey the word instantly.

When you invite the carpenter or any handyperson who comes without equipment and tools, what will you say? Job well done?

1 Samuel 15:22 And Samuel said, Hath the LORD as great delight in burnt offerings and sacrifices, as in obeying the voice of the LORD? Behold, to obey is better than sacrifice, and to hearken than the fat of rams.

Many disobedient, unequipped, unteachable people hold positions in religious churches. Paul said they have fair speeches, transformed to be the angels of light. You cannot speak the truth to them. The argument is on the tip of their tongue. Please, just obey. Peter commanded them to be baptized, and they did. Commander means to do it or receive judgment? The Word of God is the highest authority, and not obeying the Word gets the worst consequences.

God sent a prophet to preach the Bethel with a specific guideline. But down the road, another prophet was a true prophet,

1 King 13:26 And when the prophet that brought him back from the way heard thereof, he said, It is the man of God, who was disobedient unto the word of the LORD: therefore the LORD hath delivered him unto the lion, which hath torn him, and slain him, according to the word of the LORD, which he spake unto him.

Remember, when you hear the voice of God, do it. It will be easier than you think. Under all resistance, opposition, and temptation, hold on to the voice of God.

Many denominations, churches, and organizations have replaced Jesus Christ and His commandments. They have kept the Bible where they do not feel pain in the flesh. Remember, nothing is above the Word of God. Obey as the word of God says. Word of God hurt your feelings? It is to get rid of the flesh and to save the soul.

Obeying the word is cashing the promises of God. Achievement of promises results from obedience. Spirit world results in tangible as you obey. God will disconnect you as you disobey the word, which is the voice of God.

Most churches teach religions, resulting in the downfall of Christianity. Adding and subtracting to a Word of God causes the lawlessness you encounter today. Do not follow false teachers and prophets. Anyone who labels themselves as pastors, prophets, or teachers doesn't mean they are that.

Deuteronomy 28:1 And it shall come to pass, if thou shalt hearken diligently unto the voice of the Lord thy God, to observe and to do all his commandments which I command thee this day, that the Lord thy God will set thee on high above all nations of the earth.

MAY 5

The Bible says, Praise Him loudly, with clapping hands and loud musical instruments. Holy churches wouldn't. It bothers the devil. They will find an excuse, no loud prayer, clapping, or music that bothers the ear. Really? Get rid of the devil. Whatever the Bible says, yes, the devil says NO.

They can watch TV movies, but they cannot pray. They pamper the demons inside to keep them sick, fearful, bound, and oppressed. Obey the voice of God. It will do well. Many times I wake up attacked by the enemy, Satan. I turn on some worship and praise music and start worshiping God. In no time, the chain of the devil breaks off, the yoke is destroyed, and I am free again. You see an outcome, fulfillment of the Word of God by obeying, doing, practicing, and putting it into action.

Roman 5:19 For as by one man's disobedience many were made sinners, so by the obedience of one shall many be made righteous.

The supernatural Spirit of God operates differently. He only needs your obedience to prove the fulfillment of promises. When people become more thoughtful, wiser, and all-knowing, they bring calamity to themselves and others. Disobedient leaders will bring calamity to a nation. Remember the difference between David and Jeroboam. David brought safety and prosperity by obeying, but Jeroboam destroyed the land, brought removal from land, and put back to slavery by disobeying. God removed the Israelites from the ground in the year 722. If God has given you a family, a position as the ruler, or whatever, take it seriously, and get God's help. Take His Word heartily, put in life to see the power of fulfillment. The result of it will keep giving you success and bless you and the surrounding people. What you see makes you confident, but the Lord secures you unseen. He never sends you where He will not go. God wouldn't ask you to do what He can't handle. Experience and learn God by obeying His voice.

I have a memory of being at Bombay Airport. The immigration officer annoyed me. Their behavior got to me and made me upset. While I was in prayer, God singled out the man with a gesture. He wanted to know where I had come from. I said, USA. He said, you are in the wrong line; he put my baggage on the screen, stamped my passport, and said to go. It was evident that this man had a dirty appearance and clothes. Based on his appearance, I would never guess he was an officer. By following God's voice, I quickly emerged without unpacking any bags. He might not be a real man, you never know.

It is a more accessible, stress-free, and easy life if we hear His voice and obey. Life gets more manageable, enjoyable, and peaceful as we walk with God. Despite this, I still encounter trials, trouble, lions, bears, fire, sickness, and disease. Through understanding and obeying His voice, I attain healing, triumph, peace, and freedom. Aligning work with God's conditions. Eliminating Eve's personality will bring blessings, peace, and beauty to your life. Stop window-shopping, reasoning, and desiring forbidden. Stay connected to the scripture, appreciate the saying, abide by it, and experience blessings. Life is short, with many troubles and trials, but the Lord's deliverance from them all. The Lord loves us, which is why He gave us laws. It doesn't misguide us. Just obey the voice of your Father God and see what happens!

LET US PRAY

Heavenly Father, thank you. We have you. You care and have given us heavenly laws, precepts, and commandments. We thank you for your protection if we keep it. We ask for the obedient heart to love and keep without questioning. Lord, you know the best. You know the road to victory. We ask you to hold our hand to walk through the plan of the Most High God. It is amazing the God of heaven takes an interest in our lives and loves us. We have enough evidence of obeying and disobeying the voice of God. We know you have a beautiful plan for us if we obey. Help us, Lord, so we see the significant result and success in Jesus's name. Amen! God bless you!

MAY 6

ENGAGE YOURSELF WITH KINGDOM ACTIVITIES!

What Activities? Activity means action, life, hobby, busy or vigorous action, or a lot of activity in the area.

Turning to Jesus opens the door to diverse kingdom activities. You can join and keep yourself busy. It should transform into a hobby. Match the lifestyle of Jesus and His disciples in your actions and choices. The disciples indicated those who followed the Lord and persisted in practicing His teachings.
I'd like to bring up an activity mentioned in the Bible.

1 Thessalonians 5:16 Rejoice evermore.17 Pray without ceasing.18 In every thing give thanks: for this is the will of God in Christ Jesus concerning you.19 Quench not the Spirit.

Day and night, I find joy in studying the Word. YouTube is my go-to platform for accessing the finest preaching and teaching. Knowing the magnitude of what I have yet to learn is helpful. If your pursuits are for the Kingdom, you'll affirm, "I am busy but productive for His kingdom." I have no time for myself, I, and myself. It's amazing how good God is. You will go deeper, higher, wider, and overflowing. You will persist in praying, Lord, grant me more than I already have. Your journey through life will be finished before you realize it.

Engage yourself in studying the Word of God.

1 Thessalonians 4:11 And that ye study to be quiet, and to do your own business, and to work with your own hands, as we commanded you;12 That ye may walk honestly toward them that are without, and that ye may have lack of nothing.

By studying the Word of God, you eliminate the presence of false teachers and prophets. There's absolutely no room for denominations or non-denominations.

The Book of Hebrew issues a warning to those who neglect to study the Word.

Hebrews 5:12 For when for the time ye ought to be teachers, ye have need that one teach you again which be the first principles of the oracles of God; and are become such as have need of milk, and not of strong meat.

The work of getting hold of Jesus involves studying the Word, praying, laying hands on the sick, and receiving the power of the Spirit. Similar to Lord, they combined teaching and going out to work. This falls under the category of activities.

Jesus stated that his presence on Earth was to accomplish his father's business. The Bible says Jesus did so much work that if we keep writing, then there is no place to store books.

John 21:25 And there are also many other things which Jesus did, the which, if they should be written every one, I suppose that even the world itself could not contain the books that should be written. Amen.

Jesus labored tirelessly. Is your church preventing you from going beyond its boundaries? After church, go out to eat and enjoy. Did Jesus start His Kingdom in that way? They're not representing the Kingdom of Jesus, but someone else's; they're fooling you. God, who was manifest in flesh, engaged in prayer. Remember, flesh needs to connect with the spirit of God. The act of praying is our link to the higher power.

Mark 1:35 And in the morning, rising up a great while before day, he went out, and departed into a solitary place, and there prayed.

Luke 5:16 And he withdrew himself into the wilderness, and prayed.

Prayer is necessary to establish a connection with our Father as we enter the Kingdom of God. Charge up and connect with the person you work for, there's no time for anything else. Being in the presence of God is a privilege.

I pray for hours. As soon as my alarm goes off at 3:50 in the morning, I am ready for prayer. There are times when I am already awake to meet God, even before that. I dedicate a significant amount of time to being in the presence of the Lord. He addresses me and brings up different individuals to pray for. Most people don't realize that I covered them in prayer during the morning.

Once, as I finished showering, God told me to pray for someone for an hour, so I did. Then He said to pray for another person for an hour, and I did. I didn't have enough time to dry my hair or eat lunch when I checked the clock. I quickly brushed my hair in a rush. I was hungry when I went to work. I needed to run a comb through my hair. So I did it at work. I thought my hair was a mess. I did not comb my hair or set. My friend looked at me and said, your hair looks so pretty, I said thank you, Lord. I had no time for lunch and was hungry at work. The supervisor came and said, there is food. Why not go and get some? Witness how God operates. The amazingness of God's manifestation is undeniable. The Lord has all provisions according to His scheduling. It wasn't until later that I learned the individuals I prayed for were facing overwhelming family challenges.

Lord Jesus prepared us to go to other cities to preach. We must preach to other cities around us. Don't you feel you have wasted your time?

Luke 4:43 And he said unto them, I must preach the kingdom of God to other cities also: for therefore am I sent.

MAY 6

I am just informing you there is much activity to fill your life. There is no time to waste or to get bored. We have a list of activities to get busy with the work of God. How did Jesus and the disciples work? They had no time to eat?

Mark 6:31 And he said unto them, Come ye yourselves apart into a desert place, and rest a while: for there were many coming and going, and they had no leisure so much as to eat.

Have you heard people complain I am bored? I have nothing to do. I just watch TV. I just have to go to the mall, walk around, and have so many lazy hobbies. Have you noticed the multitude of problems associated with drugs, alcohol, smoking, lust, laziness, rape, murder, and more? Why? Consider, and contemplate the source of this pain for them. We must reach out to these individuals who are sick, afflicted, and bound. We are busy like Eve. We are looking at forbidden things!

Suppose if we carry on our assignment, then we wouldn't have a prison, jail, lawyers, police, hospitals, doctors, nurses, and medicine to destroy us. Evaluate your time. Where are you spending it? Is your attention on God or on church-related activities, organizations, and pastors? Are you filled with church religious activities to destroy the kingdom or to establish the kingdom? You are the Church. Get busy with the Lord. A building called a church is a den for thieves.

During my visit to India, a lady in need approached me for assistance. She sought my help in praying for her son, who was afflicted by a demon. Upon hearing this, the District Superintendent got upset. He asked why she came to you. I said, why not? The power of darkness lies in religion. Expect them to criticize you if you extend a helping hand. People will be influenced by religious authorities to go against you. Just like the Romans didn't kill Jesus but the religious authorities. Their training focuses on teaching people to worship them instead of God.

Attending drinking parties, consulting witch doctors, and getting divorced is acceptable to religious Christian authorities. Is it alright if I educate you with the truth? Make sure people don't discover the truth. Let them stay bound and broken. Is this what Jesus did? He went around and cast out the demon. Are you doing this activity? Are you convincing them of their sins? Is it an emotional problem? Take some pills. Can a pill cast out demons? Did Jesus use prescribed drugs to cast out demons? Did the drugs make people free and whole?

All tasks can be accomplished by the Lord, but He seeks service from those who have graduated from His university. We must preach the word with a sign.

Mark 16:20 And they went forth, and preached everywhere, the Lord working with them, and confirming the word with signs following. Amen!

Life will be full of joy.

Luke 10:17 And the seventy returned again with joy, saying, Lord, even the devils are subject unto us through thy name.

Acts 5:41 And they departed from the presence of the council, rejoicing that they were counted worthy to suffer shame for his name.

Engage in God's activities and witness the transformative power of His Word. Your news media will be delivering good news. Allow me to inform you that you are the chosen broadcaster. All the social and news media are under the control of the devil. They removed my YouTube channel and restricted me from Google. They label my book "I Did It His Way" as an inappropriate book. So open your mouth and testify, give God glory, do not let rock take your place.

Acts 17:6a These that have turned the world upside down are come hither also;

LET US PRAY

Lord, as you trained disciples, we also want to walk close to you so you can work with us. We want to see a drastic change in the nation. The Lord heals marriages and physical, mental, and spiritual health. The creator of the universe is very interested in our welfare. God, we want you to be our way. We want to learn to pray, preach, teach, cast out a demon, heal the sick, and do all. Please teach us, Lord. Help us not to follow lost, false teachers and prophets. We want your Spirit to teach, direct, and empower us to work. We ask for help, mighty God, to be our way, truth, and life in Jesus's name. Amen! God bless you!

MAY 7

CHARACTERISTICS OF SPIRITUAL LEADERS!

God appoints a spiritual leader to govern in His Kingdom. He has a system for selecting leaders on earth to keep us from harm and danger. A loving father always wants to save His creation, protect it, and promote it higher than any other kingdom on earth. God communicates His Creation through a distinct system in each era. The purpose of humanity's existence is to build lasting relationships. God plans to have us in His life. He desires to keep us close to Him. Yet, for this to occur, God relies on leaders who can lead His creation with integrity. The issues we face in life originate from the heart, as the Lord is aware. The heart is where life starts, and the Lord chooses those with pure hearts. God handpicked Abraham, Moses, Joshua, and several others to fulfill various roles for the advancement of His Kingdom.

We observe the remarkable character of a distinct leader chosen by God. Their beauty radiates from within and shines outwardly. They knew the Lord.

The admiration expressed by God's leaders is truly encouraging to me. It activates the miracles and supernatural seen in different situations. It contributes to the health of the hearer's ear and brings comfort to our hearts and souls.

A leader means commander, chief, superior, headman, king, queen, and you can add many other titles. God chose David to be king. A shepherd boy had some sheep to take care of. But God saw something to choose this little kid from the sheepfold. A sheepfold is carved from the rock to house the sheep. Sitting at the door, the shepherd keeps a watchful eye. David's diligent care for these few sheep did not go unnoticed by God. He risked his life to ensure their safety from the bear and lions.

1 Samuel 17:34 And David said unto Saul, Thy servant kept his father's sheep, and there came a lion, and a bear, and took a lamb out of the flock:35 And I went out after him, and smote him, and delivered it out of his mouth: and when he arose against me, I caught him by his beard, and smote him, and slew him.36 Thy servant slew both the lion and the bear: and this uncircumcised Philistine shall be as one of them, seeing he hath defied the armies of the living God.

Subsequently, He saved the Israelites from Goliath's clutches in warfare. True leaders are forged in battle. He is a bold, courageous, mighty man who fears God and acknowledges Him in every battle. All leaders, independent of others, themselves, abilities, and past experiences, find their source in God. David showed no fear when he laid eyes on the towering Goliath, who stood at nine and a half feet tall.

1 Samuel 17:4 And there went out a champion out of the camp of the Philistines, named Goliath, whose height was six cubits and a span. 5 And he had a helmet of brass upon his head, and he was armed with a coat of mail; and the weight of the coat was five thousand shekels of brass. 6 And he had greaves of brass upon his legs, and a target of brass between his shoulders. 7 And the staff of his spear was like a weaver's beam; his spear's head weighed six hundred shekels of iron: and one bearing a shield went before him. 8 And he stood and cried unto the armies of Israel, and said unto them, Why are ye come out to set your battle in array? am not I a Philistine, and ye servants to Saul? Choose a man for you, and let him come down to me. 9 If he be able to fight with me, and to kill me, then will we be your servants: but if I prevail against him, and kill him, then shall ye be our servants, and serve us. 10 And the Philistine said, I defy the armies of Israel this day; give me a man, that we may fight together. 11 When Saul and all Israel heard those words of the Philistine, they were dismayed, and greatly afraid.

King Saul, who led the Israeli army, was filled with fear at the horrifying scene. Upon seeing that scene, David's reaction was authentic, as he knew God. When King Saul saw David, he remarked that he was just a young child. According to King Saul, there was no chance of winning against the giant.

David spoke with confidence 32, *And David said to Saul, Let no man's heart fail because of him; thy servant will fight with this Philistine.*

David displayed great confidence in his Lord. He stated that I would come to you, but not using my strength and ability.

Then said David to the Philistine, Thou comest to me with a sword, and with a spear, and with a shield: but I come to thee in the name of the Lord of hosts, the God of the armies of Israel, whom thou hast defied. 46 This day will the Lord deliver thee into mine hand; and I will smite thee, and take thine head from thee; and I will give the carcasses of the host of the Philistines this day unto the fowls of the air, and to the wild beasts of the earth; that all the earth may know that there is a God in Israel. 47 And all this assembly shall know that the Lord saveth not with sword and spear: for the battle is the Lord's, and he will give you into our hands. 49 And David put his hand in his bag, and took thence a stone, and slang it, and smote the Philistine in his forehead, that the stone sunk into his forehead; and he fell upon his face to the earth.

God seeks leaders who are bold, courageous and prepared for battle. They understood that the victory in the battle would come from the Spirit of the mighty God, not from their strength. They are aware that if I engage in the battle in His name, He will fight and God's name will be raised.

David took responsibility for his actions when he committed adultery, confessing his sin, guilt, and shame without blaming Bathsheba.

2 Samuel 12:13 And David said unto Nathan, I have sinned against the Lord. And Nathan said unto David, The Lord also hath put away thy sin; thou shalt not die.

Truthfulness, sincerity, boldness, and courage are essential qualities of a leader. By following God's word, statutes, commandments, precepts, and laws, we experience His love and protection. God is drawn to individuals who possess a genuine, kind, and compassionate heart.

MAY 7

David was one human man.

2 Samuel 24:14 And David said unto Gad, I am in a great strait: let us fall now into the hand of the LORD; for his mercies are great: and let me not fall into the hand of man.

David was prepared to receive chastisement for his wrongdoing. David had no secrets, he was an open book. It's no surprise that God called David a man after His own heart. I have a great love for David's compassionate words. Seeing the little dead animal, his heart called out to the Lord in sorrow.

2 Samuel 24:17 And David spake unto the LORD when he saw the angel that smote the people, and said, Lo, I have sinned, and I have done wickedly: but these sheep, what have they done? Let thine hand, I pray thee, be against me and my father's house.

According to the Bible, David was chosen by the Lord as King over His people. Take a look at the man and his attitude. He won't abandon you and flee when trouble arises. God chose Paul, Peter, and many others; they were willing vessels, faithful unto death. I am passionate about advancing God's kingdom for His glory. God handpicks good, clean, righteous, and holy leaders. We need leaders who are righteous, bold, courageous, holy, and truthful to rescue us from Satan's grasp. The one who feels compassion when we are hurting. The one who prays and fasts when we are sick, oppressed, and possessed. Visit incarcerated individuals and assist those who are hungry, suffering, and in need.

Good spiritual leaders are the key to a flourishing kingdom.

LET US PRAY

Lord, you are the chief Shepherd. Surely you will deliver our soul from the mouth of the Devil. We thank you for being an outstanding leader, especially for giving your life on the cross. The Lord makes us great, bold, courageous, and compassionate leaders over our homes, churches, cities, and this world. Give us leaders like David, who leads his sheep beside still water. Who can deliver from the bear and lion? Lord, we desire the leaders to know you and love you. We thank you for choosing exceptional leaders for our souls. Please lead everyone to the one who is faithful and righteous to protect our souls in Jesus 'name. Amen! God bless you!

MAY 8

I AM A SPOKESPERSON OF GOD!

What is the Spokesman? A spokesman is an agent, mouthpiece, prophet, ambassador, and representative. When you become the speaker of whoever, then you know that person. You cannot speak for the one you do not know. When Jesus picked twelve disciples, they went around and spoke for Him.

In Matthew 3:1 In those days came John the Baptist, preaching in the wilderness of Judaea, 2 And saying, Repent ye: for the kingdom of heaven is at hand. 3 For this is he that was spoken of by the prophet Esaias, saying, The voice of one crying in the wilderness, Prepare ye the way of the Lord, make his paths straight.

John the Baptist came as a spokesperson of God Jehovah, who was coming to earth as Jesus Christ the Messiah, the world's savior. John was connecting the broken bridges between creation and creator. Sin remedy provided by God, but to make it available, someone has to give exact information on how to achieve it. It is the way of Jesus and not man. Thank you, Lord—the remedy of broken relations caused by sin in the Garden by Eve and Adam.

Thank you, Lord! We need an exact recipe, exact blueprint, and prescription. We cannot add and subtract even if it costs our heads. See what happened to John the Baptist.

Spokesperson speaks for God: *Mark 6:18 For John had said unto Herod, It is not lawful for thee to have thy brother's wife.*

Our responsibility is not to fit in culture, color, and nation but to speak what thus saith the Lord. It is costly.

Matthew 14:10 And he sent and beheaded John in prison.

If we become the speaker for Jesus, we will not see the birth of false churches, denominations, and polluted Bibles. Theological colleges raised the antichrist army and the population of sick adulterers and confused people. Jesus sent the spokespeople to speak and perform work for Him. The report was beautiful as they went out and did exactly what the Lord asked them to do!

Luke 9:1 Then he called his twelve disciples together, and gave them power and authority over all devils, and to cure diseases. 2 And he sent them to preach the kingdom of God, and to heal the sick. 6 And they departed, and went through the towns, preaching the gospel, and healing everywhere. 7a Now Herod the tetrarch heard of all that was done by him: and he was perplexed, Wow, the result was excellent! Do you

MAY 8

see this in your church today? Are you working for Jesus or your organization and churches without the revelation of Jesus?

70 came back

Luke 10:1 After these things the Lord appointed other seventy also and sent them two and two before his face into every city and place, whither he would come. 17 And the seventy returned with joy, saying, Lord, even the devils are subject unto us through thy name.

Jesus uses a spokesperson to preach for Him. They must know the one for whom they are speaking. God has the key and can give it to the one who knows Jesus. Jesus was the God in the Flesh.

Matthew 16:15 He saith unto them, But who say ye that I am? 16 And Simon Peter answered and said, Thou art the Christ, the Son of the living God. 17 And Jesus answered and said unto him, Blessed art thou, Simon Barjona: for flesh and blood hath not revealed it unto thee, but my Father which is in heaven. 18 And I say also unto thee, That thou art Peter, and upon this rock, I will build my church; and the gates of hell shall not prevail against it. 19 And I will give unto thee the keys of the kingdom of heaven: and whatsoever thou shalt bind on earth shall be bound in heaven: and whatsoever thou shalt loose on earth shall be loosed in heaven.

If you do not have the same key, you cannot open the kingdom of God. The remedy of sin is no more animal blood. The Lamb Jesus replaced the animal lamb. Sickness and disease remedy is available. Treatment for broken hearts is known to break the power of the demon and darkness. The gates of hell have no control only if you are building the church on the revelation of Jesus Christ. The revelation of Jesus is rock.

Paul, a scholar of the Torah and master in languages, was a learned man who did not have a clue, even as he was waiting for the Messiah. Not knowing the Messiah, Paul was long gone, and now a new dispensation started. He testified about Jesus that He was the Messiah.

Later, Paul was persecuted for the truth.

Acts 26:7 Unto promise our twelve tribes, instantly serving God day and night, hope to come. For which hope's sake, king Agrippa, I am accused of the Jews.

The revelation came to Paul at Damascus Road.

Acts 9:3 As he journeyed, he came near Damascus, and suddenly a light shone around him from heaven. 4 Then he fell to the ground, and heard a voice saying to him, "Saul, Saul, why are you persecuting Me?" 5 And he said, "Who are You, Lord?" Then the Lord said, "I am Jesus, whom you are persecuting. It is hard for you to kick against the goads." 6 So he, trembling and astonished, said, "Lord, what do You want me to do?" Then the Lord told him, "Arise and go into the city, and you will be told what you must do."

Jesus Christ revealed His identity as Jehovah in the flesh to Paul. God chose Paul to witness to gentiles. A master in many languages needs to know who Jesus is. Jesus, not a second God but Jehovah, walked by putting on flesh on earth as the savior. Later, Paul was baptized in Jesus's name and received His Spirit. Paul's life story changed. The truth makes the devil nervous. Paul was in an army of Satan. By finding the savior, he became a martyr in Rome.

Acts 19:11 And God wrought special miracles by the hands of Paul:

Some spokesperson of Christ was separated from the truth when the apostle John was still alive. He was the last disciple of Jesus to depart from the earth. He warned in his epistles.

John says they are the antichrist.

1 John 4: 2 Hereby know ye the Spirit of God: Every spirit that confesseth that Jesus Christ has come in the flesh is of God: 3 And every spirit that confesseth not that Jesus Christ comes in the flesh is not of God: and this is that spirit of antichrist, whereof ye have heard that it should come; and even now already is it in the world.

I remembered my first experience, going into the water for the remission of my sins. I came out differently, which I cannot explain. The mountain of sins was removed and felt lighter than a feather. I said wow! Christianity is real. I still did not have a revelation of Jesus.

The following Scripture gave me a revelation of Jesus.

Isaiah 43:10 Ye are my witnesses, saith the Lord, and my servant whom I have chosen: that ye may know and believe me, and understand that I am he: before me, there was no God formed, neither shall there be after me.11 I, even I, am the Lord; and beside me, there is no saviour.

When I got this revelation, my life story changed. I said Lord, how grateful I am. I became His spokeswoman with many testimonies. Before, I argued about Hindus and Muslims and had no support to prove that Jesus heals, delivers, sets free, and restores. But now I lay a hand on people, the demon runs, and the sick heal. My phone constantly rings, emails, and text messages for prayers. I hear great testimonies of healing, deliverance, and salvation. If you are the spokesperson of your religious group, have a cross on the building. If you use the Bible and are still powerless, follow the book of Acts. To use the Way of Jesus will take you where all truth is. Hell will be behind you, and Jesus will give life eternal in heaven. May the Lord make you a spokesperson of Jesus. Pray the Lord to change your life story like Paul in Jesus's name. Go out, do what Jesus did, and experience the power in His Name Jesus. This dispensation is of doing and not talking.

LET US PRAY

Lord, how wonderful it is an open invitation to humanity. Lord, how excellent to have a revelation of you and then be your spokesperson. We are grateful that you will give us your revelation if we love you and keep your commandments. We thank you for opening the treasure of the kingdom that knows Jesus. Lord, we proclaim your identity to the world so the end of these antichrist churches comes. We need to see blind eyes open, the lame walk, the dead rise, missing limbs restored, and all healing and deliverance take place in Jesus's name. Amen! God bless you!

MAY 9

LOOK FOR THE GREAT GOD!

Where is the God of Elijah!

The God of Elijah did marvelous work. Let's search for someone knowledgeable about the Great God to guide us. The desire for someone's mental fall on us who lives in the supernatural. We want the God of Elijah, Abraham, Isaac, Daniel, etc. God picked Elisha to be a successor to Elijah. Elisha followed closely to the master. His sole focus was his calling, with no other distractions. May we be blessed with an exemplary role model from the Lord? Then We can do something even more significant. Many people attend churches gaining nothing and leave achieving nothing. Sick individuals attend church and leave still sick. There is a lack of advancement in life. Many have lost hope and submitted. Many were captured by the devil's army. They were held captive, forced to obey the devil's commands. A destructive devil is bringing hell to earth.

Many people wonder where God is when it comes to healing, delivering, and setting captives free. Where can we find the solution to all problems? Where is the power which operated 2000 years ago? Why am I suffering from sickness with no means of escape? What does the future hold? Being born poor means dying poor. Every day, the prince of hell is rising again and triumphing! Does the statement "God is the same yesterday, today, and forever" leave you scratching your head and full of questions?

You won't find the answer in church organizations, medicine, pastors, government, or your military. In order to receive, you must seek, knock, and ask from God. Do you have to go down on your knees and disclose where you are? I'm in need of your help.Lord, you hold the solution to every question I have. I go to church/building, but I haven't experienced healing, deliverance, or salvation. You live in a heavenly place and hold the answer. Elisha sought out the God worshipped by Elijah. Find the supernatural God who performs extraordinary feats. The Great God was known by them.

2 King 2:13 He took up also the mantle of Elijah that fell from him, and went back, and stood by the bank of Jordan;14 And he took the mantle of Elijah that fell from him, and smote the waters, and said, Where is the Lord God of Elijah? And when he also had smitten the waters, they parted hither and thither: and Elisha went over.

Do you feel there is no way that God says I make new things daily? In light of the situation, we need to find the Great God. Fulfilling His condition is necessary for us to enter the realm of the supernatural.

God said,

Ephesians 4:24 And that ye put on the new man, which after God is created in righteousness and true holiness.

Experiment with wearing different attire or transforming yourself and observe the results. After my baptism in Jesus 'name and receiving the Holy Spirit, I began to witness and experience things I had never seen before. I started hearing the voice of God. When we aligned on the same frequency, I became a sheep under His care, and Jesus became my shepherd. It's truly remarkable how amazing God is. Do you need help finding your way? Having trouble finding Him? Uncovering an exceptional God is equivalent to finding a precious treasure. By hearing and obeying, we bring his promises to life. You become the temple of the Lord when His Spirit resides in you. Once you listen and follow His voice, your life will transform forever. Looking for the almighty in the structure will leave you feeling empty.

Isaiah 43:18 Remember ye, not the former things, neither consider the things of old.19 Behold, I will do something new; now it shall spring forth; shall ye not know it? I will even make a way in the wilderness and rivers in the desert.

What I appreciate are lovely transformations and delightful surprises. I have a passion for experiencing greater and more incredible miracles. I am declaring and in pursuit of it.

John 14:12a Verily, verily, I say unto you, He that believeth on me, the works that I do shall he also do; and greater works than these shall he do;

The great God holds the solution to all questions. He said in His word.

Jeremiah 32:27 Behold, I am the LORD, the God of all flesh: is there anything too hard for me?

During my time in the wheelchair, I felt hopeless, but I held onto His promise that I would walk and run. I trusted the Lord, who said, is there anything too hard for me? My prayers were answered when God sent the man who possessed the gift of healing and performing miracles. As he prayed, I experienced a remarkable healing where my leg grew, my spine straightened, and feeling returned to my legs. Even though my muscles were weak, I had balance. Over time, exercise made muscles stronger. The Lord wants us to find healing through seeking Him.

The manifestation of deliverance, miracles, and supernatural gifts. He will connect you with those to whom He has granted the advantages. Their faith and humble heart allow God's work to be extraordinary through them. You follow God. I please God and not man. God is great; listen to Him alone. God's mission is to set the captive free and He is still doing it today if you let His Spirit guide you.

Moses trained Joshua; Joshua served Moses.

Joshua 1:1 the LORD spake unto Joshua the son of Nun, Moses 'minister,

God picks the one who gives Him glory;

MAY 9

Joshua 4:14 On that day the LORD magnified Joshua in the sight of all Israel; and they feared him, as they feared Moses, all the days of his life.

Those who believe have no issue placing trust in the mighty God at work. People are fed up with the cycle of belief and no tangible outcomes. They make their way to Nigeria, Johannesburg, or any location where they can seek help. I am looking for someone who operates using spiritual gifts. We must look for the greater. You'll discover it if you search for it.

In India, we faced numerous barriers that made things impossible. When I come to the US, I have the opportunity to drive to different destinations in search of Him. In the modern era, people are losing interest in God as they pursue prosperity. The people of God experience prosperity by faithfully following God's instructions. We do not look for wealth; we look for the God who prosper us. I know no one gives peace, comfort, or deliverance from drugs, alcohol, and depression. We must look for the God of Paul, Peter, God of King David, and King Jehoshaphat.

The Bible is the key to finding God. Seeking Him through prayer, whether on the mountain or elsewhere. Find Him and seek His presence. Learn about God by doing what He did and what He has asked of you.

In the past, I loved going to church early to connect with God. It was a struggle to find a place to pray in many places. The noise they made prevented any possibility of praying. Everyone comes to sit and wait for the show to start. The performance has concluded, featuring stunning music, dance in flesh, and limited teaching. That's the beginning of the disappointment. But as I left India, I came to seek Him. I am constantly searching for the great God, a search that never ends. Despite being told it was a minor procedure, my blood condition prevented me from surviving the removal of my tonsil. I initiated my search for an extraordinary healer. When I had different eye problems, I started looking for my great God. I look for the great God when I have a complex issue or a family situation. If you wear the holy and righteous garment, you can discover God's presence.

Many who seek help from witch doctors, magicians, astrologers, and psychics should be careful. Through them, you will be connected to numerous other demons. They have the power to manipulate your soul. On one occasion in India, I encountered a Christian lady who did not have any children. She sought the help of several witch doctors. Due to the God of Elijah, Moses, Paul, and Peter being unwelcome, she is left without any options.

It is not allowed to speak the truth of the Bible in many places. They are being influenced by their religious beliefs. According to her, nobody in the family has kids. I promised that my prayers would result in you having children. Religion's influence prevents people from knowing Jesus and His power. Find my God who rescued me from cancer, restored my mobility, and offers healing and deliverance whenever I require it. At Jesus Bank, you can find all your needs fulfilled. Simply search for the Great God. Look for Him! Seek Him on the knee by prayer and fasting, and you will find Him.

LET US PRAY

My Lord, we seek you through the system of our churches and organization. People are disappointed and losing faith because, in this dispensation, you are in us. Help to look outside of the four walls where God can be found. The God that Paul and Peter preached is what we want. We look for the Lord said with withered hands healed, blind eyes open, and the dead arise. Your spirit is what we want to lead and guide us. We need the Holy Spirit to be our teacher and Instructor to look for the Great God. This world needs to know the Great God, not our religious leaders, pastors, or organizations. We want the hopeless world to find hope by finding the great God in Jesus 'name. Amen! God bless you!

MAY 10

SOMEONE USHERED YOU!

How would you define the term "usher"? To help someone get from one place to another, especially by showing them how to lead.

Mary ushered in Jesus. Mary trusted in the Lord's report. She accepted the word of Angel Gabriel.

Luke 1; 30 And the angel said unto her, Fear not, Mary: for thou hast found favor with God. 31 And, behold, thou shalt conceive in thy womb, and bring forth a son, and shalt call his name Jesus. 32 He shall be great, and shall be called the son of the Highest: and the Lord God shall give unto him the throne of his father David: 33 And he shall reign over the house of Jacob forever, and of his kingdom, there shall be no end.

By believing, Mary brought forth the Lord Jesus, the King of Kings, the world's savior.

38 And Mary said, Behold the handmaid of the Lord; be it unto me according to thy word. And the angel departed from her.

Hanna Ushered in the great Prophet Samuel! Someone who couldn't have children pleaded with God and vowed to give back in His service.

1 Samuel 1:10 And she was in bitterness of soul, prayed unto the Lord, and wept sore. 11a And she vowed a vow, and said, O Lord of hosts, if thou wilt indeed looks on the affliction of thine handmaid, remember me, and not forget thine handmaid. Still, wilt give unto thine handmaid a man child, then I will give him unto the Lord all the days of his life, 20 Wherefore it came to pass when the time was come about after Hannah had conceived, that she bare a son, and called his name Samuel, saying, Because I have asked him of the Lord.28 I have also lent him to the Lord; as long as he liveth, he shall be lent to the Lord. And he worshipped the Lord there.

Hannah presented Samuel immediately after he stopped breastfeeding. Samuel received recognition for his commitment to walking in God's statutes and precepts.

1 Samuel 9:6 And he said unto him, Behold now, there is in this city a man of God, and he is an honorable man; all that he saith cometh surely to pass: now let us go thither; peradventure he can shew us our way that we should go.

None of his words fell to the ground. What Samuel spoke became true. To present great prophets, we must have the presence of a mother with godly qualities. The presence of genuine prophets would lead to a decrease in interest for physics, witch doctors, magicians, and astrologers. Jesus is coming soon.

1 Samuel 3:19 And Samuel grew, and the LORD was with him and did let none of his words fall to the ground.

The role of a woman in ushering the great man was more significant. Their position was confirmed by the one who guided them.

Jesus enlisted 12 disciples at first, and later gathered 70 more, who accomplished remarkable deeds on this planet. How you introduce something determines its outcome.

The nation is exposed to drugs, alcohol, gangs, witches, satanic practices, and evil by numerous ushers. The country will be destroyed by ushering false teachers and prophets. Make sure you usher in the children, who can significantly impact this world. Women are called by God to raise children who are God-fearing. From childhood, is it important to instruct children in God's ways, precepts, statutes, and commandments?

You invite God into your country through the guidance of the great prophets and prophetesses. They bring prosperity to both the Spiritual and physical dimensions. By removing barriers and providing guidance, the Prophet helps you navigate and solve puzzles. God Almighty appoints the Prophet as their leader and worker.

The Great Prophet Moses was introduced by Jochebed. Moses received his knowledge of the truth from his God-fearing mother. A leader and redeemer was brought by Mother to free the Hebrews from slavery. He introduced the great commandments from the One True God. The God of the universe was introduced to the world by Moses. Nations trembled in fear of this powerful God.

Allowing ourselves as vessels, we bring in the true God. At the altar, repentance brings about our death. Then we usher in the God almighty. You were directed to the place where you are currently sitting.

The prisoner's final wish was to see his mother. Upon her arrival, he chews her nose. According to him, you led me to hang on these gallows. If you had noticed, you would have prevented me from stealing. You transformed me into a criminal.

I knew one lady; she told the children to steal things from the cart that came by the house. Due to his habit of stealing, her son lost a good-paying job. Are you welcoming in individuals who are robbers, prostitutes, alcoholics, liars, deceivers, and so on? This brings the nation to calamity.

There's a story I heard about a man who got in trouble with his grandma because he didn't return a pencil he found at school. She guided the small boy to the principal, instructing him to return the pencil he had found on the school playground. It's a valuable lesson to be learned. I have no doubt that he learned his lesson.

A woman brings the child into the world. However, she played a crucial role in leading them to where they are today. Allowing God to guide your future through a mother who follows Him. Help them navigate the Word of God accurately, without leading them astray.

MAY 10

Regardless of the title we give you, the role of the mother is the most practical and powerful. Mother is ushering Satan or Lord. Satan gained power and authority as Eve welcomed him. Usher in the Word of God, Commandment, statutes, precepts, and laws of God is the key to success. Our connection with God is maintained through the knowledge we have of Him. The ability of God has do's and don't. If you establish a connection with God, He will remain your guiding force until your departure.

Helping a child find their path is more significant than their entry into this world. May the Lord have many Ruth Moabites who demonstrated great love to the God of Israel!

Her Word was.

Ruth 1:16 And Ruth said, Intreat me not to leave thee, or to return from following after thee: for whither thou goest, I will go; and where thou lodgest, I will lodge: thy people shall be my people, and thy God my God:

Ruth kept the name of the dead. She came to Israel as a widow but ushered in the most incredible man down the road. Boaz, the wealthiest man in Israel, married Ruth. Ruth was the great-grandmother of King David. Ruth ushered Great King David to rule in Israel.

Ruth 4:21a Boaz begat Obed, 22 And Obed begat Jesse, and Jesse begat David.

The great King David ushers the Messiah into this world.

Something is introduced to the world by us. Keep close attention to what we are ushering in. We make a big difference. Poverty can turn into riches, slavery into freedom, and much more if we usher in the Prophet, preacher, and saints of the Most High God.

LET US PRAY

Lord, we come before your altar, asking for a believing heart. Heart like Mary who ushers in Jesus, Jochebed who ushers in Moses, Mariam, and Aaron. We pray, this world to change. Lord, let our minds be made up to raise the powerful man and woman who brings God in. We desire your truth to set us free. May the Lord Bless each woman and man with a determination to usher in great men and women who make a positive impact. May the Lord help us usher in His word back in our home and country to be blessed again in Jesus's name. Amen! God bless you!

MAY 11

YOU CAN'T UNDERSTAND. JUST DO IT!

God of heaven plans to lead you to safety, prosperity, and higher. It will be an unexpected surprise for all. Relax and make yourself comfortable. If you require healing, it's right here. If you're looking for fish, you've come to the right place. If you need water, here it is. If you seek peace, comfort, and protection, let me be your guide. No need to worry, I'll take care of everything. We have a problem of overthinking and analyzing when confronted with obstacles, resulting in laziness, fear, and irrational thoughts.

1 Corinthians 2:14 But the natural man receiveth not the things of the Spirit of God: for they are foolishness unto him: neither can he know them, because they are spiritually discerned.

The Bible teaches that wisdom comes from fearing God. Knowing the Lord and His power ensures that no problems will take place. Only after getting to know someone can a relationship be established. If they can't be trusted or believed, then what they say is unreliable.

Lord Jesus commanded pairs of individuals to go forth and demonstrate His power by driving out demons, curing the sick, and resurrecting the dead, all in the name of Jesus. Upon Jesus 'arrival to preach about the Kingdom of God, He was well-received by the people. Individuals need to have information about the product before purchasing it. Once they experience the Lord, they'll be amazed! You are an absolute wonder!

1 Corinthians 1:25 Because the foolishness of God is wiser than men; and the weakness of God is stronger than men.

Our human minds struggle to make sense of God's words. Are you in need of something that makes sense? Why? It is God who does the supernatural. That's why He holds the title of God. Taking only two fish and a few pieces of bread, God blessed them and demonstrated a miracle. Hand over your worries to God, and blessings will follow. God was given small pieces that began to multiply. It's simply mind-blowing! God demonstrates the miracle of abundance! It is beyond, and no need to add or subtract when He is leading; just relax.

1 Corinthians 1:18 For the preaching of the cross is to them that perish foolishness; but unto us which are saved it is the power of God. 21 For after that in the wisdom of God the world by wisdom knew not God, it pleased God by the foolishness of preaching to save them that believe.

MAY 11

A leper Naaman, captain of the host of the King of Syria, heard from a little maid from Israel about healing. The great God of Israel and His ways were unknown to Naaman. He arrived in Israel to meet Elisha, the prophet.

2King 5:10 And Elisha sent a messenger unto him, saying, Go and wash in Jordan seven times, and thy flesh shall come again to thee, and thou shalt be clean.11 But Naaman was wroth, and went away, and said, Behold, I thought, He will surely come out to me, stand, and call on the name of the Lord his God, and strike his hand over the place, and recover the leper.12 Are not Abana and Pharpar, rivers of Damascus, better than all the waters of Israel? May I not wash in them and be clean? So he turned and went away in a rage.

Naaman disagreed with Elisha. An obedient person can never predict the result of following God's commands.

The faith must be in God. His order or matter is only understandable to a few. Familiarize yourself with the Lord and believe in His principles.

Lord decided to rename Jacob as Israel. Jacob carried out the Lord's instructions. Just say yes to the Lord.

Matthew 14:36 And besought him that they might only touch the hem of his garment: and as many as touched were made perfectly whole.

Some people acted by faith, but only a fraction of them. They labored according to their desires to obtain their miracle. There was controversy surrounding the healing of a blind man. Why? Show us what we expect and do as I ask. God manifests Himself in diverse ways. Follow the instructions and witness the outcome. Instead of questioning, we should follow God's order and press on.

John 9:6 When he had thus spoken, he spat on the ground, and made clay of the spittle, and he anointed the eyes of the blind man with the clay, 7 And said unto him, Go, wash in the pool of Siloam, (which is by interpretation, Sent.) He went his way, therefore, and washed and came seeing.

Take a moment to ask yourself, would you do this? Does it make sense? You might be wondering why? Yet, the humble man comprehends the ways of God.

Isaiah 55:8 For my thoughts are not your thoughts; neither are your ways my ways, saith the Lord.

I mentioned to the Lord during my morning prayer that I've seen many miracles happen when I prayed for them. I've personally witnessed miracles where the deaf could hear and the lame could walk, but I haven't seen the blind regain their sight. Can you make use of me to bring sight to the blind in your name? Later that day, I drove to the store on K Avenue in Plano, TX. God said, make a left turn here. He pointed to the store, and I parked. Although the parking lot was full, a car moved out right next to mine, and a new vehicle swiftly occupied that spot. I was talking while on the phone. I noticed a man exiting the vehicle while using a white cane to walk. He walked into the store and quickly returned. I asked his wife about his eyes, and she said, he is blind. I had a thought about offering a prayer for him. Wife asked the man, and he said yes. I said a prayer for a man and then drove off. I was clueless about where to find the blind man. That morning, I prayed for God to use me to restore sight to the blind. The Lord knew, so He led me to this blind man.

I went to the children's hospital to offer prayers for a young man. I do not know why they kept him in the children's hospital since he was 22. He had cancer in the past and amputated his leg when he was 16. Cancer kept coming back continually. He asked me to visit him, so I did. During my prayer for him, I extended the offer of prayers to others. His mother asked for prayers, saying, "Please pray for me." I was praying, and God said to sit down and pray for her leg. Despite my back pain, I sat down and reached out to touch her leg. There was a piece of thread I found encircling her ankle. She said she tied it there. I asked what it was about. However, the son responded to me saying it was given by a witch doctor as a form of protection. Later she removed her, and her younger son did the same. See, I wouldn't know about the thread; I lay my hand on her head, but God asked me the put my hand on her leg. He wanted to reveal something to me.

Take the direction that Jesus is showing.

John 14:6 Jesus saith unto him, I am the way, the truth, and the life:

Keep following God's path, even if it doesn't feel right or convenient. It is the correct way of life.

Proverbs 14:12 There is a way which seemeth right unto a man, but the end thereof [are] the ways of death.

Ephesians 5:17 Wherefore be ye not unwise but understanding the will of the Lord [is].

Never try to figure out God or His ways. If God is calling you to jump in, then simply go for it. Whether it's the lion's den or fiery furnace, you have nothing to fear.

The government of God is organized. You will be fine obeying Him. No one knows the way of God. Only through trust can the miracle be achieved. No fear, only faith!

Jeremiah 29:11 For I know the thoughts that I think toward you, saith the LORD, thoughts of peace, and not of evil, to give you an expected end.

What are you expecting today? Let the Holy Spirit serve as a GPS, providing direction and guidance. Take all orders and do it? The Lord has all the power to make crooked ways straight. By the Lord's power, the mountains vanish and the dry ocean becomes land. Thank you, Lord. Is there anything too hard for God? He said I could do everything; nothing is impossible. Why are you questioning? What is the cause of you being a stumbling block? Keep in mind that a limited mind cannot comprehend it supernaturally. If you can't grasp it, recognize that it's all because of God. Just do it.

LET US PRAY

Lord, we come before your altar, asking for a believing heart. Heart like Mary, who ushers in Jesus, Jochebed, who ushers in Moses, Mariam, and Aaron. We pray this world changes. Let our minds be made up to raise the powerful man and woman who brings God in. We desire your truth to set us free. May the Lord Bless each woman and man with a determination to usher in great men and women who make a positive impact. May the Lord help us usher His word back into our home and country to be blessed again in Jesus's name. Amen! God bless you!

MAY 12

WORD GIVES PLATFORM TO GOD OR ENEMY!

Your choice of words can determine life or death.

Proverb 18:21 Death and life are in the power of the tongue: and they that love it shall eat the fruit thereof.

If a situation arises, remember to pause and take a deep breath before speaking. Exercise wisdom when choosing your words. React to the challenge by looking to the promises of God. The Word of God gives the platform to perform His powerful act. Read more words so the Bible becomes the primary book of life.

I have seen people receive promises as they claim. Stay committed to your work and always be honest with your words. Always be attentive and respectful to God's guidance.

I've noticed that when I pray for people, they speak in order to receive something. A tendency to talk negatively results in chronic illness for some individuals. They mentally prepare themselves for feeling unwell on the upcoming day. There will always be the next day. I ask them to speak instead; I will be better tomorrow, say; I am better now. God, heal me now; deliver me now. All should be now. God works that very moment if you stay positive.

Matthew 12: 35 A good man out of the good treasure of the heart bringeth forth good things: and an evil man out of the evil treasure bringeth forth evil things. 36 But I say unto you, That every idle word that men shall speak, they shall give account thereof in the day of judgment. 37 For by thy words thou shalt be justified, and by thy words, thou shalt be condemned.

God operates according to His true word, which has been tested seven times and remains unwavering. Beauty is found in believing and obeying the word. I believe that the Word of God is everlasting. There are 5,467 promises given in the Bible. It is all available without sweat; just speak to claim it.

Let me help with your vocabulary. You should never say that it is not God's will, maybe; I think He would not do or I do not know. These words give Satan a platform. Do not make any negative remarks. Read the word, make personal promises, and speak to redeem the securities. As you live for God, you become one of His. No matter what, God is in charge of your body, soul, spirit, family, and everything concerning you.

The truth is what a wise man will always say. Religion finds fault when the Holy Spirit speaks. Some dare to give the platform to the devil. They never see the victorious outcome. They overwrite the Bible through their actions. God did not do an excellent job of writing it? Do not fall into the trap of fitting in or lusting for flesh, eyes, and pride in life. I see them always in the wishing cycle. Seeing their energy, Lord have mercy. When God separates us from religious people, do not try to reconnect.

Deception has become rampant as the end draws near. You may wonder what happened. It is simply the word of God not followed. Their actions prove it. The Bible says that if you speak the talk but do not act.

James 2:26 "For as the body without the spirit is dead, so faith without works is dead also."

The devil recognizes you through your words. You can attend church and pray daily, but what you speak counts the most. A positive person has fewer problems since their mind does not think about all the adverse outcomes of the situation.

The situation can be simple, but speaking negatively will make the weight heavier. Similarly, if you say positive Words, they will lift the load up. Words have the power to destroy and construct. Remember, if the situation could be harmful, keep positive comments to turn it around. Say, the Lord will turn it around in my favor.

Proverbs 16:24 Pleasant words [are as] a honeycomb, sweet to the soul, and health to the bones.

Proverbs 15:1 A soft answer turneth away wrath: but griev-ous words stir up anger.

When you meditate, you will speak. Meditate on good and positive things.

Psalms 19:14 Let the words of my mouth, and the meditation of my heart, be acceptable in thy sight, O LORD, my strength, and my redeemer.

Every one of us experiences difficulties and challenges, but our actions shape the final outcome. When you say the Lord will see me through, you are challenging God. All challenges are taken by God. Say, all is well; it will be well. I'll make it happen, and you will too. When sickness comes, then say, I will be healed. Declare the Lord is my healer. State confidently that God is in control, no matter how things may appear. The Lord will provide from His abundance when we are in need. We fail ourselves by constantly searching for our own mistakes. Do not curse yourself.

Jeremiah 17:5 Thus saith the Lord; Cursed be the man that trusteth in man, and maketh flesh his arm, and whose heart departeth from the Lord.

Our prayer through the Word of God is the key to success. In short, we create our world. Our life should be a book one would like to read. Our testimony should be someone's stepping stone. We're the book that people read without asking for your permission. Your actions have an impact on life, even if no one trusts your words. The spice of life is found in overcoming challenges. In life, actions have more impact than words. People learn 85% of your example. Once, I was a shepherd; now, I have a crown on my head. The reason you don't sit on the throne is because your life hasn't impacted God.

MAY 12

Merely acknowledging God in your situation won't necessarily convince Him. God, I want you to know that I surrender to you and trust you to guide my life. I trust you for my life, knowing who you are. My life can't be the same since my problem is beyond my control, and you take care of it. I perceive the situation as you do, with one side having a thousand and the other side having ten thousand. I know they cannot harm me. You are my defender. Many are my troubles, but you brought me out of them all. I have seen with my eyes the fall of my enemy. Give peace and comfort in a time of my calamity. What more can I say? The Lord gives victory, healing, joy, tranquility, comfort, promotion, and all. Once you develop your relationship with the Lord, you are on the road to victory. God is all that you need.

That is why: Philippians 4:6 Be careful for nothing; but in everything by prayer and supplication with thanksgiving let your requests be made known unto God.7 And the peace of God, which passeth all understanding, shall keep your hearts and minds through Christ Jesus.8 Finally, brethren, whatsoever things are faithful, whatsoever things are honest, whatsoever things are just, whatsoever things are pure, whatsoever things are lovely, whatsoever things are of good report; if there be any virtue, and if there be any praise, think on these things.9 Those things, which ye have both learned, received, heard, and seen in me, do: and the God of peace shall be with you.

The understanding of God is the key to success.

Proverbs 4:5 Get wisdom, get understanding: forget it not; neither decline from the words of my mouth.

I win souls; some of them are a joy. When the trial comes, the situation goes over the head; their words are always positive and healthy to the hearer. When faced with trouble, they cry but claim to hand it over to God. As expected, the devil has no power over the situation. I have personally witnessed God untangling the confusion. Always remember, you have the power to build your world. Master the art of selecting the right words for divine intervention. Stand your ground and make your claim known in this particular scenario. See what happens. Your journey will be filled with consecutive victories, constantly ascending higher, and life will be infused with the fragrance of success.

LET US PRAY

We thank you for the Word of God. It is the life- giving word. It gives nutrition to my spirit and protection to my soul from harm. Lord, let my words be right and acceptable in your sight. My words give birth to evidence to trust in your beautiful name. God almighty, we need you to provide understanding and wisdom through your word. It is life giving and healthy to the hearer-more of you than we desire. The Word of God should illuminate our path. You gave these beautiful words to speak with authority and power in the name of Jesus. Amen. God bless you!

MAY 13

YOU ARE MY RESPONSIBILITY, IF!

The Lord can take care of us only if we follow His voice. If we allow Him to be our shepherd and be His sheep, then we never have to worry about pastures, water, and protection. He leads sheep in places where there is safety. He keeps the devourer away from His sheep. How wonderful! Do sheep have the ability to protect themselves? They will run away from a predator. Instead of fighting, they choose to flee. Just remember, having a shepherd ensures your safety. David kept his sheep and fought against the Bears and Lions. The true shepherd, Jesus, will fight and deliver us from the predator. If we allow Him to be, the Lord is our creator, father, and Shepard.

We become His responsibility when we are born again. He also has given you a unique Shepherd just for you. So, depending on God, take His lead to find a Shepherd specially chosen for you. There are many shepherds, but God will designate some for your journey.

Jeremiah 3:15 And I will give you pastors according to mine heart, which shall feed you with knowledge and understanding.

A man had two sons, and one went away from every benefit, being the son of a wealthy father. The father had servants, flocks, farms, and riches. He took off, not realizing what he thought was a deception of Satan. He found rejection, starvation, and all opposite of what he thought. We decide to go astray from Him is the end of all benefits and privileges. A prodigal son is in Luke 15 is the parable of what happens if you think of going astray from the Lord.

God is the provider if you stay under His rules and regulation. God is not for the rebellious, disobedient, and covenant breaker. Our wages are much more than we can imagine if we obey His commandments.

When we say "God becomes our Elohim," it signifies that Adonai is our supreme master. Our El Bethel the House of God, El Elyon, the highest God, He becomes El Emunah, the faithful God; we can say He is my Elohei tehillati, my praise, El Hakabodh, my God of Glory. This mighty God will show by acting on each occasion and situation that arises in our life.

He will become Elohim Chayim, the Living God, El Hayyay, the God of my life. Elohim Machase Lanu, God, my Refuge. When you need strength and fortress, He becomes your Elohei Ma'uzzi. In trouble, he becomes El Rai, the God sees us. Regardless of your location - be it the desert, unfamiliar territories, or in

MAY 13

spirit or body - He will uphold you. Lord, Becoming your rock of salvation means El Sali. He is El Shaddai, the Almighty. He is our salvation, meant deliverer, healer, and redeemer Elohe Tishuathi.

Walking in His statutes and precepts, He becomes our righteousness: Elohe Tsadeki. Because God is Elohei Haelohim, the God of gods, you have no reason to be afraid of other gods, goddesses, witchcraft, or demonic forces. He will use His Sword to protect since He is Jehovah Cherub. God will fight all our battles, Jehovah Gibbor Milchama, the Lord mighty in battle. Our God is Holy. He is Kadosh. God is a Spirit God, Rauch Elohim; God is our Ab, our father. Jehovah is Malakh, our Angel. He is now Emmanuel; God is with us.

Remember, we might find an easy way by establishing or following a religion and turn back like the prodigal son. You can experience the Great God at the highest level. You won't believe the power and might of Him that will blow your mind away. In times of need, he will act according to your requirements. Picking and choosing from various churches and denominations is illustrated by the concept of a prodigal son.

There was a time; I was also seeking Him. If you find yourself lost, follow the example of the Prodigal son and make a u-turn and come back. Like a lost sheep, His arms are open to receive you. The Prodigal Son did not find rest for His soul, where he wandered from place to place. He said there is no other way but to repent. As we follow God's way, we find all the truth to set us free.

I challenge you that there is nothing better than truth. I am searching for the truth. The devil manipulates the fact by hiding, removing, burning, adding, and subtracting. It will not work for true lovers. Precious Lord is merciful to take us in if we say, forgive me, Lord; I am wrong.

Let us read.

Luke 15:14 And when he had spent all, there arose a mighty famine in that land; and he began to be in want. 15 And he joined himself to a citizen of that country; and he sent him into his fields to feed swine. 16 And he would fain have filled his belly with the husks that the swine did eat: and no man gave unto him. 17 And when he came to himself, he said, How many hired servants of my father's have bread enough and to spare, and I perish with hunger! 18 I will arise and go to my father, and will say unto him, Father, I have sinned against heaven, and before thee, 19 And am no more worthy to be called thy son: make me as one of thy hired servants. 20 And he arose, and came to his father. But when he was yet a great way off, his father saw him, and had compassion, and ran, and fell on his neck, and kissed him. 21 And the son said unto him, Father, I have sinned against heaven, and in thy sight, and am no more worthy to be called thy son. 22 But the father said to his servants, Bring forth the best robe, and put it on him; and put a ring on his hand, and shoes on his feet: 23 And bring hither the fatted calf, and kill it; and let us eat, and be merry: 24 For this my son was dead, and is alive again; he was lost, and is found. And they began to be merry.

God grants a sense of peaceful reassurance. Sleep peacefully; you can't take care of yourself. It provided lifetime coverage for you. God, I am your servant, take charge of provision, protection, and all.

Isaiah 46:4 And even to your old age I am he; and even to hoar hairs will I carry you: I have made, and I will bear; even I will carry and will deliver you.

May the Lord bless us with a discerning mind and comprehension of His ways. What we have is not because of our effort or intelligence. It is because of our great God. The nation prospers as a result of the forefather's commitment to following God's Law and commandment. They feared and served the Living God.

Psalm 33:12 Blessed is the nation whose God is the Lord; and the people whom he hath chosen for his own inheritance.13 The Lord looketh from heaven; he beholdeth all the sons of men.14 From the place of his habitation he looketh upon all the inhabitants of the earth.15 He fashioneth their hearts alike; he considereth all their works.16 There is no king saved by the multitude of an host: a mighty man is not delivered by much strength.17 An horse is a vain thing for safety: neither shall he deliver any by his great strength.18 Behold, the eye of the Lord is upon them that fear him, upon them that hope in his mercy;19 To deliver their soul from death, and to keep them alive in famine.20 Our soul waiteth for the Lord: he is our help and our shield.

Lord, grant us the strength to abide by statutes, commandments, laws, and precepts, and to embrace love in our hearts. May the Lord give us a desire to seek Him? Lord, give us the strength to keep going until the end. The darkness has come, but the Lord will be our light if we follow Him.

Any nation that leaves God can compare with the prodigal son. We can have all and more if we just stay under His umbrella of Grace and mercy. May the Lord send us the True Shepherd, prophet, and Teachers. Who is willing to sacrifice their life for the sheep? May we be blessed with leaders similar to Moses, Joshua, and David. He is straightforward with his answers, saying yes or no without hesitation. Open your Bible and dig deep, seek and see what happens. He is present to provide guidance and support for you. You'll find safety in your father's house if you return. May the Lord bestow His blessings upon you!

LET US PRAY

My Lord, we need you till we depart. We want to be your sheep; we want to follow the true shepherd. Deliver us from a hireling. May the Lord give us His Word to keep us from going astray. There is nothing but evil out there. The peace, protection, and help are with you. Lord, we handle our choices. Please give us the wisdom to make the right choices. Lord your mercy, and grace never depart from us. I speak the blessing of God over you and your family. May Lord keep you from all appearance of evil and guide you till you meet Him in Jesus's name. Amen! God bless you!

MAY 14

WHAT IS YOUR ROLE IN THE KINGDOM?

I once inquired of God about my purpose in serving the Kingdom. He informed me that I have been chosen as a prayer warrior.

2 Peter 1:10 Wherefore the rather, brethren, give diligence to make your calling and election sure: for if ye do these things, ye shall never fall:

I find great joy in praying. I pray whenever I can find a spare moment. At work, I eat during break time which is only 15 minutes. I hide in some corners during the lunch break and pray for 30 minutes. After work, I pray with my coworker. I pray for God to send someone to join me in prayer. The Bible says if two or more agree on anything is done. I'm always on the lookout for someone to join me. I see this as my true calling and have a strong desire to excel in it.

Matthew 18:19 Again I say unto you, That if two of you shall agree on earth as touching anything that they shall ask, it shall be done for them of my Father which is in heaven. 20 For where two or three are gathered together in my name, I am in the midst of them.

I had a coworker who also participated in fasting and praying. We must respond to our calling to the best of our ability. We have won many battles by praying to gather. Many prayers have been answered by now. Prayer is a necessary tool to fight the enemy. Prayer is the hiding place with the Lord! I pray while driving, in the shower, any time, all the time. Now I do not work, so I wake up to pray at 3:50 am or before that. I get a prayer request call or text message all day and night from people around the world.

Staying connected through prayer keeps us in His presence. May every household be blessed with a prayer altar from the Lord. A Godly man always seeks a place to pray. King David prayed all the time. He loved to be in the presence of God. He built the Temple where they prayed.

If your leader prays, your nation will experience peace, protection, and prosperity. No place in the world is better than the presence of God. Solomon built a magnificent Temple, and said, Lord, answer our prayer when anyone prays at this place. What the nation needs are prayer towers and prayer places, not churches without prayer.

God called Moses to redeem Hebrew from slavery. Can I consider this a small task? Only God knows who is capable of handling this task. Stick to the tasks assigned by God, don't take on someone else's duties. And don't advise since God is the director.

Exodus 4:10 And Moses said unto the Lord, O my Lord, I am not eloquent, neither heretofore, nor since thou hast spoken unto thy servant: but I am slow of speech and a slow tongue.11 And the Lord said unto him, Who hath made man's mouth? or who maketh the dumb, or deaf, or the seeing, or the blind? have not I the Lord?12 Therefore, go, and I will be with thy mouth, and teach thee what thou shalt say.

Those who are called by God are not necessarily qualified, but they become qualified through His calling. Lord also performed many signs and wonders in Egypt through Moses. When God calls, just say yes, Lord. He is doing all; you are a surrendered vessel in His hand. Many times, He will ask me to go places to pray or counsel people. As I go, I see miracles, healing, and deliverance.

Jeremiah 1:5 Before I formed thee in the belly I knew thee, and before thou camest forth out of the womb I sanctified thee, and I ordained thee a prophet unto the nations.

The majority of individuals lack knowledge about their role in the Kingdom. God picks your role, but you must also understand your role in His Kingdom. If a person does not know their role, they will wander like a ship without a sailor. If a person knows their part, they must hold on to God. He will position you. There is no big or small role, but playing the role with diligence will establish God's purpose.

1 Corinthians 1:26 For ye see your calling, brethren, how that not many wise men after the flesh, not many mighty, not many noble, are called: 27 But God hath chosen the foolish things of the world to confound the wise; and God hath chosen the weak things of the world to confound the things which are mighty; 28 And base things of the world, and things which are despised, hath God chosen, yea, and things which are not, to bring to naught things that are: 29 That no flesh should glory in his presence.

If we are called a manager, supervisors, teachers, doctors, or whatever, we try our best. If not, then there are chances of losing our position. Many work for money and give themselves 100% to the secular job but treat God's creation as secondary. They will do it if they feel like it or they have time. I want to do God's work to the best of my ability. We must be faithful to our calling.

Philippians 3:14 I press toward the mark for the prize of the high calling of God in Christ Jesus.

When God calls, He will go with you all the way. He will not send you to the field and disappear. His purpose on earth can only be fulfilled if He finds the workers for God's high calling.

1 Thessalonians 5:24 Faithful is he that calleth you, who also will do it.

God called us to work for His purpose and not ours. We must get His guidance and instruction to carry on His blueprint to fulfill His kingdom plan. Receive His provisions, protections, and unique extras.

2 Timothy 1:9 Who hath saved us, and called us with a holy calling, not according to our works, but according to his own purpose and grace, which was given us in Christ Jesus before the world began.

MAY 14

He said do not add and subtract. Our major problem is we add and remove from His plan. We see no result but sickness, curses, and bondages. We know the confusion, discouragement, and ruin of the beautiful dream of God.

God said go,

Mark 16:15 And he said unto them, Go ye into all the world, and preach the gospel to every creature.

We must go out to preach the gospel. Many times we say, it's not for me, that's the excuse we give. Always say, oh yes, I go to church. Listen to what God said, go, and preach the gospel. That is mine and your job. I must pray and preach the gospel— the good news of healing, deliverance, and salvation.

He who calleth us is faithful; He will go with us. Jesus said to preach the gospel, cast out the demon, and heal the sick. If they believe in Jesus, then baptize them in the name of Jesus. God called us to do this high calling of God. You and I join the church and follow the plan and agenda of the church. That is not God's plan. God came to set the captive free and heal the sick, break the chain, and yoke Satan. Jesus Gave power over serpents, scorpions, and poisoned food. We must respond to our calling. We must preach the gospel if we go to work, market, or anywhere. The Lord will perform supernaturally. He has called many people.

Jesus likes Hearer and doer.

Mark 16:20 And they went forth and preached everywhere, the Lord working with them, and confirming the word with signs following. Amen.

One afternoon, a lady and I went to Pioneer Blvd in California. We went shop to shop and preached the gospel. We visited the last shop and asked the couple if they needed prayer. A couple was sad and said; please pray for us; we lost a young son. As we prayed over them, the Holy Spirit touched the couple. See, Jesus came to heal the broken heart. Many are doing the evil thing. Why? Their heart is broken. Only Jesus heals the broken heart. His Holy Spirit comforts the heart; He healeth the deep wounds.

Jesus wants someone to do as He planned. Do not add. How many churches are there? Nothing is happening except their business and how they designed it. They have replaced the plan of God with theirs. We fail God all the time. It is humans who fail God, not God fails us. God is faithful.

Respond to God's calling. We have many churches; some are crowded, but they are the organization's followers, not God. God can further His Kingdom if He finds a faithful servant. Perform your role sincerely.

Matthew 25:21 His Lord said unto him, Well done, thou good and faithful servant: thou hast been faithful over a few things, I will make thee ruler over many things: enter thou into the joy of thy Lord.

LET US PRAY

Lord, we are grateful for calling us to work in your Kingdom. We desire to be faithful. Lord, many are called, but few are chosen. We want to call the chosen one. Lord, it is the high calling of God. You will not leave us on the field but work with us to deliver from all worry and fear. Many questions, but let us say, yes, Lord, your servant hearth. Speak, Lord. The Lord blesses thousands of generations who work for Him.

We desire blessings to run in our family. Let unlimited benefits come into our life, so we find favor. We always want to have over and above His abundant blessings in Jesus's name. Amen! God bless you!

MAY 15

DIE TO SELF SO CHRIST CAN LIVE!

To increase wheat production, wheat needs to die underground. In order for you to live, your flesh must die. The soul finds life in the death of the self's flesh. The soul's existence relies on the choices made between flesh and spirit, Satan's domain being the flesh and Spirit God's domain being the spirit.

Roman 6:8 Now, if we be dead with Christ, we believe that we shall also live with him.

Eve and Adam failed in their fleshly trials, but Christ triumphed over them all. It takes someone to die of the lust of eyes, the lust of the flesh, and the pride of life. To live eternally, we must be crucified with the Lord. God told Adam that he would die the day he ate the fruit. That is the eternal death of an immortal soul in the lake of fire.

The same thing happened; now, we must overcome what Adam and Eve couldn't. Jesus provided all assistance to conquer the flesh, specifically through the spirit of repentance. The spirit of repentance is the realization of sin with the determination to make a U-turn toward the cross. What a privilege to have the excess of the Blood of Jesus to wipe out every sin and death of flesh in the baptismal tank in Jesus 'name.

Study the book of Acts to learn about the significance of baptism in Jesus 'name and receive the forgiveness of your sins by being baptized in his name. It is the marvelous experience of rising in the newness of life. When you go into the water, they bury the sinner man in the name of Jesus.

Do not change anything in the word of God. Do not add or subtract. Give it serious consideration, as the God who spoke to Adam and Eve is speaking to you today, cautioning that disobedience results in death. Choose to die to your flesh, burying your old sinful nature, and God will bring forth a new person. To help you reach the end of your life's journey, He will give His Spirit.

I choose to sacrifice my earthly self and follow Jesus, allowing God's Spirit to guide me for eternal life.

Roman 6:6 Knowing that our old man is crucified with him, that the body of sin might be destroyed, that henceforth we should not serve sin.7 For he that is dead is freed from sin.

Christianity is the result of God's creation being redeemed. His blood was the price God paid to reclaim what was lost in the Garden of Eden. The Lord's plan is always the best, but it still requires following the procedure. We know God speaks the truth, but Satan speaks the lies. To reach your destination in life, keep the word of God, which is the voice of God, in your heart. If you choose to live according to your sinful nature and allow the enemy to lead you astray, you will find yourself condemned to hell for eternity, similar to what happened to Adam and Eve. Do not destroy the New Testament Plan that was bought back by God's Blood. God's spirit took on a physical form to offer its blood for us.

Once saved, always saved, and simple faith is the Logo of the devil. It is not the truth of the Bible. According to the Bible, we should continue in truth by exploring and searching for it. The devil will say to enjoy; you are saved, so do whatever. The devil is still leading many astray, causing the cross to have no impact. In order to mislead God's creation, the devil has established multiple religions.

John 8:31 Then said Jesus to those Jews which believed on him, If ye continue in my word, then are ye my disciples indeed;32 And ye shall know the truth, and the fact shall make you free.

Make sure to always seek truth from the Word of God. It will continue to help to crucify flesh to keep you close to Christ. Our flesh does not possess anything good within it. The transgression of disobedience allows Satan to defile flash. Sin entered the flesh, which was not there before. Adam and Eve did not know right from wrong. Once you allow it, this cancer of corruption needs to continue to weed out from within. Maintain the act of killing flesh on a daily basis.

Romans 7:18 For I know that in me (that is, in my flesh) dwelleth no good thing: for to will is present with me, but how to perform that which is good I find not.19 For the good that I would I do not: but the evil which I would not, that I do.20 Now if I do that I would not, it is no more I that do it, but sin that dwelleth in me.

Let's remember that this is a process because we have all sinned. Sin enters right from the beginning. The devil attempts a new tactic to make you stumble, as you continue to be crucified. Many new devices of Satan exist to harm you, but you can triumph over them daily by denying, dying, and crucifying your own self.

Galatians 2:20 I am crucified with Christ: nevertheless, I live; yet not I, but Christ liveth in me: and the life which I now live in the flesh I live by the faith of the Son of God, who loved me and gave himself for me.

By replacing worldly desires with a holy lifestyle, you pave the path to victory.

Romans 8:12 Therefore, brethren are debtors, not to the flesh, to live after the flesh.13 For if ye live after the flesh, ye shall die: but if ye through the spirit do mortify the deeds of the body, ye shall live.

Many churches will never teach about sin, but the Bible repeatedly talks to remind us. Sin is the problem, and Jesus is the answer, not churches. Your body serves as the church. If Adam and Eve had held onto the word in their hearts, the story would have been different. It's important to hold onto the word of God in your heart. Keep word knowing dos and don't. Take the warnings and cautions from God in the Bible seriously and avoid them.

To live in the spirit, you must die in the flesh. Living right requires the assistance of the Spirit of God; it's not something you can achieve on your own. You need true teachers and prophets to help you.
David was led astray by sin. There is no choice but for him to perish. It's an everlasting damnation in hell. See, once you die to the flesh, which has all sin, then you can live.

MAY 15

2 Samuel 12:13 And David said unto Nathan, I have sinned against the LORD. And Nathan said unto David, The LORD also hath put away thy sin; thou shalt not die.

Prosperity comes from heeding the words of the Prophet. Do we have the Prophet today? The Prophet will point out the sins, and you can get forgiveness if you repent. Sinners cannot go to heaven, period.

What causes you to die eternally that must die? All sin hiding in the flesh must mortify, kill, uproot, and destroy. May the Lord give us the strength to kill our desire, lust, and pride, which causes eternal death. May the Lord grant His Spirit to us, so we live eternally. The Spirit of God is the greatest gift ever to guide, lead, teach, empower, and speak to the enemy. The enemy may have the beautiful package to seduce, but the Holy Spirit will reveal the disguiser. A hunter of my soul, the enemy of the cross, and hater of the light! The deceitful and manipulative aim to destroy me by luring me into sin. I do not window shop.

I see many hang-ups; suicides kill and die without Jesus. They needed to die in the flesh to live. It is imperative that we confront and reject the devil's deceptive tactics of distorting and manipulating the Word of God, as it can have horrible consequences for our eternal salvation. Lord, grant us your teachings, guidance, and words, that we may crucify our flesh and suppress the longing for Jesus to reside within us. When you do not hear God, check where the sin lies within you.

May you receive the Lord's blessing of clarity and discernment to avoid the eternal punishment of hell. God is the one who loves you. That is why he gave the commandment. Eve and Adam felt they had missed out and were deeply saddened.

1 John 5:3 For this is the love of God that we keep his commandments: and his commandments are not grievous.

May we think in the same way as John the Baptist.

John 3:30 He must increase, but I must decrease.

Luke 9:23 And he said to them all, If any man will come after me, let him deny himself, take up his cross daily, and follow me. 24 For whosoever will save his life shall lose it: but whosoever will lose his life for my sake, the same shall save it.

LET US PRAY

Lord, we must die by repenting all sin and burying ourselves in the water. Our appreciation goes to the cross, representing the triumph over our physical desires. We know nothing is good in the flesh; even the aging process speaks to us. Let us die and let the Lord live in us. We desire this world to see the Lord if we fail to self and its desire. We want to rule with you forever. Our desire is to spend eternity living together with you. Your precious blood speaks on our behalf, and we are grateful. It is better than Abel's blood crying out from the ground. May Lord help us die to our flesh every day, so our Lord lives through us and in us. In Jesus's name. Amen! God bless you!

MAY 16

WHY AREN'T YOU USING THE TREASURE?

Are you familiar with the process of withdrawing the treasure? It takes more than just converting to Christianity. Once you convert to Christianity, you will discover a multitude of wonderful blessings waiting for you. In order for you to learn, someone needs to teach. Jesus taught the Disciples. Paul, Peter, and other apostles spread their teachings to Galatians, Corinthians, Ephesians, and cities in Greek and Asia. Do not just take people to church; lead, counsel, and pray with them. Did you know that you represent the church? Keep them under your wings while teaching and training them. It is a job; I love it.

When you bring children into the world, you don't abandon them; you look after them. Take care of, attend to, and assist until they become fully developed. When you bring someone to the Lord, approach teaching them in the same way you would with a baby.

Once I learned the truth, I began reading and studying the Bible every day. Upon hearing people's testimonies, I took it as my own. I prayed for God to do the same thing. The condition of God must be obeyed by us. If we do, we open the treasure. I teach many today, so they understand extending and expanding their territories. Receive the hidden treasure existing if you obey the Scriptures of God. Many wonder why they're not experiencing the same blessings as others. You can if you learn how. May the Lord give us many true teachers and prophets. Knowledge is the Key.

Ephesians 4:11 And he gave some, apostles; and some, prophets; and some, evangelists; and some, pastors and teachers; 12 For the perfecting of the saints, for the work of the ministry, for the edifying of the body of Christ: 14 That we henceforth are no more children, tossed to and fro, and carried about with every wind of doctrine, by the sleight of men, and cunning craftiness, whereby they lie in wait to deceive.

Prayer and teaching are necessary every day. Think of the media; you can reach the world through your teaching and preaching. It's possible to cast out demons or cure the sick through a phone call.

See the ancient churches.

Acts 2:42 And they continued steadfastly in the apostles' doctrine and fellowship, and in breaking of bread, and in prayers.

Jesus worked every day; disciples worked every day, and so we do. Ignorant Christians are frequently responsible for creating a negative image. This is the reason why individuals question, comment on, and

MAY 16

distance themselves from the living God. Your home should serve as a gathering place, fostering connections and education. A baptistry in the backyard can cleanse the sins of those who repent and believe. As you work like Jesus, you can have treasure.

It is important for us to study and educate our children about the word. Their education is not something we should worry about. Our system has taken away our money, focus, time, and children, all from God. It is important to educate them on praying, expelling demons, receiving blessings, and accessing heavenly treasures. Learning should be based on the principles of God. Treasure will can come to us.

Matthew 6; 33 But seek ye first the kingdom of God, and his righteousness; and all these things shall be added unto you.

In addition, we have the opportunity to be wealthy in heaven.

Matthew 6:20 But lay up for yourselves treasures in heaven, where neither moth nor rust doth corrupt, and where thieves do not break through nor steal:

From the start, I learned the importance of giving. It was the best part of life to give to God. I witnessed the door being opened by God. The key to financial protection and blessings lies in giving to God's laborers, widows, orphans, the poor, and the hungry.

Blessings come from giving to the right places. Each Promise in Word is the rope to pull your blessings on earth. The manifestation of the promise depends on you. The necessity lies in using the word of God as a key. If not, you are just wasting time and living in darkness! Refuse to accept anything less than what you deserve.

Deuteronomy 28:11 And the Lord shall make thee plenteous in goods, in the fruit of thy body, and in the fruit of thy cattle, and the fruit of thy ground, in the land which the Lord sware unto thy fathers to give thee 12 The Lord shall open unto thee his good treasure, the heaven to give the rain unto thy land in his season, and to bless all the work of thine hand: and thou shalt lend unto many nations, and thou shalt not borrow.13 And the Lord shall make thee the head, and not the tail; and thou shalt be above only, and thou shalt not be beneath; if that thou hearkens unto the commandments of the Lord thy God, which I command thee this day, to observe and to do them:14 And thou shalt not go aside from any of the words which I command thee this day, to the right hand, or to the left, to go after other gods to serve them.

I witness Christians experiencing poverty, illness, bondage, and despair. The truth was not accurately taught by someone. Day and night, tirelessly seek out what you're lacking, what you're failing to do, and where the blessings have been stolen, destroyed, or vanished. Look no further, the answer is right here.

Deuteronomy 28:1 And it shall come to pass, if thou shalt hearken diligently unto the voice of the LORD thy God, to observe and to do all his commandments which I command thee this day, that the LORD thy God will set thee on high above all nations of the earth: 2 And all these blessings shall come on thee, and overtake thee if thou shalt hearken unto the voice of the LORD thy God.

True teachers and prophets are crucial in interpreting the Word of God for me to receive my inheritance. Can you imagine where your nation can be today if you teach truth? If we prioritize the Word of God and live by its teachings. These additional dangers can be eliminated. Our home is secure without the need for security systems, prisons, credit cards, or debt. We shouldn't borrow and submit ourselves to the devil's control. They have disconnected us from God without realizing it.

Luke 22:35 And he said unto them When I sent you without purse, and scrip, and shoes, lacked ye any thing? And they said nothing.

Our needs can meet if we go out and preach the word. Be careful of false teachers and prophets if you seek treasure. When God called me to work, He made a promise to take care of me. I am so happy; I have been without a job for the last 23 + years. God has taken care of my need. I never have to worry about tomorrow. May Lord give you a revelation of how to withdraw His treasure. There are many ways.

Let us see when you help the poor,

Proverbs 19:17 He that hath pity upon the poor lendeth unto the LORD; and that which he hath given will he pay him again.

Be mindful of how you give. *Luke 6:38 Give, and I shall give it unto you; good measure, pressed down, shaken together, and running over, shall men give into your bosom. With the same measure that ye mete withal, it shall be measured to you again.*

Friends, you can be rich, overflowing, and blessed. Your individual contribution determines the prosperity of the nation, leading to wealth for the entire country. Decide, do not go astray to worship dumb and deaf idols. They are millions of evil spirits. They do nothing good for those who worship them. Idol worshippers wander from place to place for a better life. Take a look at their country. How poor are they? To receive blessings in Jesus's name, open your Bible and faithfully observe its laws and commandments. Amen!

LET US PRAY

Our great and precious One true God, possessors of heaven and earth who bless a thousand of a generation who love and obey you. We asked you to bless us with divine understanding and an obedient heart to receive your treasure on earth and in heaven. This treasure is better than making ourselves tired of working on earth. Help us teach our children the divine laws and commandments so we live as a rich, healthy, and wealthy generation. May God give us the heart to trust, believe, and obey his commandments. Lord, thank you for loading us daily with benefits. May Lord give us all treasures of heaven, so His name is blessed and magnified in this world in Jesus's name. Amen! God bless you!

MAY 17

KNOW GOD, BE STRONG, AND DO EXPLOITS!

Satan knew God and was in the presence of God for millions or trillions of years. He had an excess of moving in and out of the presence of God. Thus, He is aware of God's strength and power. Yet, our connection was broken when we committed the transgression known as disobedience.

Our knowledge of God is based solely on our obedience to His Word.

God reveals Himself to individuals through dreams, audible communication, or introducing His ministers, known as Angels. God comes in a vision or plan. Long ago, there was no access to the written word of God.

Genesis 15:1 After these things, the word of the Lord came unto Abram in a vision, saying, Fear not, Abram: I am thy shield, and thy exceeding great reward.

The righteous man and woman receive messages from God. He gives orders, provides instructions, and issues warnings.

Genesis 20:3 But God came to Abimelek in a dream one night and said to him, "You are as good as dead because of the woman you have taken; she is a married woman."

Relationships between us and God are built through His Word, ordained prophets, and priests. Now we tell them pastors, evangelists, prophets, apostles, and Teachers. Having His Spirit with us is a privilege as He teaches, talks, leads, and guides us to all truth. It's usable at any time. By understanding how, we can easily connect with our divine God.

This is a wonderful period to be alive. Walking and talking with God is possible if we faithfully follow His instructions and guidance. We need to pray and familiarize ourselves with Him through Torah and the Bible in order to develop a relationship. God has provided us with the book known as the Bible. The correct path was lost because of Satan's misleading. By employing the old strategy of lies and deception, he continues to steal, kill, and destroy.

Babylon had Daniel as an enslaved individual. He possessed knowledge about his God. To know God in His might and power is very important. God is a covenant keeper if we fulfill our condition. Our God

Jehovah is a supreme, everlasting father, alpha and omega, beginning and ending, first and last. Now He is a healer, healer of the broken heart, and the deliverer. God said nothing is impossible, and all things are possible.

Once you're informed, the thought of perishing in the lion's den won't scare you. When you have a relationship with God, the devil will fear you.

The Lord directed me to pray for the Pastor of the Church during our early morning prayer. I prayed over Him, not knowing he had cancer. Releasing a mighty 500-watt surge, it crushed the cancer demon. A multitude of patients experienced healing after my prayer in an ICU room. I knew the devil was there to kill and destroy. During our phone conversation, I prayed for the lady in the ICU. She spent several days there but came out on the same day. I knew the devil was holding her. She could not catch her breath. According to her, she was communicating with fallen angels in the ICU. Having knowledge is crucial for accomplishing great and powerful tasks.

It's hard for an ordinary person who attends church to believe in His might and power. The average church attendee would continue relying on medication, surgery, and satanic media assistance. If you possess the truth, sickness will go away. God's knowledge will be communicated, and that is the truth. Send the word like, I just touched the garment, and let your shadow pass heal me.

Our keys to knowledge are stolen by false prophets and teachers. It is my job to get it back to what belongs to me. The Bible is my life manual-a hidden treasure to do exploits. My strength comes from knowing God.

Daniel 11:32 And such as do wickedly against the covenant shall he corrupt by flatteries: but the people that do know their God shall be strong, and do exploits.

Paul ignorantly killed people who believed in Lord Jesus. Paul gained strength and exploited after receiving knowledge of Jesus.

Listen to Paul:

Philippians 3:8:Yea doubtless, and I count all things but loss for the excellency of the knowledge of Christ Jesus my Lord: for whom I have suffered the loss of all things and do count them but dung, that I may win Christ,10 That I may know him, and the power of his resurrection, and the fellowship of his sufferings, being made conformable unto his death;

All knowledge of this world is enmity. The greater your knowledge, the more it will challenge your faith in God. You are catching yourself in a thicket of confusion. Once you have a relationship with God, Satan's reign is finished.

Man can establish a relationship with God by trusting in Him. There is nothing like it. The powerful motion in the celestial sphere will be visible to you. The one who steals, kills, and destroys throughout time will need to change their location. May the Lord raise many Paul, Peter, and John these days! We require an individual who has the audacity to declare "so be it".

Mary's fearlessness resulted from her deep connection with God.

MAY 17

Luke 1:38 And Mary said, Behold the handmaid of the Lord; be it unto me according to thy word. And the angel departed from her.

Overcome the fear of people, death, society, and rejection. We know the power of a lion, fire, water, heights, and all-natural harm, but once you know, the power of God will make you fearless. Quitting is not an option when you have knowledge of God. Daniel prayed for 21 days, and Moses was on the mount for forty days. They patiently waited until they obtained what they were seeking. A lot of people will start praying but will quickly become disheartened and give up. When you pray, your answer is on its way. God is looking for people who have perseverance.

What is the story of today's generation? Our search is focused on finding the witch doctor or another medium. The moment we receive a small favor or promotion, we often quit serving God. Remember, we are strangers and pilgrims. We are searching for the perfect city where you can live forever. We must remain steadfast in our faith in God, who has remained unchanged throughout the ages. Lying is not something he will do. He doesn't show favoritism towards anyone. May we be blessed with individuals like David, who had a deep understanding of his God.

2 Samuel 18:3b now thou art worth ten thousand of us: therefore now it is better that thou assist us out of the city.

Daniel was familiar with his God, the one who unveiled secrets.

Daniel 2:23 I thank thee, and praise thee, O thou God of my fathers, who hast given me wisdom and might, and hast made known unto me now what we desired of thee: for thou hast now made known unto us the king's matter.

Lord, assist us in becoming as faithful as the men and women you have chosen. I seek to find God in every situation I encounter. My hater even sought me out for prayer at the workplace. Their trust in my willingness to help was unwavering. I constantly prayed and received answers from God. May His compassion be extended to all, as the Lord wills. The soul was won through my dedication to prayer and fasting.

A lady was engaged in both Wudu Buddu and witchcraft. I had a vision in my bedroom where I saw God exposing her involvement in witchcraft. The Holy Spirit provided me with guidance while I was praying. The Holy Spirit, who is my teacher, spoke and returned to her in the name of Jesus. She became possessed by four demons that she was sending after someone, unbeknownst to me. Both she and her daughter appeared angelic but were cunning in their actions. However, during the night, God unveiled the truth. The spiritual realm governs the physical world.

There are many who go around complaining that they are stagnant and experiencing a blockage. Knowing your God will make you strong. Kneeling in prayer, fasting, reading the word, and obeying are ways to know God intimately. It's possible to get rid of the devil by following a certain approach. When introducing the devil to people, we can describe him as powerless, a loser, and a liar. Knowing your God requires your determination. May the Lord give us that desire to know Him in His might and power in Jesus's name.

LET US PRAY

Lord, we come before you to know you. Lord, give us that bulldog determination to find the God of the New Testament who said I could do greater. Teach us to do more wondrous works than what you did. Oh God, you depend on us to show the authority and power you have given us. Please help us do what it takes. We need to come to you. Let your Spirit be our teacher. It requires total submission and obedience; we surrender to you, Lord. Have your way in our life in Jesus's name. Amen! God bless you!

MAY 18

GOD MANAGES THE EARTH WITH EXPECTATION!

God does the Earth's establishment and management with a condition. God made beautiful Earth with all provisions to sustain His creation.

Psalms 115:16 The heaven, even the heavens, are the LORD'S: but the Earth hath he given to the children of men.

Humans reside on the Earth that was created by the Lord. God's creation, which included Adam, Eve, and Earth, began at the start. Through the creation story, we learn that disobeying God's commandment can result in a cursed land for the one who disobeys. Mercy is a characteristic of God. We understand what needs to be done because he is straightforward in his speech. May Lord give us a heart and ear to hear and obey.

Genesis 2:7 And the Lord God formed man of the dust of the ground, and breathed into his nostrils the breath of life; and man became a living soul.8 And the Lord God planted a garden eastward in Eden; and there he put the man whom he had formed.

God punished the land with a curse because of man's sin. Pay attention to God's voice. You can give any excuse not to obey; it will not work.

Genesis 3:17 And unto Adam he said, Because thou hast hearkened unto the voice of thy wife, and hast eaten of the tree, of which I commanded thee, saying, Thou shalt not eat of it: cursed is the ground for thy sake; in sorrow shalt, thou eat of it all the days of thy life;

Why is the land cursed? I witnessed the premature dropping of the fruit by the tree. Either through flooding or drought, God destroyed the crops, causing famine. God governs the Earth by means of our proper actions. Some may call it a small transgression. Remember, a little sin leaveneth the whole lump.

Sodom and Gomorrah were destroyed by God as a consequence of people's disobedience to His laws and commandments. The Lord burnt the land with fire.

Genesis 19:24 Then the LORD rained upon Sodom and upon Gomorrah brimstone and fire from the LORD out of heaven;

Before pouring out judgment, God looks for someone to intercede for the land. Abraham attempted to save Sodom and Gomorrah, but God insisted on reducing the number to 10. Lot's family of four, being righteous, were saved. God led four honest out.

Burning sulfur destroyed the land. You cannot use that land to build again. Any land that was once blessed and later worshipped as a place of gods and goddesses will eventually decline.

In India, Christians endured terrible persecution in the year 2000. That year, an earthquake came where they beat up missionaries. The epicenter experienced the release of saltwater. Now, in that land, you cannot have any crops. See, the Earth belongs to the Lord. Should you ever decide to harm the followers of Jesus Christ, remember that you are not going against Christianity, but the one true God Almighty. God has given us temporary stewardship of the Earth. Expect judgment if you fail to properly care for the planet He entrusted to us. God's hand is powerful enough to reach you. Consider carefully before you act. With God's power, winning is out of the question. His people will receive assistance from God. The Word of God was tested in the fire seven times. It's unwise to go against the people who bring prosperity to your country. Those who are ministers to so-called gods and goddesses eat pounds of food because of a demon that craves excess. By deceiving people, the lie ensures they receive food and believe they will be blessed. According to the Bible, feeding the poor brings blessings. All animals were created by God. Instead of worshipping animals, you worship the one who created them. May God remove their spiritual blindness and guide them to love Him and find blessings.

May the Lord give us a sense of responsibility to live on Earth. God's unique favor involves the creation and blessing of the Earth, ensuring that no one goes hungry. By following His laws and commandments, the Earth flourishes and prospers.

Lord, help us abandon false deities and instead dedicate ourselves to a God who is alive. Our Lord bestows blessings upon the land. The key to success is knowledge. Discovering the true God leads to receiving all blessings. Whether you move abroad or not, failing to acknowledge God will result in a cursed land.

Genesis 39:3 And his master saw that the LORD was with him and that the LORD made all that he did to prosper in his hand.

The house of Potiphar in Egypt experienced blessings thanks to Joseph. Blessings followed Joseph wherever he went.

Deuteronomy 11:14 That I will give you the rain of your land in his due season, the first rain and the latter rain, that thou mayest gather in thy corn, and thy wine, and thine oil.

During the time when Great Britain governed India, my mom claims there was plenty of rain. She confirmed once again that she encountered both the first and last rain. The poor were able to survive because it was so inexpensive, even with limited funds. Once the Christian government departed, the curse descended and famine plagued the land. The poverty in India is overwhelming. We need to find out how the poor are surviving. It's a never-ending cycle of complaints with them. The lack of blessings from the true God

MAY 18

renders a majority inadequate. Despite the passing years, my recent visit revealed that the poor are still in the worst condition. I hope they discover Jesus, the true God.

Deuteronomy 28:12 The LORD shall open unto thee his good treasure, the heaven to give the rain unto thy land in his season, and to bless all the work of thine hand: and thou shalt lend unto many nations, and thou shalt not borrow.

We have the right to enjoy all the abundance that Earth offers. Living abundantly is within our reach. Allowing Jesus can eradicate corruption, deception, and poverty. Jesus is the way of truth; a solution is Jesus. There are reports of the Indian government supporting the destruction of churches and the persecution of Christians, while also seeking rain and blessings. To what extent are these individuals spiritually blind?

Psalm 24:1 The Earth is the Lord's, and the fulness thereof; the world, and they that dwell therein. 2 For he hath founded it upon the seas, and established it upon the floods.

Detailed information about the Earth can be found in the Bible, as given by God.

Psalm 104:5 Who laid the foundations of the Earth, that it should not be removed forever.

Be cautious when considering the rental or purchase of the property. Although you may grasp the area where curses are linked, you won't grant blessings. Tell the truth; the truth will set people free. Without proper education, they will carry poverty, sin, and sickness wherever they go.

I consistently anoint the exterior with Holy oil. Through the anointing, all yokes and curses over the land will be destroyed. Go out and use Blessed Olive Oil to anoint stores, parks, downtown trees, schools, and land. It gets the job done. May the Lord make us doers of the word and not hearers.

To curse God's creation, the devil has established a law that encourages us to keep our mouths shut. May the Lord grant you love for the soul and the bravery to speak the truth.

Blessings came my way when someone shared a truth with me. We are accountable for urging others to worship the true Spirit of God, the one who brought humans into existence. His name is Jesus. Idol gods and goddesses are helpless. Please pray that idol worshipers find the way to truth and eternal life. God is seeking a courageous, bold, righteous mediator who can lead. Lord, let love for Jesus fill the hearts of those who worship idols.

Ezekiel 22:30 "I looked for someone among them who would build up the wall and stand before me in the gap on behalf of the land so I would not have to destroy it, but I found no one.

May God shower blessings upon those who stand in the gap and pray for others. May the Lord direct us to an individual who can serve as a mediator between God and humans, offering intercession in the name of Jesus.

LET US PRAY

Lord, we handle all blessings or curses on Earth. We can give any excuse, which is lies. Our prayers today are focused on the cursed land, devoid of God's blessings, as a consequence of our sins. May Lord raise the true prophets and teachers to carry on the mission of God. Your task is to bless us by acknowledging God and His Laws. May the Lord bring forth individuals like Joseph, Isaac, and Abraham, who birthed the land of Israel. The blessed land to inherit for the special people of God. May the Lord give His creation ear to hear and eyes to see. May Lord help us teach our children the knowledge of God where our strength and blessing hide. We want to continue in your blessing, so help us, Lord, in Jesus 'name. Amen! God bless you!

MAY 19

DETERMINE TO WAIT ON THE LORD!

If we receive divine eyesight and mental clarity, we will rely on the Lord's guidance. Lord, hinder the impatient from moving ahead of You.

Lord, may you reveal your plan.

A lot of people make plans for their lives. Early one morning, I was invited to someone's house and asked to pray for her grandchildren to become doctors. Christianity was the religion of this grandmother. She wished for her plan to be integrated into the lives of her grandchildren. I chose not to pray in this way because of my Christian faith. I mentioned that God has a better plan than yours. I will ask God to bring His plan to materialization in their life. These scriptures are something they should know.

Jeremiah 29:11 For I know the thoughts that I think toward you, saith the LORD, thoughts of peace, not evil, to give you an expected end.

Learn the importance of waiting on God's plan. Keep your children's and grandchildren's lives intact. I pray on their behalf, but I don't control their future.

A lot of Christians lack understanding of the concept of Christianity. May the Lord grant them the insight that we must patiently wait for Him when we seek His guidance. May Your will succeed, not mine. Let God take control of the planning. Let your thoughts and plans, higher than mine, be fulfilled in my life. God bless His people with the strength and courage to wait. There will be many tests and difficulties that we must overcome to hinder and dismantle the achievement of God's plan. Stay aligned with God's plan and He will empower you to perceive the Lord's beautiful plan. His plan will be fulfilled, and your life will bloom. May Lord give newness of mind and life. Let every chapter of our day be new. Lord, may your plan and thoughts be revealed to the world through our actions. Lord, use us as a powerful instrument in your hand. God becomes the Potter, and we are clay in His hand.

God, the mighty Lord, desires someone who will place complete trust in Him and surrender. Our intention is to demonstrate His faithfulness by surrendering to His control. It needs the relationship and knowledge of God to allow Him to carry on our life.

At times, I observe that ladies and gentlemen cannot contain their impatience and start deviating from the path. They ask why, what, and how my life has become a disaster. I'm in need of support to grasp the situation. Master the art of being patient. The outcome is determined by making a wrong move. If you jump into a fire, expect to get burned. What is the outcome of jumping into water without knowing how to swim and without being dragged? Lord, give us a teachable spirit.

Isaiah 40:31 But they that wait upon the Lord shall renew their strength; they shall mount up with wings as eagles; they shall run, not be weary, and they shall walk, and not faint.

Lord, grant us wisdom in waiting for you faithfully. King Saul's disobedience resulted in his removal from power by God. The story would have taken different modes if he had waited for God. God provides us with promises and strength when we patiently trust in Him. He knows where He is taking us. The plan is from God, but timing is part of the package. We're always unsure of the path as we make each turn. May we have the patience and trust to accept that God's plan is beyond our understanding.

Psalms 27:14 Wait on the LORD: be of good courage, and he shall strengthen thine heart: wait, I say, on the LORD.

God assigns each of us a specific mission and plan when we are born. May the Lord guide our parents to have patience in waiting on Him, so they can teach their children. Lord, please give us parents like Jochebed, Mary, Joseph, and Manoah,

Judges 13:2 And there was a certain man of Zorah, of the family of the Danites, whose name was Manoah; and his wife was barren, and bare not.3 And the angel of the Lord appeared unto the woman and said unto her, Behold now, thou art barren, and bearest not: but thou shalt conceive, and bear a son.4 Now, therefore, beware, I pray thee, and drink not wine nor strong drink, and eat not any unclean thing:5 For, lo, thou shalt conceive, and bear a son; and no razor shall come on his head: for the child shall be a Nazarite unto God from the womb: and he shall begin to deliver Israel out of the hand of the Philistines.

The Bible provides us with instructions on how to teach our children. We hope for a parent who imparts the wisdom of God's Word to us. May the Lord make us anointed teachers of the truth! The Lord has entrusted parents with the duty of instructing their children in the proper path.

Proverbs 1:8 My son, hear the instruction of thy father, and forsake not the law of thy mother:

All day long, I teach and win the soul for the Kingdom of God. Resting, hunting, golfing, and vacationing are not my things. I pray and fast for them. At night, I am awakened by the heavy burden of the soul. Why? In order to receive guidance from God. Many individuals are in search of guidance for their life. They are in a state of intense sorrow or have become entangled and are unable to find a way out. Lord, assist in leading others back to the correct way. Let their mistake serve as a valuable lesson. Shall we serve as a source of light for those who are lost and led astray?

We need much patience and faith to carry on the plan of God.

Satan presents a view of the ocean, mountains, destroyed bridges, and no escape. Let me remind you, the Lord said I am a maker; I make new things. I transform dessert into a pool of water. I can turn your sorrow into joy, sickness, to health. I can help heal your broken heart. Remain patient and have faith in the Lord's plan. Remember not to go before me and avoid leading yourself astray. Lean on me. Allow me to be your God, for I am God. Avoid listening to your surroundings. Stop informing yourself what you feel and how

MAY 19

your situation is. May we be blessed with the comprehension to see beyond our circumstances, as granted by the Lord. What is the purpose of having a God? What is the purpose of reading the Bible? What is the purpose of the Holy Spirit being given to us? Do not keep going around the same way. May the Lord provide you with help to overcome the slavery of Satan. May the Lord bless your trust in Him, even when you can't see the way.

I took a friend to a store; I wasn't shopping, so after a while, I sat down. Simultaneously, a woman sat next to me and we exchanged smiles. I asked her if she needed help. She replied no. Nevertheless, her face displayed the pain she felt when she placed her hand on her leg. I offered the prayer, which she accepted. She weeps as tears stream down her cheek. As we talked, she stated her commitment to following God's commands. I always obey God's commands without hesitation. If He asks me and finishes His work, I'll go anywhere. She said If I do not, then who will? I said wow. Her words were that I was about to settle the bill and head home. Since the line was long, I decided to sit down and meet you in order to receive healing. I saw the change on her face, so I asked about the pain. She said the pain was gone. Wow! If you wait, Lord has a plan.

Acts 17:28a For in him we live, and move, and have our being;

Life can be enjoyable if we learn to lean on God. You won't have to deal with the mess caused by your actions. Waiting will bring forth something new and beautiful. May God grant us the patience to wait for Him with all our hearts. This scripture is meant for those who have the patience to wait for the Lord.

Isaiah 43:16 Thus saith the Lord, which maketh a way in the sea, and a path in the mighty waters; 17 Which bringeth forth the chariot and horse, the army and the power; they shall lie down together, they shall not rise: they are extinct, they are quenched as tow. 18 Remember ye not the former things, neither consider the things of old. 19 Behold, I will do a new thing; now it shall spring forth; shall ye not know it? I will even make a way in the wilderness and rivers in the desert.

Embrace the practice of waiting on God and encourage others in your generation to do the same.

LET US PRAY

Lord, we are grateful to you; you are God, not man. Help us be like Moses, Daniel, and King David, who waited on God. May the Lord give us patience and strength to endure during the waiting time. May the Lord give us the understanding to wait rather than make a mess of our life. You are the same God who sent us with a brilliant plan. Lord, there is no plan, small or great. All plans of God are higher than our plan. May the Lord give us a generation of obedient and submissive to allow the Plan of God to accomplish! Our God is real. Help us, Lord, to wait on you in Jesus's name. Amen! God bless you!

MAY 20

DO NOT LET YOUR HEART FAIL WITH FEAR!

When there is fear, there is no faith; fear is the attack of the enemy and the weapon of Satan. Satan's presence brings fear. The presence of God around you brings both love and peace. Perfect love casteth all fear. May the Lord feel our hearts with His Love. Remember, God is love.

The night perfectly represents darkness. People feel fear in the dark. The ignorant are terrified by Satan during this time.

The Word of God is light. When I feel fear, I speak the Word of God.

2 Timothy 1:7 - For God hath not given us the spirit of fear; but of power, love, and a sound mind.

The word of God takes the form of a sword. The word of God is a powerful weapon against the demon of fear. I have used it many times; demons ran and never came around. It is incredible how the right word of God becomes an offense to the enemy; believe me, it works. If fear holds you captive, use this word as your weapon. Lord, thank you for giving me the spirit of love, power, and a sound mind. Recite it. See what happens. God gave the word to exercise in our life. May the Lord make us mighty in the knowledge of His Word. Our trouble will disappear as we practice the word by obeying and submitting to it. Light is the presence of God. God is light. Lord, enlighten us about your creation of darkness and the authority you have bestowed upon it. God has control over the night.

Fear stems from the presence of defeat, being trapped, and encountering unfamiliar places. May the Lord provide us with guidance during times like this. I pray to the Lord to give you Peace when you see darkness.

Proverb 29:25 The Fear of man bright a snare: but whoso putteth his trust in the LORD shall be safe.

The Lord is our Shepherd; we shall not fear. Sheep has a Shepherd to watch over them. Jesus is our Shepherd and we are His sheep. Following the crucifixion, fear gripped the disciples of our Lord.

John 20:19 Then the same day at evening, the first day of the week, when the doors were shut where the disciples were assembled for Fear of the Jews, came to Jesus and stood in the midst, and saith unto them, Peace be unto you.

MAY 20

Jesus is with us. He said I wouldn't leave you or forsake you. The ability of God to manifest Himself anywhere, even behind closed doors, serves as evidence of His promises. We need our confidence in the Lord.

Psalms 56:3 What time I am afraid, I will trust in thee.

Lord said the stressful time would come. In times when everything conspires against you, and a storm becomes an unstoppable force, causing the water level to rise, just trust in the Lord! Trust is more significant than faith. Trust is when you are going through a dreadful time and still have Peace in your heart. This is what Job is talking about. Job was surrounded by trouble, trial, and sorrow, yet he expressed only confidence in God through his words.

We all pass through some shape, form, and type of fear. Fear of losing children, job, marriage, health, or whatever.

However, confidently speak words of faith. In the face of the lion's den, Daniel uttered the word "faith." David spoke of faith, not fear, while facing Goliath. Satan is trying to silence us, but we must not be afraid to speak the name of Jesus in times like this. Witness the power and outcome of speaking the Word of God. Fear will flee. There are those who choose not to mention the name Jesus. The name of my God is Jesus, and even the devil is subject to this name.

Luke 10:17 And the seventy returned again with joy, saying, Lord, even the devils are subject unto us through thy name.

The devil is afraid when you say the name of Jesus. The devil knows the power hidden in the Name of Jesus. They are protesting specifically against the name of Jesus. It terrorizes Satan. Satan trembles when he hears the word 'Jesus'. Spirit world knows who Jesus is. When Jesus cast the demon out, they revealed Him. The demon said we knew who thou art. Satan, Fallen Angels, and demons are spiritual beings. They know Jesus as the Holy one and not Holy Trinity. He is the God in the flesh, alpha and omega, beginning and the ending, first and last, the one spirit God. May we be blessed with understanding from the Lord, so that we do not fear.

The Bible says the trouble will be everywhere:

Matthew 24:21 For then shall be great tribulation, such as was not since the beginning of the world to this time, no, nor ever shall be.

Every great war gives birth to a new dispensation. Before the crucifixion, it was a great war, and the power of darkness took over. At the end of Jesus 'mission, the devil was caught off guard by the unexpected revival that took place on earth. When God's blood purchased the New Testament Church, the devil had unpleasant news. The devil had a migraine when he saw the Blood of Jesus over born again, baptized in Jesus 'name to be born of water. God applies the blood as they go into the water in the name of Jesus, sins will be wiped out, and sins will also be remitted. Hallelujah! Disciples were trembling and hiding in the upper room. Fear left as the Holy Spirit came down. The gates of hell cannot prevail against repented, washed sins in the blood by baptizing in Jesus's name and receiving the Holy Spirit. It terrified the devil when all started praying in the tongue. The Devil didn't understand at all.

Fear is the weapon of the devil for the ignorant. Peter denied Jesus three times because of fear. He received the Holy Spirit, received power, and spoke with authority and without fear. Although he had a revelation of Jesus, God did not bestow the Holy Ghost at that time. If you do not have the Holy Ghost, I urge you; time is near, repent of your sins and baptize in the precious name of Jesus. Under the name of Jesus, God buried the blood of the lamb. When I received the Holy Ghost, I received the power. I had no fear of the enemy. The truth will set you free from the power of fear.

Psalm 23:4 Yea, though I walk through the valley of the shadow of death, I will fear no evil: for thou art with me; thy rod and thy staff they comfort me.5 Thou preparest a table before me in the presence of mine enemies: thou anointest my head with oil; my cup runneth over.

When you're in the valley of the shadow of death, you encounter trials, darkness, sorrow, and all sorts of trouble. God has no limits, so don't put any on Him. Persecution is everywhere. The devil hates the light, truth, and Word of God. People are afraid of the devil. Satan is working through the authorities. However, there is good news in the promise of the Word of God.

Isaiah 41:10 - Fear thou not; for I [am] with thee: be not dismayed; for I [am] thy God: I will strengthen thee; yea, I will help thee; yea, I will uphold thee with the right hand of my righteousness.

Churches are burning, and pastors and Christians are being persecuted with the help of the authority in the name of so-called gods and goddesses. Pray as you have never prayed, fast as you have never fasted to receive assistance from the Lord. Remember Daniel, King David, Shadrach, Mishak, and Abednego. Remember Queen Esther and the Jews who prayed and fasted. Calling on God is necessary to receive help from our faithful Creator. Get His attention by praying and fasting. Lord, guide Christian leaders to fast and pray, progressing ahead. We must be the house of prayer. We will arise to do mighty if Lord pours his spirit on us.

Christianity is founded on love because God is love. God will not move on people to kill, steal, burn, and destroy but to help, protect, and bless.

May our God feel us with wisdom and knowledge! God gives us genuine leaders to lead us to the truth. May Our Lord protect and bless us! Bible already prophesied in the book of Revelation,

Revelation 2:10 Fear none of those things which thou shalt suffer: behold, the devil shall cast some of you into prison, that ye may be tried; and ye shall have tribulation ten days: be thou faithful unto death, and I will give thee a crown of life.

The Bible says in Matthew 10:19,20 I will put the word in your mouth what to say to the authorities.

God gave the end-time warning in the Bible; it should not surprise the Christian since it was spoken by the Holy Spirit two thousand years ago.

Matthew 10:26 Fear them not, therefore: for there is nothing covered, that shall not be revealed; and hid, that shall not be known. 27 What I tell you in darkness, that speak ye in light: and what ye hear in the ear that preach ye upon the housetops. 28 And fear not them which kill the body, but are not able to kill the Soul: but rather fear him which is able to destroy both Soul and body in hell. 29 Are not two sparrows sold for a farthing? And one of them shall not fall on the ground without your Father. 30 But the very hairs of your head are all numbered. 31 Fear ye not; therefore, ye are of more value than many sparrows.

LET US PRAY:

Our great heavenly father, we thank you for the truth you have spoken in the word of God. We see the time of your coming is near. Persecution is extreme throughout the world. May Lord open the blind eyes to see and deaf ears to hear. Lord turns the heart to the living God from false gods and goddesses. We love the Soul of the lost. Lord, show them mercy that they do not suffer in hell. You forgive those coming against your people. Forgive them since they do not know what they are doing. Lord, give them your dream and vision to see you. Lord, we cover those persecutors 'sins under your precious blood, wash them in your blood, save them, and change them before it is too late, in Jesus's name. Amen! God bless you.

MAY 21
PLACE LOANED TO LIVE WITH CONDITION!

Place loaned to live with Condition!

Remember, we arrive in this world without clothes and leave without clothes. We bring nothing and can't take anything with us.

In order to possess anything, we must acknowledge Jesus as God. Take a moment to think about your past homes and jobs. Is it possible to enter without any permission? Sorry, but that's not possible. Press the doorbell and ask for permission to come in. If they allow, then you can; otherwise, you can't. I was born in India; I do not hold citizenship. If I want to visit, I have to get a visa to visit, and I have to stay for a limited time.

The same way God says.

Psalms 24:1 The earth is the LORD'S.

As long as you obey God's laws, you can remain on earth. May God bless us with understanding, allowing us to find joy in our earthly existence. Abraham was favored because of his faith in God. Abraham obeyed the voice of God. So God gave Abraham an extraordinary blessing.

Genesis 17:8 And I will give unto thee, and to thy seed after thee, the land wherein thou art a stranger, all the land of Canaan, for an everlasting possession; and I will be their God.

May we remain faithful to carry out the perfect will of the Lord God. So our generation finds favor. My actions affect the next generation. Teaching the laws of God to the next generation guarantees a joyful existence for them. When God promises, He never forgets what He promised. Despite the passing of centuries, he ensured that Abraham's descendants reached the promised land. May God remember you today. May you also receive promises by listening and obeying the Word of God. God is faithful, be faithful to receive the promises. God is a reward for those who seek His face diligently. Each pledge must be fulfilled in order to receive blessings.

Bibles say.

MAY 21

Psalms 37:25 I have been young, and now am old; yet have I not seen the righteous forsaken, nor his seed begging bread.

Lord, help us realize the danger for the next generation if we don't do as God said.

God promised a land to Abraham, which was defiled by sins and transgression. Jehovah God uprooted all natives of that land. Sinning against God will result in God wiping you out. When the wicked take positions and power, that results in curses on the land, and they lose the territory. Do not think you can act and react the way you love. People of the land were practicing sins. That was the reason God removed them and gave land to Abraham.

Genesis 15:18 In the same day, the LORD made a covenant with Abram, saying, Unto thy seed has I given this land, from the river of Egypt unto the great river, the river Euphrates:

We must teach the Word of God to our children and future generations, so they can inherit the land.

God kept the promise: *Joshua 11:23 So Joshua took the whole land, according to all that the LORD said unto Moses; and Joshua gave it for an inheritance unto Israel according to their divisions by their tribes. And the land rested from war.*

Later, neglecting the Word, Israel fell into the same trap repeatedly. It is essential to teach children the Word of God first. Take nothing for granted. Lord, help us teach our children, so they inherit the land with peace, protection, and blessings. People continued to follow God until Joshua, and their elders lived. By obeying God's laws, they experienced benefits. May God give us true prophets and teachers to teach us the laws of God! It is filled with God's blessings that are incomprehensible to us. It is necessary for me to grasp the teachings and guidance of the Holy Spirit in order to obey. I just go ahead and do it. No need to analyze to comprehend; just do it. The commandment is not for debate but to obey.

Abraham never questions the idea of sacrificing his son.

He marched around the future country of his descendant. What would have happened if Abraham did not leave the land of Ur with his family? He did it by believing in the Lord. Believe and obey every word written in the Bible. What chaos would you cause by not following the word exactly? When you conform to the world system and change your lifestyle, you're causing trouble for your successor.

As people started going astray from the Lord, God began sending oppressors to oppress the people. All God's blessings come with a condition. As they went whoring after other gods and goddesses and forgot the laws of God, see what happened to them.

Judges 3:8 Therefore the anger of the LORD was hot against Israel, and he sold them into the hand of Chushanrishathaim king of Mesopotamia: and the children of Israel served Chushanrishathaim eight years.9 And when the children of Israel cried unto the LORD, the LORD raised a deliverer to the children of Israel, who delivered them, even Othniel the son of Kenaz, Caleb's younger brother.

The land experienced a period of rest, but the people forgot about the Lord and began worshiping different gods and goddesses. Practice regularly so that you remember the laws, commandments, and statutes. God sent the Median for seven years to oppress. When they turned to God, He sent help to deliver them from the oppressor. How important is your role, especially when you repent and return to God wholeheartedly?

God raised Gideon to help Israel.

Judges 10:6 And the children of Israel did evil again in the sight of the LORD and served Baalim, and Ashtaroth, and the gods of Syria, and the gods of Zidon, and the gods of Moab, and the gods of the children of Ammon, and the gods of the Philistines, and forsook the LORD, and served not him. 7 And the anger of the LORD was hot against Israel, and he sold them into the hands of the Philistines, and the hands of the children of Ammon.

The Lord allowed oppressors to oppress for not keeping God's laws, statutes, commandments, and precepts. The oppressor distressed Israelites. God raised the deliverer again when they repented. Do not forget God and His commandments. May God give us the wisdom to do what it takes. Land can be blessed, delivered, and protected only if we live by the Word of God. We often prioritize the laws of the land over the rules of God.

I heard the news; it says in 2018 alone, there were 22 shootings in the school. It results from land occupied by many idol worshippers, other gods, and goddesses. The laws, commandments, and statutes of God need to be practiced by leaders. God has the power to free us from oppression, fear, homelessness, sickness, addiction, and marital separation. Protection is available for both us and our children. The Israelites cried out when they were tired of persecution. The land needs healing. The land has been in trouble ever since we left God. We forgot the Word of God. Children are in prison and die early. Do not look for help anywhere; kneel, repent, cry out, open the Bible, and read the word to practice.

Do you require assistance in understanding how your rights were lost? Read the book of judges and cry out to the Lord. You have the ability to make a powerful impact through your actions. If you study the word to obey, you will leave a legacy of blessings. Having a place to live on earth is a generous gift. If you do as God Jehovah said, you have done all.

Cry out to the Lord! Currently, surrender is what we need, not sympathy. Surrender and say, I am wrong; I am a sinner; I have transgressed your laws and commandments. Please forgive me and help me, Lord. The Lord will raise someone to help us. It needs leaders to lead us out of trouble. Pray for our leaders. May God protect and bless them. May they be blessed with wisdom as they lead the nation on the righteous path. Kneeling is necessary for us to demonstrate our humility.

2 Chronicles 7:14 If my people, which are called by my name, shall humble themselves, and pray, and seek my face, and turn from their wicked ways; then will I hear from heaven, and will forgive their sin, and will heal their land.

It is the same situation that repeats over and over. Pray God brings the Bible and prayer back to the school, home, and individual life with repentance. And we never put it on the back burner again. God says to keep my commandment, laws, and precepts. Seek God before anything else, pray, and witness the outcome.

LET US PRAY

Lord, we ask for the forgiveness of all our sins. We invite you to forgive the transgression of our land.

MAY 21

We have committed sins, Lord. Please help us do what we are supposed to. Please be with us as we face the challenges ahead. We need spiritual teachers and prophets in our land. Let us pray around the clock before we lose all our rights. Lord, forgive our wrongdoing. Take us to the path of righteousness. Give us the obedient and submissive spirit to your will. May Lord make us a doer of the laws and not hearers. Please, Lord, heal our land in Jesus's name. Amen! God bless you!

MAY 22

TAKE IT BACK FROM SATAN!

The day God created man, *Genesis 1:26 And God said, Let us make man in our image, after our likeness: and let them have dominion over the fish of the sea, and over the fowl of the air, and the cattle, and all the earth, and over every creeping thing that creepeth upon the earth.28 And God blessed them, and God said unto them, Be fruitful, and multiply, and replenish the earth, and subdue it: and have dominion over the fish of the sea, and over the fowl of the air, and over every living thing that moveth upon the earth.*

God has graciously blessed and given us the power to subdue and have dominion over everything on earth, in air and sea. The Lord Jehovah is an owner. He blessed us by giving us all that He created. How wonderful! The king passes the throne to His firstborn to rule after him.

Please acknowledge we have ownership of all, but with a condition. We lost all our rights, blessings, and freedom when we transgressed. Jehovah God put on flesh and came to recover what we lost. He put on flesh to shed the blood.

1 Timothy 3:16a. And without controversy great is the mystery of godliness: God was manifest in the flesh.

His ultimate act of putting on flesh to shed blood was more significant. Jehovah God destroyed the power of death by dying in the body of Jesus for us. Giving His sinless blood was to redeem our souls from the wages of the death penalty. Let the name of Jesus be revered and magnified for His great sacrifice and love. He never intended us to wonder or suffer on earth. Lord God exposed the plan of Satan and their characteristics.

John 8:44 Ye are of your father the Devil, and the lusts of your father ye will do. He was a murderer from the beginning and abode not in the truth because there is no truth in him. When he speaketh a lie, he speaketh of his own: for he is a liar and the father of it.

The Devil is a liar and murderer. He took the lives of Abel, the Prophets of God, Jesus Christ, and His prophets. How? The Devil operates on those who hate the way of God. These are religious people whom the Devil uses to destroy the saints, work, and ways of God. If you want to be blessed, then follow Jesus and His ways. May our vision be enlightened by the Lord's mercy. Satan wants to steal your blessings and brings the sugarcoated plan of destruction. God wants to bless you, and the Devil wants to curse you by misleading you.

MAY 22

Remember the Word of God.

John 10:10 The thief cometh not, but for to steal, and to kill, and to destroy: I am come that they might have life and that they might have it more abundantly.

Gain the understanding of truth for freedom and to stay free. Jesus gave His life and returned to heaven by taking a key from the Devil. The temporary job of Jehovah in the human incarnation of Jesus is to redeem us by His sinless blood.

Revelation 1:18 I am he that liveth, and was dead; and, behold, I am alive for evermore, Amen; and have the keys of hell and of death.

Don't worry, God holds the key to hell and death. He also granted you authority over scorpions, serpents, demons, Satan, and fallen angels.

It was the disciples who established the New Testament Church. Follow the book of Acts to demonstrate God's Church in you. Holy Spirit power is available if you cease to pursue misguided false pastors, churches, denominations, teachers, prophets, and the antichrist Spirit. How can you determine they are anti-Christ? Simple, they will not baptize in the name of Jesus to wash away sin. Baptism is where the blood of the lamb is needed over sinners. Lord's blood is hidden under the name of Jesus. They lack the revelation of Jesus as Peter and Paul had.

These structures are labeled as churches, but they are anti-Christ in nature. Stay away from these buildings. May the Lord give us the revelation of Jesus as He did to Peter and Paul. Satan has started many theological colleges and churches and has modified the Bible. To be on guard, the Devil is a liar. You are the church, not the building.

We do not establish the new basis recognized by various names, organizations, denominations, and non-denominations. However, our fundamental principle is rooted in the teachings of the Apostles and Prophets. Remember, Jesus appeared to shed blood and show how to live for Him in this dispensation.

Ephesians 2:20 And are built upon the foundation of the apostles and prophets, Jesus Christ himself being the chief cornerstone;

John 13:15 For I have given you an example, that ye should do as I have done to you.

Revelation of Jesus 'apostles who possessed the key established the church on the day of Pentecost. Pentecost meant the fiftieth day. They established the original church by baptizing in Jesus's name and receiving the Holy Ghost. Gates of hell cannot prevail against the church built on the correct foundation. Jesus taught us to continue in the truth; we will be set free, delivered, and healed. Hallelujah! Do not get stuck in the building. Keep seeking until you find the mighty work of the Holy Spirit in operation. Do not stagnate, trapped in the trap of religion established by Satan. Do not fall in the ditch, but proceed in the word to obey. You will find a solution. You will defeat the enemy. He is holding and hiding your blessings. May the Lord grant us a seeking, hungry and thirsty heart. Fast and pray to regain forcefully what the Devil has stolen. Get violent in battle with the Devil and its fallen angels.

Some time ago, the Holy Spirit led the preacher to a small town in the US. A couple was fasting and praying around the clock. One prays for four hours while the other rests. The town had a bar and a liquor store. The owner challenged, saying we do not need the church in our village. When missionaries came to town, bar and liquor owners ganged up against them. Within a month, very first meeting the bar and liquor owner gave their life to the Lord.

Did you see what the missionary did? Why aren't you taking authority over the Devil of your town? Hide in your closet to pray around the clock. Please get rid of all the power of darkness working in your village. The Devil knows he is defeated; Jesus has the key. Now the authority is given to us. Get violent against Satan by fasting, praying, binding, breaking their power, and casting them out of our home, city, and county. We cannot be too busy and lazy to live for God and allow the Devil to steal, kill, and destroy. We are having power than using it. Why can we not drive away the Devil, his angels, and demons? Because we do not pursue Jesus and no prayer with fasting, which works.

One sister in the Lord wanted to hear a talk show at midnight. At night she came to the bedroom and turned on the radio to listen to a talk on Ouija Board. She started seeing a demon entering her room. On the side, she noticed a man who appeared to be her husband. He leaped over her, she struggled to catch her breath. Man's eyes were like deep hollows. He pressed her down and choked her. As she continued uttering the name of Jesus, fallen angels released her and jumped off her. It walked away in the hallway. She was scared and called me the next day and asked if I could fly to her place. There was a powerful presence of evil in her house. I said, no need to fly to California. Please put me on speakerphone, and you go around the house and speak in tongues. She did, and I commanded the demon to leave the house in Jesus 'name. It left. See, we have the power to cast them out.

The Bible says we do not give place to the Devil. She had no business listening to the live Ouija Board performance. Later that same year, I visited her home. The evil presence hid in her garage, so we commanded her to leave and demanded not to come back again. Please use the power to cast them out, and do not invite Satan. May Lord Give us wisdom with knowledge. I hate the Devil, so I learn the weapon of truth to destroy it. We wrestle not against flesh and blood but against an evil spirit.

God gifted me the power, so why must I play with darkness? Do not watch, read or put something that brings the Devil into your home, city, or county. May the Lord give you knowledge of the truth through the word to guide and direct. Baptism of the Holy Ghost is to empower us. Exercise the authority granted by God. Fast, pray, and read the word. I remember someone telling me that God always answers the prayer if we pray between 3 and 4. Guess what? I meet God between 3-4 am when I need to handle spiritual matter. But I regularly pray from 3.50 am till 7. Take it back from Satan what belongs to you. Snatch it from the Devil's hand and say to get out from my case in Jesus's name, Amen!

LET US PRAY

Mighty God in your name, we asked you to fill us with the Holy Spirit. We need the power of Holy Ghost to come against the power of darkness.

Lord, we defeat the enemy devil, who comes to steal, kill, and destroy. Lord, we thank you for giving the word of God as our sword, only offensive weapon against the devil. Teach us your word as we read. I command north, south, east, west, up, and down to lose our blessings. We command the demons who kill, steal and destroy to be confused, blinded and destroyed in Jesus 'name. We speak life to resurrect now in the name of Jesus. Amen! God bless you!

MAY 23

A LITTLE LEAVEN

LEAVENETH THE WHOLE LUMP!

The Bible discusses the potential harm of sin, whether it's small or large. Sin is a sin. God compares sin with leaven. What is leaven?

The definition of leaven is the substance causing the expansion of doughs and batters by releasing gases within such mixtures, producing baked products with a porous structure. (From https://www.britannica.com/topic/ leavening-agent)

God compares sin with leaven and has the power to spread in the body like a leave-in dough or lump. Our body has a similar experience of leaven by having the sin within. Sin is food to Satan. Recognize the demon and find where he is hiding. Satan needs little sin in the flesh to enter, kill, steal, and destroy.

Sin causes sickness in our bodies. Sin allows the devil to take the reign of our life. God is the only one who can help care for and give a great new day every day. God can give us success, blessings, and progress at light speed.

Our life has an adversary called flesh. Our carnal nature/flesh is our greater and bigger enemy than Satan. Walk in the light of His word, so we do not fall into the trap of sin. We wish to avoid repeating the snare of Satan over again like Adam and Eve.

I have witnessed people have the spirit of jealousy, envy, and pride. Those religious people will fight, control, and hurt you. This is the dangerous growth in our flesh.

Paul said: 2 Corinthians 7:1 Having, therefore, these promises, dearly beloved, let us cleanse ourselves from all filthiness of the flesh and spirit, perfecting holiness in fear of God.

How can you cleanse yourself from fleshly sins? You pray and fast against it every day. In the flesh, we have fleshly sins. We all must dedicate time and confess the sin to get cleaned up. The power of confession is the key to letting the devil know he cannot hide from us. We have to seek God's forgiveness for our sins, and we also forgive ourselves.

MAY 23

1 John 1:9 If we confess our sins, he is faithful and just to forgive us and cleanse us from all unrighteousness.

Galatians 5:9 A little leaven leaveneth the whole lump. What kind of leaven is sin? Galatians 5:19 Now the works of the flesh are manifest, which are these; Adultery, fornication, uncleanness, lasciviousness, 20 Idolatry, witchcraft, hatred, variance, emulations, wrath, strife, seditions, heresies, 21 Envyings, murders, drunkenness, revellings, and such like: of the which I tell you before, as I have also told you in time past, that they which do such things shall not inherit the kingdom of God.

These sins are the gateway for the evil spirit to come into us. As it enters in us, it transforms into a murderer like Satan. Satan causes destruction if you allow through sins listed above in Galatians 5. it will steal your joy, salvation, health, peace, and family. As it enters into you and brings more evil demons and makes your body their residence.

Roman 6:12 Let not sin therefore reign in your mortal body, that ye should obey it in the lusts thereof.

Matthew 16, Jesus has a powerful explanation of the leaven. The religious teachers spread the false teaching or false doctrine known as leaven. That is what we see in the world. What is the cause of having many religions? Well! God never created these religions, but the false teacher, leaders, and prophets did.

Matthew 16:5 And when his disciples were come to the other side, they had forgotten to take bread. 6 Then Jesus said unto them, Take heed and beware of the leaven of the Pharisees and of the Sadducees. 7 And they reasoned among themselves, saying, It is because we have taken no bread. 8 Which when Jesus perceived, he said unto them, O ye of little faith, why reason ye among yourselves, because ye have brought no bread? 9 Do ye not yet understand, neither remember the five loaves of the five thousand and how many baskets ye took up? 10 Neither the seven loaves of the four thousand and how many baskets ye took up? 11 How is it that ye do not understand that I spake it not to you concerning bread, that ye should beware of the leaven of the Pharisees and of the Sadducees? 12 Then understood they how that he bade them not beware of the leaven of bread but of the doctrine of the Pharisees and of the Sadducees.

Entering buildings where you find the cross can be risky since they have their doctrine. I remember one brother in the Lord who carries an abundance of God given gifts. So he began going to churches to visit. Pastors witnessed the mighty work of God through him. Later, the Pastor left the message to this brother not to come back to their church. This shows God is not welcome! Since God's supernatural intervention did miracles, healing, and deliverance and not the brother.

He visited a place of worship (it is a building, not a church, you are a church). People began getting healed and delivered. Instantly, Satan's eyes got big, and authorities stopped him. It was the same encounter he had in California. May the Lord deliver people from these false teachers and prophets. It would be best if you flee from these false prophets and teachers. With your money, you are being fooled.

The word of God testifies in the Bible that Jesus came to heal the broken in heart, heal the sick, and deliver the people from sins, demons, and sicknesses. Seek what is available, as the Bible tells us. I will not compromise.

I want true doctrine and true teaching. The leaven of false teaching and philosophy is so deep that people have forgotten the real meaning of the coming of the Lord Jesus.

Accepting all, even wrong, without questioning is false. Nations have been contaminated since truth is hidden from false teachers and prophets.

2 Corinthians 4:3 But if our gospel be hid, it is hid to them that are lost:4 In whom the God of this world hath blinded the minds of them which believe not, lest the light of the glorious gospel of Christ, who is the image of God, should shine unto them.

Luke 11:52 Woe unto you, lawyers! For ye have taken away the key of knowledge: ye entered not in yourselves, and them that were entering in ye hindered.

I see the significant challenge is not people but the leaders of the religious Churches. They will notice you and will gang up against you. Many false teachers and false prophets stole my books; printers stole money and destroyed the work of God.

What is the motive behind this?

Mark 15:10 For he knew that the chief priests had delivered him for envy.

John 12:6 This he said, not that he cared for the poor; but because he was a thief, had the bag, and bare what was put therein.

In the same scenario, money has become a god. They de-sire power and position more than God.

Many authorities in establishments or religious sects look for votes. Make sure to familiarize yourself with their lifestyle. Many have shared with me that people in the religious world have alcohol, adultery, gambling, addiction to pornography, and greed problem. Many go from house to house for food and money.

What about driving out the demon, fasting, praying without ceasing, and healing? Do not even talk about it.

So if you notice this situation, we are about to enter a new dispensation. God's way of saving souls has had no effect because of the leaven of sin in the organization, religious sects, and non-sectarian groups.

It is not little leaven, but much leaven has entered the dough. Sin, which is leaven, has joined the Body of Christ. It is time you cry out and repent. It is time you look for one who loves your soul, not your financial help, or vote. May Lord help us remove the leaven of sins within us and the body of Christ. Wake up, repent, and wash away your sins by baptizing in Jesus's name and receiving the Holy Spirit to empower you to live right in Jesus's name.

LET US PRAY

Lord, we know the wages of sin are death, eternal death in hell. Lord, we confess our sin that we all have sinned. Please forgive all our sins. May your grace and mercy never depart from our family and us! Keep us from evil and its grip on us. We thank you for the cleansing blood to wash away our sins. Lord, cleanse us from all our unrighteousness and sins. Let your plan be accomplished for us. Lord, we thank you for putting on flesh to pay my wages of sin and giving me eternal life in heaven. Help us preach the truth; so many find this truth in Jesus's name. Amen! God Bless you.

MAY 24

USE YOUR HELPER, HOLY SPIRIT!

The Lord always provided us help. Jehovah God created Eve to be a helper for Adam. He made lots of Angels to help His multiple departments.

The heir of salvation needs the assistance of the angels. Reason Behind the existence of the material domain is the spiritual realm. The tangible world exists because of the spiritual world's operation. Invisible God brought forth all visible things, and not made by the one you see. May Lord help us.

Hebrew 1:14 Are they not all ministering spirits, sent forth to minister for them who shall be heirs of salvation?

The Almighty cares for His creation and knows our limited spiritual world knowledge. He made laws, precepts, and commandments to help and protect from the harmful celestial realm.

Our ignorance of Lucifer and its 1\3 unclean angels thrust out from heaven before our existence. We are unaware of the existence of millions of fallen, corrupted angels chained to the darkness. We have to trust God and His ways to avoid all troubles, trials, traps, ditches, and problems created by the devil.

Two kingdoms are at war with each other. The devil and its kingdom of darkness is moving towards God's Kingdom with a destructive plan. The devil has a nonstop deception scheme and uncountable programs to make us fall. God is trying to keep our focus on Him so we do not fall into the trap again, like Adam and Eve.

The devil tries and will try, but keep your focus right and be led by the Lord. Keep yourself in His commandment, precepts, and laws. We will come out clean and protected. In the flesh, we have limitations, but follow the eternal truth of the word, to defend. The Lord has always given us much help. Jesus, also in flesh, presented us with an example, demonstrating how faithful He is. When Lord Jesus went on a painful trial, he passed all His lust of eyes, the lust of the flesh, and the pride of life test. Angel appeared and ministered to Him.

Matthew 4:11 Then the devil leaveth him, and, behold, angels came and ministered unto him.

In this day and age, we have Holy Spirit, which is God Himself in us. Just we have to use His help. We are not using aid from the helper called Holy Spirit. There is always a memory issue. We choose the wrong route and never learn to know the way of God. It is the power of obedience. Blind trust in the word of God to see the result you expected. Stop being a grownup and listen to the omniscient. Stop being extremely prideful and arrogant follow Jesus. Look around what kind of world we are living in. We have the Holy Spirit to lead and guide, but do we care to accept the assistance? The decision is no. Why? We just have the same problems as Eve and Adam. Learn to walk in the Spirit, not flesh, to avoid many life accidents. Are you staying on earth forever or passing by?

May the Lord give us wisdom, ear to hear, and eyes to see. May the Lord help us retain in mind Jesus will not leave us without help.

Matthew 26:53 Thinkest thou that I cannot now pray to my Father, and he shall presently give me more than twelve legions of angels?

Legions are many thousands, so 12 legions are many more. It is the Lord who wonders. You just have to do what is required.

At this end time, God has given us the Holy Spirit as a helper

John 14:16 And I will pray the Father, and he shall give you another Comforter, that he may abide with you forever; 26 But the Comforter, which is the Holy Ghost, whom the Father will send in my name, he shall teach you all things, and bring all things to your remembrance, whatsoever I have said unto you.

John 15:26 But when the comforter is come, whom I will send unto you from the Father, even the Spirit of truth, which proceedeth from the Father, he shall testify of me:

It is the best help anyone can have. When I need assistance, I always take help from the Holy Spirit. The Holy Spirit reminds me as soon as I leave the house. Anytime you seek support, ask the Holy Spirit, and it will.

Once, I needed a tablecloth. Instead of making multiple stops at different stores, I asked the Holy Spirit to take me where the TableCloth was. I was across the mall; the Holy Spirit took me straight to the right to the store and department, upstairs where the tablecloth was.

Many use Ouija Board, psychics, or any other help. You will be better off with the Holy Spirit. It is the best help because it is the Spirit of truth. There is no lie in the Holy Spirit. Thank you, Lord, for your Spirit. If you love the truth, then use the Holy Spirit.

One of my prayer partners needed prayer. She is an aged lady who took care of herself and her grandchildren. The Holy Spirit told me what to pray for her. The Holy Spirit asked me to pray for her peace, and I did. When it was their morning, she called me. She said please pray for me. I said the Holy Spirit asked me to pray for peace. She said I dropped peace in her heart as I prayed for her. She got up and went around to do her business. Isn't the Lord wonderful?

I use the Holy Spirit for my direction, guidance for the day, and even shopping, which store to go to or not to go to. I take the help of the Holy Spirit to make my plan. The Holy Spirit is our helper. You just have to speak to the Holy Spirit rather than a horoscope, false prophets, friends, parents, or others.

MAY 24

While offering spiritual supplication over people, the Holy Spirit will tell me where the pain or problem is. And it is always accurate information. Lord, give us a sensitive ear, so we have less confusion, trouble, trial, or toiling. The Lord has given us a spirit of truth to guide and lead us.

A friend at work asked me to pray for her. She has to make a big decision. I heard her story and thought all were falling into the right places. I said God had already taken care of you. What do you want me to pray for? She repeated the same story. So I asked the Holy Spirit what to pray for. The Holy Spirit said, rebuke her nervousness. As soon as I rebuked it, she came to my department an hour later and said; I am fine. So I shared how the Holy Spirit helped me to pray. She agreed, yes, I stopped eating and eating. She shared that when I get nervous, I keep eating. When people get nervous, they use food as a pacifier or shake their legs, bite nails, touch their hair, and develop strange habits. Remember to take help from the Holy Spirit. The Holy Spirit is a helper, comforter, teacher, professor, and guide.

The Holy Spirit will help us pray.

Roman 8:26 Likewise, the Spirit also helpeth our infirmities: for we know not what we should pray for as we ought: but the Spirit itself maketh intercession for us with groanings which cannot be uttered. 27 And he that searcheth the hearts knoweth what is the mind of the Spirit because he maketh intercession for the saints according to the will of God.

When you are praying, not knowing what to pray, Holy Spirit takes over and prays through you in the tongue. The Lord is praying through you. Refrain from leaning on your understanding. Allow the helper to help you.

Lord said Holy Spirit is a leader and advisor to take you to correct path.

John 16:13 Howbeit when he, the Spirit of truth, is come, he will guide you into all truth: for he shall not speak of himself; but whatsoever he shall hear, that shall he speak: and he will shew you things to come.

One time I needed particular blouses, so I sought guidance through prayer. One afternoon, I was working on a computer and Spirit asked me to go to a particular store. I usually would prefer to go to some other than that shop. I started looking, not knowing why I was there. Thank you, Lord. I found beautiful blouses in that store at a reasonable price. Let me tell you, use the Holy Spirit before you mess up your life. Many take help from the Holy Spirit after they mess up their lives. So why not protect yourself and others? Humble asks for help.

LET US PRAY

Lord, we humbly come before you. Please help us lean on the Spirit of God. Let the Spirit of God lead and guide you to all the beautiful plans you have prepared for us. Lord, let your Spirit lead us beside still water. Let your Spirit teach us to know the hidden and deep secret things. Lead us through our prayer. May the Lord give us the wisdom of Daniel and Joseph, lead us Spirit of God. God, you are Spirit and we want you to help us in Jesus's name. Amen! God bless you!

MAY 25

CATCH AND LOOSE!

The Lord grants us the wisdom to understand the plan of God for winning the soul. Jesus went around preaching the kingdom of heaven. He trained disciples and sent them to preach. You can win the soul and lose them in the world to preach the Kingdom of God with the power of healing, setting free from bondage and deliverance. We should never identify ourself or new convert with denominations, non-denomination, or organizations. Catch souls and lose them to preach the good news. Amen!

He never saw one family but thought of the world as one family. A neighbor is someone not related to your family. Lord, make us understand you died for the sin of this world. When Lord said neighbor, He wanted you to understand that you should receive the world like a good Samaritan and not treat how Priest and Levi did. Churches, pastors, and Levi think of them only, or some appear similar to them. In today's perspective, if the church is built on a specific doctrine or some belief that I believe, then it is my responsibility to help. Religious leaders assist individuals who contribute a significant amount of money. Some believe in assisting only those of the same color, same nationality, or whatever excuse we give to get away when we see a need.

May the Lord give us a heart of compassion. After Jesus had sacrificed Himself for all of humanity, Jesus gave an open invitation to all. We can share the message of the gospel without considering the goal of converting them to our church, denomination, or organization. When you win a soul, make sure you win for the Kingdom of God. So God can utilize them in this world. May Lord give us an outstanding picture of the dying world. None of us died but the Lord. He alone helps with our needs.

Luke 10:29 But he, willing to justify himself, said unto Jesus, And who is my neighbor? 30 And Jesus answering said, A confident man went down from Jerusalem to Jericho, and fell among thieves, which stripped him of his raiment, and wounded him, and departed, leaving him half dead.31 And by chance there came down a certain priest that way: and when he saw him, he passed by on the other side.32 And likewise a Levite, when he was at the place, came and looked on him, and passed by on the other side.33 But a certain Samaritan, as he journeyed, came where he was: and when he saw him, he had compassion on him,34 And went to him, and bound up his wounds, pouring in oil and wine, and set him on his own beast, and brought him to an inn, and took care of him.35 And on the morrow when he departed, he took out two pence, and gave them to the host, and said unto him, Take care of him; and thou spendest more, when I come again, I will repay thee.36 Which now of these three, thinkest thou, was neighbor unto him that fell among the thieves? 37 And he said, He that shewed mercy on him. Then said Jesus unto him, Go, and do thou likewise.

MAY 25

An injured man requires your help. Jesus said the Priest, Levite, and the Religious ran away. But the individual who was not of full jewish descent came to help. May Lord send only kind-hearted Samaritans when we need help. Do not be devoted to any particular faith. The title is not important, but virtue is. The Lord gracious and compassionate came to set the captive free. Make sure you are like Jesus and be gracious and merciful. Do not look away from the needy. Do not believe each person who is on the pulpit or holding the microphone. But take note of how they treat those who are in need. Do they care for the impoverished? Do they show humanity to others who are not their church members? Keep an eye out for whether they offer help to a stranger in their time of need or not.

At one point in my vacation, I joined the Christian team in India. We were in some city and venturing out to preach the gospel. I remembered, we went out two-two, and I was with a foreigner lady. She was a nice Christian girl. We knocked on the door and as the man came out; he was not mad at her but told a foreigner lady, why don't you preach to your people? He had an unpleasant experience visiting the nation where she was from.

So do not confine your Christian faith within the realm of a place of worship, but be christening out there. We exemplify Lord Jesus and not ourselves, the church, organization. Jesus healed, set free, and went preaching from town to town and city to city. Jesus restored the broken hearts. May Lord rescue us from following the priests, churches, denominations, and organizations. Follow Jesus! If we do, then we experience the sovereignty of God's realm on earth.

Color, power, money, language, people, or religion can not control the Gospel of Jesus Christ. We have the Gospel of Jesus to teach and preach with the power hidden within us. It is the Power of God to save, heal, and deliver. May the Lord transform us inside out. Make us kingdom laborers. Rescue us from the power of synagog, bondages of churches, denominations, non-denominations, and organization.

For a long period of time, I was in search of the truth. The Bible declares that the truth will set us free. Yes, free us from the accusation of Potiphar's wife burning a fiery furnace and lion's den.

If you desire to receive the promises of the Word of God, then obey the Word of God. Do not fear anybody or anything.

2 Corinthians 13:8 For we can do nothing against the truth, but for the truth.

John 8:32 And ye shall know the truth, and the truth shall make you free.

For a long time, I attended some denominational churches. I noticed that the church dedicated a significant amount of time to prayer and fasting. Music, preaching, and teaching were there, but something was missing. I could not figure it out. I know they held the title of pastor, saints, preachers, missionaries, and all kinds of things. But I did not feel right in my spirit. One day I asked God, Lord, everything is correct, but something is missing here. What is it? Am I in the puzzle? The Holy Ghost stated that they have no Love. If no love, then all is religion.

It is best to go to God, His spirit is called the spirit of truth and will reveal the truth. The Holy Spirit is not afraid of the pastor, his wife, church, organization, or denomination.

1 Corinthians 12:31 But covet earnestly the best gifts: and yet shew I unto you a more excellent way.

There is an excellent way, and what is this excellent way? Charity, 1 Corinthian 13 chapter is the journey of Love, which is charity.

1 Corinthians 13:1 Though I speak with the tongues of men and of angels, and have not charity, I am become as sound-ing brass or a tinkling cymbal. 2 And though I have the gift of prophecy, and understand all mysteries, and all knowledge; and though I have all faith so that I could remove mountains, and have not charity, I am nothing. 3 And though I bestow all my goods to feed the poor, and though I give my body to be burned, and have not charity, it profiteth me nothing.

The preaching and teaching of Jesus are to love as He loved the church. Dedicate all for the kingdom. Submit to Him. We capture the soul, then lose it for the work of the kingdom. Do not introduce them to churches, groups, or organizations, please, but Just Jesus. Followers of Jesus cared for the oppressed, depressed, hurt, and possessed.

Capture and release them to build the kingdom of Jesus. If you do, then they will swim to the locations to reach the needy. They will have the ability to move into this world without any constraints. The Holy Spirit will be in control again. There will be no burden to stamp them with the wrong labels. Understand that you are the church. You are the temple of God. He comes to you; He wants you to make you a fisher of man. We can have Jesus rule again if we catch and lose saints for the kingdom services. I believe this world would have a new image. Catch and release born again saints for the Kingdom of God and not to the kingdom of religion. Amen! Blessings!

LET US PRAY

Thank you, Lord, for coming on earth to buy back the author-ity we lost in the Garden of Eden. Lord, you have called us to work for your kingdom. We can do all that you did and more. This world will see heaven on earth if we allow the Holy Spirit to operate in and through us. It is God ruling in us if we free ourselves from the bondage of religion and allow ourselves for His kingdom. We pray, Lord, to send us laborers for the harvest. May Lord give us a burden for the needy, sick, poor, oppressed, depressed, and dying world! Lord set us free from all bondages, to win the soul for the kingdom. Lord, let us win many souls and lose them back for the services of the kingdom, in Jesus's name. Amen! God bless you!

MAY 26

GOD WATCHES AND KEEPS AN ACCOUNT!

God watches you from heaven and always sees what you are doing. He too has books where he records your wrongs and rights.

We also have notebooks, voice recorders, and video cameras to keep the record. Our planetary system also saves records on the computer. The country maintains a record of different things (Like the police department and birthdays, God is eternal and meticulous in His business. the bank keeps its record. We file to support a vital record).

Malachi 3:16 Then they that feared the Lord spake often one to another: and the Lord hearkened, and heard it, and a book of remembrance was written before him for them that feared the Lord, and that thought upon his name.

Rev 20:21 And I saw the dead, small and great, stand before God; and the books were opened: and another book was opened, which is the book of life: and the dead were judged out of those things which were written in the books, according to their works.

God is eternal and meticulous in His business. He watches what you are doing all the time. You cannot hide from God. I believe the Lord will play our recorded actions with a goal before us. It will be your documentation of life.

2 Chronicles 16:9 For the eyes of the LORD run to and fro throughout the whole earth, to shew himself strong in the behalf of them whose heart is perfect toward him. Herein thou hast done foolishly: therefore, from henceforth, thou shalt have wars.

Is God a dictator, or love you enough to take care of you? May the Lord give us an ear to hear, so we obey and give God the joy of forming us. God was filled with sorrow for creating the human.

Genesis 6:6 And it repented the LORD that he had made the man on the earth, and it grieved him at his heart.

Parents supervise the kids to guide them on the right path. Some children need additional correction, while others require less. We each have our own individual characteristics. Children have been assigned responsibilities by the one who created them. The Bible affirms there is a judgment, and there are consequences. To go through loss is on our side. God has all written works in heaven, and one is the Bible. The Bible is the one by which our judgment will be based. The Bible is not there to continue gathering dust. It is the only set of directions given to us by the Lord. Life could be wonderful if you take heed of it. If we read to obey, then the life of an individual and nation will be smooth and peaceful.

God knows how to write. He gave ten commandments engraved by His finger.

Exodus 31:18 And he gave unto Moses, when he had made an end of communing with him upon mount Sinai, two tables of testimony, tables of stone, written with the finger of God.

Jesus never went to school, but He had the ability to read and write.

John 7:15 And the Jews marveled, saying, How knoweth this man letters, having never learned?

Keep in mind, God is omniscient and omnipotent. God has knowledge of the future, presence, and past.

In the end, God is ultimately going to open the Word of God, the Bible. The divine scripture will judge us. Believe Lord Jesus is the decision-maker today and in the future. If you do wrong, then the Judge will punish you, as the book says. The Judge is not above the Law; Law is above the Judge. You cannot escape if you murder, lie, steal, kill, or go against the law.

May the Lord give us the wisdom to keep the laws written in the Bible! The word is, above all, His name.

Psalms 138:2b. for thou hast magnified thy word above all thy name

John 12:48 He that rejecteth me, and receiveth, not my words, hath one that judgeth him: the word that I have spoken, the same shall judge him in the last day.

If you are a living individual, then please repent of all your sins today. Baptize in Jesus's name to wash away all your sins and receive the power of the Holy Spirit to continue living the Holy life.

In the digital age, we understand how the delete key works. God is wonderful. He will remove our awful record from His computer as we do on ours. We have no obligation to file the paperwork. Our past will be removed from the heavenly book as we obtain forgiveness in water baptism. It is the most incredible experience when we receive a clean conscience by baptizing in Jesus's name. I can't find anything that matches this supernatural experience.

Baptism is not a formal procedure, but an experience. Baptism is not to enroll your name in an organization but to get cleared up sins recorded in heaven. God knows how to take care of us. We need instruction to continue living a holy and clean life. Does God have the record of all? God wrote 66 books in the Bible, took 1600 years, and used 40 different people in different eras and places.

With all of this, God is merciful. He forgives if we repent. God shows mercy to them who make the Bible their personal guide and life manual. If the nation embraces this book and educates based on it, then that country will have peace, protection, and safety. Society appreciates Bible to learn right from wrong. The Bible instructs them to love one another. Love would not cause any damage to the neighbor. God is love, and love is streaming through this book.

MAY 26

Lord, help us apply the Bible in our daily lives.

On the day of judgment, He is going to separate the sheep from the goat. Your work will define you as a goat or sheep. He will find out from your record in the book whether you fed hungrily, clot naked, visited a sick and in prison, gave water to thirty, or gave shelter to a stranger. Do you care when you see someone sick and take care of them? Have you visited a sick person in the hospital? Do you buy food for the hungry? Do you cover naked? Do you help strangers?

While visiting the convalescent home, I met one elderly lady. Her garments were tight. I saw no blankets in winter. So I went shopping. Got all that she needed. We know at the end, when God opens the book, I have done what I can. Do not give any excuse. Do not say, I have no availability, maybe their relatives will take care of the elderly, or it is not my responsibility. I have to attend church, busy working for denominations. It is your job to go out and help. All individuals requiring assistance are our neighbors, and you can be that good samaritan.

I also visited many other convalescent home. I took some gloves and shocks; their reaction was, oh, I needed this. One lady said, how do you know I needed gloves and shocks? Another person bought some scratchers. These people are in homes; we must go visit and talk to them. Help them and spend some money on their needs. Provide their requirement, which is without. I love to give to those who cannot return to me. Why? Why expect back? God depends on us. God called some goats, since their record did not show what God required from them. Jesus said follow me; I gave you an example. Did Jesus build a pulpit or Den, I mean, was He a thief stealing money? Jesus gave an example and said, follow me, not building a cross. Go out to support the underprivileged. Do what Jesus did. Given in the laborer's hand will go to the needy. Remember to give the laborer you will be blessed. The Bible is a multimillion business for the thief. Jesus had a business of healing, delivering, and setting captives free. Study how thieves conduct themselves, and not their word. When you do to strangers, it is doing unto the Lord.

Matthew 25:40 And the King shall answer and say unto them, Verily I say unto you, Inasmuch as ye have done it unto one of the least of these my brethren, ye have done it unto me.

Can you imagine what will be the benefit for those who do all that God requires of them? If you do what God requires of you, you will be happy and surprised by seeing the reward on the day of judgment.

Matthew 25:34 Then shall the King say unto them on his right hand, Come, ye blessed of my Father, inherit the kingdom prepared for you from the foundation of the world

LET US PRAY

My God, we want the heart of gold. We want our hands to be fruitful. Help us plant our work to needy people. May the Lord give us a sensitive ear and heart to feel others 'hunger, cold, pain, thrust, and hopelessness. Lord, we are your hand and leg. You have given us many resources, so the Lord gives us a merciful heart. We love doing what you have assigned us. Lord, help us visit the sick, oppressed, and possessed. God, you labored and said you do what I did. Lord, help us go around doing your work. It is not just for our family but helps us, so we are the family of those who do not have a family in Jesus's name! Amen! God bless you!

MAY 27

MAKE ROOM FOR GOD!

Are you too busy for God? Have you distanced yourself from God? Have you become the slave and servant of the devil, your employer? Had you kept your priority in order as the Lord ordered, you would not be where you are. The Go machine has become yours. Being tied up with a job that is around the clock, you have no free time. You got too busy and had no time for God. With no other options, you must accept your enslavement.

It was easy in the Garden of Eden; God provided all, but replacing God with your lust and pride made you a slave of the devil. By being your own problem, you hinder your progress. May the Lord give us the ear to hear and eyes to see. Once you learn to listen and obey, I am sure your life will be much easier. How disobedient we are to such a wonderful God!

By putting materials and pride first, some end up missing out on easy blessings, which is why they always need to correct. I have won many people, and they become prayer warriors, but later become busy and have no time to pray. Who is important? God or organization program? May God give us the wisdom to keep our priorities straight. Let us reprogram our life according to the order passed by God. With each passing moment, it is getting worse.

Once, I had a dream of a couple whom I had won for the Lord. They got involved in so-called church activity. They were on this train going so fast that they couldn't escape. If you are on this short-life train, be careful. The procession will not stop until its route or program is finished. God will come, and you will be in trouble.

While being occupied with activities, some neglect God and His project. Martha was busy. She got engaged, prioritizing the less important part. Mary seemed to enjoy her life by hearing and eating the word of God. In order to maintain the Lord in His rightful place in life, submit to His teachings.

Instead of having two jobs, working like a dog, and still needing more, people would have been free. Eventually, their family will break up. While hearing this, I cannot afford expenses. Instead of taking the proper route of the Lord and being free from stress, you have made a terrible choice. By opening the door for the Lord in your life, you can be stress free.

Sadly, Christians have no time for God due to being too busy. Ignoring God's assignment, they had no time for Jesus. By ignoring God, not visiting poor widows and prisons, and failing to preach from home to home

MAY 27

and city to city, the bloodshed now becomes visible everywhere. Does God instruct us to attend church and be spectators, or does He instruct us to go and preach, cast out demons, and heal the sick? What are you doing? You are simply trying to justify your actions! Make some room for God.

Following churches/buildings and encountering lost pastors, false teachers, and prophets, this generation has become the most confused and mixed-up. You need to wake up. God said to preach, pray, fast, and study the Word of God. Jesus said, follow me. You learn the word of God by practicing means doing, in the sense it says.

While there are many churches/buildings, the presence of bloodshed, drug use, alcohol abuse, divorces, depression, discouragement, and suicide remains widespread. In order to find solace, go to God and utter, "Lord, I am lost." I have no time; I have become the slave again. Untangle me from my problem. The Lord's ability to deliver, heal, and bring you out is unquestionable. When we mess up, God cleans up if we allow Him to. Having messed up life in debt, poverty, and sicknesses, many can be brought out of all by the Lord. Put God first. Although he sees you, you also need to see Him. Meet your maker. Check yourself; where are you standing with Him today?

When the devil consumes all your money and time, stealing your life, Jesus becomes the only way out. By kicking the devil out, destroying the time stealer, and giving your time to Jesus, you can overcome. Make sure to follow Jesus, for he overturned the table and declared it a den of thieves.

As I recall, my life was very busy when I lived in America. The job became challenging as I worked for God and maintained a full-time Post Office position. When He called me for His full-time services one day, He assured me that He would take care of me. Lord said, I will take care of you if you take care of my work. By listening in, I caught many of my friends and family complaining about my finance situation. I always answer their complaints about having no money by affirming that the Lord is my provider.

You are busy for nothing, friends. Getting a job and touching the cheque may feel good since it is tangible. Although I do not see tangible money, it still feels good to rely on His provision. It brings greater joy. May the Lord give us hunger and thirst for Him. While his people are dying, sick, hungry, and hurting, you move around in your vehicle from one church to another. It has no meaning. You are the church; your body is the temple God created to dwell in.

What do we have to care for in this dispensation? God said to visit the orphan, widow, and hurting. Make some space for Jesus. By being His yielding vessel, he will do all.

Jesus went to the man.

John 5:5 And a certain man was there, which had an infirmity thirty and eight years. 6 When Jesus saw him lie and knew that he had been now a long time in that case, he saith unto him, Wilt thou be made whole? 7 The impotent man answered him, Sir, I have no man, when the water is troubled, to put me into the pool: but while I am coming, another steppeth down before me. 8 Jesus saith unto him, Rise, take up thy bed, and walk. 9 And immediately the man was made whole, and took up his bed, and walked: and on the same day was the sabbath.

It was a Sabbath day. Perhaps, you say it is Sunday, the day designated for attending church.

To ensure you arrive at church on time, wear the best shoes, clothes, and suits. But Jesus went seeking a man who was sick. God looks for the sick, hurting, oppressed, and possessed to help them. Prepare yourself by fasting, praying, and studying the word. We don't need buildings in this dispensation, but we are the church. We are Jesus's hands, feet, and mouth.

It is the sickness of not having enough money. Most of the money goes to nails, hair, shoes, clothes, eating out, shopping, vacationing, sightseeing, and all other lust and pride of life. Your desire to live for God is secondary. May Lord deliver us from all slavery of lust and pride in life. You are slave of the devil.
Have you ever read this word?

Matthew 6:33 But seek ye first the kingdom of God, and his righteousness, and all these things shall be added unto you.

Let me tell you, this is not to memorize or read; it is the promises of God. Your life can be transformed by applying the powerful promises of God.

Ever since He took away my job, I have been working for God. Through my experience, I have found His promises to be trustworthy. In drawing my provisions, I rely on the heavenly bank account. No matter how I look at it, I never see myself as poor or broke, but rather as rich, wealthy, blessed, and overflowing. By contributing from my small paycheck, I assist many people and still have leftover funds.

When I am sick, Jesus serves as my doctor, a physician. Having no knowledge about my body, I don't need to go to someone. Having the knowledge of how to fix, heal, and perform a miracle, the creator of my body possesses great power.

The one who has made them for Himself goes unheard by people because they are too busy. Due to being occupied with church building activities, there is no time to carry out God's work for His Kingdom. How sad! Did they die for you? Did they say I would give you eternal life? Follow Jesus and do not die lost.

Upon casting the demon out, it revealed itself as a choir member. In hell, one can see a lost singer and musician of the church.

Matthew 6:31 Therefore take no thought, saying, What shall we eat? Or, What shall we drink? Or, Wherewithal shall we be clothed? 32 (For after all these things do the Gentiles seek 😊 for your heavenly Father knoweth that ye have need of all these things. 34 Take therefore no thought for the morrow: for the morrow shall take thought for the things of itself. Sufficient unto the day is the evil thereof.

Before you ask or even when you think, would you like to receive it? Make room in your life for Jesus. We watch all evil around us but walk like a zombie, insensitive, blind, and lost. What is our problem? The problem is you are misguided by the devil. You are hand cleft and leg cleft to sit on the pew year after year by accepting false teaching and joining the lost club. Through allowing yourself to walk by your lust for flesh and pride for life, you have fallen prey to them. Allow Lord Jesus to come in.

May the Lord give us an understanding of the word. Differently from older times, elderly complaints have changed, reflecting the change in people.

Despite being given good news by God, you handed it over to the devil, similar to Adam and Eve.

MAY 27

Despite Adam's failure, Jesus triumphed over it and reclaimed what the devil had taken, bestowing it upon us. But we are also not faithful servants and good stewards over it. May we make some room for Him to take care of His business? In Jesus 'Name, Amen!

LET US PRAY

Lord, we have limited time on earth. Help us not to entangle in the dark. We live amongst the lost. We have time for everything but you. So help us, Lord, to bring back our lives, home, town, school, city, and country. We see the mess of not being a good steward of your business by being too busy. Lord, help us trust you for our health, finance, provision, children, and life. May the Lord give us wisdom, knowledge, and understanding to be the best laborer. Lord, if we make room for you, you will load us with all benefits. Thank you, Lord, in Jesus's name, Amen! God bless you!

MAY 28

HEALING WILL COME IF YOU CLEAN FROM WITHIN!

Every human has a body, spirit, and soul. It is important for us to understand that mechanisms in the body cannot die. In order to prevent the disease, we continue making suitable cells in the body. Depending on the operation of spirit and flesh, our soul's destiny is determined. Through fleshly sin, our sicknesses manifest. A person who is filled with love, joy, peace, long-suffering, gentleness, goodness, meekness, and mercy will not experience illnesses.

It is undeniable that transgressors will suffer from illnesses. Committing a transgression involves stepping on God's commandment. Sickness, as God's correcting rod, brings about correction. God, in His love, uses sickness as a rod of correction to slow us down and teach us the lesson of action. Experiencing pain for eternity is much worse than feeling a little pain. People often experience headaches, vomiting, and high blood pressure due to sin reigns inside. We think of no importance to it. Frequently, we experience a headache when we get upset. Unforgiveness is our worst enemy; immune system problems are the reason for bad temper. Acidity causes a terrible reaction. There are many who give excuses, saying that they were compelled to get upset. In order to be fine, it is necessary to have forgiveness and forget. You will have no health issues. When you harbor bad feelings, it will cause you multi sicknesses.

Having one sickness leads to another. By repenting of your sins, you can find the best way out. Maybe you say, repent of what? I have reason to get upset. No, you do not; you are not suitable for yourself. In my entire life, I had never encountered a headache. So when people talk about headaches, I do not understand.

However, some people constantly experience headaches. I know them; they have a terrible temper. In their opinion, no one can say anything to them. Suffering from a mental disorder is a consequence for those who are envious, jealous, and prideful.

I had a coworker; who always took counseling from me. Consistently, I offer counsel and pray for her. After feeling better for a while, she will go back to the same problem. She had a past. When she was younger, her sister treated her unfairly. A stepmother made her finish the food which she did not like. You may say, all these are not major. Despite her attempts to move on, she still held onto the past. She collected garbage within. She was frequently admitted to a psychiatric hospital. Without any reason, she will often get upset with others. Regrettably, she forgot her medicine, as people commented.

MAY 28

It is acceptable if she mistreats others, but if anyone utters a single word, she will become upset, angry, cry, and throw tantrums. As we understand, bullying is a common occurrence here in the US. Despite that; it is our health, not to harm ourselves.

Those who do evil to others may also go crazy. Some bullies at work turn to alcoholism. In order to deal with their mental instability, they have to stay away from work. It is evident that school shootings occur as a result of students becoming frustrated. The cause of mental trauma is inner anger, bitterness, and helplessness. Make sure you treat people with kindness. Show some compassion and love. It is free.

Anger, unforgiving, hurt, heartbreak, and many other sinful issues are the reasons why hospitals are full of sick people. Not wanting to believe they are sinners, we do not label it a sin.

Since we are in the flesh, it follows that all flesh has sinned. The inevitable disease grows within every human; you must subdue and chop it off. Let the root be out. May the Lord bless us with individuals like Paul, John the Baptist, and honest teachers and preachers. Due to sin, sickness is a worldwide cause. The sicknesses that destroy you are brought into your body by your sin.

Liz, despite our fight, my coworker told me that you spoke to me the next day. I said what you meant. If I fight with Asians the way I fight with you, she said they will not talk to me. We Asians are different. Regardless of her nationality, I do not want to mention it. She said we wouldn't even look at each other if we fought. But you are different; when you see me, you greet me, saying, Hello, Lucy. She said, I kind of wonder why. Years later, I observed that she was confronted with life-threatening illnesses in her body. I explained to her; please do not let this temper control you. It has the potential to ruin you. She admitted, "I know, but I couldn't help." With many prayers and counselings, she took baptism and now mellowed down.

See if you see this kind of situation, please pray for them. By helping them and not hurting them, we can make a positive impact.

God gave me a dream of a particular person before I visited a family. Unfortunately, she was suffering from severe diabetes. With God exposing her jealousy, it was revealed. Following her mother's teachings, she learned not to show love to her in-laws. What she brought up turned out to be very confusing. Parents, please teach children right. As a result of your wrong advice and evil teaching, your children have become sick.

From India, one girl came by marrying a guy from the US. She had many evil spirits. She was full of jealousy, envy, lies, and pride. That affected her emotions. She started cutting herself. They invited me to pray, and we cast out demons from her. I found her rude and jealous. Little did we know, she was also the prayer leader of the denomination. Despite my efforts to help her, her raise turned out to be bad. Instead of trying to teach, her parents allowed the daughter to use her mouth against her in-laws. Despite not speaking, parents utilize their children's mouths against in-laws. By causing illnesses to you and your children, that will result in hell.

Knowing that people have HIV, aids, cancers, and diseases caused by sins, I understand. No one but you has to suffer from sickness.

By getting tough on your flesh, mortifying and uprooting all sinful nature with sins, you will please. Do it by prayer, fasting, and obeying the word. Instant forgiveness helps. Buy some gifts or bless by giving to those who do wrong to you. It brings peace to the enemy.

By utilizing the scriptures, you can overcome your flesh and eliminate it. When dealing with anger, search for all scripture about temper, read them, and pray against it. To obtain victory, you must overcome the desires of the flesh. Although you may have to pray a few times daily, continue praying against it. Pleading the blood of Jesus over your body, soul, sin, and spirit is essential. Ask the Holy Spirit to help you. Ask someone to pray for you. Only those who can pray for you should be confessed to, not to everyone.

John 1:9 If we confess our sins, he is faithful and just to forgive us our sins and to cleanse us from all unrighteousness.

Psalms 32:5 I acknowledged my sin unto thee, and mine iniquity have I not hid. I said, I will confess my transgressions unto the LORD; and thou forgavest the iniquity of my sin. Selah.

Remember, God is merciful. If you say, Lord, forgive my sin. Confess sins to God, not to father, sisters, or whoever, since sin is against God. God gave us laws, statutes, precepts, and commandments; if you transgress, you sin.

Proverbs 28:13 He that covereth his sins shall not prosper: but whoso confesseth and forsaketh them shall have mercy.

Having a relationship with God, David experienced a deep connection. Having a deep understanding of His God, David knew Him. When the prophet confronted him, David reacted with a confession. Remember to not be like Cain. By no means say that I do not know what you are talking about.

2 Samuel 12:13 And David said unto Nathan, I have sinned against the LORD. And Nathan said unto David, The LORD also hath put away thy sin; thou shalt not die.

Your sins cause sickness.

Psalms 103:3 Who forgiveth all thine iniquities; who healeth all thy diseases; 4 Who redeemeth thy life from destruction; who crowneth thee with loving kindness and tender mercies;

By loving ourselves, we can foster a positive mindset. By loving, you are willing to do anything and everything to support yourself.

By helping us, God can change our guilty conscience into a clean consciousness. Gradually, God will remove the old sin power grip from consciousness. Go in the water and wipe out your sin in Jesus's name. Before baptizing, it is important to study the Book of Acts. Through submerging in the water in Jesus's name, you will be granted healing, deliverance, and salvation. I love you, and may God bless you.

LET US PRAY

Lord, you are the answer for the sins. We ask you to forgive and wash our sins in your blood hidden behind the name of Jesus. Lord, we all have sinned, born in sinful nature. Help us to always keep a watch over

MAY 28

ourselves. We confess to cleansing ourselves from the filthiness of flesh and sin. Our fleshly nature causes us many troubles, helps us, Lord, and forgives us, Lord. Help us also to forgive others and help us pray for others who are sinning. Not to talk against, but to pray for others in their weaknesses in Jesus's name. Amen! God bless you!

MAY 29

THE DEVIL IS HIDING BEHIND RELIGIOUS CHURCHES!

It is the best place to hide, no question about it. It is impossible for anyone to tell that you are demon-possessed or operated by the demonic world systems. In organizations, denominations, and non-denominations, it is the place where Satan is hiding.

Above all, the Lord placed love for Jesus in their heart, prioritizing love for the truth over religion.

In the book of Revelation, the Lord addresses the different churches in Asia. Unbelievably, the Lord is confronting the churches. Those are the churches? Not synagogue, temple, or another worship center. The most dangerous place to be careful about. When Satan is preaching, controlling, teaching, or prophesying, run from them. In order to avoid being misguided or deceived, don't pay attention to the titles. In identifying the facts of their spiritual condition, Jesus is providing clarity. How strange is it that your body creator has chosen your body as their residence and referred to it as a temple?

Being a liar, the devil is also a twister and the most wicked. Diligently working day and night, he aimed to deceive the one who does not love the truth. The book of Revelation is meant to be for the future. The book of prophecy is what that is. By revealing to John, it was shown that Jesus is Judge, King, and God, and that he died in the flesh for you. The manifestation of the spirit God of the old testament is Jesus. By receiving revelation, you know this rather than through teaching or attending theological college.

Revelation 1:1a The Revelation of Jesus Christ, which God gave unto him,

Upon having this revelation, your journey to victory begins. If not, then you will be on the road of confusion and darkness. May the Lord grant us a revelation of Jesus, just as He did to Peter, Paul, and others who love God. It was a fantastic experience to have the revelation of Jesus. Regardless of a person's backsliding, he will not believe that there are many gods. Since the Spirit of God wrote the word, all words of God require revelation.

When the Lord is talking to 7 churches, it is important to remember that these are churches. Built on rock, this church had its foundation rooted in truth. Rock is a revelation of Jesus as the Spirit of Jehovah in the flesh. Carefully, they should study what warnings and corrections are given to them. Though it is not I who is saying, but the Lord. In order to escape from the hellfire, may Lord correct us today. Given that Jesus is

MAY 29

the way, religion, commonly referred to as the broadway, is considered the most dangerous path. While you believe you are right, the fact is actually the opposite.

To fit in society, certain churches compromise with culture and lose their first love for Christ. At this end-time, they have adopted the heathen way for each Christian festival. There are seven types of lifestyle adopted by us, it is mentioned as churches.

The Church of Ephesus did hard and single-minded work, but it died. After rebuking you, the Lord said that you have abandoned your first love. God warned Ephesus to remember and return to their first love. It is a matter of life and death. Always remember it is talking about hell and heaven. Eternal death in hell or eternal life in heaven! So friends do not get connected with anyone but the Lord. His word is above all His name. Obey the word and submit to the Spirit of God to learn the word. The Holy Spirit is given by God not for speaking in tongues only, but to be led by it in order to do powerful work.

As a result of bad persecution, the Church of Smyrna faced poverty. When a country persecutes Christians at work, it destroys their property and businesses, affecting finances. Poverty takes a heavy toll on them. In spite of persecution or poverty, the Lord instructs to stay faithful and not be afraid. In heaven, we own a mansion.

While initially founded on true faith, the Church of Pergamon later compromised. Seeing the churches compromising is also happening at present. To repent is necessary for them, which also applies to us. Having started outright and going astray, it is necessary to repent and come back.

In an incredible way, the Church of Thyatira had its beginning. Although great faith and services were present, immorality has now crept in.

They must repent in order to reconcile. Despite being a church, the Church of Sardis was lifeless. The church was filled with superficial people, causing it to lose its authenticity. By waking up, repenting, and holding on to the truth, they must ensure their spiritual growth.

In its faith, the Church of Philadelphia stands strong. This church is not subject to reprimand. Being good and reliable is how we describe it.

Without being hot or cold, the Church of Laodicea needs to repent, be earnest, and demonstrate a serious commitment to the work of Jesus.

Praising is found in all churches except for the Sardis and Laodicean churches.

Without any rebuke, the Church of Smyrna and Philadelphia are praised and given advice to continue.

The actions, reactions, praise, and rebuke of these seven churches demonstrate that God will not govern in any other manner. In order to repent, we must all turn from the sin we are practicing. While grieving, we must carry on with the truth. Churches will compromise, become superficial, or even lukewarm. Immorality will creep in and move away from the first love, but if we repent and turn to God, He will forgive and receive us.

God is merciful! God is the same yesterday, today, and forever. Without any variance, He remains constant. So if you have adopted any worldly way, repent, and remember, you are the church. He is giving chance after chance to turn to Him. May the Lord give us an understanding of Him.

Sin is in all these churches except two, so you understand all five churches have compromised. May the Lord give us love for truth and help us continue in the truth. Do you believe Satan is hiding in the churches?

It is a fact that churches in Corinth, Gallatin, Ephesus, collisions, and many other churches mentioned in the Bible have rebuke and praise. Many learned the truth but left and started following false prophets and teachers.

We are living in an end-time that gives us greater understanding. We see how people want freedom and join a social club. Dislike a rebuke. Despite disliking corrections, they have to make changes to their lifestyle. God has a standard, and we have to go by His template called the Bible. Remember, no matter how many denominations, organizations, or churches we start; it will not work. Jesus is the way, He said follow me.

The devil, in order to misguide you, can stand on a pulpit. It is said in the Bible to follow Jesus. Repent, turn from your wicked ways. Sin is sin in the eyes of God. You cannot redefine, justify, or rewrite the Bible by accepting worldly lifestyles. Let the Spirit of God lead, guide, teach, and empower you to remain faithful to Him. If church authorities approve, wrong doesn't mean God endorses it. You can sit in the church, but then what? Do you have any chance on the day of judgment? Love your soul. God can deliver, set you free, and save you if you repent and turn to God. May the Lord give us leaders like Jesus. May Lord give us the shepherd ready to die for the truth, but teach the truth only. It is the greatest example of Jesus dying for the truth and holding on. He said it was finished. The persecution of Christians today reminds us many will compromise, but some wouldn't. Praise God!

It is time; we must refresh ourselves with prayer, fasting, and the Word of God. Satan will try to corrupt many by hurting and bribing with money, power, and position. The devil has changed the Bible but stays faithful to the Lord. The Lord is faithful! Do not get deceived by Satan.

I have seen the organization compromised, left fasting, shallow prayer, no testimony, and going down the hill. Follow Jesus; His word will make you and keep you.

I remembered the day when I stood by the church's altar by myself and cried out to God. I was praying for righteousness to come back and for righteous people on the pulpit. As he got up from the corner, the man who resembled the church pastor pushed me. A fallen angel manifested and pushed my forehead; I almost fell backward. This was not a dream; it happened to me in that church. I still did not move. I kneeled on the altar and started praying. As I prayed, I asked the Lord to bring back the prayer and fasting. Same time I saw a vision. The same pastor's wife walked to the middle and stood between the pews. Although none of them were present, the spirit behind them was present. This is how the devil gets hold of the leader of the churches. When it happens, get direction from the Lord and get out. If the organization, church, or denomination gets contaminated, then please get out of there. We should not be called to nurture the pastor, his wife, and the building, but get out and do what the disciple did. Please love the truth and hold on until the end. You will make it. Jesus did not call you to follow anyone but Him. The powerful weapon is the truth of the word. Hold on to the word. May the Lord deliver you from pew, den of thieves and remove the leg handcuffs so you go out to Jerusalem, Judea, Samaria, and the uttermost part of the World.

MAY 29

In order to be saved, we ask the Lord to deliver us from anything and everybody. Who contaminates? May the Lord give us the truth to be free. Let us repent every day and be faithful till the end. In Jesus 'name, Amen!

LET US PRAY

Lord, we recognize, we wrestle not against flesh and blood but against the spiritual wickedness ruling in high places. Give us the power of your word as a sword to destroy the evil work of Satan. May the Lord make us obedient and submissive to the word of truth. Lord, this is the end time. Everything is changing before our eyes but you. We thank you because you change not; you fail not; you are our savior and Lord. Help us be faithful till the end and hold on to you. Our hearts overflow with gratitude for every prophecy and warning in the Bible. Everything you say in the word is fulfilling before our eyes. Lord, help us watch and pray, so we escape from all coming against us in Jesus 'name. Amen! God bless you!

MAY 30

THE DEVIL IS A LIAR, AND THE HOLY SPIRIT IS TRUE!

Everyone is aware that the Devil is a liar. That is why God gave us the Holy Spirit to lead us in all truth. But my question is, do you allow the Holy Spirit to lead to the fact? There is no denying that, by permitting others, we allow them to take over and replace the Holy Spirit. Do you seek help from the Holy Spirit to direct you? Deceiving us, many use different dressings, titles, labels, churches, and organizations as disguises. Do you allow the Holy Spirit to let you lead, speak, or guide to all truth? It is a great comfort given to us. We made a mess in the garden of Eden by disobeying one commandment. The Devil has found many more ways to deceive.

2 Corinthians 2:11 Lest Satan should get an advantage of us: for we are not ignorant of his devices.

While searching the garden of Eden, Satan discovered something subtle to further its agenda. It cannot be denied. There is no one available to play the role of the deceiver. The Devil is a liar, and he needs someone to play the role of a liar. With the intention of deceiving the creation of God and snatching it from the hand of God.

God's Blessings are on His handiwork, made in God's image.

Genesis 1: 26 And God said, Let us make man in our image, after our likeness: and let them have dominion over the fish of the sea, and over the fowl of the air, and the cattle, and all the earth, and over every creeping thing that creepeth upon the earth.

Knowing we have dominion overall, the liar acknowledges it. The Devil was only interested in what the Lord placed in our hands. He planned to steal from us by lying and deceiving creation. This way, men will lose their rights again. Does ignorance counts? No, it doesn't. The Devil is able to manipulate the talent, money, and power for our own destruction because our ignorance plays into Satan's hands. If you do not keep your eyes and mind on the given possession by God, you will become perishable. God gave all gifts with conditions, so memorize your dos and don'ts.

Matthew 10:16 Behold, I send you forth as sheep in the midst of wolves: be ye therefore wise as serpents, and harmless as doves.

MAY 30

God called the serpent subtle, which means crafty or cunning. In encountering cunning, crafty people, they have the intention of getting something out of your hand. Being careless, the devil can take away something from you.

To take something away from you is the purpose of all evil devices or plans. The only protection is the word of God, the truth. The Word of God is faithful. The Devil is a liar; he uses conniving and misleading devices. You were better off with the Holy Spirit's guidance by standing on the word of the truth. You cannot survive any other way. Look what happens to those skilled singers, musicians, gifted and intelligent people.

Pay attention to the Lord; hear His small voice.

While traveling on the freeway in California, I was stopped by a police officer in the middle of the night. I saw a flashing light, so I pulled over to the side and stopped. My job hours were 4 pm to midnight, if overtime, then 1 or 2 am.

I heard the voice of the Holy Spirit, which prompted me to refrain from opening the car door. As soon as the police officer arrived, he asked me to open the door. I opened the window slightly by rolling it down. Curiously, I noted that his question was strange. He asked me a personal thing like; you look familiar. Where are you coming from? Are you a nurse etc.? The Holy Spirit had already warned me, so I did not have to obey the command of the policeman, even though he dressed like a police officer driving in a police car. Without opening the door, I answered all His questions and he responded with a smile, saying okay, go. See, the Devil is a liar. He was not a police officer. If you have the Holy Spirit, you will not be deceived by the Devil. The Holy Spirit will lead you to all truth.

Once on vacation, I was in a hotel room. I wanted to eat breakfast. The Lord warned against going in the restaurant downstairs. I was hungry and thought I would get it from a safe place. Due to having an emergency, I had to immediately return to my room without stepping off the floor. Later, I found out that the site was packed with criminals. I was on tour, so I needed an idea about which hotel they booked. We must understand the Devil can personate anyone. Learn to love the truth and obey. Is there a place where you see the miracle? Probably no where. Make sure the Spirit of God leads you.

2 Thessalonians 2:9 Even him, whose coming is after the working of Satan with all power and signs and lying wonders,10 And with all deceivableness of unrighteousness in them that perish; because they received not the love of the truth, that they might be saved.11 And for this cause God shall send them strong delusion, that they should believe.

According to the Bible, many organization leaders are considered devil's agents.

2 Corinthians 11:3 But I fear, lest by any means, as the serpent beguiled Eve through his subtilty, so your minds should be corrupted from the simplicity that is in Christ.14 And no marvel; Satan is transformed into an angel of light.

Remember that the blessing of God was stolen. One of the worst things to happen to humanity was eternal death, taking place in hell. Can you again give the reason that, oh so and so, deceive me as Eve gave reasons?

Genesis 3:13 And the LORD God said unto the woman, What is this that thou hast done? And the woman said, The serpent beguiled me, and I did eat.

Can you say I went to this place of worship, and now I am in hell, so and so beguiled me? Be careful; the highest authority is the word of God. Let the Spirit of God steer you away from the manipulative devil.

1 John 4:1 Beloved, believe not every spirit, but try the spirits whether they are of God: because many false prophets are gone out into the world.

I completed my three-day and night period without food and water. Yet again, God asked me to fast for three days and nights for someone who needed deliverance. So I carried out the action, but in between, I seeped water. I communicated to God I would take one seep. As I immediately seeped the water, the Holy Spirit said you have to go one more time for three days and nights. I called for you to abstain from eating and drinking for three days and nights, no food and water for the deliverance of a person. So I went for the third time. I am so glad that I did. At that time, I never could even imagine that in my lifetime, I see that fasting would turn into a kosher diet. The Devil's deceptive interpretation is called Daniel's diet. The Devil beguiled Eve and still not stopping? I bruised your head with my heel. I do not have High Heal, but I have the truth and will destroy your devices.

May the Lord give us a vision of hell and heaven. We need to feel the fire and the hottest hell. Just stare at burning lava. Might get a little idea.

Sometimes I scratch my head and wonder where the true prophets and teachers whose sole focus is God wholly. If we embrace the truth, then no fear in the school or mall, no fear of kidnappers. Children can enjoy outdoor recreation. My Lord grants us wisdom, you need the fear of God, not the freedom of the world. No one manages your soul but you. I have seen substance abuse, alcoholics, mental illnesses, suicide, bullying, depression, discouragement, and name it. Do you ever question what took place to the old-time religion? Let me bring to your attention that the training of Jesus contradicted the modern-day churches.

Don't enter the structure when you see the cross on it, you will be sorry. It is time to explore the Bible and let the Holy Spirit teach, guide, and empower us to stand against the will of the enemy.

Ephesians 6:11 Put on the whole armor of God that ye may be able to stand against the wiles of the Devil.

Listen to the Holy Spirit. You will renew, rejuvenate, and get back on the track called the narrow way to heaven. May the Holy Spirit be the sound you hear in Jesus 'name. Amen!

LET US PRAY:

Thank you, Lord, for giving us the word as light, lamp, and sword. Help us here to the spirit of the truth more than our lust and pride. It is the old method the Devil uses to harm us. Lord Gives us love for ourselves. We send ourselves to hell, not the Devil or false churches. So love the word, which is also the spirit. The spirit of truth is the Word of God. Give us boldness, courage, submission, and obedience to the Holy Spirit. We need the rest within and for our country. Having many churches, we see hopelessness and despair, since Satan is misleading us again. The Devil disguises himself behind the labels of spiritual authority. Help us guided by the Holy Spirit and the Holy Spirit alone in Jesus 'name. Amen! God bless you!

MAY 31

BUILD YOUR ALTAR AND NEVER LOSE IT!

Genesis 12:7 And the Lord appeared unto Abram, and said, Unto thy seed will I give this land: and there built he an altar unto the Lord, who appeared unto him.

So What is the Alter? An Alter is a Structure on which they made offerings to a deity. The Hebrew word for Altar is Mizbeah [;eBzim], from a verbal root meaning "to slaughter." From the Bible Dictionary, Greek renders this word as thusiasterion [qusiasthvrion], "a place of sacrifice.

How to build an Alter? Since God is not only the God of Abraham but also of His numerous descendants, God provided specific instructions to the Israelites.

Exodus 20:24 An altar of earth thou shalt make unto me and shalt sacrifice thereon thy burnt offerings, and thy peace offerings, thy sheep, and thine oxen: in all places where I record my name I will come unto thee, and I will bless thee.25 And if thou wilt makes me an altar of stone, thou shalt not build it of hewn stone: for if thou lift thy tool upon it, thou hast polluted it.

God wanted Abraham to build an altar, with the intention of honoring His name. As is true, God knows His people and meets them personally. While I was in India, I observed Hindu temples scattered here and there for their idols.

Moreover, we established the Altar where we commune with our living God. God reveals himself to the righteous, holy, and obedient people. He comes to the one seeking God with unwavering commitment and walking on God's path! God is real. He remembers the locations where we meet. Isaac, son of Abraham, also established an altar where He met God.

Genesis 26:25a And he built an altar there, and called upon the name of the LORD,

The promise of Abraham was passed down to his son Isaac and his son Jacob. Jacob was passionate about God and His blessings and not about meals. His father and grandfather testified to him about God. Jacob was on the hunt for this great God. His yearning to have all but from God alone. Isn't it nice that somebody is ready to do anything and everything to get to God? I am very impressed with my God. It is my understanding that not everyone wants to call on God for their needs. God perceives how much faith we have in our hearts. Your connection begins with God when you trust and believe in Him. Indeed, you will encounter Him like God encountered Jacob.

Genesis 28:13 And, behold, the Lord stood above it, and said, I am the Lord God of Abraham thy father, and the God of Isaac: the land whereon thou liest, to thee will I give it, and to thy seed; 14 And thy seed shall be as the dust of the earth, and thou shalt spread abroad to the west, and to the east, and to the north, and to the south: and in thee and in thy seed shall all the families of the earth be blessed. 15 And, behold, I am with thee, and will keep thee in all places whither thou goest, and will bring thee again into this land; for I will not leave thee, until I have done that which I have spoken to thee of. 16 And Jacob awaked out of his sleep, and he said, Surely the Lord is in this place; and I knew it not. 17 And he was afraid, and said, How dreadful is this place! this is none other but the house of God, and this is the gate of heaven. 18 And Jacob rose up early in the morning, and took the stone that he had put for his pillows, and set it up for a pillar, and poured oil upon the top of it. 19a And he called the name of that place Bethel:

Under God's command, Jacob was returning back after 20 years to the promised land. God commanded Jacob to journey to the place where He once met him.

Genesis 35:1 And God said unto Jacob, Arise, go up to Bethel, and dwell there: and make there an altar unto God, that appeared unto thee when thou fleddest from the face of Esau, thy brother. 7 And he (Jacob) built there an altar, and called the place Elbethel: because there God appeared unto him, when he fled from the face of his brother.

We all should build our Altar. I had a friend who was a mighty prayer warrior. She informed me about having alters in a small closet. She kept her bedding and prayed there practically all night. God utilized her mightily in the church, and for me as well! Upon being sent to Texas by God, I initially struggled with my health and also encountered numerous oppositions in California.

With no one around, my destiny was under attack by the devil. Since I was getting very sick, I questioned whether it was the will of God to move to Texas or did I miss the signs. During the Sunday Church service, the Pastor invited the saints of God to come to the Altar. He said this altar call is for the faithful servants of God. I was instantly convinced that it was for me. I went to the Altar and kneeled. During my prayer, I asked God, "Lord, what is Your will for me today?" Is this your will for me to be here, or do I miss it?

This lady who is committed to praying was on the Altar as well. She turned around, put her hand on me, and started speaking in a heavenly language and interpreting. God communicated through her mouth. 'Why do you doubt me, I brought you to this place. Can't you have faith in me? 'She kept repeating this. As she prayed, the sickness vanished, and I felt lighter. She did not know what was happening to me.

She said I thought you were someone who had a smoking habit. She was confused since I smelled a cigarette, she said. Then she said, I realized that when I smell cigarettes, that is the consequence of fear. So I knew I was being targeted by Satan. I was so thankful for the people who created the Altar. I do not know her spiritual walk with God today. Keep your Alter. Never lose it. The devil wants to target your meeting place.

I had a friend in California who mentioned that she has her altar. In the park, she prays and connects with God under a particular tree. She said, I always encounter God at that place. We must have our meeting place with God. The place where you meet God will stay holy from generation to generation.

Jeroboam defiled the place of Bethel, who became the first monarch of the Northern Kingdom. His motive was wrong. He did not want people to meet God but to distance them from the living God. When you have

MAY 31

a deceitful heart, the devil manipulates the motive and desire. He took counsel from others. He put Calves and made Israelite idol worshipers.

Calves are not God. Jehovah God brought them to the promised land from Egypt, not the calves.

1 King 12:28 Whereupon the king took counsel, and made two calves of gold, and said unto them, It is too much for you to go up to Jerusalem: behold thy gods, O Israel, which brought thee up out of the land of Egypt. 29 And he set the one in Bethel, and the other put he in Dan.

A false god replaced the devotion to the true God. May the Lord help us not to lose our motive.

Later, the Israelites lost their country and were expelled from the promised land.

Today, God has promised us the one selected for the mansions in heaven. Make sure you have the Altar and diligently pray day and night. Meet God in the place He picked to contact you. Let your children see you praying and calling on Jesus. Let your children learn one thing from you: they need an altar to meet their God. We do not make our God of gold or stone. Our God has created us. He also loves to fellowship with us. God talks to those whose hearts are perfect toward Him. Our prayer is like perfume, a sweet-smelling perfume. He wants to smell your prayer. Come before Him and pray.

Psalms 141:2 Let my prayer be set forth before thee as incense; and the lifting up of my hands as the evening sacrifice.

God has an Alter in Heaven.

Revelation 8: 3 And another angel came and stood at the Altar, having a golden censer; and there was given unto him much incense, that he should offer it with the prayers of all saints upon the golden Altar which was before the throne. 4 And the smoke of the incense, which came with the prayers of the saints, ascended up before God out of the angel's hand. 5 And the angel took the censer, and filled it with the fire of the Altar, and cast it into the earth: and there were voices, and thunderings, and lightnings, and an earthquake.

LET US PRAY

Lord our father of faith, Abraham had a meeting place. He called it an Alter. We desire to meet you where we can say, Lord, this is my Altar. Lord, there we come and meet you. Please give us an ear to hear from you. Give us the Altar where promises of God are renewed in ours, our children, and their children's lives. We want Alter never to be replaced with the wrong motive and lose our promises. Lord, we do not want to lose our blessing and land. May the Lord help us remember our meeting with Him is more important than calves, idols, or anything. We perceive the reason for losing the promised land since people were hungry for power. Help us never to repeat the same mistakes in Jesus's name. Amen! God bless you!

JUNE

JUNE 1

FEAR THE JUDGE JESUS!

Deciding right from wrong falls upon judges in the secular world. People have to appear before the judge when they do wrong. Knowing that your life depends on judgment when you stand before the judge. Based on his judgement of the law, the judge can choose to show mercy or punish or do what he believes is right. Having a law enforcement, judge, and judicial system is a requirement for each nation, country, state, and city. By following laws and statutes, the system of the world can prosper and be blessed. A system of overseers is needed to enforce the law. Regrettably, something is missing or not right in every world's government.

Since He has a kingdom, we also refer to God as the judge. He has laws, commandments, and precepts. All His do's and don'ts are for our safety and benefits. Our Lord, being fair and the highest judge, reigns over the earthly judge. He is the judge over all judges. His kingdom is all over the earth. By writing His laws in our hearts, we can ensure that they are always with us. God is searching for someone who will follow His laws. He desires for someone to watch it and make sure it is enforced. Instead of talking about it, he wants someone to follow it.

Isaiah 33:22 For the Lord is our judge, the Lord is our lawgiver; the Lord is our king; he will save us.

The Lord, having given us the law, ensures that nothing is beyond His laws. To bring the kingdom of God to earth, one must diligently observe the law without violating it by disregarding its boundaries. By obeying His laws, commandments, and statutes, you will find enjoyment during your stay on earth. Temporarily residing on earth, humans decide where they want to spend eternity. Choosing the righteous path is what wise people do on Earth.

Failing to keep the law will result in you being cursed and removed from the earth. In God's kingdom, there is a law enforcer for each kingdom as stated in the Bible. The judge fulfills the requirement of The Rule of Law by walking according to the law.

Therefore, let the king render back to the law what the law gives him, namely, dominion and power; for there is no king where will, and not law, wields dominion." So wrote Henry de Bracton.

The judge should be punished if he breaks the law, as stated by the law. God, being the judge of all His creation, exercises judgment. Revealing the judgment against Sodom and Gomorrah was his action. At the start, Abraham initiated his appeal for the cities. In showing the trespasses and transgressions of those cities, God establishes Himself as the King who acts by His commands.

Genesis 18:25 That be far from thee to do after this manner, to slay the righteous with the wicked: and that the righteous should be as the wicked, that be far from thee: Shall not the judge of all the earth do right?

God said that had He found ten righteous in both cities, He would have spared them.

Genesis 18:32 And he said, Oh let not the Lord be angry, and I will speak yet but this once: Peradventure ten shall be found there. And he said I would not destroy it for ten's sake.

Had the Lord found a few good people, He would not have been ready to overthrow the nation. Per their sins, God rendered judgment upon them. The sin of homosexuality, when committed, brings judgment and wipes out sinners along with their cities. There is no remedy for sin unless repentance is sought. Because this kind of sin is directly against God, chances of repentance are very low.

Roman 1:28 And even as they did not like to retain God in their knowledge, God gave them over to a reprobate mind, to do those things which are not convenient;

No one can escape from His judgment, for there is none above the laws. To amend your ways is the best approach. There is little possibility of turning back in situations like homosexuality, with only judgment awaiting. God, having given the land to the descendants of Abraham, saw the sins of that city being over the head. They were waiting for the judgment.

Genesis 15:16 But in the fourth generation they shall come hither again: for the iniquity of the Amorites is not yet full.

To execute judgment, the land must first reach the height of sin. If people have committed such-and-such sin, God has the power to evict them from the land. If not, the Lord will be unable to carry out the judgment of removing them from their land.

Deuteronomy 7:1 When the LORD thy God shall bring thee into the land whither thou goest to possess it, and hath cast out many nations before thee, the Hittites, and the Girgashites, and the Amorites, and the Canaanites, and the Perizzites, and the Hivites, and the Jebusites, seven nations greater and mightier than thou; We may only stay in the land of the living if we observe the laws of God.

Psalms 127:1 Except the Lord build the house, they labour in vain that build it: except the Lord keep the city, the watchman waketh but in vain.

Your city can be safe and secure only if God is watching over it. If you desire God to secure you, keep His commandments and laws. Do not go over the limit or step over His laws. There is a blessing and security if we live by the laws of God. We hear news of rape, child molestation, fornication, and adultery continuously due to women removing their clothes. After realizing their nakedness, the first correction in the Garden of Eden was the cloth. To shield evil from our eyes, the Lord made a robe, since the apron will not cover us. Seeing the devastating result we see today is a consequence of not following the laws of God. To avoid surprise, simply get wiser.

JUNE 1

Clothes serve the function of covering your body. If you cannot afford a bodyguard, refrain from displaying your body. Despite the Devil's efforts to make you fall and destroy you, get wise and live according to the word of God. Observing the requirement leads to the blessings discussed in the Bible. By not obeying God, you will face curses as the judgment. Different sins are committed by us, both as individuals and as countries. If an individual sins, there is a judgment of sickness, poverty, famine, flood, plague, and more. All your actions will determine the effect where you lacked, deviated or trespassed on the laws and commandments of God. When you go to the extreme, you will be out of the land given to you. God is the Chief Judge with eyes and ears to see your action. Fear God and no one else. If you fear the Lord and amend your ways, you will be reestablished.

Before the destruction, God warned the sinful city of Nineveh. He sent His spokesman Jonah to warn them. Revealing a plan of judgment and time, Jehovah God warns them to repent.

Jonah 1:2 Arise, go to Nineveh, that great city, and cry against it; for their wickedness is come up before me.

In His justice, God is also righteous. In all circumstances, he will always do right.

Jonah 3:4 And Jonah began to enter into the city a day's journey, and he cried, and said, Yet forty days and Nineveh shall be overthrown.

As they heard the preaching, from the king to the lowest person and animals, they all repented. The Lord saw the change of action and repentance.

Jonah 3:5 So the people of Nineveh believed God, and proclaimed a fast, and put on sackcloth, from the greatest of them even to the least of them.

God rewards those who diligently seek Him. The land needs repentance like Nineveh. It starts with the chief of the nation. King, queen, prime minister, or president. If leaders lack knowledge of the Lord, then the land suffers, lacking in resources such as food, water, and job opportunities, resulting in barrenness and lack of prosperity. Open the Bible, and start doing what God says. To realign your life, follow the word of God! Rededicate your life and country! The ruler must have a healthy fear of God. Those who are lawless, rebellious, and disobedient will face judgment. God excused no one.

1 Peter 4:17 For the time is come that judgment must begin at the house of God: and if it first begin at us, what shall the end be of them that obey not the gospel of God?

The Lord will judge us and, based on our actions, either reward or punish us.

2 Corinthians 5:10 For we must all appear before the judgment seat of Christ; that everyone may receive the things done in his body, according to that he hath done, whether it be good or bad.

Fear the Judge of the Earth. His name is Jesus!

LET US PRAY

Our heavenly Father, thank you for giving the earth to stay. Our stay is temporal with a condition, so help us do exactly as you have commanded. We want to live and be blessed on this earth. Help us follow the word of God. The Lord grants us wisdom by choosing the fear of God, allowing us to have peace in our temporary abode on earth. Give us true prophets and teachers to explain the ways of God. We want to find the ways of God to be blessed and have eternal rest in heaven in Jesus's name. Amen! God bless you!

JUNE 2

GET EGYPT OUT OF YOU!

In a country called Egypt, they held the Hebrews in enslavement. By going to Goshen in Egypt, the Hebrews could survive the famine. As time went on, when Joseph passed away under new authorities, they became enslaved people in Egypt. For 430 years, the Israelites, also known as Hebrews, resided in Egypt.

Exodus 12:40 Now the sojourning of the children of Israel, who dwelt in Egypt, was four hundred and thirty years.41: And it came to pass at the end of the four hundred and thirty years, even the selfsame day it came to pass, that all the hosts of the LORD went out from the land of Egypt.

Israelites were in Egypt for over four generations! God was merciful to the descendants of Abraham. Eventually, the Lord fulfilled His promise to Abraham by bringing the Hebrews out of slavery in Egypt. Bringing the Hebrews out of Egypt took a few weeks, but bringing Egypt out of the Hebrews took 40 years. Witnessed in Egypt, the Lord revealed many miracles to the Hebrews. The Israelites knew God had a long hand to save them, and He kept the mighty difference between His people, called Israelites or Hebrews and Egyptians. May the Lord give us an understanding that our God is a covenant keeper. He remembers the covenant forever, but the problem is we forget it or can't wait.

The Lord showed miracles to prove His power of deliverance. Your God can deliver, heal, provide, fight, set free, and work wonderfully.

Many must document all God does for us, so we can remember and learn not to complain.

Isaiah 40:28 Hast thou not known? Hast thou not heard that the everlasting God, the Lord, the Creator of the ends of the earth, fainteth, neither is weary? There is no searching for his understanding.

This is the everlasting God. He is Alpha and Omega, beginning and ending, first and last. The Word of God declares His wisdom, knowledge, and authority.

Remember, the Lord said, nothing is impossible; all things are possible to Him. Learn your God by obeying the Word; He proves Himself. With no way out, the Israelites were beaten up by their master in Egypt. Witnessing all the amazing signs of the Lord, they danced and rejoiced.

Disregarding their faith in God, they began to question His existence when faced with difficulties. Their fears, criticisms, and constant complaints only invited further misfortunes. In order to showcase His strength, the Lord unleashed ten devastating plagues upon the Egyptians, using them as a weapon. These plagues were a demonstration of His power. Although God is a spiritual being and does not possess a physical hand, the term "mighty right hand" represents His capability to perform miracles and operate His power. The true essence of this phrase lies beyond its literal interpretation.

By parting the Red Sea, God rescued them. The opposing troops were buried in the sea, ending their existence. By displaying God's power, these are known as the works of God's right hand.

Although Egypt still lived within them, the Hebrews kept forgetting this.

Exodus 15: 23,24 And when they came to Marah, they could not drink of the waters of Marah, for they were bitter: therefore the name of it was Marah. And the people murmured against Moses, saying, What shall we drink?

While situated in the wilderness of Sin, they expressed their discontent with the food.

Tell me about what you are complaining about. Remember the deliverance of God to your soul from the bondage of sins and sicknesses. It is best to avoid complaining or desiring to go back to your old vomit. I pray the Lord grants us a heart filled with gratitude. There is nothing in this world. By letting go of the world, keep your heart peaceful. In order to remove the world out of your heart, you need to take action. Failing to do so will lead you into bondage and destroy you. You should not forget the taste, smell, and feel of the world. You should refrain from complaining. After the Lord gets fed up, you will eventually lose your salvation.

Exodus 16:3 And the children of Israel said unto them, Would to God we had died by the hand of the Lord in the land of Egypt, when we sat by the fleshpots, and when we ate bread to the full; for ye have brought us forth into this wilderness, to kill this whole assembly with hunger.12 I have heard the murmurings of the children of Israel: speak unto them, saying, At even ye shall eat flesh, and in the morning ye shall be filled with bread; and ye shall know that I am the Lord your God.

God sent the Manna from heaven to feed the Hebrews and pampered them in the wilderness, and they forgot the harsh slavery in Egypt.

In Rephidim, they complain about water.

Exodus 17:3 And the people thirsted there for water; and the people murmured against Moses, and said, Wherefore is this that thou hast brought us up out of Egypt, to kill us and our children and our cattle with thirst?

They tried to stone Moses and wanted to go back to Egypt. See, they were free from slavery but not free from the bondage within.

The Lord heard their complaint:

6 Behold, I will stand before thee there upon the rock in Horeb, and thou shalt smite the rock, and there shall come water out of it, that the people may drink. And Moses did so in the sight of the elders of Israel.

JUNE 2

They tempted God, saying, is there a God among us? That place is called Massah (meaning temptation or testing). Do you carry Massah within? Are you tempting God in your trial or trusting?

The Lord tired of the Israelites. They never got rid of Egypt from their heart. Egypt is the World. You remove the world and do not talk about the pleasure you had in the world. Remember the goodness of the Lord. Many go astray after testing His love, seeing the goodness of God, and deliverance. Not removing the world from our hearts will be an obstacle. Remove the World from within.

Number 14:11 And the Lord said unto Moses, How long will this people provoke me? and how long will it be ere they believe me, for all the signs which I have shewed among them? 12 I will smite them with the pestilence, and disinherit them, and will make of thee a greater nation and mightier than they.

God saw the heart of His Servant, Caleb.

Number 14:24 But my servant Caleb, because he had another spirit with him, and hath followed me fully, will I bring into the land whereinto he went, and his seed shall possess it.

After rescuing you from the Word, God can destroy, disown, and disinherit if you do not get the world out of you.

Number 14:28 Say unto them, As truly as I live, saith the Lord, as ye have spoken in mine ears, so will I do to you: 29 Your carcasses shall fall in this wilderness; and all that were numbered of you, according to your whole number, from twenty years old and upward which have murmured against me.

Let us repent and remember to remove the world from within. In the world, there is sorrow, trouble, and distress. Remove complaints and murmurings, and replace them with good, kind words by giving God glory.

Express gratitude for every trial, deliverance, and goodness of God. He does all good. You will never lose your salvation as long as you have a thankful heart. In order to remove the taste, smell, and desire of the world, one must take action. In order to fully enjoy the promises of God, we must do so. There are over 5 thousand promises for you if Egypt is removed from you.

LET US PRAY

Acknowledging our fragility, Lord, we tend to forget. We forget what you did for us yesterday. But if we give you glory and honor for mighty deliverance, we will never forget what you did for us. May the Lord help us remove the world's deceitfulness from our hearts. There is a lust for eyes, the flesh, and pride for living in the world. We can lose our salvation, healing, and deliverance if we do not hold it tight. We thank you for your provision, peace, and the comfort of the Holy Spirit. You have delivered us from all our enemies and set us in high places with you. May our Lord put praise on our lips and thankfulness in our hearts in Jesus's name. Amen! God bless you!

JUNE 3

HOW TO ACTIVATE YOUR MIRACLE!

The Lord Jesus proclaimed He is the way. In order to activate all promises, including your miracles, you must use the way of God rather than relying on your own.

In order to redeem promises, it is crucial for you to play your part in the action, with obedience as the key.

God says, do as it sounds. Add not, subtract not. You understand it is risky if you miss it.

The Bible says in

Revelation 22:18 For I testify unto every man that heareth the words of the prophecy of this book, If any man shall add unto these things, God shall add unto him the plagues that are written in this book:19 And if any man shall take away from the words of the book of this prophecy, God shall take away his part out of the book of life, and out of the holy city, and from the things which are written in this book.

Following God's instructions is both easy and safe.

In the fellowship meeting, the prophet asked for offerings. A lady gave that amount for offering, and the prophecy came forth for her. Does it mean you are selling the prophecy? Prophecy comes from God; the prophet doesn't know the situation without God's intervention. It is the Lord who provides information to the prophet. So God is selling it, or you are activating our prophecy by giving an offering. You can activate your miracle by making either a sacrificial offering or a unique one. To obey the word of the prophet is necessary. Understanding obedience is better than sacrifice.

1 Samuel 15:22 And Samuel said, Hath the LORD as great delight in burnt offerings and sacrifices, as in obeying the voice of the LORD? Behold, to obey is better than sacrifice, and to hearken than the fat of rams.

To be the king of Israel, King Saul was chosen by God. To receive the position for himself and his descendants, he needed to pass some tests. In order to work for the kingdom of God, there are rules to obey. Similarly, the prophets, Levites, and kings must also follow the rules. If you don't obey, then you will be thrust out without receiving a blessing.

Allow me to provide you with a few examples. God sent the prophet Elijah to Zarephath to a widow. A widow? Yes, a widow!

JUNE 3

1 King 17:12 And she said, As the LORD thy God liveth, I have not a cake, but a handful of meal in a barrel, and a little oil in a cruse: and, behold, I am gathering two sticks, that I may go in and dress it for me and my son, that we may eat it, and die. 13 And Elijah said unto her, Fear not; go and do as thou hast said: but make me thereof a little cake first, and bring it unto me, and after make for thee and for thy son. 14 For thus saith the LORD God of Israel, The barrel of meal shall not waste, neither shall the cruise of oil fail, until the day that the LORD sendeth rain upon the earth. 15 And she went and did according to the saying of Elijah: and she, and he, and her house, did eat many days. 16 And the barrel of meal wasted not, nor did the cruse of oil fail, according to the word of the LORD, which he spoke by Elijah.

By what means did the widow activate the miracle? It is your action that triggers the miracle. If God is looking for a widow, poor, sick, and oppressed to perform the mighty miracle, are you willing to do what it requires?

In India, I heard many messages about giving. People were sincere during that time. Believing and learning to share were important to me. When I started giving, the miracle began happening in my finances. By donating to leprosy missions, blind missions, and other places, I contributed to various charitable works.

In my regular giving, I always include tithes, offerings, and missions. Upon receiving my first check from the new job, I offered the first checks to God. By giving to God, I have noticed that I can use, eat, and enjoy my money. Despite their efforts, sickness, robbers, devourers, and stealers cannot deprive me of my cash. Jesus purchased us by His blood, and now we are the temple of Jehovah God. So you may wonder how and where to give. In this dispensation, remember to give offering to the laborers working for Jesus, the poor, the naked, the hungry, the orphan, and the widows. Lord overthrew the table and told the building a den of thieves.

Malachi 3:11 And I will rebuke the devourer for your sakes, and he shall not destroy the fruits of your ground; neither shall your vine cast her fruit before the time in the field, saith the LORD of hosts.

In order to activate miracles, may the Lord grant us understanding. A little boy had two fish and some bread. He gave it to Jesus and activated the miracle of plenty. If you want plenty, learn to give at the right places where you see money in the money-making machine.

Although I know some people, they have never learned to give in the prophet's hand or seen miracles. How sad! Everyone reads the Bible. Some obey, but some are skeptical. They never learned to give. They count money like a widow lady. I have a little oil and flour to eat and die. In order to activate the miracle, learn to put your oil and flour as instructed by the prophet. By following carefully, you will behold a miracle of survival. She charged her miracle by doing her part.

True and faithful, the Lord remains steadfast. Remaining stingy, some people lack their lives, sicknesses, and misery.

During the early years of my learning, I witnessed that when I obeyed the voice of God, it yielded a a great result. Because I was suffering from severe sinus problems, I could not sleep. While the worship service was taking place, God both spoke me to danced. I jumped out of my seat and started dancing. After clearing out everything that was clogging my sinuses, I felt a sense of relief as I breathed easier. I felt relieved. Not only that, I never had that problem again.

In order to advise you, I suggest speaking only a few words. Like my headache, my fever, and my High Blood pressure. It is not yours; it is from Satan and it has to go. Do not claim the curses of sicknesses the devil tries to give you. You have to rebuke and destroy all pieces of sickness baggage in the Name of Jesus. With the Lord's guidance, may we gain the knowledge of how to activate over five thousand given promises of miracles.

Whenever I encounter the sick, I have a habit of laying my hands on them and praying. As I observe, there is the activation of healing, deliverance, and miracle.

Every time you receive a monetary blessing or increase in income, give God first and not last. See what happens. As the Lord finds the nation obeys the laws of God and the ways of God, what happens?

Malachi 3:12 And all nations shall call you blessed: for ye shall be a delightsome land, saith the Lord of hosts.

We live in a time where the nation is changing the laws of the land. It is more like the time of Daniel. But remember, God's laws override the laws of the land. It is supernatural. No one can say or do anything against the supreme power of God.

He knows how to shut the lion's mouth. He knows how to protect us from fire and water. God is God; a superpower cannot fight against or resist. The maker of heaven and earth knows how to create, overthrow, bless, and a curse. It all depends on you, yes, you. You activate blessing and cursing on earth, your land, and your life. Get the knowledge and wisdom from above. Open up the Bible, read, study, and listen to obey. God will bless you to see many miracles. God does not call you to think or figure it out, but to act on it. Let us be like all who believed and operated in the voice of the living God and amazed the world.

John 21:25 And there are also many other things which Jesus did, the which, if they should be written every one, I suppose that even the world itself could not contain the books that should be written. Amen!

How did this happen? Someone knew how to activate the miracle. Please obey since it requires your action. Jesus is the same yesterday, today, and forever. It is your role that brings heaven down on earth. May we all do His will! Pray so we all have His way to activate all miracles in Jesus' name. Amen!

LET US PRAY

Our Lord and Savior, we know the way of God has many supernatural blessings. We need the Holy Spirit's guidance to enter the supernatural realm. Help us, Lord, to believe and do. Believe and act to receive the great miracle. It is not in anyone's control to do supernatural things, but in yours. We need actions, so help us do precisely what you want. May the Lord do many miracles to amaze the world in Jesus's name. Amen! God bless you!

JUNE 4

DO WE HAVE A NOBLEMAN?

Acts 17:10 And the brethren immediately sent away Paul and Silas by night unto Berea: who coming thither went into the synagogue of the Jews. 11 These were more noble than those in Thessalonica, in that they received the word with all readiness of mind, and searched the scriptures daily, whether those things were so.

Just like the Berean, do you go home and check what the different denominations, organizations, and non-denominations teach and preach? Since John has written in his message, I would not believe all spirits since we have an antichrist spirit working amongst us. Of course, under the heading of organization, denominations, etc. Be careful of them.

1 John 4:1 Beloved, believe not every spirit, but try the spirits whether they are of God: because many false prophets are gone out into the world.

Once you hear from the Lord, you should only obey to His instruction. The Bible is the highest authority. The Word of God is above all His names. The devil knows, but do you? The Lord used the word against the devil's plan to tempt Jesus's flesh, the lust of eyes, and the pride of life. He used the word as a sword and destroyed his schemes. Without doing so, we would be left with numerous denominations, nondenominational, and organizations. Instead of seeking a broadway or convenience to the carnal mind, it is important to learn how to divide the word of God. In order to establish any doctrine, it is necessary to look for two or more scripture. Without discovering multiple scriptures practiced by the true prophets and teachers, it is impossible to establish the doctrine or teaching.

Although the Prophet can lie, the word of God remains truthful. Every word of God, after being tried seven times, has proven to be true. When God has spoken to you directly, there is no need to consult prophets or teachers.

1 King 13:18 He said unto him, I am a prophet also as thou art; and an angel spake unto me by the word of the LORD, saying, Bring him back with thee into thine house, that he may eat bread and drink water. But he lied unto him.

What about Angels? Do not listen to the angels when it comes directly from God.

Galatians 1:8 But though we, or an angel from heaven, preach any other gospel unto you than that which we have preached unto you, let him be accursed.

You lack knowledge of the whole truth of the Bible, the place called heaven, and the presence of God, whereas the devil is familiar with them. To ensure you believe only what the word said, it is best for you to go home, study what you heard. To establish the doctrine, find two or more scriptures as evidence. In order to avoid being influenced, do not listen to someone's opinions.

2 Corinthians 11:14 And no marvel; for Satan himself is transformed into an angel of light.

You, yourself, get the correct information from the Lord. Do not depend on people's prophecy or teaching. No seminary teacher or prophets are above the Lord. Get into the Word of God. In this age and time, there is no one pursuing God. Many times, people identify man as a liar, greedy, Pharisee, or hypocrite. Many people can't see it since they need to do homework or know what he is talking about. Frequently, I have seen pedophiles, adulterers, or thieves speaking, yet nobody realizes what lies beneath the surface of the person, organization, or pulpit.

In the land today, antichrist demons are becoming more subtle. Get into the word and study to know the truth.

To misguide you, many will come up with different teachings and doctrines. Be careful, do not repeat Eve-Adam's character.

Genesis 3:1 Now the serpent was more subtil than any beast of the field which the LORD God had made. And he said unto the woman, Yea, hath God said, Ye shall not eat of every tree of the garden? 2 And the woman said unto the serpent, We may eat of the fruit of the trees of the garden: 3 But of the fruit of the tree which is in the midst of the garden, God hath said, Ye, shall not eat of it, neither shall ye touch it, lest ye die.

As Eve did, do you respond to the false teacher? Do you know that God didn't say you should not touch? God's instruction was to refrain from eating. Once you answer the question, the devil gains insight into your knowledge of the Word of God. By being subtle, the devil will catch you in the trap of questioning you, never taking a direct approach. Satan traps us through our lust and pride.

2 Corinthians 8:2 Providing for honest things, not only in the sight of the Lord but also in the sight of men.

2 Timothy 2:15 Study to shew thyself approved unto God, a workman that needeth not to be ashamed, rightly dividing the word of truth.

Now, remember that the word of God is above everything. By preparing yourself, you can come against the wrong teaching of the devil that he has started from the beginning. He sends many to hell while keeping all of us in mind. Do you know what you have to do against the false teaching? As Jesus did, do you ever challenge the words? As false teachers and prophets of that time challenged Jesus, he stood firm as the word.

Psalm 138:2 I will worship toward thy holy temple, and praise thy name for thy lovingkindness and for thy truth: for thou hast magnified thy word above all thy name.

JUNE 4

Use the Word of God and see how the devil gets defeated. He runs from the truth, a light and mighty sword of the Word. Friend, carefully divide the word of God according to the order given by God. Do not accept hell for your soul.

As the one who holds the keys, you have the power to either preserve or deny the truth. In what way is the devil deceiving you today? They deceive us by teaching powerless sugar-coated false doctrine. No healing, no salvation, no healing of the broken heart, and still blind, deaf people accept it.

2 Timothy 3:1 This know also that in the last days, perilous times shall come. 2 For men shall be lovers of their own selves, covetous, boasters, proud, blasphemers, disobedient to parents, unthankful, unholy, 3 Without natural affection, trucebreakers, false accusers, incontinent, fierce, despisers of those that are good, 4 Traitors, heady, highminded, lovers of pleasures more than lovers of God; 5 Having a form of godliness, but denying the power thereof: from such turn away.

In order to do the work for God, receive training from the true prophets and teachers. You will get the results of deliverance, healing, and healing of the broken heart to continue the mission of Jesus. With each passing day, I am tasked with learning different things through a new assignment. Disciples of Jesus came back rejoicing and happy, and you will too.

Jeremiah 15:16 Thy words were found, and I did eat them; and thy word was unto me the joy and rejoicing of mine heart: for I am called by thy name, O LORD God of hosts.

Psalm 119:162 I rejoice at thy word, as one that findeth great spoil.

Let the Word of God be accepted with repentance and sincerity.

Matthew 13:23 But he that received seed into the good ground is he that heareth the word, and understandeth it; which also beareth fruit, and bringeth forth, some a hundredfold, some sixty, some thirty.

What we oppose is only what opposes the word. Accepting the truth is our way to escape from the devil's tactic and plan to kill, steal, and destroy.

Beginning today, make it a habit to open the word of God. Receive the Spirit of God. The sinner needs to repent and wash away their sins in the blood hidden under the name of Jesus. Water baptism without a name 'Jesus' has no power to remit sins. You go under the water with stains of sins and come out the same if you do not use the name Jesus.

John 5:6a This is he that came by water and blood, even (kai=even or that is. Name)Jesus Christ; not by water only, but by water and blood

The doctrine of Jesus is kept hidden. People like Berea will find it if they search. It is not mom, dad, or family instruction. It is God's order through the word. The Lord will not hide anything from you once you seek, ask, and knock, as the word of God said. He only hides from;

Cor 4:3 But if our gospel be hid, it is hid to them that are lost: 4 In whom the God of this world hath blinded the minds of them which believe not, lest the light of the glorious gospel of Christ, who is the image of God, should shine unto them.

God's wrath will come upon those.

Romans 1:18 For the wrath of God is revealed from heaven against all ungodliness and unrighteousness of men, who hold the truth in unrighteousness;

Having the Spirit of God, which is True, is essential in order to find the truth. It will set you free from the power of sins. Strive to enter the narrow path.

1Cor 2: 10 But God hath revealed them unto us by his spirit: for the spirit searcheth all things, yea, the deep things of God. 12 Now we have received, not the spirit of the world, but the spirit which is of God; that we might know the things that are freely given to us of God.15 But he that is spiritual judgeth all things, yet he is judged of no man.

Amen!

LET US PRAY

Lord, give us the heart to keep the word in the order given in the word of God. It is, above all, confuse religious doctrine. It confuses people and keeps them from getting delivered, healed, and healed of their broken hearts. We need the truth to spread the good news of blind eyes opened, deaf ears opened, the lame walk, and broken hearts healed. Wonderful hope to the hopeless. We pray to keep our eyes and ears open to see the truth and keep it diligently in Jesus' name. Amen. God bless you.

JUNE 5

CONTINUE TILL YOU FINISH!

Workers who come every day to work constantly are needed by God. Whenever you call, they are there. They are sensitive to the need. By understanding, many sincere people left a good example of what it takes to be a champion and what it takes to receive a trophy. To accomplish it, all of you are needed.

Jesus came on earth to work and committed to the plan. Lord Jesus worked all the time without resting and often not even eating. He trained the disciples to follow in His footsteps. I admire those who stand with the will of God. With the Lord's help, we can commit ourselves to the will and work of God.

Our God is faithful. With the Lord's help, may we come to understand that there is a force working behind every success. The force is self-discipline and giving your total attention. For the mission you wish to establish, condition your heart, mind, soul, spirit, and strength. In your mercy, Lord, bless us with the understanding of how to reach God's standard.

By visiting a friend in another state, I had a great experience. I asked her to lay her hand on my back and pray. While praying, something moved on my back. She removed her hand and went to work, showing no sensitivity to the Spirit of God. She is a workaholic. Although I was at her house, she never laid hands and prayed despite my request.

The Bible says, Mark 16:17c And these signs shall follow them that believe; In my name shall they cast out devils; they shall lay hands on the sick, and they shall recover. Jesus, by laying hands on people, healed them.

Luke 13:13 And he laid his hands on her: and immediately she was made straight, and glorified God.

Mark 7:32 And they bring unto him one that was deaf, and had an impediment in his speech; and they beseech him to put his hand upon him.

To pray for someone effectively, it is important to both know the scripture and be guided by the Spirit of God. Without fail, I do the complete job whenever I pray. People who do not complete their job exhibit laziness, carelessness, and insensitivity to the work God calls them for. When I told my sister, I mentioned that the tumor on my back moved when you laid your hand on it. Despite this, she did not care. How sad! They join the social club/building called church and diligently work every Sunday and midday for their organization. Why are we replacing Jesus for all organizations, denominations, and non-denominations?

We witness chaos, it's natural that we struggle to continue with the Lord's assignment. When I have to follow Jesus, I do it right so as to bring Him Glory. Of course, we face different giants in the land called churches. Well, my body is the church. Jesus lives in me, and I choose to follow Him alone.

I have prayed with different people; they saw the power of prayer, but still, they discontinued the work of God. Although they go to the building they call a church, they ignore the mission God called them for.

The devil, instead of focusing on God's assignment, will prioritize other things. Regrettably, people neglect the work assigned to them by God. I feel sorry for people. Instead of putting God first, they put jobs and church first. Many great things will happen if we prioritize according to the ways of God. Once you become the hand, mouth, and feet of God, God will shower you with blessings. By following the instruction of God, I learn this. Remember, you already have authority in Jesus' name, which was yours and lost in the garden of Eden. In Jesus's name, you now possess authority. Second, the Lord has given power through His Spirit; then, you must receive it. You do not have it automatically, but once you take the step given by Peter, repent, baptize in Jesus' name, and then receive the Holy Spirit by evidence of speaking in tongues.

Is it too hard to work for God? By working for God, He said that He will care for you.

In the year 2002, I accepted the will of God. God spoke to me; you take care of my work, and I will take care of you. Since then, by keeping God first, I have been blessed beyond measure. Because I always preferred God, He called me to work for Him. With the Lord's assistance, may we come to understand that God will not lie. God is faithful. In a manner unknown to you, God can do supernatural things. He will make something out of nothing.

Hebrews 6:10 For God is not unrighteous to forget your work and labor of love, which ye have showed toward his name, in that ye have ministered to the saints, and do minister.

Even if we do just a little, God will still reward us. To get compensation, we must do something. By being an operating tool in the hand of the almighty, we facilitate the Lord to do supernatural healing, deliverance, and provision.

Lord, give us the understanding of your awesomeness. He will not disappoint you.

Although she is diligent in attending church agenda, paying tithes, and attending parties and functions on time, that sister in the Lord neglected to continue laying her hand on my back. Although she prioritizes the pastor's agenda and church policy, she neglects her time for God. In saying that Mary had chosen the right thing, the Lord emphasized the reason.

In addition, he mentioned in the Bible numerous other examples, such as five wise and five fools, sheep and goat.

I was very disappointed seeing not caring about the pain in my back. If you work for God, God will do great things for you and your children. Maybe she thought I had to follow the organization's agenda to fit in. To tell you the truth, she is a hard worker and very faithful to building activities and pastors. They love her very much, but she has disappointed God. She is unfaithful to His work. Do justice to the Lord, and you will never be alone.

JUNE 5

Deuteronomy 7:8 But because the Lord loved you, and because he would keep the oath which he had sworn unto your fathers, hath the Lord brought you out with a mighty hand, and redeemed you out of the house of bondmen, from the hand of Pharaoh king of Egypt. 9 Know therefore that the Lord thy God, he is God, the faithful God, which keepeth covenant and mercy with them that love him and keep his commandments to a thousand generations; 10 And repayeth them that hate him to their face, to destroy them: he will not be slack to him that hateth him, he will repay him to his face. 11 Thou shalt, therefore, keep the commandments, and the statutes, and the judgments, which I command thee this day, to do them.

For the Lord has called you, it is important to continue His business. God will bless your 1,000 generations as a result. Lord, teach us the things we are missing out on by not listening and following Your agenda.

Through our agenda, denominations, non-denominations, and organization programs, people are left broken, behind bars, on drugs, suicide, lost, and hurt. Our God is awesome and will do a marvelous job if you hear and obey His voice. Rather than searching for work in the building they called church, direct your attention towards God's work. After indirectly hearing from one minister, it was conveyed to me that I am my pastor and God is not using me. The good news is that I am working for God's purpose, not for their pocket or to continue their organizations. Despite my refusal to let them put me on a pedestal and give me a position, they taunted me. While doing it, I was responding to God's call to pray and intercede. Remaining indifferent to their comment, I disregarded their harassment and folly. While browsing the internet, I occasionally come across people sitting in the same den with their legs in handcuffs. What a waste of life!

If we go out and do the will of God, consider the possibilities. Never do we see people work, as the Lord said. Having seen people laying hands, casting out demons, preaching the Gospel, and going from city to city daily, what are your thoughts? This should happen everywhere. I see people jogging early in the morning, exercising, going out to work, and children going to school. Everyone has a schedule for everything except for the work of Jesus.

The Bible says,

Matthew 6:33 But seek ye first the kingdom of God, and his righteousness; and all these things shall be added unto you.

Regardless of your education or wisdom, the Lord grants promotions. David, who was a shepherd boy, was promoted to king. Continuing under God's direction, he kept His agenda. To establish His kingdom, do not hinder yourself and God. Interfering with yourself is something that only you do. By getting out of the world's way, finding Jesus' way, and continuing in His truth, you can attain eternal rest for your and others' souls.

I enjoy working for God. I work around the clock. I stay busy with the kingdom. Regardless of when or how many calls there are, I always hear, pray, and minister to their needs. If I do not, then who else will take on the task? In the expectation that the Lord God blesses us with laborers who diligently work until the job is accomplished.

It is possible that many of us have disappointed people who may be sick, hurting, oppressed, depressed, or whatever. Do not look anywhere; use your hand to help. May your feet reach places to preach the Gospel and touch the sick! Many people don't care about how much they spend when it comes to their hobby, yet they hesitate to give to God. You must fulfill the prerequisite to achieve His promises. Continue working for the Lord until you finish. You will be rewarded by Jesus for the job well done.

LET US PRAY:

Lord, you have called, and if we do well, you will choose us. Please help us choose a good part, like Mary. Lord, make us faithful as you are faithful. Lord, we are your hands and feet; we want to work for you so your glorious name will be blessed. Many work for man-made churches, organizations, and secular jobs for money, but the highest reward comes from working for your kingdom. When we work for you, we bring blessings to ourselves, our families, and our nation. Help us be sincere, and diligent, and do the best of the best for you, in Jesus's name. Amen! God bless you!

JUNE 6

THE SPIRIT OF JEALOUSY IS A KILLER!

Jealousy, as the worst enemy of a person, can bring about significant damage. Jealousy is an ill condition. It is the self-killing sickness within. You can get delivered by praying and fasting against it.

Despite someone's denial that I am not jealous of them, there is a hiding place for Satan in you.

The jealousy is possessed by a mad and a dull spirit at the same time… Johann Kaspar Lavater.

How can you recognize if you are jealous? When someone receives a blessing, gets elevated, has achievements, and has good things happen to them, it will bother you. The inability to tolerate good things happening to others is a symptom of an inner-growing sickness. The jealous friend wouldn't stand the happiness in your life. All the time, jealous people are curious about what happens in your life. They derive pleasure from being better than others. For that reason, jealousy competes against everyone. They are always required to be better, as their relationship is not secure, and this is apparent in their behavior.

Despite criticizing you, they will also attempt to pull you down.

But the Lord is good. Confessing it is necessary if you want to get rid of jealousy. Just say, Lord, I am jealous, and help me. He will help you. God will back you up. Confessing will result in the Lord cleansing you. This disease, which is self-destructive, prohibits you from experiencing peace.

1 John 1:9 If we confess our sins, he is faithful and just to forgive us our sins and to cleanse us from all unrighteousness.

God is merciful.

Proverb 6:34 For jealousy is the rage of a man: therefore he will not spare in the day of vengeance.35 He will not regard any ransom; neither will he rest content, though thou givest many gifts.

Jealousy arose in King Saul when he heard people admired David. Upon hearing admiration from the people, he found it unbearable to face the truth. King Saul, instead of being happy about having David in his troops, wanted to slay him. Jealous people will bring you down.

1 Samuel 18:7 And the women answered one another as they played, and said, Saul, hath slain his thousands, and David his ten thousand. 8 And Saul was very wroth, and the saying displeased him; and he said, They have ascribed unto David ten thousand, and to me, they have ascribed but thousands: and what can he have more but the kingdom? 9 And Saul eyed David from that day forward.

King Saul continuously sought to kill David. In order to avoid Saul's presence, David kept running. He kept hiding in a cave, the woods, and the wilderness. God was His refuge and fortress. God kept him from the sword of the enemy. Because of that, David wrote so many worship, praise, and songs of refuge to the Lord. Despite the death at hand, David saw it, but the Lord saved his life from the sword.

We know the enemy; the devil is jealous of the Lord. Knowing that there is one throne in heaven, he desires to have it. Out of jealousy for what Jesus was doing on earth, the devil plotted a plan to kill him. The devil does the opposite of the word of God; he steals, kills, and destroys.

Jealousy is found among the power-hungry and greedy people.

Mark 15:10 For he knew that the chief priests had delivered him for envy.

They killed innocent Jesus. Jealousy, being cruel, will result in murder.

Listening to the story, I discovered that the woman was killed by her jealous husband on the day they were going to separate after their last dinner together. See, jealousy is evil; we must separate from it immediately.

While remembering, I realized that my good friend was acting hateful toward me. I never thought she could be jealous because I was there to help her in every trial and trouble. She was my friend for years. Strongly, she would come against me every time I said something. Surprisingly, she was carrying the demon of jealousy despite my belief that she was my friend.

It continued for a while. Curiously, I inquired of God what this is, Lord. Despite being my friend, why does she maltreat me? I found out from God that she was jealous. One night, God told me in my dream that this friend and another blood- related lady were jealous of me. The Lord, through a dream, revealed to me the similarities between these two individuals that I always thought they had. With gratitude, I acknowledged, Lord, and said thank you. I would never have labeled them as jealous. Due to the spirit of jealousy in them, some who we believe are friends will act and react harshly towards you, although they are not.

Here is another example of Cain that I'll give you. With a heavy heart, Cain witnessed God accepting his brother's offering. Abel was being righteous, and God blessed Abel, but not Cain. Cain was evil and did wrong to his brother. He killed his brother. We all have some jealous family members who will desire to destroy us.

The problem was common between Rachel and Rebecca, who were sisters. Rachel was jealous of Rebecca. Jealous people will always compete. There is an apparent nature within them. Jealousy has a torment within.

If you are suffering from jealousy, get rid of it immediately. It is deadly. You will lose your sleep and mind over this. It is the truth that you need help from the Lord.

JUNE 6

Most people, when under the influence of jealousy, cannot stand the person they are jealous of. Please stay away from them. There is no medicine to help, so stay away from them if they do not want to be delivered. Jealous people will harm and damage your life. Many extremely jealous husbands or wives end up killing each other or divorcing.

After Lord Jesus appeared on earth, He noticed that the religious authorities were consumed with jealousy. It was when people kept the label of their position with extreme self-righteousness, knowing the Torah but envying God of Torah. They were like Satan Because they desired to have a power position, control, and greed.

Isaiah 14:13 For thou hast said in thine heart, I will ascend into heaven, I will exalt my throne above the stars of God: I will sit also upon the mount of the congregation, in the sides of the north:

Having an opponent is a possibility if someone is jealous of your circle. Conflicts arise as a result of jealousy. When you observe the strife, you will notice it among the jealous. It will go smoothly if there is no jealousy. If one comes with a jealous spirit, that person will sabotage everything.

In many families, between a husband and wife, among siblings, at school, the workplace, and in churches, you can find jealousy problems.

If you don't take necessary action, sick-minded people may unnecessarily harass or abuse you. No matter who you are, there is always someone who is against you. You should be cautious of these wicked jealous people. They are sick individuals, there is nothing wrong with you, but the jealous person has the sickness in them.

May the Lord deliver people from the spirit of jealousy and set them free. Internally, it is a sickness that poisons the self. Having all, they still cannot enjoy themselves and can't be happy. Jealousy is the worst thing to have. Because of causing themselves unfair treatment, they suffer the consequences.

Sometimes, they end up in prison, kill someone, or go crazy. By not confessing, fasting, and cleansing, Christians allow jealousy to be present in them.

They forget 2 Corinthians 7:1. Having; therefore, these promises, dearly beloved, let us cleanse ourselves from all filthiness of the flesh and spirit, perfecting holiness in fear of God.

Make sure to address not just jealousy, but also all forms of filthiness. God Bless you.

LET US PRAY

Lord, jealousy and envy are the most dangerous for one who carries them in them. Help us, Lord, that we overjoy when someone gets blessed. It is our privilege to be happy and not sad when someone elevates their life. Lord, we want you to give us that spirit of peace and love. Help us bless our enemy, knowing it is the right thing to do. We appreciate God for our heavenly father, who has no variance. Who blesses His children? Let there be no jealousy found in us in Jesus's name! Amen! God bless you!

JUNE 7

THE DEVIL USES SUMMER AS AN EXCUSE!

Seeing more nakedness is common during the summer. It is always the woman who falls into the trap of Satan.

For women to guide, they need protection, guidance, and supervision. God chose Adam to guide Eve; instead, Eve misguided Adam. Clearly, Adam was not paying attention. It is concerning to see the nation where man has put down, given in, and given up their authority. Despite being given the role of responsibility by God, man does not want to play it.

God says: 2 Chronicles 16:9 For the eyes of the LORD run to and fro throughout the whole earth, to shew himself strong in the behalf of them whose heart is perfect toward him. Herein thou hast done foolishly: therefore, from henceforth, thou shalt have wars.

Having an imperfect heart toward God, you will encounter many sorrows, wars, trials, and trouble that could have been avoided by hearing, listening, and obeying God. It is unnecessary to have all the problems if we learn to listen.

Hebrews 4:13 Neither is there any creature that is not manifest in his sight: but all things are naked and opened unto the eyes of him with whom we have to do.

While you don't, God sees the far-off issue of all you do. With knowledge of today's culture, God dressed Adam and Eve. With no provocative cloth designers available, and no pornographic and rebellious generations forcing their lifestyle upon others, that time was quite different. One person brought a flood to destroy the world, and today is no better. Due to our disobedience of God's word, our society is confronted with numerous problems. By obeying the word of God, life is safeguarded. By choosing in accordance with the Bible's instructions, we can attain peace, protection, and provisions in our life despite having total freedom to choose.

Following God's instructions, the High priest was given a dress code.

Exodus 28:2 And thou shalt make holy garments for Aaron, thy brother for glory and beauty. 4 And these are the garments which they shall make; a breastplate, and an ephod, and a robe, and a broidered coat, a

JUNE 7

miter, and a girdle: and they shall make holy garments for Aaron thy brother, and his sons, that he may minister unto me in the priest's office. 42And thou shalt make them linen breeches to cover their nakedness; from the loins even unto the thighs they shall reach:

In the New Testament, we are referred to as the temple of the Lord. The saints of God are those who have repented of sins, been baptized in Jesus's name, and received His Spirit. When we are not meeting His standard, how can the Lord live in our bodies?

1 Corinthians 6:19 What? Know ye not that your body is the temple of the Holy Ghost which is in you, which ye have of God, and ye are not your own? 20 For ye are bought with a price: therefore glorify God in your body, and in your spirit, which are God's.

Lord knows what He is doing, and so are the people.

Genesis 3:7 And the eyes of them both were opened, and they knew that they were naked, and they sewed fig leaves together and made themselves aprons.

In my observation, kids tend to cover themselves once they reach a certain age. They dress by covering their body. It is common to hear about open rape in our country today. Failing to cover the body leads to rape. Satan creates chaos, but humans adapt or react to the devil's plan. There is no need for you to respond to Satan's ideas. While visiting certain nations, I have observed women walking alone in the middle of the night. While reading notices on beaches, I realized the importance of wearing modest clothes. Due to the lack of knowledge about what they are doing, many ladies are cared for by the country.

In order to protect their little bodies, parents teach and choose modest clothes. After seeing people raised in modest countries, I have noticed how they move to freestyle nations and easily adapt to their immodest dressing. Why? Their lack of choice forced them to be modest, as modesty was not in their heart. People should remember that clothes are meant to cover the body, not for style.

1 Timothy 2:9 In like manner also, that women adorn themselves in modest apparel, with shamefacedness and sobriety; not with broided hair, or gold, or pearls, or costly array;

With the influence of the media, nowadays the world encounters more challenges. People who do not have the word of God as a guideline have taken over it.

Romans 12:2 And be not conformed to this world: but be ye transformed by the renewing of your mind that ye may prove what that good, and acceptable, and perfect, will of God is.

Our God never clothed us. We walked naked until we knew good and evil. God has to step in when humanity disobeys the command of the Lord. The time of innocence was the best. Crime wouldn't creep in since the Lord knew all good and evil and never entered our consciousness.

Even today, we can get pure consciousness if we repent of all our sins, baptize to wash away our sins, and get power receiving His Spirit to fight evil out. Remember, the father who created us has more knowledge than corrupt media and society. Even religious authorities, in fact, misguide us. Follow Jesus. He has truth to lead and guide and deliver us. 2000 years ago, many embraced the truth since false doctrine did not degrade it. Truth sets us free, but religion traps us in cages, forcing us to feel free.

I heard on YouTube that many women and children are being kidnapped. In a time like such, nothing is stopping offenders. How sad, isn't it? By continuing the truth, the problem can be solved by true apostles, prophets, teachers, pastors, and preachers.

We need to edify our Lord in our bodies.

Ephesians 4:12 For the perfecting of the saints, for the work of the ministry, for the edifying of the body of Christ: 13 Till we all come in the unity of the faith, and of the knowledge of the Son of God, unto a perfect man, unto the measure of the stature of the fulness of Christ: 14 That we henceforth are no more children, tossed to and fro, and carried about with every wind of doctrine, by the sleight of men, and cunning craftiness, whereby they lie in wait to deceive; 15 But speaking the truth in love, may grow up into him in all things, which is the head, even Christ: 16 From whom the whole body fitly joined together and compacted by that which every joint supplieth, according to the effectual working in the measure of every part, maketh increase of the body unto the edifying of itself in love.

A laborer is needed today to bring the Kingdom of God to earth. The Kingdom of God is in heaven, where our heavenly father lives. We can have it on earth if we have laborers working for Him and not for religious organizations. Amen!

LET US PRAY

Heavenly Father, we invite you to be our master and King. We are lost without you. Please guide us with your true teachers and prophets. We need the path of righteousness to lead and guide us to the truth. You said I am the way of truth for eternal life. Give us the truth and love for it. Make us a teacher of truth to teach our next generation, in Jesus's name. Amen! God bless

JUNE 8

THE SOLUTION IS TO UPROOT THE CAUSE!

The Good Lord has given us the knowledge of the truth. Every seed of the word we plant has a root.

Satan plants some of his seed. If you have land around you, you will notice and say; I did not plant this; where did it come from?. The Lord said to Adam when he transgressed.

Genesis 3:17 And unto Adam he said, Because thou hast hearkened unto the voice of thy wife, and hast eaten of the tree, of which I commanded thee, saying, Thou shalt not eat of it: cursed is the ground for thy sake; in sorrow shalt, thou eat of it all the days of thy life; 18 Thorns also and thistles shall it bring forth to thee; and thou shalt eat the herb of the field;

The root of all curses was a transgression. A transgression is when you step on the commandment of God deliberately. If you transgress, then you are too bold. In what way can you violate the laws set by God? Humans root out the good seed of God planted as the word of God and overstep it. Their actions let God know; that I do not care. Contrary to God's instruction, they would do the opposite if told to do one thing. Being disobedient is our behavior during this end time. People have forgotten to do what God wants us to do. Suffering the consequences is what happens when we don't seek God for the situation and let our flesh take over.

Many families, by not caring to know the root of the destruction, are losing the souls of their loved ones. Instead of finding the origin of the sickness, they find the solution by taking medicine. Medicine is not a solution. Find the sin that causes sickness, then repent. Rather than shedding tears, please see the roots that cause the illnesses.

If you have true prophets of God, you will find a remedy. They will not worry about your feelings, but deliver the message of a cure with boldness.

God said the root of the curse on the ground is the transgression of Adam and Eve. In sorrow, we eat our bread. Why? Out of the earth, we observe thorns and thistles sprouting. The curse came to the land because of the transgression of Adam and Eve. We cause much sorrow when we uproot God's good seed from our life. The Lord's words are the good seed.

1 Chronicles 10:13 So Saul died for his transgression which he committed against the LORD, even against the word of the LORD, which he kept not, and also for asking counsel of one that had a familiar spirit, to inquire of it; 14 And inquired not of the LORD: therefore he slew him, and turned the kingdom unto David, the son of Jesse.

The solution is to uproot the Cause!

How sad! The Bible is as clear as black and white, life and death, true and false, and light and darkness. So help me, Lord! Mend life by planting the Word of God to search for the root causes. To prevent repetition, refrain from sharing the same life story. No one has the authority to change the word, as it is the Lord's commandment. The devil's misguidance hinders us from following God's good guidance as given in the Bible. To follow Jesus, we must follow His Word.

May the Lord, by helping us, drop the word as a seed in our hearts and our children's hearts and enable us to continue the blessings. God is good! With his loveliness, he always leads and guides us on the right path.

In India, I remembered a family. Every family member was under a curse. Someone always committed suicide, either by burning or killing themselves. The mother, living a sinful life, was the cause. By causing much trouble, it affected her children. It is best to stay away from the cursed family. Although we all know there will always be someone rebellious in the family, refrain from getting attached to the cursed one. If you stand on the word of God and obey, you can escape from the family's curses.

By discovering and tending to the root of the cause, the curse can be resolved. David, knowing God, took time to find the cause of the famine in the land. Your action can bring curses and blessings. So when there is a curse, find the root and solve it. Go to the source of the cause and take care of it. Ignoring the curses for generations and continuing is not recommended.

2 Samuel 21 Then there was a famine in the days of David three years, year after year; and David inquired of the LORD. And the LORD answered. It is for Saul and his bloody house because he slew the Gibeonites.

Gibeonites were not Israelites, but they were living in the land. King Saul was not famous, so he tried to please the Israelites. To gain favor from the Israelites, he killed many Gibeonites. Inquiring of God, King David resolved the problem caused by someone, unlike King Saul who shed much innocent blood.

2 Samuel 21:5 And they answered the king, The man that consumed us, and that devised against us that we should be destroyed from remaining in any of the coasts of Israel, 6 Let seven men of his sons be delivered unto us, and we will hang them up unto the LORD in Gibeah of Saul, whom the LORD did choose. And the king said I will give them.

That solved the problem. God's commandment is to remember not to uproot the good seed. Doing so will result in inviting trouble. Only God knows how to make the wrong right. To achieve our goal, we must do whatever it takes. Our action counts, uproot the evil root, and plant the good seed. To prevent bringing sickness and curse to our lineage, may the Lord aid us in not being too bold. Do not seek money. Seek God. He is of greater significance and better than money.

When we see a dangerous situation, ask God how to fix it. Go to God and find the cause; treat the cause.

JUNE 8

Observing prophetic services in various nations has been a common occurrence for me lately. By visiting churches in other countries, Christians seek to find the solution to the trouble. It surprises me when people seek help from the witch doctor. What abilities does Satan possess? Satan sends more demons to destroy you since his job is to steal, kill, and destroy. In their attempts to find a solution, they only bring more sickness and curses. When you pray and do not find the answer quickly, it is important to wait for God. He will come on time. King Saul is the best example of an impatient person. An impatient person will take the wrong route. Wait on the Lord.

Psalms 27:14 Wait on the LORD: be of good courage, and he shall strengthen thine heart: wait, I say, on the LORD.

Everyone encounters some sort of problem in life. To find a solution, we must turn to God. Do not take any wrong avenue. It is a waste of time and money. We are, thereby causing more headaches and trouble. To resolve the problem, many in India go to the witch doctor and spend money. When they call, I strictly tell them, please stop; the devil cannot heal, deliver, or give life. Let me pray to Jesus; only He can do it.

I remember not having the truth; I always felt confused, helpless, and sad. Sadness and brokenness stemmed from the inability to find the solution. By leaning on Him, the Lord solves and brings peace to our lives. By using His prophets, the Lord can accomplish all good things.

2 Chronicles 20:20b Hear me, O Judah, and ye inhabitants of Jerusalem; Believe in the LORD your God, so shall ye be established; believe his prophets, so shall ye prosper.

If Adam-Eve, King Saul, Priest Eli, and others had done right, I cannot imagine what would have happened to them.

By resorting to drugs, divorces, shootings, killing, and many other crimes, people attempt to find solutions. To uproot the evil seed, one must plant the good seed, which is God's word. By keeping His commandments, precepts, and statutes, you will witness a turnaround in your life and country. The Lord's Word (seed) brings blessings when we keep them in our hearts. By hiding the seed in your heart, you can prevent yourself from sinning and transgressing.

With the Lord's help in uprooting the cause of curses, may we find a seed that brings blessing and peace, in Jesus's name.

LET US PRAY

Lord, we are grateful to be your children. We desire mercy and grace never to depart from our family and us. I incline our ears to receive the Word of God as a good seed in our hearts. We desire your word to be planted in us to bring blessings. Lord, you have the truth, which can free us from the curses. Only you have the facts and not the media. May our Lord help us uproot the cause and provide the remedy to turn our sickness into health, curses into a blessing, and heartache into gladness, in Jesus's name. Amen! God bless you!

JUNE 9

LEARN TO GIVE YOURSELF!

Learn to give. The act of giving results in receiving. That is why the Bible says.

Luke 6:38 Give, and it shall be given unto you; good measure, pressed down, shaken together, and running over, shall men give into your bosom. With the same measure that ye mete withal, it shall be measured to you again.

When you give as the Lord has asked, there is a return or a blessing that comes from God. Giving has more of a profound effect than what you think. If given where the Lord has advised, the seed will receive blessings. The blessings will extend to many generations. Consequently, your actions have an outer effect on the family, city, and country. By determining the cause of the blockage on receiving, you can find a solution. Profoundly, the sins of Achan and losing the kingdom of King Saul left a lasting impact. If you continue sinning, you may be expelled from your land. The generational curse can be caused by the country practicing witchcraft or using an Ouija board, even if Hollywood is involved. The act of shooting, killing, and shedding innocent blood is considered evil. Believing in religion will result in chaos, as stated in the Bible. Religion offers no help. There is no God in religion. You have a lot of charisma, but that's all.

Considering God is the same as yesterday, today, and forever, why is there chaos? Parties, police, and the like are who we blame. Seek to know from God where the sin lies. For a better grasp of the content, make it a habit to read the Bible more. With the help of the Holy Spirit, you will grasp the concept. If you see a blessing, it means that someone has done something good, whereas the presence of a curse indicates that sin is being practiced somewhere in the family. By studying the life of David, we can grasp how he received the blessings. By coming through His bloodline, the Messiah revealed Himself. To study the legacy they left behind, one should examine the lives of Daniel, Joseph, and Moses. When it comes to talking and teaching, it is the Holy Spirit, not religion, that presents itself as a snake. If you don't follow the timing agenda, religion will handcuff you and subject you to harassment and expulsion. By breaking the chain and kicking the pew and the table, one can be free, in accordance with the example and teaching of Lord Jesus.

You will see what happens if you go out and work as Jesus did. You will see the change in the city and the country. By anointing the places with holy blessed olive oil, you can sanctify them wherever you go. By offering your time, you can support the Lord's ministry. In order for the yoke of drugs and alcohol, sin chain, and darkness to break off, it is necessary to play the shofar and see. In our actions lies the cause of blessings and curses. By His Spirit, the Lord granted us authority and power in His precious name. Despite having many security systems, there is no security today. In broad daylight, criminals are engaging in acts

JUNE 9

of robbery, kidnapping, shooting, killing, and rape. The problem is something we need to address. The church can be of assistance in this situation, can't it? By overthrowing the table, the Lord labeled them as thieves who built a den. Why are you supporting religious organizations, denominations, and non-denominations, which the Lord labeled as the den of thieves who collect money and overthrew their table? It is important to go and feed the hungry, clothe the naked, care for the widow, and visit the sick and those in prison. It is my and your responsibility. Some false teachers and prophets deceitfully stole the truth. By seeking the truth, one can find freedom and liberate others through truth-sharing.

Remember, you are the temple; you are His house. With His hand, God created you to live in you. Yield to the Spirit of God and plant the seed, which is the word of God. Watering the seed means praying and nurturing it by giving it teaching and directing it to Jesus. By following in Jesus 'footsteps, you will be blessed abundantly, but if you refuse to align with God's ways and instead join various organizations to build a social club, you will be responsible for the current state of affairs. Crucially, both my part and your part are important. By taking Jesus as an example, acknowledge that He is the only way and truth for eternal life. With the power and authority given by Jesus, we are able to do as He said. In your search, find the true prophets and teachers who are unafraid to speak the truth. Do not fight them; it is your choice, so choose right. Some individuals, acting as the mouthpieces for their false preachers and teachers, will engage in a battle of words with my prayer line. They quench the spirit. Those who are the mouth of their pastors speak for them. Those individuals exhibit the spirit of Jezebel and are considered antichrists. The teaching and leading of the Spirit of God are completely unrelated to them. Because of their busyness, they will never enter His rest.

While they think they are against Elizabeth, they are not. Despite protecting their religion, safeguarding their lifestyle, and rising in their flesh, they often come against me. In their own way, each of them justifies themselves. With shootings, killings, etc. occurring in their city, their family and life are cursed. To ensure obedience, please read and follow the Bible. You will only harm yourself by collecting dollars. Prioritize the well-being of your children and grandchildren, offering help, education, and guidance in the ways of God. Your job is not complete simply by sending them to Sunday school. After the false teachers said to bring children to church, the question arises: where does it say in the Bible to take them to a building? By living like one, it is stated that you are the church, resulting in blessings for your family. By showing them the lesson, teach them to lay hands and anoint one another, portraying your life as a Christian. To show them what they should do, take them out and demonstrate how to cast out the demon and heal the sick. That the lame walk, the blind see, the sick are healed, and deliverance from drugs, alcohol, and cigarettes is given is the good news of the Gospel. Regrettably, the power given to us by God remains unutilized in our country. By working instead of sitting on the pew and listening to the same old, you can avoid wasting time and money. While you believe you are going somewhere, you are actually going nowhere. Protecting oneself is possible by staying away from false teachers and prophets. By simply not engaging in fights with God, you can maintain peace. To get rid of the demons associated with different religions, organizations, and denominations. Let's bring revival in the land of the living by going city to city and town to town, for we are the temple of God. You will not reach heaven if you live this lifestyle. In the followers, we observe the same deception as the priest, which is being greedy and jealous. Have you not realized that God desires to use our hands and feet in order to provide care for the poor, widow, naked, hungry, and laboring? Without teaching them to hear and obey God, they focused solely on teaching them the benefits of money. Envy is felt by some people towards God.

Besides offering position, power, promotion, and demotion, God also provides. When you come against the queen, king, or people in powerful positions, then you will be in trouble, but stand on truth. God will rescue your soul. Get out of your comfort zone, the four walls of the den, get out of the house and do what Jesus did and see what happens in your town. Giving your testimony, a Bible study, tea, coffee, or anything else will give the needy a reason to live. Do you understand that forty percent of people are losing their minds? Why? Because we are not doing what we are supposed to. The wrong network brings the evil spirit. Teach each other to connect with the Spirit of God. Join with God, not with the building they call churches.

Keep in mind that the battle is against the Devil, fallen angels, and demons. By learning through doing what the Lord says, you can teach them to use the word and be a teacher. You will never learn by simply sitting in a pew and joining the organization. Since you are the church, be open to the Lord using you to baptize and lay your hand to receive the Spirit of God. To baptize them, you can keep a baptistry in your backyard or take them to the river. So that their sins are washed away in the blood, baptize them in Jesus 'name. If you give yourself to God, you can be one of the laborers we need. Only by following the ways and will of God can one find the right path. Jesus is the way to the truth and life. Do not be a fool by believing in a church, as Jesus said you are the church and He purchases His residence by His blood. By repenting of your sins and going under the water in Jesus 'name, you can now allow Him to wash away your sins and receive His Spirit. When I started going out to preach and teach, I understood the word. Choosing to follow Jesus, I prioritize this over my degree despite the pressure from the denomination and non-denomination authorities. By choosing prayer, I decided to forgo higher education.

There was a day He sent me out. Though many are called, not all are chosen, but the one who obeys the will of God is chosen. The one who pays more money or goes to the building called the church is not who he is chasing, but the one who hears and obeys His voice.

In Jesus 'name, give what you have and raise them, not silver or gold. Inviting them to a religious building is something you should never do. When you lay hands on them and pray, observe what the Lord is doing and acknowledge that He alone deserves the glory. Although a building is not a church, you are classified as a church. So-called authorities will kick you out if you follow the Spirit. They kicked Jesus out as well. You will see the result when you go from place to place and do what the Lord did.

You wouldn't see drugs, alcohol, baggers, etc. The hospital will shut down. When you give a laborer a good productive ground, blessings of 30, 60, and 100 folds will come to you. Blessings will come to your family and country. In the act of taking care, do not forget the God-sent apostle and the prophet. Many people come to my house from different states. Sometimes, I have to bring them in without knowing them, lay hands on them for healing and deliverance, and minister to them. Giving to the kingdom of God involves giving yourself, opening your home, and sharing with those who need spiritual help. As you see the blessing coming into storehouses, security from God and multiplication of your food and money will be evident. Through his unwavering work, Jesus paved the way for us to encounter countless true prophets, teachers, and missionaries, and we have to offer them direct support.

Under no circumstances should money be given in the den to thieves. During the previous dispensation, they were required to give tithes and offerings to the temple(storehouses), whereas, in the current dispensation, we must support laborers. Give joyfully and gladly. If you give your talent, money, and knowledge to the kingdom of God, it will be appreciated. By giving to God, you will receive in the measure that you give, and you will be repaid in that same measure. Give cheerfully. In the way that Jesus gave and taught us to give, simply give.

JUNE 9

LET US PRAY

We must give to the Lord who gave all. Help us give to the needy, hungry, and homeless. You have instructed us to give ourselves to teach, baptize, cast out demons, heal the sick, and visit the widow and orphan. Our hearts overflow with gratitude as we sow our money into the kingdom of God, supporting laborers and shunning the thieves. Help us read and understand the word. You gave an example of giving, and we also want to give in Jesus 'name. Amen! God bless you.

JUNE 10

DIFFERENCE BETWEEN RELIGIOUS AND SPIRITUAL!

Religious people and spiritual people differ in their beliefs. While religious people know of God, spiritual people actually know God. What makes one sacred? Instead of being guided by God, we often find ourselves being guided by our flesh or by others. The religious mind, being fearful, is unable to surrender to God, as it directs God rather than allowing God to guide it, like a child commanding God instead of God guiding the child. To deceive oneself and others, it is an empty shell with only big words.

How sad! Instead of having these types of leaders, it is better to actively seek God and develop your relationship with Him.

By counseling people worldwide, I came to the realization that religious individuals have never truly experienced God. Although they read or memorize the scripture, they do not apply it to their situation. When a trial, trouble, or question arises, religious people, who are on shallow ground, fail to remember God. God cannot make use of people who are rebellious and self-centered. The Lord seeks those who are obedient, submissive, and who trust Him unconditionally. God's richness is evident in all aspects of his creation. He doesn't want you to offer Him Lollipops. With the statement from the Lord, I learned that He owned the cattle of 1,000 hills.

Psalm 50:10 For every beast of the forest is mine, and the cattle upon a thousand hills. 11 I know all the fowls of the mountains: and the wild beasts of the field are mine. 12 If I were hungry, I would not tell thee: for the world is mine, and the fulness thereof.

What is it that God wants?

Because of their prideful, selfish, and arrogant nature, religious people repeatedly make mistakes. Ever learning and never coming to the knowledge of the truth! Religion exhibits a deep down, unteachable, unruly, and fearful spirit.

Not surrendering to Him can result in losing everything that God will give them. The beginning of your relationship with the Lord starts by offering to Him. The Lord will bless you and love you. By submitting, you allow the Lord to take the reign of your life and assume control. Learning the Lord happens when we

JUNE 10

give Him everything. In order to use you for His Glory, God has called you. By learning from your success story, others can realize how awesome He is.

People like Eve, King Jeroboam, Jezebel, and King Ahab started a religion. Despite lacking evidence, signs, or wonders of God, religious churches only rely on empty words and beautiful songs to entertain your flesh. It is a business run by humans and their followers. Your flesh feels comfortable because no Holy Spirit can correct and convict you. The Holy Spirit convicts you in order to discourage the acceptance of manufactured rules. Although your flesh feels safe, your soul does not.

The Spiritual can allow God to move when surrendering to His will and ways. The spiritual person perceives the hand of God. Believing that sickness can transform into health and deliverance from the power of darkness, the spiritual person's love of God knows that their trial will turn into testimony.

There is a story to tell when one enters on a spiritual walk with God. You should ask them what the secret is behind their life story. In order to give the devil a black eye, my life story must be shared. By giving glory and blessings to His great name, my life story becomes significant. It should amaze the world. By theologians building churches everywhere, it is business without the Spirit of God.

During one prophetic meeting, the Prophet revealed to a Pentecostal Pastor that although you are aware of God, you do not truly know Him. What do you mean by the understanding of God? It is simply a straightforward answer.

They never surrender to God in order to know Him through their trial and trouble. The dying, empty religion is what brings hopelessness. God has nothing to do with it, but everything is for themselves! Religion attracts those who are fearful and disobedient to God. Religion is adding and subtracting in the word of God.

1 Samuel 15:24 And Saul said unto Samuel; I have sinned: for I have transgressed the commandment of the LORD, and thy words: because I feared the people, and obeyed their voice.

Wholeheartedly, people who know God will follow His direction. Their life is directed by Lord Jesus, the Author of the Bible. Having our blueprint ready, we all can achieve a powerful testimony, surpassing that of Daniel, Shadrach, Meshach, and Abednego. Should you choose to follow Lord Jesus, would you?

Starting your religion is achieved by going ahead of God. God will answer if you ask. Having questions won't make him tired of you, no matter what.

Judges 6:17 And he said unto him, If now I have found grace in thy sight, then shew me a sign that thou talkest with me.36 And Gideon said unto God, If thou wilt saves Israel by mine hand, as thou hast said,37 Behold, I will put a fleece of wool in the floor; and if the dew be on the fleece only, and it be dry upon all the earth beside, then shall I know that thou wilt save Israel by mine hand, as thou hast said.38 And it was so: for he rose up early on the morrow, and thrust the fleece together, and wringed the dew out of the fleece, a bowl full of water.39 And Gideon said unto God, Let not thine anger be hot against me, and I will speak but this once: let me prove, I pray thee, but this once with the fleece; let it now be dry only upon the fleece, and upon all the ground let there be dew. 40 And God did so that night: for it was dry upon the fleece only, and there was dew on all the ground.

Do you see how good God is? Every time Gideon asked, he answered.

I had been going through some significant life changes. Despite my opposition, the Lord had a plan for me. In my submission to Him, I asked Him to reveal it in my dream and made sure it wouldn't wander away. The Bible says the Lord speaks to us in a dream. In my dream, God spoke to me not once but three days in a row, just as I asked, and confirmed His plan. Upon my surrender, he was immediately included in the plan. The only condition was to reveal me in the dream. May the Lord remove our agenda, fear, rebellion, and disobedience in Jesus's name. You are safe, being in His plan. Surrender!

Those who are spiritual will have no personal agenda. In accordance with the plan of God, they achieve the expected end.

By walking according to the plan of God, He will make known whose heart is perfect for Him.

2 Chronicles 16:9a For the eyes of the LORD run to and fro throughout the whole earth, to shew himself strong in the behalf of them whose heart is perfect toward him.

Understand God by obeying His voice. You learn God's way by trusting and obeying His Word. May the Lord help us understand the voice and Word of God. Our relationship starts when we trust and obey the Lord. A relationship has two parties, and both have to walk together. It is not a relationship between you and people. If so, then it's called the religious. It is the right relationship if it is between you and God. He is not a co-pilot but the pilot of your life. Depending on how high you allow Him to, He will take you. Not your will, but the will of God to receive surprises, happiness, and a joyful end.

May the Lord elevate your faith like never before! May your relationship be healthier and more powerful. Be the vessel or instrument in His plan. The masterpiece will come out if you allow the Lord. Don't be a director. Let God be the director of the story. If you direct the plan, it will end up in religion. The end will be happy if God is the director.

Matthew 25:21 His Lord said unto him, Well done, thou good and faithful servant: thou hast been faithful over a few things, I will make thee ruler over many things: enter thou into the joy of thy Lord.

LET US PRAY

Our heavenly father, as father desires his children, so we desire you as our father. Today we surrender our selfishness. Help us, Lord. Open our ears and eyes to see and hear your voice. We commit our lives to your plan, not ours, but you will be done. We know God plans to bless and give success to you on earth. Help us surrender each day and do as you ask us to. Lord, your word says that we can call you to do great and mighty things which we do not know. We call you today to take us on that route of great and strong. We surrender to you, mighty God, in your powerful authority in Jesus's name. Amen! God bless you!

JUNE 11
LEARN TO BATTLE WITH UNSEEN ENEMIES!

We are called to work for King Jesus.

Revelation 17:14 These shall make war with the Lamb, and the Lamb shall overcome them: for he is Lord of lords, and King of kings: and they that are with him are called and chosen, and faithful.

King Jesus's plan is being fought against by an unseen enemy. Both have a system or agenda. We all have to follow the one we choose to work for. Let us read the schedule of both parties correctly.

John 10:10 The thief cometh not, but for to steal, and to kill, and to destroy: I have come that they might have life and that they might have it more abundantly.

In the role of a king, Jesus arrived to offer abundant life, while the devil, observing all your abundance, seeks to steal, kill, and destroy. We should learn to protect what God has given us. God, with many ways, has the ability to protect it. Let us see some of them.

Before anything else, we must gain knowledge of the Word of God and wield it as a sword. To care for our abundance, we should also utilize the power through the Holy Spirit and the authority in Jesus 'name. The first security, as mentioned in the Bible, is our money. By giving to the laborer, the workers in the field, the widows, orphans, the poor, naked, and hungry, the remaining money can be protected from Satan. In the previous dispensation, your security bank served as God's storehouse, but now all laborers minister to everyone.

2 Corinthians 9:6 But this I say, He which soweth sparingly shall reap also sparingly, and he which soweth bountifully shall reap also bountifully. 7 Every man according as he purposeth in his heart, so let him give; not grudgingly, or of necessity: for God loveth a cheerful giver.

Luke 6:38 Give, and it shall be given unto you; good measure, pressed down, shaken together, and running over, shall men give into your bosom. With the same measure that ye mete withal, it shall be measured to you again.

Mark 9:41 For whosoever shall give you a cup of water to drink in my name because ye belong to Christ, verily I say unto you, he shall not lose his reward.

Matthew 10:42 And whosoever shall give to drink unto one of these little ones a cup of cold water only in the name of a disciple, verily I say unto you, he shall in no wise lose his reward.

Jesus said that by following his ways, you can secure your finances. How wonderful it is to bring an offering and continue the work of God's instruction given by the Lord. God will protect all things from Satan. Remember to give in order to have God's protection over your vine, fruits, and field. Devourers cannot enter to destroy what belongs to you.

Another weapon is the authority to bind them.

Matthew 18:18 Verily I say unto you, Whatsoever ye shall bind on earth shall be bound in heaven: and whatsoever ye shall loose on earth shall be loosed in heaven.

In Jesus 'name, we have been given power and authority by God to bind and destroy the power of all demonic spirits, fallen angels, and Satan. Please speak with your mouth to activate it. Learn how to use the authority and power God gave you.

We should learn how. After coming from work every night, I pray for over an hour. Having finished my prayer one night, I went to sleep and felt something fall on my feet. The Holy Spirit spoke through my mouth; I bind you, Satan, and break your power in Jesus's name. I heard the scream of pain and hurt. That night, I discovered what happens when you speak the Word of God. The word is quickened or comes alive when you talk. By speaking correct scripture out loud over the situation, one breathes life into the word.

Another weapon is to plead the Blood of Jesus. At work, I noticed two employees were quarreling. The Holy Spirit spoke through my mouth, I plead the blood of Jesus over them. Right away, they calmed down and separated. The devil cannot cross the blood of Jesus. The blood of Jesus destroys Satan's work. The blood frees us from Satan. By using the blood over yourself, your family, all the people of the earth, buildings, and everything, you can make a significant impact. As you say, I plead the blood of Jesus, it works against Satan and its army.

The blood of Jesus speaks, the blood has life, and the blood delivers and sets us free in the name of Jesus.

Another powerful weapon is the shofar, an instrument given by God. Play the shofar while walking around the house, in the market, or anywhere. The demons around or in your home will be swallowed up by it.

Once I experienced extreme pain in my leg. The Lord asked that I play the shofar in the house. By walking and playing the shofar, I covered each room of my house with sound of Shofar. Following that, I took a nap. Having a dream, I witnessed my phone swallowing the slithering lizard. Upon waking up, the pain had disappeared. Giving pain on my leg, the lizard acted like a creeping demon. It sticks to any part of the body to give pain.

By trying different Biblical remedies, you may find relief for the pain in your body. Carefully, anoint over the body where the pain is using holy oil. Every day, I anoint my body with holy anointing oil. Spiritual problems can be resolved if you are aware of which weapon to use.

JUNE 11

The weapon of our warfare is not carnal but mighty through God. Use God's instruction to destroy this devil.

Another weapon: Anoint your house with Holy oil by reading the Word of God. I read Psalms 91 while touching the things in my house. Practice this every day. You will notice the presence of the Lord will come strong wherever you anoint. People will be free in your house. When the demon of drugs, cigarettes, religion, sickness, and all kinds of demon oppression and possession, along with its power, is destroyed, it will be a significant victory.

Isaiah 10:27 And it shall come to pass in that day, that his burden shall be taken away from off thy shoulder, and his yoke from off thy neck, and the yoke shall be destroyed because of the anointing.

Lord, guide us in comprehending how to achieve victory by utilizing simple yet powerful weapons of warfare. With a powerful testimony, I can attest to the effectiveness of using anointing oil. I will share a few of them. After anointing and witnessing what happens, you can then testify to others about your victory.

The Hindu lady, who converted to Christianity, had an angry husband. Once she began putting anointed holy oil in their food, he started vomiting, causing all the demons to come out and making him calm and sweet towards her.

Another mother and daughter used holy oil and anointed the entire house, reading Psalms 91 daily. Successfully overcoming addiction, her father and brother were freed from the drugs. I have seen in my dream a lizard demon dying after anointing the yard and burying 2" x 2" anointed pieces in the dirt. How wonderful! Try this at your work, at home, and in your city. It will work. Read the Bible and practice as it says. If you start using all the different weapons everywhere, the drugs, raping, sickness, killing, stealing, and every devourer will run from your town.

Another weapon: Anoint your laundry clothes before putting them away.

I keep Holy oil in my bathroom, and after the shower, I anoint my body with oil—an instant remedy to destroy the enemy's yoke.

You should always anoint the sick and pray by placing your hand over them. The sickness will go away if you practice continuously. Autism, paralysis, stroke, cancer or any deseases will be gone. It is God's powerful remedy against the unseen enemy. You can use it if you believe and trust it. With power comparable to weapons, the Word of God is mighty.

Use the Word of God: For example, say no weapon against me can prosper. I am first; I am head; I am above; I am highly favored. Speak the Word of God to use the disguised power to see the result.

I put the Bible as a pillow under my head. It works mightily. Using the Bible as a pillow, you can make the devil flee if you experience attacks, nightmares, caesura, night walking, PTSD, anxiety, or anything similar. Also, anoint your head with holy oil and see what happens.

When I have stomach problems, putting an open Bible on my tummy works miraculously. Covering every part of my face or body with the Bible, I sought victory, healing, and deliverance from the enemy.

Hopefully, this will be of assistance to you. By getting the directions and teaching of the Holy Spirit, you will see the result. By actually doing the word, you can witness its powerful effect. By calling upon Jesus' name, know the way of God. The enemy will be defeated. Hallelujah!

LET US PRAY

Lord, we come before your altar. By helping us, you enable us to be the doer of your word and not just a hearer. We know the word can work if we put it into action. Lord, as we go in this world, help us to get a victory. The Battle belongs to the Lord, but we are the soldiers in the army of the King of Kings, Jesus. We are victorious if we pay close attention to your command and direction. We ask you to make us mighty laborers in the field of the Lord. In the name of Jesus, we want to do the job well. When we go home safe and sound, we say Hallelujah! Glory to God for the mighty victory. Thanks for revealing the truth in Jesus' name. Amen! God bless you!

JUNE 12.

WHAT KIND OF EXAMPLES ARE YOU?

To somebody, we all serve as an example. As a parent, you serve as an example to your children. As someone observes and imitates you, they are studying your behavior. By watching their roles, someone is imitating the actors or actresses. Since your childhood, someone has had an impact on your life. The pattern of someone you have imitated is reflected in how you talk, dress, and think.

John 13:15 For I have given you an example, that ye should do as I have done to you.

By following the example of Jesus, we should strive to do the same. No other but Jesus! A perfect example of our Savior. Having twelve disciples, the Lord Jesus instructed them to follow him, and they submitted.

1 Peter 2:21 For even hereunto were ye called: because Christ also suffered for us, leaving us an example, that ye should follow his steps:

In order to follow in the footsteps of Jesus, we must reproduce His actions and teachings. Rather than discussing what Jesus did, take action and do what He did. Although many people know how to prepare and preach a great sermon, what about their work? We must always see the fruits of their labor. By following Jesus, you must remember to have the appropriate lifestyle.

Jesus came to set the captive free. With compassion, the Lord healed the broken heart. By casting out the demon, he demonstrated his power. By going from place to place, he took care of the sick, possessed, and oppressed, successfully resolving their issues.

Jesus taught to those who were spiritually hungry while teaching against the jealous and greedy religious authorities. In his confrontation, he showed that he did not care for the corrupted leaders ruling over His creation.

Instructing us to pay attention and follow Him alone, Jesus emphasized the rejection of religious groups. Jesus said we could stop the contamination in Christianity if we became salt. Being light can be understood by people. By following Jesus and not a false prophet, teacher, or religious group, we can become light.

Have you seen the followers of a movie star or someone who is a big player? From time to time, they even follow someone in school, a friend, or someone they look up to.

Many have lost interest, hope, and faith and are discouraged by seeing the church authority doing wrong. Remember, you are the church. Let Jesus come in, and allow Him to manage your life. The proper action would not contaminate. If you put good fruit with good fruit, it will stay good. But if you put bad fruit with the good, it will infect all.

The truth is not contaminating, but false is. False teaching can corrupt everything. It is likely that many of you have noticed pastors exhibiting some form of contamination. Perhaps due to favoritism, being biased, having a preference for the big money giver, prejudice, or simply disliking their family. This contaminates the work of God. We know that Christianity, which is based on truth, will work as it is the work of God. Seeing problematic church authorities, be aware that their children will not survive for long and their grandchildren will be neglected. Having already contaminated their family, they face the consequences. You are the church. He wants you and me to do what He did. As Christians, if we are doing wrong, we should know that evil spirits will attach to us. Jesus overthrew tables and labeled buildings as a den of thieves, but we label buildings as the church today.

No matter how many times you fast, pray, or speak in tongues, if your lifestyle does not match the Word of God, you will not last long. Your lifestyle must follow the word of truth. It is the power of deliverance. The truth has preservation property and will keep you from harm and danger. Never mind the one who preaches from the pulpit, simply follow Jesus. Paul said follow me as I follow Jesus. Yes, Paul was not standing in one place. He did what Jesus did and also trained his disciples to do the same.

Every day, your lifestyle preaches. Though you may not think you are preaching, your actions, reactions, and lifestyle speak louder than words. Teach your children good conduct from a young age in the same way that you teach them manners. In order to teach, you must set an example. Your actions and reactions play a role in the raising of children. Please do not take people's words but observe what they do.

Jesus said you must be born again. Why? So we can start a new life. It is a fantastic experience if you know how to be born again. Do you know how to be born again? Follow the teaching and preaching of His followers, disciples, prophets, and apostles. I had an amazing experience the day they baptized me to wash away my sins by going under the water, in Jesus's name. Like an old sinner, I was buried in water and resurrected as a new person. As the Lord Jesus instructed His disciples, I want you to take the route of the book of Acts. The Lord Jesus is the chief cornerstone, so do everything in Jesus's name. You can learn by following the example of water and Holy Spirit Baptism from the book of Acts. It would be great if you could carry on with the book of Acts. By following the authentic example of how disciples started the one church, you ensure that the Book of Acts will never end. Please continue the book of Acts. Despite being labeled as a church, many buildings do not follow the truth. Do not establish a new religion or organization as a means to replace the book of Acts. By engaging in true or false actions, history repeats itself. Our actions will help us find the right or wrong path. No matter how you put it, you represent either good or bad. So be careful how you talk, dress, act, and live.

Being told by someone, I learned that if a country practices an immoral lifestyle, Jesus would be merciful. This statement surprised me! How would the Author of the Word of God allow unholy people in His kingdom? What a privilege for them if they repent and are baptized in Jesus's name. They can get a new life by getting a clean conscience.

JUNE 12

Do yourself a favor, find the KJV Bible, and study the life of Jesus by obeying His Word. Find the key to open the kingdom of heaven; Peter had the key, and He gave it to us, use the key. Disciples, apostles, and prophets of Jesus are an example of the new birth experience of how to enter the kingdom of heaven.

Not everyone practices the truth. Do not enter the building because you see a cross. In order to follow a good example, carefully heed the teachings of Jesus. Do not go after corrupt false denominations, non-denominations, and organizations. If we follow Jesus, we still are working in the streets, city, and country, turning the world upside down.

Remember to consider that your life talks. People like to see your actions. The confusion arises when your actions and words do not match. Jesus taught the disciples to do all kinds of work, like what He was doing. Do you need a building when the Lord said to go places and set the captive free? As the second Adam, Jesus has the plan, but by staying inside a building, you are inhibiting and undermining the plan of the Lord Jesus.

The fruit has a name; what name do you carry? Similarly to the Apple, orange, and banana, we also have our pattern. We make our pattern just like a fruit. Let's carry the Name of Jesus.

Matthew 7:15 Beware of false prophets, which come to you in sheep's clothing, but inwardly they are ravening wolves. 16 Ye shall know them by their fruits. Do men gather grapes of thorns or figs of thistles? 17, Even so, every good tree bringeth forth good fruit; but a corrupt tree bringeth forth evil fruit. 18 A good tree cannot bring forth evil fruit, neither can a corrupt tree bring forth good fruit. 19 Every tree that bringeth not forth good fruit is hewn down and cast into the fire. 20 Wherefore by their fruits ye shall know them.

You are an example of what you represent. Regardless of not holding a title or position, it is your character that defines you.

The vital lesson to learn. Think how the people of God crucified the God whom they were serving. By simply following the one who was following fleshly authority and not God, people were led astray. Checking the religious authorities you are following is important. It is very dangerous to follow the lost one. If we follow Him, I believe God has a mission for every one of us. It is the same mission that started in the Garden of Eden. Focus on Jesus. No one but Him!

Have you heard the parable of five wise and five fools? The same time is here today. Five wise follow the Lord and five fools follow their flesh.

By establishing churches on the rock, Peter and other disciples began their mission. Rock meant having a revelation of Jesus. Jesus was their example. A disclosure is made when one knows that Jehovah is walking in the body of Jesus and that the saving name of Jehovah is Jesus.

Noticing that evil teachers, supervisors, or authorities have the power to control people. When wicked rulers take over, all chaos, division, exploits, and abuse of power dominate, and all is not well. Do not follow in their footsteps. Wait on the Lord and follow Jesus's example.

2 Corinthians 3:2 Ye are our epistle written in our hearts, known and read of all men:

Someone can read our example. Without needing to ask, it is clear whether you are a Christian or a sinner. Or are you Muslim? Or who do you follow?

Do not let the agenda of denominations or organizations contaminate you. Jesus paid an enormous price, so take His example. Without uttering a word, people will still recognize whose footsteps you are following. Amen!

LET US PRAY

Lord, we know you are the living example for us. Help us, Lord, to follow you. Our desire is to be an excellent example in a dark, lost world. We desire you and want to know more and more about you. Many know of God, but we want to know you by living for you. Your word says we recognize our fruits, let our fruit be good. We want all nine fruits and nine gifts of Spirit. Teach us to love our enemy and to be kind to others. Help us preserve your word by being salt in Jesus's name. Amen! God bless you!

JUNE 13

CONFUSION OF GIFT OF TONGUE AND SPEAKING IN THE TONGUE!

It is necessary to have clarity or understanding about speaking in tongues and the gift of the tongue. The gift of the tongue, which delivers a message to the individual or people, is followed by interpretation.

When referring to 1 Corinthians, chapter 12 talks about nine gifts of the spirit. These nine gifts, which are also referred to as charisma, are accessible to all who desire it. Not all have these nine gifts, but only all those who covet them.

I remembered working with one saint of God, who had some spiritual gifts. The Bible says it is the same God, the Same Lord, and the same spirit that comes in you to administrate for operation of the charisma/gift. Read carefully that this is given to all and those who desire it. Someone has to lay hands on you to transfer the gifts.

1 Corinthians 12:31a But covet earnestly the best gifts:

So keep the nine gifts of the spirit distinct from the baptism of the Holy Ghost. When the Spirit of God comes in you to do diversities of operations, that is when the nine gifts of the spirits are. Naming these nine gifts, let me mention that a word of knowledge followed by a word of wisdom works simultaneously. Gifts of faith, miracle, and healing are self-explanatory. Discerning the spirits will identify the spirit. The same Spirit of God will detect through you if you have God's discerning Spirit. The gift of Tongue and interpretation of Tongue works at the same time. The gift of tongues brings the message, and God moves on someone to interpret the message in the tongue. Tongues means language. If the message comes, then allow someone to interpret it. It is not a translation, but an interpretation of the message.

1 Corinthians 12:30c. Do all speak with tongues? Do all interpret?

See, the answer to each question is no. Not all have these gifts, but some do.

Few have the gift of the tongue. One, two, or three at the most will give a message in an unfamiliar language, and one will interpret the message, whoever has the gifts of interpretation of tongues. Whoever yields the Spirit of God can interpret through that person. If no one yields, then they won't understand the message. A gift of the tongue is necessary. God is speaking to the church and uses one to interpret what He is saying.

Interpretation means explanation or clarification, it is not a translation. These gifts are especially to edify or for correction or a special message to the individual or the many. This gift gives honor to Jesus as God.

Now, let us discuss the Holy Spirit Baptism that Jesus mentioned to Nicodemus. The Holy Spirit Baptism gives you the power to witness; it will be your teacher, will guide you, and much more. This tongue is in Greek Glossa. They will speak the tongue that is Glossa. When one receives the Holy Spirit, called the baptism of the Holy Spirit. Glossa means the language or dialect used by a particular person distinct from that of other nations.

The Lord is letting you know that when you baptize in Jesus's name, then you will receive the gift of the Holy Spirit, also called the baptism of the spirit. How would you know you have received the Baptism of the Holy Spirit? The only way to know is when you are speaking in Glossa, a language. A language you did not learn or did not go to learn at a university. With the Spirit of God, you are given the ability to speak. What it is, is your prayer language.

Let us see some examples of people who received the Baptism of the Holy Spirit.

Acts 2:7 And they were all amazed and marveled, saying one to another, Behold, are not all these which speak Galileans? 8 And how hear we every man in our own tongue, wherein we were born?

All can receive the Holy Spirit if they are baptized in the name of Jesus. Some received the baptism of the Holy Spirit before water baptism in Jesus's name. The key sign of receiving the Holy Spirit is when you hear people speaking in an unknown language.

The Prophet Joel already prophesied about this Holy Spirit baptism.

Joel 2:28a And it shall come to pass afterward, that I will pour out my spirit upon all flesh; and your sons and your daughters shall prophesy, 29 And also upon the servants and upon the handmaids in those days will I pour out my spirit.

John 3:5 Jesus answered, Verily, verily, I say unto thee, Except a man be born of water and of the spirit, he cannot enter into the kingdom of God.

Given to the disciple of God, the unknown language is a sign to recognize that the person has received the baptism of the Holy Spirit. After the resurrection, Jesus asked the disciples to wait until they received the Holy Spirit's baptism. It has not poured out on the earth yet. On the day of Pentecost, the Holy Ghost was poured out on earth.

Mark 16:17a And these signs shall follow them that believe;17c they shall speak with new tongues;

In Greek, the new tongue is called Glossa.

Now the day of Pentecost has fully come.

Acts 2:4 And they were all filled with the Holy Ghost, and spoke with other tongues, as the spirit gave them utterance.

JUNE 13

Acts 19:6 And when Paul had laid his hands upon them, the Holy Ghost came on them; and they spake with tongues, and prophesied.

Peter knew Cornelius received the Baptism of the Holy Spirit when he heard him speaking in tongues.

Acts 10:44 While Peter yet spake these words, the Holy Ghost fell on all them which heard the word. 46 For they heard them speak with tongues and magnify God.

No one has to interpret this language. It is called the baptism of the Holy Spirit. It was nice that God filled them with the Holy Spirit on the day of Pentecost. On the day of Pentecost, people from all over the world flocked to Jerusalem. Though they heard it, they did not comprehend that yes, it is a language. Though it is your prayer language, your understanding remains silent.

Paul explains this well.

1 Corinthians 14:2 For he that speaketh in an unknown tongue speaketh not unto men, but unto God: for no man understandeth him; howbeit in the spirit he speaketh mysteries. 4 He that speaketh in an unknown tongue edifieth himself; but he that prophesieth edifieth the church. 14 For if I pray in an unknown tongue, my spirit prayeth, but my understanding is unfruitful.

Paul explains in verse 18; I thank my God, I speak with tongues more than ye all:

After arriving in the US in 1982, I received the Holy Spirit. I came from India in 1980. Before that moment, I had never witnessed anyone speaking in the language of the Holy Spirit. I was against speaking in tongues until I received and experienced it.

Loving this subject comes from my understanding of the gifts of spirits and the gift or baptism of the Holy Spirit. In India nowadays, many people have been baptized in the Holy Spirit, speaking in a heavenly language. I have heard them praying in the Holy Spirit language.

Through the act of praying, your prayer language takes control, assisting you in praying for the matter. If you are interested in knowing about this subject, I advise you to inquire with someone who is knowledgeable about it. If you are not careful, ignorance will misguide you.

Roman 8:26 Likewise, the spirit also helpeth our infirmities: for we know not what we should pray for as we ought: but the spirit itself maketh intercession for us with groanings which cannot be uttered.

While praying for people, I spoke in the Holy Ghost language without understanding the words, as the spirit prayed through me.

By praying in the tongue, I can strengthen my faith. I read this article written by a pastor who received the Holy Spirit. Having been baptized with the Holy Spirit, he never spoke in tongues. With a sense of badness, sadness, hopelessness, and dryness, he felt overwhelmed. He went to another pastor, who understood the reason. The pastor explained that you have to pray in a tongue which is an unknown language every day for one hour or more, even though you do not understand. It is your heavenly language. You will get more and more words later on.

Jude:20 But ye, beloved, building up yourselves on your most holy faith, praying in the Holy Ghost,

When you continue speaking in your tongue, your spirit will well up and build up.

LET US PRAY

Lord, we need the Baptism of the Holy Spirit. We are grateful to you as you said you wouldn't leave us comfortless, but you would come to us. The Holy Spirit will teach and guide us all to the truth. It will empower us to witness. We thank you that now you are working for us through us. We thank you that the Holy Spirit Gift is free and prays through us for the things we are unaware of. May you, Lord, help us not to reject but to receive your spirit. As they rejected you while working with the Israelites as King, then you came on earth in the flesh. They crucified you, and now your spirit works, and they rejected it. We ask you to remove the blinder of our minds so we understand in Jesus's name. Amen! God bless you!

JUNE 14

GO DEEPER TO FIND THE ROOT OF THE CAUSE!

The Bible is the source, root, and answer to all questions. Our wonderful God knows all. His name is Jesus!

Hebrew 4:13 Neither is there any creature that is not manifest in his sight: but all things are naked and opened unto the eyes of him with whom we have to do.

Isaiah 46:9 Remember the former things of old: for I am God, and there is none else; I am God, and there is none like me,10 Declaring the end from the beginning, and from ancient times the things that are not yet done, saying, My counsel shall stand, and I will do all my pleasure:

When facing any problem, make sure you go to the Lord. He has the answer and no one else. May the Lord give you direction! Someone told me the Lord answered prayers and prayed between 3 am-4 am. We might say, Lord, it is the best time to sleep. But if you seek the answer, you must face your sleep and find the Lord.

I have connections internationally. A lady told me that witch Doctors, Satan worshipers, and all dark mediums do their work at night. The Lord knows the demon gets an assignment in the night. The enemy diverts your destiny before you meet your day.

Psalms 77:2 In the day of my trouble I sought the Lord: my sore ran in the night and ceased not: my soul refused to be comforted.

We call this the made-up mind to find the answer.

Psalm 6:6 I am weary with my groaning; all the night make I my bed to swim; I water my couch with my tears.

To fully understand the root of all problems, delve deeper. That is what the Prophet of God does. The prophet will find the root cause and subsequently seek remedies. In order to find the root cause and how it occurred, the prophet will connect with God and seek its remedy.

People usually go to a doctor when they are sick. Like a radiologist, he sends you to diagnostic tests such as X-rays, MRIs, ultrasounds, blood tests, and urine tests. Having curses like High Priest Eli leaves you with no remedy. You will witness young people dying and suffering as they grow older.

1 Samuel 2:33 Yet I will not cut off from My altar every man of yours; some shall survive to weep and mourn [over the family's ruin], but all the increase of your house shall die in their best years.

In this manner, why does God bless His people? What was the cause of the curses that affected the Holy Priest's family? Let us find the root.

Samuel 2:29 Wherefore kick ye at my sacrifice and at mine offering, which I have commanded in my habitation; and honourest thy sons above me, to make yourselves fat with the chiefest of all the offerings of Israel, my people?

While his children were sinning, Eli should have taught them the ways of God and not ignored their actions. Correct your children by guiding them when they are going astray.

By exploring the origins, let us uncover why King Uzziah became a leper.

2 Chronicles 26:21a And Uzziah, the King was a leper unto the day of his death, and dwelt in several houses, being a leper; for he was cut off from the home of the LORD:

Leprosy, being the curse of God, is a devastating disease. In the Priest, King, or people of God, it is not to be found. We must find the root to remove it. Uzziah must find the answer from God and not from other sources.

18 And they withstood Uzziah the King and said unto him, It appertaineth not unto thee, Uzziah, to burn incense unto the LORD, but to the priests the sons of Aaron, that are consecrated to burn incense: go out of the sanctuary; for thou hast trespassed; neither shall it be for thine honor from the LORD God. 19 Then Uzziah was wroth, and had a censer in his hand to burn incense: and while he was wroth with the priests, leprosy even rose up in his forehead before the priests in the house of the LORD, from beside the incense altar.

See, Uzziah trespassed on the commandment of God. You do not transgress the Laws and commandments of God. After you, it is the most dangerous move for you and your family.

Knowing your roots is knowing your curses or blessings. Remind and review the condition. Know and accept your dos and dont's or face the consequences. God said I am the same yesterday, today, and forever. Don't look for a shortcut. The Lord makes us bold to follow Him and not bold to transgress. The result is the same for the high to the low position. You are an example of either good or bad. Now Uzziah may have thought, who is this priest? I am King; I am the highest authority. No, but God is the Highest authority and not a king, queen, Priest, or High Priest. Stay within your boundary, and you will find blessings.

As the son of King Jehoshaphat, Jehoram takes center stage in this story. In order to secure his position, Jehoram killed his six brothers. Learn from his example.

JUNE 14

2 Chronicles 21:18 And after all this the LORD smote him in his bowels with an incurable disease. 19 And it came to pass, that in the process of time, after the end of two years, his bowels fell out by reason of his sickness: so he died of sore diseases.

God knows your motive. Are you greater than God? Be careful! Pay close attention to the Lord; the Judgment of God lingers no more. By turning away from your sins, you should repent of them. By aligning your life with the plan of God, you find purpose. The Lord has called us to fulfill His goal and not ours. Pay attention to your actions and reactions. You are not above the law and commandments of God. Although God is in Heaven, He needs someone to take care of His business on earth.

2 Chronicles 21:4 Now when Jehoram was risen up to the kingdom of his father, he strengthened himself, and slew all his brethren with the sword, and divers also of the princes of Israel. 6 And he walked in the way of the kings of Israel, like as did the house of Ahab: for he had the daughter of Ahab to wife: and he wrought that which was evil in the eyes of the LORD. 7 Howbeit, the LORD would not destroy the house of David because of the covenant that he had made with David, and as he promised to give light to him and to his sons forever.

The Lord protects your health, wealth, position, power, and success. The Lord called you with the plan, so stay connected by keeping His commandments.

Another powerful piece of information;

1 Timothy 6:10 For the love of money is the root of all evil: which while some coveted after, they have erred from the faith, and pierced themselves through with many sorrows.

To truly comprehend the significance of our calling, we must understand that nothing else matters. By keeping integrity and knowledge of the redeemer, creator, and savior of your soul, you can stay grounded. The outcome of everything rests on how you handle your life.

According to the Bible, sickness is rooted in sin. In order to solve the problem, find the source and uproot it. If you possess traits such as being power hungry, an adulterer, a liar, wicked, or any kind of sin, sickness will disappear when the root of evil is removed. The Lord is faithful and just. May we receive humbleness from the Lord. Acknowledging their guilt, they will ask the Lord for forgiveness. If you come out of all trouble, sickness, and curses, you will be blessed again. Hallelujah!

LET US PRAY

My Lord, we know you are merciful. We stand for our family and us to be forgiven and washed in the blood of Jesus. Lord, we confess our flesh has nothing good. We desire your spirit to lead, teach, and guide us for the truth to receive the blessings of God. Lord, we desire the stream of blessings to flow in our bloodline to our descendants. We need you to be our protector, health, and hope. We want the root of all sicknesses to be removed as we repent. Revive us and bless us in Jesus's name. Amen! God bless you!

JUNE 15

IT WILL NOT WORK!

By following the instruction of God without adding or subtracting to it, you can establish what the Bible claims, recognizing it as truth. No matter how advanced science, astrology, astronomy, technology, medicine, or satanic knowledge may be, they cannot replace the truth of the Bible. It is a fact that the Bible is the only source of truth from its origin. Without anything to replace it, the Bible's ways, plans, instructions, commandments, laws, and precepts remain unmatched. If you changed it, it simply wouldn't work. Check the history from the beginning. Instead of following the commandment of the Lord, Eve tried her own ways. She failed herself, the plan of God, and the world. Her choices did not work, and she destroyed the plans of God. When the Lord gives us accurate information, simply follow and not question. People who question are rebellious, disobedient, and driven by pride and lust, or Satan. If you find another way, honest disclosure, it will not work.

Having help from the omniscient God, we are more than blessed. The owner of the product knows the facts and not the fiction.

God's test for obedience is to search whether you deserve blessings. Enjoy the benefits after obeying what the Lord asked you to do. The original plan has more flavor than an artificial one.

Our Lord has given many ways to help His creation and guide them through their earthly journey. You know science, medicine, witches, warlocks, and mediums are not based on truth. From the beginning, science keeps changing its books. Astrologers have been proven wrong. Medicine has killed many. The Bible will determine whether you have collected the information claiming to be facts as right or wrong. The Bible is the source of all the treasures you cherish. Wherever you go, the Bible is beneficial for all ages, cultures, and countries to achieve, prosper, and establish. Make sure to understand that the Bible is a book not to question, debate, or allow to collect dust. The Bible is not the book to read to kill time. Open the book by opening your heart and mind. Read prayerfully, do not dare to change by adding or subtracting. It is the book for God's followers.

Write it down. You will fail if you try anything instead, thus saith the Lord. Your future will be just like Eve-Adam, King Saul, and Priest Eli. Do not dare to go against the Lord. Although God created and called you, anointed and used you mightily, still you can make mistakes. If you decide to take any other route but the Lord's, you will go down. You will be out of the promised land. All your assignments, appointments, and calls will be replaced by the ones who will believe, obey, surrender, and do as asked.

JUNE 15

Do not let the history of rebellion and disobedience repeat in your life. May the Lord give us an ear to hear and eyes to see. No matter who you are, king, priest, low or high, you will have to bow before the King of Kings and the Lord of Lords. If you are wise, humble, and sincere enough to see significant results without putting yourself in trouble, then obey God's voice.

Let me ask you, are you smarter than God? Are you greater than God? Are you omniscient, omnipotent, or omnipresent? You are not. You are dust and will become dust. Look at the dust and say, Lord, I look to you for my direction.

Open the Bible and study the life of a successful man and woman. Success was not because of their smartness but because of the one they obeyed. God guards your back. They called on God for help. My friend, without getting a big head, follows the Bible without opinion. God does not want your view over His facts. The devil and his followers are opinionated. They have done the job against the truth. But anyone who recognizes the power and authority on high has no problem. It is wise not to add to or subtract from the word. What is adding and subtracting to the truth?

Revelation 22:18 For I testify unto every man that heareth the words of the prophecy of this book, If any man shall add unto these things, God shall add unto him the plagues that are written in this book:19 And if any man shall take away from the words of the book of this prophecy, God shall take away his part out of the book of life, and out of the holy city, and from the things which are written in this book.

So, are you ready for the plague or to remove eternally from the presence of God? Are you ready to face the darkness on earth and in hell forever?

Branded religion is a replacement for truth.

The Bible says, John 8:32, And ye shall know the truth, and the truth shall make you free.

The survey showed how many people say they are Christians. You might say, many. The world's largest population is still Christian. Then why are people still bound, possessed, oppressed, and have many problems? Simply, people have taken a shortcut called the route of religion. Some were born into a family that believes in Jesus. See, the Scripture is clear and straightforward.

John 8:31 Then said Jesus to those Jews which believed on him, If ye continue in my word, then are ye my disciples indeed;

You need to continue in His true Word. Do not deviate from joining denominations, non-denominations, organizations, or any form of religion. Open the Bible, study, meditate, obey, and submit to the word of truth. See what happens. Let us see what the early church practices are.

Acts 10:48a And he commanded them to be baptized in the name of the Lord.

See, it is not a suggestion; it is a commandment. Do without questioning.

Romans 9:20 Nay but, O man, who art thou that repliest against God? Shall the thing formed say to him that formed it, Why hast thou made me thus? 21 Hath not the potter power over the clay, of the same lump to make one vessel unto honor, and another unto dishonor?

I remember my search was over the day they baptized me in the name of Jesus, as the prophets, the apostles, and the disciples of God practiced. There was no question after my experience of receiving the forgiveness of sin. I felt lighter than a feather. I felt like I could walk on water. The heaviness of sin like a mountain was removed as I came out of the water. Wow! I am glad I did as they wrote it in the Word of God.

I have seen druggy, alcoholic, sick, and those deep in sin washed in the blood come out of the water as new men.

The Bible says to follow the apostle, prophet, and disciple.

Ephesians 2:20 And are built upon the foundation of the apostles and prophets, Jesus Christ himself being the chief cornerstone;

The foundation was laid in the Book of Acts. The Apostles and prophets were taught in the New Testament. The first church (the church is not a building) continued in the truth and had seen marvelous experiences, signs, and wonders. Hold on to the truth of the Bible and get rid of the false teaching of adding and subtraction. To follow the truth, you need boldness, courage, and love for the truth. Family, friends, and religious people can reject you. Do not worry; they always reject the followers of the truth.

Acts 2:42 And they continued steadfastly in the apostles 'doctrine and fellowship, and in breaking of bread, and in prayers.

Be steadfast and continue to follow the book of Acts. Start a born-again life by first repenting of sins, then wash all sin away in water by baptizing in the Name of Jesus and receiving the gift of the Holy Spirit.

Jesus said.

John 14:6 Jesus saith unto him, I am the way, the truth, and the life:

I minister to many converted Christians. Some of their family has not experienced the true God Jesus yet. So many times, they pressure new converts. But the truth is so powerful that they have no fear at all. They cannot deny the deliverance, healing, and forgiveness experience. They cannot deny the revelation. You can kill, persecute, put them behind bars, throw them in the well, or burn them. The truth cannot be denied, argued, replaced, or compromised, but only obeyed. Experience the power of deliverance and healing by obeying the truth.

LET US PRAY

Lord, we come before your altar, open our eyes and ears to hear your voice to obey. The Lord speaks to our hearts through His Word of truth! Teach us how to divide the word of truth in the right way. Truth has the power to set us free from sickness, disease, bondage, chains, and darkness. We do not want religion, but a relationship. May our Lord give us victory by directing us in absolute truth! May we become living example followers of Jesus and not religion! The Lord shows us the way of truth to find eternal life in Jesus's name. Amen! God bless you!

JUNE 16

POWER OF CONFESSION!

Confession means acknowledging or disclosing one's sins in the sacrament of reconciliation (Miriam Webster). A statement made admitting guilt of an offense. With His omniscience, God already knows right and wrong. In the event that we do wrong, God will not forsake us as sinners but will create an opportunity for an escape. If we admit our faults or trespasses, then God will forgive us. God can forgive, but your confession is crucial to discharge guilt against yourself. Confessing the mistake you made is not a justification. With a clear conscience, you say, I admit my fault; please forgive me.

Realizing sin or trespasses and then admitting, 'I am guilty, will cleanse your record in heaven. This is our most powerful blessing from a merciful, loving father. Acknowledging that we are not divine, God knows that we are created from dust. Let us see some examples of confession. There are also consequences for not confessing sins. It is a known fact that the Lord is merciful. God, knowing our origin in dust, opened a way for us to find an escape. To confess is the path to freedom from trouble, punishment, and curses.

God's promises are contingent upon us confessing our faults and seeking forgiveness.

1 John 1:8 If we say that we have no sin, we deceive ourselves, and the truth is not in us. 9 If we confess our sins, he is faithful and just to forgive us and cleanse us from all unrighteousness.

By sinning, we all earn death, which is eternal punishment in hell. If you confess, "Lord, I am guilty," you will escape from hellfire.

2 Samuel 11-12 After engaging in adultery with Bathsheba, David then conspired to kill her husband, Uriah. Occasionally, you do something wrong without recognizing it as a sin. The heart, although a human organ, has areas of blindness. A just and kind King, David did not know his deed.

David was confronted by Prophet Nathan, who spoke on behalf of God.

II Samuel 12:13 And David said unto Nathan, I have sinned against the Lord. And Nathan said unto David, The Lord also hath put away thy sin; thou shalt not die.

The phrase "put away" signifies the act of disposing or abandoning. If you want God to dismiss your sin, you need to confess. Our God is truly great, isn't He? God knew David was sinning without recognizing it. Often, we sin without realizing our mistake due to our lack of awareness. Being in the presence of the Lord helps us identify and understand our sins. The fact that sin causes sickness is well-known. Being humble is essential for maintaining good health. You possess no more wisdom than God. By not confessing your sins, you are causing harm to yourself. Confronting yourself requires courage. Search for God and acknowledge your wrongdoing. It will help you regain your health. Surprisingly, a simple confession led to a powerful outcome.

Find the cause of your peace loss by examining your conscience. The body often experiences sickness as a result of sin.

Also, John 9:31 Now we know that God heareth not sinners: but if any man is a worshiper of God, and doeth his will, he heareth.

Hiding sin is not a good idea.

Proverb 28:13 He that covereth his sins shall not prosper: but whoso confesseth and forsaketh them shall have mercy.

I can still remember the moment I started my job at the post office. My supervisor, or rather general supervisor, made my life incredibly difficult. This supervisor was a highly influential harasser. She used her power to come against me. I was angry about her dirty games and persecution. She used others to turn against me. I came home daily mad about the ongoing harassment and even lost sleep over this wicked supervisor. During that time, I was taking Bible classes. The lesson was about forgiveness. I thought about how to forgive. I said, if I forgive, I will go through the same thing repeatedly. So I spoke to the preacher about the whole matter. He told you to ignore her and see what happens. Well, one day, I went to my room and said, Lord forgive me; I was angry with this woman who was evil to me. And I also ignored her. From that night on, I started sleeping again. Don't you see when you forgive others, you get forgiveness? God has forgiven me for my anger toward this lady. I confessed to God I was angry because she was harassing me. No problem; God came through the matter. My confession forgave my sin of anger. As I ignored her, I slept well! The next time I saw her, I was not bothered; she did everything evil in her power, but I was free from the bondage of anger.

Later, the company demoted the woman supervisor. To take revenge is the Lord's. I know I did not want to confess since I was angry. I thought I had a reason to get upset because she caused it. Remember, sin is sin no matter whose fault. I am not sure I can help with taking revenge. I have to forgive and not get angry. Many people who cannot say Lord forgive me, I did wrong, will have some kind of sickness.

Psalm 103:3 Who forgiveth all thine iniquities; who 161ealth all thy diseases;4 Who redeemeth thy life from destruction; who crowneth thee with loving-kindness and tender mercies;

Do you see the benefits of confession? You are granted forgiveness and healing both. Verse number 4 says no destruction has power over you; you receive loving-kindness and tender mercies. Hallelujah!

Lord, grant us the bravery to confront our own flaws. As the Bible says, there is no hearing for the liar. You are inviting trouble if you say it is her fault and not mine. Saying sorry and admitting fault can lead to positive changes. God will instantly grant you forgiveness and shower you with blessings.

JUNE 16

Educate your children on the importance of confessing, so they grow up to be truthful. Honest kids will succeed, but those who learn to conceal their mistakes will face consequences in the future.

Cain was unwilling to confess his fault. Instead of providing the correct answer, he responded proudly. He replied, how do I know? If you find the courage to answer to God, there's no reason to fear hell's punishment and curses.

Genesis 4:12 When thou tillest the ground, it shall not henceforth yield unto thee her strength; a fugitive and a vagabond shalt thou be in the earth. 14 Behold, thou hast driven me out this day from the face of the earth; and from thy face shall I be hid; and I shall be a fugitive and a vagabond in the earth, and it shall come to pass, that everyone that findeth me shall slay me. 16 And Cain went out from the presence of the Lord, and dwelt in the land of Nod, on the east of Eden.

Romans 10:10 For with the heart man believeth unto righteousness, and with the mouth, confession is made unto salvation.

Healing, deliverance, and salvation are all encompassed by the concept of salvation. For eternal salvation, it is essential to confess sins. My we be blessed with the strength to always speak the truth. There is no hearing for liars on the day of judgment, only a direct ticket to hell for not confessing your sins. It's advisable to seek a place for confession and encounter God's mercy.

LET US PRAY

Lord, thank you for giving us a conscience to feel the torment of sin. Sin should never rule over us. We confess our faults, trespasses, and immorality.

Lord, you are faithful in forgiving all our shortcomings. Please forgive us. Thank you for the grace and mercy of your creation. Lord, come to our rescue when we are at our lowest point. Let your compassion and grace, Lord, never depart from us. Lord, we plead with you to not withdraw your Holy Spirit from us. We need your Spirit of truth to lead and guide us until we reach heaven. Our God is Holy and righteous. God wants us to be honest, so help us, Lord, in Jesus's name. Amen! God bless you!

JUNE 17

THE FOLLOWER OF JESUS USE HIS AUTHORITY!

Those who follow Jesus utilize His God-given authority through His name. By giving them authority in his name, Jesus trained his disciples on the field. Knowing Jesus 'identity is even more remarkable as it reveals His connection to the creator. Jesus handcrafted Adam and Eve with purpose, not merely to wander aimlessly in this world.

Paul walked in Torah and consequently missed out on the grace and manifestation of the Messiah. He discovered the Lord when he was afflicted with blindness. The one who truly knows God reveals His identity, but our religious beliefs blind us to this truth.

Stay away from individuals who wrongly classify themselves as teachers, pastors, or apostles. Choose to follow Jesus instead of the religion established by the serpent. In such a case, you'll find yourself helpless and unable to fly, even with assistance.

When Jesus unveils His true identity, He equips and sends you to serve His kingdom. He is dedicated to freeing captives, healing, delivering, and restoring those who are in ruin. Hold the hand of Jesus; do not go aside, betray, or look for the forbidden fruit that has the power to make you like God. It is all a lie; when Jesus said do not, then do not. You will lose authority and power again after He reestablished you from the sins of Adam and Eve.

Jesus didn't want His followers to be limited by denominations, religions, or external authorities during their training. The Bible says that after shedding blood, he came out of the temple. Later temples were later plowed and destroyed. Moreover, the Lord entered the temple and forcefully flipped the table, denouncing them as thieves and condemning the building as a den of thieves. Why do you like to go there, which can put you in the name-brand cage and cannot get out of it? Jesus paid for your freedom with His blood and instructed you to liberate others. Are you repeating the same mistakes as Eve and Adam?

He came to free you by giving back the authorities we lost in the garden of Eden by the transgression. Be mindful of obeying the given instructions. It has the power to free you and continue to keep setting you free.

JUNE 17

Luke 9:1 Then he called his twelve disciples together, and gave them power and authority over all devils, and to cure diseases.

Matthew 10:1 And when he had called unto him his twelve disciples, he gave them power against unclean spirits, to cast them out, and to heal all manner of sickness and all manner of disease.

We have a responsibility to train, appoint, and teach more people, permitting them authority and practical experience in the name of Jesus.

Luke 10:1 After these things the Lord appointed other seventy also, and sent them two and two before his face into every city and place, whither he would come.

If you follow Jesus and do what He did, He will not hold you back. However, it will increase your power even more. Your growth will be constantly amplified by Him.

Mark 9:39 But Jesus said, Forbid him not: for there is no man which shall do a miracle in my name, that can lightly speak evil of me. 40 For he that is not against us is on our part.

The Lord wants us to use authors by following His example completely. He desires to reunite with His bride and restore everything that was taken by the cunning devil.

Matthew 28:18 And Jesus came and spake unto them, saying, All power is given unto me in heaven and in earth. 20 Teaching them to observe all things whatsoever I have commanded you: and, lo, I am with you always, even unto the end of the world. Amen.

Use His given authority in His name to do supernatural things.

Mark 16:17 And these signs shall follow them that believe; In my name shall they cast out devils; they shall speak with new tongues 18 They shall take up serpents; and if they drink any deadly thing, it shall not hurt them; they shall lay hands on the sick, and they shall recover.

Go and spread the message everywhere, don't just sit in the pew, the Lord has given you authority.

Mark 16:20 And they went forth, and preached everywhere, the Lord working with them, and confirming the word with signs following. Amen.

By believing and taking the next step of baptism, old sins can be buried and new life can be found through the name of Jesus. It was in 325 AD that Satan exploited a particular scripture to create confusion surrounding the trinity, seeking to undermine Christ and emphasize the distinct offices within the Godhead. Father, Son, and Holy Spirit serve as the headings for the one God. All last names are contained within the name Jesus.

Mark 16:15 And he said unto them, Go ye into all the world, and preach the gospel to every creature. 16 He that believeth and is baptized shall be saved; but he that believeth not shall be damned.

You've been granted the authority and instructions. Now complete the task.

The Holy Spirit manifested within us to further the endeavor of healing, delivering, and reclaiming what was taken, stolen, and destroyed.

Acts 1:8 But ye shall receive power, after that the Holy Ghost comes upon you: and ye shall be witnesses unto me both in Jerusalem, and in all Judaea, and Samaria, and unto the uttermost part of the earth.

At every location I visited, they made efforts to restrict me within the confines of their religious sects. Furthermore, they conduct training programs for individuals affiliated with their denomination, organization, and non-denominations to earn money. Lord didn't do that; instead, He liberated them to advance His Kingdom's work.

If you work for Jesus, you'll witness and experience His power, authority, and supernatural work, bringing you joy.

Mark 2:12 And immediately he arose, took up the bed, and went forth before them all; insomuch that they were all amazed, and glorified God, saying, We never saw it on this fashion.

If you submit to and obey Jesus, the Lord has great power and can do amazing things. Continue in His word. Seek, ask, and knock; do not faint or compromise. Do not give up or give in.

1 Corinthians 2:9 But as it is written, Eye hath not seen, nor ear heard, neither have entered into the heart of man, the things which God hath prepared for them that love him.

You will have joy when you see life restored and things happen beyond man's ability.

Luke 10:17 And the seventy returned again with joy, saying, Lord, even the devils are subject unto us through thy name.

Rejoicing for the right reason is what the Bible teaches us.

Luke 10:20 Notwithstanding in this rejoice not that the spirits are subject unto you; but rather rejoice, because your names are written in heaven.

To carry on His work, you must learn by following Jesus. You will do great.

John 14:12 Verily, verily, I say unto you, He that believeth on me, the works that I do shall he do also; and greater works than these shall he do; because I go unto my Father.

Believe in more excellence; the sky is a limit, nothing is impossible, and all things are possible. Accurate knowledge of His word can be obtained through following, obeying, and submitting.

Jesus's name was used for the baptism of Peter, Paul, John, Thomas, and the individuals at Pentecost. They were bestowed with the Holy Spirit, traveled afar, and proclaimed the salvation of their souls from the lake of fire through the authority and power of Jesus's name and the Holy Spirit. Being born of water and Spirit is the essential requirement for entering the kingdom of God.

JUNE 17

Unlock the kingdom of God by using the key, and be the first to show others, urging them to repent from all sins.

LET US PRAY

Heavenly Father, thank you for giving us authority in Jesus's name. We are so glad that we can follow you anywhere, anytime. Your love to repurchase us from the devil is beyond our understanding. May the Lord help us that we use authorities, setting all free, and the devil runs from us. My Lord, your name can heal, deliver, heal a broken heart, and set the captive free. Free us from the demon of religion, organization, denominations, and non-denominations to go forward and do what you did. Lord, we are in need of help and guidance. Just like the disciple, we submit. We drop all like the drop on their net to follow you. Anoint us with your Holy Spirit in Jesus's name. Amen! God bless you!

JUNE 18

LEVEL UP YOUR LIFESTYLE TO GOD'S EXPECTATIONS!

The creator of the universe showcases their style through the world's breathtaking beauty and endless variety. Heaven, earth, everything around us, beneath the earth, and all great things we see or do not see are part of the creative mind of the creator. The desire of our Heavenly Father, who is our creator, is to bless His creation. However, the children refuse to meet God's expectations. We disappoint our earthly parents by failing to meet their expectations.

Job's lifestyle led to the Lord granting him everything. He was referred to as the richest man in the world as God doesn't hesitate to bless him abundantly. The child of a king will never have to beg for food or go without it. The King's children are bestowed with the highest quality, and He expects you to raise your standards to meet His level. Bringing your life to God's standard involves obeying His statutes, commandments, and keeping His precepts. According to the creator, one who meditates day and night will never live a normal life.

Job 1:1 There was a man in the land of Uz, whose name was Job; and that man was perfect and upright, and one that feared God, and eschewed evil.

God protected man on every side from the attack of the enemy.

Job 1:3a so that this man was the greatest of all the men of the east.

God keeps the standard of His children high so that no one can compete with us. The Lord gives and takes it away.

Joshua 1:8 says that your success is in your obedience to the laws and commandments of God and not in your smartness. Do not try any craftiness. You will fail yourself. God makes you rich.

Proverb 10:22 The blessing of the Lord, it maketh rich, and he addeth no sorrow with it.

Our question is, how do I receive blessings? Deuteronomy speaks about how to receive blessings.

Deuteronomy 11:26 Behold, I set before you this day a blessing and a curse;

JUNE 18

Deuteronomy 30:19 I call heaven and earth to record this day against you, that I have set before you life and death, blessing and cursing: therefore choose life, that both thou and thy seed may live:

God knows how to protect you from the devourer seeking to harm, destroy, and steal from you. When God gives instruction, the response should be doing, obeying, and submitting, not thinking, debating, or questioning. Fulfilling promises doesn't involve reading, but rather submitting without hesitation.

Deuteronomy 4:6 Observe them, for this will show your wisdom and understanding in the sight of the peoples, who will hear of all these statutes and say, "Surely this great nation is a wise and understanding people."

Walking with God grants us His superpower, protection, wisdom, knowledge, understanding, blessings, and riches, empowering us to navigate through life. This is not you but your God whom you put your trust. Abraham placed his faith in the Lord and followed His commands. To believe is to fully trust and commit without any reservations. Abraham believed.

Romans 4:3 For what saith the scripture? Abraham believed in God, and it was counted unto him for righteousness.

By trusting God, Abraham departed from his relatives, people, and homeland.

Hebrews 11:8 By faith Abraham, when he was called to go out into a place which he should after receive for an inheritance, obeyed; and he went out, not knowing whither he went.

Abraham, trusting in God, was ready to sacrifice his only son, the child he had at the age of 100, who was a promised child.

Genesis 13:2 And Abram was very rich in cattle, in silver, and gold.

How and why did he become so rich? He followed God's command faithfully. When you come to understand that the Lord is your superior and the one who created everything. If you want to be blessed by Him, you must observe His command, lead, and counsel. Nothing can prevent you from attaining His promotion, honor, riches, and blessings.

Don't forget, your blessings come from giving, but explore fresh ways to invest in the New Testament. To receive the blessings of 30, 60, 100, and unlimited, seek out the laborer of Jesus who serves as His prophet, evangelist, apostle, teacher, missionary, and pastor. The blessings of God can be spoken by them. They serve as conduits of God's message, but you are blessed for your devotion and adherence to God's will.

Matthew 25:34 Then shall the king say unto them on his right hand, Come, ye blessed of my Father, inherit the kingdom prepared for you from the foundation of the world:35 For I was hungered. Ye gave me meat: I was thirsty, and ye gave me drink: I was a stranger, and ye took me in:36 Naked, and ye clothed me: I was sick, and ye visited me: I was in prison, and ye came unto me.37 Then shall the righteous answer him, saying, Lord, when saw we thee an hungered, and fed thee? Or thirsty, and gave thee drink?38 When saw we thee a stranger, and took thee in? or naked, and clothed thee? 39 Or when saw we thee sick, or in prison, and came unto thee? 40 And the King shall answer and say unto them, Verily I say unto you, since ye have done it unto one of the least of these my brethren, ye have done it unto me.

This king is the creator and has compassion, love, concern, and understanding for the creation. Make sure to visit sick individuals when you encounter them. Don't be quick to judge when you encounter someone in prison; instead, make an effort to visit and pray for them. If they're hungry or thirsty, provide them with food and a drink. If you encounter naked individuals, be sure to provide them with suitable attire and offer hospitality to any unfamiliar people you meet.

According to the Bible, the Lord holds an important standard. If you obey His teachings, you will experience transformation.

Joseph was sold by his jealous and envious brother. Due to his integrity, he refused to remain a slave and was subsequently elevated to a position beside the king. Daniel remained faithful to God's commandments without any compromise. Among magicians, enchanters, astrologers, and diviners, he was the greatest. Keep Him first, and He will keep you above everything else.

Remaining faithful to God's covenant brings blessings.

Malachi 3:12 And all nations will call you blessed, For you will be a delightful land, Says the LORD of hosts.

Your battle will be fought by the Lord to bring you freedom. Your captivity will turn around. He will set you free and make you prosperous overnight. Seek God, humble yourself, and forgive my sins, which have separated me from you. Seek forgiveness for my wrongdoing, including adultery, fornication, witchcraft, lying, idolatry, hatred, variance, emulations, wrath, strife, seditions, heresies, envying, murders, drunkenness, reveling, and the like.

The danger within is greater than the danger around you.

2 Peter 2:7 And delivered just Lot, vexed with the filthy conversation of the wicked:

The Bible testifies.

Genesis 13:5 And Lot also, which went with Abram, had flocks, and herds, and tents. 6 And the land could not bear them that they might dwell together: for their substance was great so that they could not dwell together.

Remember, God makes you rich if you keep Him first and obey His commandment. Are you aware of what God expects from you today? Wash away your sins by being baptized in the name of Jesus. Take the next step and receive His Spirit to guide, teach, and empower you in the world. Uncover Him through the sacred text known as the Bible. Obtain the accurate KJV Bible for blessings on the land.

In the modern era, people want what they can see for themselves.

In Matt 6:33 But seek ye first the kingdom of God, and his righteousness, and all these things shall be added unto you.

It is adding the machine of the Lord, not yours.

JUNE 18

When you align with God's will, you won't feel the need to undermine or criticize others who are more successful than you. Learn the lesson on how to go higher and do the same. Don't repeat Cain's mistake by killing your brother. Learn from King Saul's mistake and don't let jealousy drive you to harm others, like his attempt to kill David.

1Peter 2:9 But ye are a chosen generation, a royal priesthood, a holy nation, a peculiar people; that ye should shew forth the praises of him who hath called you out of darkness into his marvelous light; 10 Which in time past were not a people, but are now the people of God: which had not obtained mercy, but now have obtained mercy.

By wholeheartedly following the Lord Jesus, you become Royal as He is the King of Kings and Lord of Lords. All is in your lap, so pay attention to your heart since your heart is the origin of your life. The heart is a deceptive and wicked organ that demands cleansing from evil in order to reveal its virtuous core.

Proverb 3:5 trust in the Lord with all thine heart; lean not unto thine own understanding. 6 In all thy ways acknowledge him, and he shall direct thy paths.

Do not acknowledge Him after you mess up for not taking the counsel of God. A big job is to keep your ways, heart, and life aligned with the Lord.

Psalms 139:23 Search me, O God, and know my heart: try me, and know my thoughts: 24 And see if there be any wicked way in me, and lead me in the way everlasting.

Bring your level to God's expectation. His expectation is high.

Micah 6:8 He hath shewed thee, O man, what is good; and what doth the LORD require of thee, but to do justly, and to love mercy, and to walk humbly with thy God?

LET US PRAY

Father God, your expectation for your children is always great. We know we mess up by having our wicked ways. Lord, help to take counsel first with you. Keep us continuing in your laws, commandments, and ways. We want to be recognized as wise and good people of God. Our citizenship is in heaven if we keep walking and following you. Our Father, which is in heaven, thy kingdom come, and thy will be done on earth as it is in heaven in Jesus 'name. Amen! God bless you.

JUNE 19

GOD IS THE SAME ALL THE TIME!

God remains unchanged and is resistant to any influence that might cause Him to change. If you follow His plan, you will witness God's merciful nature. Accepting His rescue plan grants forgiveness and deliverance from hellfire. God created hell for Satan and His Fallen Angels. We should always keep in mind the importance of following God's plan to save ourselves and those around us. In order to align with His word, we must change as He has not and will not. All who search for His presence, He discloses His plans.

Psalms 102:27 But thou art the same, and thy years shall have no end.

Malachi 3:6 For I am the LORD, I change not; therefore ye sons of Jacob are not consumed.

There is only one God, not two, three, or many. Keep in mind that Jesus is the manifestation of Jehovah who shed his blood. Jesus wasn't the second God, but rather the embodiment of God's spirit in human form to sacrifice himself. He came to pay the penalty for our sins. He required a blood price that was without sin.

In what way can a divine spirit afford the price of blood? That's why Spirit God took on a physical form and sacrificed Himself. Awesome!

Revelation 22:13 I am Alpha and Omega, the beginning and the end, the first and the last.

The only thing you should seek is God. I can assist you in finding the solution to your problem. He is first and last. No matter what ancient gods and goddesses are there, Jehovah God was before them. They could be obsolete but not as old as our Lord!

As you know, the devil, his fallen angel, and all demons can lie that they are ancient. Yes, they are, but the creation is not as ancient as the creator. Those ancient gods and goddesses are evil spirits.

Jehovah God is the beginning and the ending, first and last. The Lord was the only one who was first.

In the beginning, the earth was created by the Lord. It is a fact that the earth has been proven to be ancient. God's word's credibility is supported by history, although history itself is not divine. The final word belongs to the Lord!

God is the only one you have to believe in.

JUNE 19

Revelation 5:12 Says with a loud voice; Worthy is the Lamb that was slain to receive power, and riches, and wisdom, and strength, and honor, and glory, and blessing.

Come to the Lord for strength and power. With the arrival of the Lord's Spirit, Samson engaged in a mass slaughter. The power of God comes when you receive His spirit. The Holy Spirit can help you find the correct route. The Spirit of Truth, also known as the Spirit of God, remains constant.

Do you need riches? The Lord owns the cattle on the thousand hills. The Lord can multiply the fishes. If you have faith in the true God, Jehovah, you can have anything you need - water, food, diamonds, treasures, or whatever it may be. Rather than wondering where to find wealth, seek Jesus. God is the provider. What does a nation suffering from poverty need? Jesus, the real God.

Those who were once poor and turned to Jesus bear witness to the supernatural provision of the Lord. Those who have converted to Christianity declare their transformation from having nothing to now possessing food, shelter, a freezer, and even the means to lend money. The Christian faith does not involve monetary contributions for conversion, instead, believers trust in Jesus as the Provider. Never think that Christians bribe people to convert to Christianity. People often dream of a better life in prosperous countries, but when they bring their gods and goddesses, they end up facing poverty and homelessness, just like back in their own nations. Our role is to guide and share the information given by the true God. The true Father would never forsake us or allow us to starve. Jesus, the CEO of the world, demonstrates excellent management for the creation who acknowledges Him as the One true God.

God remains unchanged for all eternity. Only the Bible contains information about creation, unlike any other religious book. The Lord Jehovah has created heaven and earth. God is responsible for all creation, while Satan and its crew of fallen angels and demons are behind all killing, destruction, and stealing.

Satan cannot bring you contentment, goodness, or satisfaction. Satan will consistently remind you of your mistakes. Satan will cause you to experience sadness and distress. He possesses the skill to deceive and leave you feeling disappointed. In a nutshell, being ensnared by the devil means being trapped in a constant cycle of confusion. Take a look at the country caught in the cycle of caste system, poverty, multiple languages, and class divisions. There is no way out of its trap except the Lord.

When you come out of those wish cycles, study the Bible. Allow the Holy Spirit to be your teacher and guide throughout your journey. The devil has many tricks, devices, and plans to keep you away from the Lord. Make sure not to sell yourself to the Christian religious organizations established by the devil. Our God delivers us, heals our wounds, saves our souls, and bestows blessings upon us. He is a rich and never-changing God.

You may be anywhere, but if you seek, you will find him. You can find Him anywhere. No matter where you are, he will be there to hear your cry and offer help.

1 King 20:28 And there came a man of God, and spake unto the king of Israel, and said, Thus saith the LORD, Because the Syrians have said, The LORD is God of the hills, but he is not God of the valleys, therefore will I deliver all this great multitude into thine hand, and ye shall know that I am the LORD.

When you repent, that is to turn from sin, thenceforth live a holy, righteous, and God-fearing life. Trust me, your connection with God will be extraordinary. You will experience the truthfulness of the word.

Experiencing His peace is beyond us; only God can give. Those who seek the truth will find that Jesus is a God of love and mercy.

Traveling the world as a minister, I see firsthand the wonders of God for those who seek Him. The key to unlocking wealth is in your possession. For a covenant to be established, both parties must fulfill the condition. Since God never changes, who needs to change? It's important to consistently remember God and His blessings, or else we may lose them.

Poverty is not a part of God's plan for his people. He gives in abundance.

Deuteronomy 28:12 The Lord shall open unto thee his good treasure, the heaven to give the rain unto thy land in his season, and to bless all the work of thine hand: and thou shalt lend unto many nations, and thou shalt not borrow. 13 And the Lord shall make thee the head, and not the tail; and thou shalt be above only, and thou shalt not be beneath; if that thou hearken unto the commandments of the Lord thy God, which I command thee this day, to observe and to do them:

Our problem arises from ignorance about God, the ultimate CEO of the universe. You can rest assured that God's emotions and state of mind are not your concern. The God I am introducing you is not 2000 years old, but He is from eternity. He came in the flesh to shed blood 2000 years ago. His existence is eternal. The testimony talks about who He is.

The Israelites were the only nation with access to the True God. When the Israelites strayed from the truth, the Lord offered His blood as a way for forgiveness to those who believed in Jesus. Through purifying our sins with the blood of Jesus, we are able to access His throne room. The testimony's power confirms that He is a healer, deliverer, savior, and great God, meeting people of all nations, walks, and ages. Abraham encountered the creator of heaven and earth. God, who is the owner of the universe, needs no advertisement or introduction. However, just by mentioning His name, everything shifts. The very mention of His name causes hell to tremble. It is our job to reach out to the sick. You don't have to wander in the dark. There is no point in creating gods or goddesses out of silver, gold, or stone, as they are incapable of providing assistance. I have received assurance from the creator that I can transform the dry land into green, the barren land into fruitful, and a wilderness into a pool of water. To continue your search, open the Bible and read the ancient testimonies. It was preserved by God in the book called the Bible. Verify and evaluate its authenticity. His word remains just as powerful now as it was from the beginning. Salvation is not limited to the Israelites; it is a great privilege for all who believe. Forgiveness and eternal life have been granted to all creation through His blood. The only condition is to submit and obey. God's warnings and testimonies have assured us for centuries that He remains constant. I'll give you the information you need to find the way out if you're willing to change. The devil is working on the earth since his time is not up yet to be thrown into hell for eternity. Hear the voice of God; His name is Jesus, and His Spirit is called the Holy Spirit or Holy Ghost. There is only One spirit, and God is that spirit. May God help us grasp His essence as He meets our needs and performs specific actions to aid His creation in the current time and situation. Jehovah incorporated a multitude of adjectives into the name Jehovah. It's not a different God, but rather a characteristic of God. All the knowledge we need to know has been granted by his power.

God possesses holiness, self-sufficiency, wealth, omnipresence, omniscience, omnipotence, faithfulness, wisdom, and mercy. The list can go on and on. He excels in all areas. God is love; God is good. Your life will be completely different once you understand and shift your focus away from other gods and goddesses. He has given promises, benefits, deliverance, and healings that are beyond comprehension. To know Jesus,

JUNE 19

one must have a revelation. If you have faith, he is capable of anything. There is nothing impossible if you believe. To obtain it, you need to believe, trust, and stand firm on His promises. We cannot stop praising and worshipping this great, unchanging God?

LET US PRAY

Heavenly Father, we thank you. You are the same yesterday, today, and forever. Thank you for your assurance. We thank you for your power and love beyond our imagination. Lord, we thank you for creating us in your image to serve you and love you. We ask you whole heartily to give us your attribute, so the world sees you in us. We thank you for your new mercy every day. Thank you for your provision and protection. You are faithful, and you will never fail us in Jesus 'name. Amen! God bless you!

JUNE 20

LIVE FOR JESUS!

Live for Jesus in all seasons of the year. You live for Jesus in any country, continent, or city. Live for Jesus at the seashore, church, home, market, gym, and all places. On all occasions, live for Him. Live for Jesus as He desires how His bride should represent her in the world. You are His bride by the seashore and in the market as well. You are His bride in any nation and walking in any season. There is not a season too hot or cold in the world.

There is an Attire for the bride of Jesus and the harlot's attire.

Proverb 7:10 And, behold, there met him a woman with the attire of a harlot, and subtil of heart.

The Prostitute has a clothing style. You do not have to guess second seeing one in a specific dress style. Right away, you can figure it out. Oh, she is a prostitute. But what happens when society wears harlot or prostitute clothing? We see the change in the world—the significant change in thinking and interest.
If you see a Muslim woman walking on the street, no one lusts for her, but a woman walking half naked, a man will have a problem looking at her flesh.

I heard one preacher say a lady will start wearing little shorter clothes when she is not finding a boyfriend. Why? So she can seduce the man. David saw the naked woman and was enticed by her body. It is in the man who sees the body to lust. Who is guilty? The one who caused her body to be naked, or one who saw the naked body and allowed the dirty mind to take over? You judge yourself.

It is the lack of knowledge on both sides. God gave the first lesson in the garden of Eden to wear a robe by disapproving of the Apron. The mind was innocent before eating the fruit of knowledge of good and evil. Now the senses are charged to know bad and good. It arouses sexual desire in a man by a woman, showing the flesh, so she shouldn't. So when you are raped or sexually harassed, find out where to make changes. If you have parents unaware of this, they are equally guilty. God has given total authority to parents to raise, train, and teach correctly. Dress to cover your body, be modest, and teach the same to your children. I am so glad I came years ago to the US, where they taught about the dress code according to the Bible and not Hollywood. May the Lord help us protect our children by telling them the truth.

The Bible has recorded God's testimony of people's actions. God knows the difference between rebellious and obedient.

JUNE 20

Genesis 18:19 For I know him, that he will command his children and his household after him, and they shall keep the way of the LORD, to do justice and judgment; that the LORD may bring upon Abraham that which he hath spoken of him.

Genesis 17:9 And God said unto Abraham; Thou shalt keep my covenant, therefore, thou, and thy seed after thee in their generations.

God asked parents and grandparents to teach the laws of God to their children and grandchildren. Please teach and guide them, do not be afraid so they do not get raped or molested by a stranger, cousin, grandfather, or father. Even anyone who can reach them. Most relatives molest most girls.

I talked with an elderly lady friend. She said her daughter's husband did something wrong with the 7-year-old granddaughters. My elderly lady friend said, Elizabeth, the little girl, wears very few clothes. See? This 90-year-old lady knows the correct dress since her mind has not accepted Satan's dress code. Further, she said, her daughter's husband is in jail for three years. The daughter divorced her husband for inappropriately touching her daughter's little body. A little girl is innocent, but the daughter's husband is not. But if you allow the little girl to wear whatever, then do not blame the man. You dress your children to cover their bodies.

I remember reading a court article about a woman walking in a little too short a dress. Now, this is in India, where people are cautious of modesty. Even today, Indian women love modesty. Now everywhere, someone has a prostitute mentality. Mother or grandmother, do not dress your little daughter to victimize their little body. Remember, God made a robe to cover, not to reveal the body.

The Lord said I do not change, so please do not conform to the world's standard. The carelessness of not teaching causes our children emotional trauma!

This is from the Huff post:

Every 98 seconds, they sexually assaulted someone in the US. That means every single day, 570 ladies experience sexual violence in the country. Stay out of trouble by dressing according to the Bible code. Do not give an open invitation to a man by wearing the wrong clothing. Cover up, and people will respect your body. Learn to respect your body by dressing right.

1 Timothy 2:9 In like manner also, that women adorn themselves in modest apparel, with shamefacedness and sobriety; not with broided hair, or gold, or pearls, or costly array;

How will the Lord feel when He sees His creation walking half-naked? It hurts the creator more than you imagine since He gave instructions very plain and clear. But your parents and grandparents think you must look like the world and act like the world. How sad! Dressing right is wise. It is not conservative or old-fashioned. God has always warned us of the effect disobedience and rebellion. You are too bold if you dress your kid, knowing the consequences. Are you ignorant or flat have no sense? Or both?

Whenever a woman needs a favor, she will put on provocative dresses. She is simply saying; you are welcome. Just give me a favor. Many women do not know that God gives favor. We won't see mentally disturbed children in our society if we do the right thing.

They raped many and now cannot function well. Their mind is already damaged. Society does not help much. I see the mother and father walking with their young girl, almost naked, from the swimming pool to their house. I just look at the other side and don't want to see the nakedness. Too bold to be naked in the middle of the street. Get ready for them to be kidnapped and sold into prostitution. Who allowed this? You are not following the correct instructions given to Adam and Eve. When the media represents naked girls, they need bodyguards. Can you afford one? The mind that rapes is carnal and filled with pornography. You must not violate your freedom. God knows best for His creation and gives you the laws and precepts, not advice. It is not a suggestion; it is a commandment.

Many times I question, what are you thinking? What are you wearing and walking in the middle of the street?

Some will argue that it is my body. I do what I feel like doing. You also have to be ready for judgment if you are violating the laws of God, who made your body. God has created you for Him. God is Holy, so dress Holy. Dressing unholy will give Satan control over you. How to keep the devil out, just get holy, modest apparel. Learn from the Muslims; they know better than Christians as far as dress is concerned.

God is a judge, but you cause the judgment to execute against you by stepping over God's commandment. God knows what is best for you, while the devil finds how to destroy you. Enjoy your life by keeping His laws, commandment, and precept in your heart. That is best for you and your little soul. God has promised to keep and hide you in His wings. He will bless you only if you submit your ways and will to God's commandments and laws. If you transgress and disobey, then you are not His responsibility. Judgment will be on the way.

Genesis 3: 23 Therefore the Lord God sent him forth from the garden of Eden, to till the ground from whence he was taken. 24a So he drove out the man;

Soon, life will be over. The Lord said you would surely die the day you eat the fruit of good and evil. Death means eternal death in hell. Are you hot? Know the hell.

Luke 16:24 And he cried and said, Father Abraham, have mercy on me, and send Lazarus, that he may dip the tip of his finger in water, and cool my tongue; for I am tormented in this flame.

Hell has no air-conditioning to cool its tongue or body. So think about those people who are hot and dress naked. What will happen if they go to hell for not covering the body?

Be careful; God meant what He said. May the Lord give us the far sight of eternity to see the power of God ruling in the future.

LET US PRAY

Lord, give us teachers to make us knowledgeable of the truth. The truth can set us free. The truth is a powerful weapon against the enemy. We cause judgment. If we are parents, then we must handle our children. Jesus, give our friends, family, pastors, and teachers the truth to teach. We do not care about the sugar-coated lie; it is harmful to our souls. Our bodies will be back in the dirt, but our souls will suffer if we do not act according to the word of God. Help us, Lord. We do not want our family or loved ones in

JUNE 20

hell. I thank you personally for teaching me the Word of Truth. It has blessed my soul. I am passing by on earth, so keep me from tricks, traps, and devices of Satan in Jesus's name. Amen! God bless you!

JUNE 21

TIME TO STAND FOR THE TRUTH!

The truth is the most powerful weapon against lies. The liar has no hearing. Their destination is hell. The matter is resolved once you speak the truth. The truth is spoken in the Bible. Satan is anti-truth. God is the truth. That's why Satan is fighting against Jesus. It's true that Satan fears the truth. Satan lies, and liars cannot stand before God.

John 8:44 Ye are of your father the devil, and the lusts of your father ye will do. He was a murderer from the beginning and abode not in the truth because there is no truth in him. When he speaketh a lie, he speaketh of his own: for he is a liar and the father of it.

Jesus is a faithful God, and Satan flees from Him. Satan left the body of a possessed man when Jesus walked by him. With Jesus living in him, Peter's shadow became a conduit for healing, deliverance, and freedom. If Lord Jesus lives within you, your presence can overpower the devil's actions. In God, there is unwavering faithfulness and absolute truth.

When two or more witnesses agree, it's a closed case. Our belief rests on the absolute truth of the Word of God. It is a done deal. Once we declare the truth, everything is complete.

During the late 1970s, while immersed in my law studies, the Spirit of God visited me and explained a specific case. Showing me the connection between this law and that law, he revealed that winning the case is possible. I agreed by saying "Yes." But the Lord honors divine law only. The Lord has no hidden lie to corrupt the system. I perceived the mistake of applying the law to that specific case and comprehended it thoroughly. I would have achieved success by favoring one law over another. If you choose a career in law, the Lord says you will engage in lies.

I've realized the untruth. Wow! Thank you, Lord. So, I accepted a job with very little pay, but I would have earned my monthly salary in a day if I had practiced law. Many people have criticized my decision to not pursue law. I received advice from many people. You don't need to practice law, just sign and authorize court documents. The moment I heard the Lord, I realized I couldn't pursue a career in law. Money has a tendency to be elusive. Furthermore, the sovereign of heaven speaks. It is the ultimate word you wish to listen to. There is no plan better than His plan. The Lord rescued me. The truth is found in God's teachings. It brings me immense happiness that I can hear God's voice.

JUNE 21

God and you can have a smooth and uncomplicated relationship only when God speaks, and you hear and obey. The key to maintaining a truthful relationship is obedience. Your path can be very smooth if you listen and obey.

The devil has fear and lies. He'll deceive you by pointing out obstacles in the ocean and the absence of water in the desert. The water is bitter. Let the devil know the Lord is coming to the rescue. Start praising God for all that He has done for you. The devil will run. Write all He did and say the Lord will add one more miracle for me. There is nothing that God cannot do. Nothing is too difficult for the Lord. This is the truth.

Today's generation would benefit if they no longer relied on government support, such as social services, welfare, and food stamps. To prevent harm to themselves and children, they must stay away from adultery, fornication, body abuse, and misusing the future. Drawing a bigger paycheck should not be the reason for having children. Provide for your family's needs. You were blessed by God with two hands for work and a brilliant mind. Use it. Please protect people, succeed, and think of their well-being. It's important for you to support your children by staying true to yourself, rather than relying on them for support.

Standing on the truth of God can lead to a brighter future for our society and our children. The devil's strategy is to confuse and misguide you. Don't be deceived by the devil's offer in the money package; instead, uncover the hidden sin in the box. Our source must be the Lord; our provision should come from Jehovah Jireh. Your life will blossom with scripture if you rely on it. Give Jesus a chance by standing on true, unadulterated truth in the Word of God. Fear, greed, or circumstances lead us astray from the truth. May the Lord help you stand tall! May the Lord grant you the courage to trust in its unwavering effectiveness!

I remembered a co-worker telling me about going to almost all the churches in Los Angeles. He did not find the truth. He was the friend of a lady co-worker. It was a sad story. When we first crossed paths, he had no idea about my beliefs. Despite that, he lacked moral character in his actions. I discussed the truth with my co-worker and watched it unfold for over an hour. When the anointing touched her, she realized her life was in danger and turned to the Lord. Living a sinful life is no longer an option for her. Seeing her friend's concern, I took over the Bible study and he was adamant about being baptized. On baptism day, the demons were pulling him, and at one moment, powerful monsters came over to tear him and the Bible. Through the intercession of the saints, he accessed the right mindset to defeat the devil in a crucial moment. As soon as they baptized him in the name of Jesus, his problems were over. He had been taking drugs, drinking, committing adultery, and many things called sin. He was even attending a church without the knowledge of God and having nothing to do with the truth of God.

God said:

Deuteronomy 11:13 And it shall come to pass, if ye shall hearken diligently unto my commandments which I command you this day, to love the LORD your God, and to serve him with all your heart and with all your soul, 14 That I will give you the rain of your land in his due season, the first rain and the latter rain, that thou mayest gather in thy corn, and thy wine, and thine oil. 15 And I will send grass in thy fields for thy cattle, that thou mayest eat and be full.

The fulfillment of Bible promises hinges on how you act and react to God's laws and commandments. Both co-workers were baptized in the name of Jesus and received the power of the Holy Spirit to fight evil. It is pitch dark out there in the world. It is dark where all follow whatever they feel like. People know of Jesus but do not know Him as a deliverer, healer and problem solver. False teachers and prophets have not taught me to know God. The commandments are never taught as something to practice or abide by. That is the reason people fall into the trap of Satan.

The Lord's words of truth are universal, reaching every continent, country, and nation. He does not deviate, vary, or mix up the idea of the culture, color, and people. Sinkholes and lava cannot shake the foundation of truth. It's proven and will continue to prove that the only solid ground is the truth of the Bible. Satan's strategy is evident through the media, movies, and technology, which aim to momentarily satisfy you. If you are looking for help to rescue your soul or protection over your life, you must go to the truth of the Bible. The signs and wonders prove the soundness of the word of truth. Whether poor, rich, white, black, or of any nationality, testimonies reveal the Lord's truth, healing, deliverance, heart-mending, and life-giving attributes. Peace, joy, comfort, and guidance are gifts from the Lord. He has proven nothing is impossible; all things are possible.

May we be blessed with the wisdom of Daniel, the faith of Abraham, and the determination of David to follow the Lord.

Every day, you will be blessed with His new mercy and grace. He said it and meant it. The Lord fulfills the roles of a shepherd, provider, and protector for our souls, families, nations, and the world. God will never leave us and forsake us. May you proclaim throughout the world His truth in Jesus's name. Amen!

Daniel 6:25 Then king Darius wrote unto all people, nations, and languages, that dwell in all the earth; Peace be multiplied unto you. 26 I make a decree, That in every dominion of my kingdom, men tremble and fear before the God of Daniel: for he is the living God, and steadfast forever, and his kingdom that which shall not be destroyed, and his dominion shall be even unto the end. 27 He delivereth and rescueth and worketh signs and wonders in heaven and the earth, who hath delivered Daniel from the power of the lions.

LET US PRAY

Lord, many Bible characters have proven that you are living God by standing on the truth of your word. Lord, use us as well. It is our duty to read the Bible and obey it. The Bible is the book of Life. It is the life manual to correct, reform, and get the direction of the highway of heaven. Lord, we need the power of truth to stand. Everything is shaking, falling, and moving away. But if we stand on the truth, the water cannot bury us, and fire cannot burn us. Lord, raise the standard against every storm of life. Hide us in your wings and shadow as we stand on your word of truth in the name of Jesus. Amen! God bless you!

JUNE 22

LONG SUFFERING OF GOD!

The suffering endured by parents is well-known. It's quite a task to raise and care for each child.

But when we see the patience of our Lord, it is beyond our comprehension. God is patient and gives His creation time to repent. Repent means to turn from your wrongdoing. Wrongdoing can take you to hell. He constantly talks to us differently, using different people or correction rods.

I have seen people realize the consequences of their stubborn ways at the end of the road. They now understand that I've reached the point of no return and it's the end of the line. Even so, God holds the power to grant forgiveness for sins.

Remember the man on the cross, He said.

Luke 23:40 But the other answering rebuked him, saying, Dost, not thou fear God, seeing thou art in the same condemnation? 41 And we indeed justly; for we receive the due reward of our deeds: but this man hath done nothing amiss.

Look at the thief on the cross who said; I deserve this punishment because I am a sinner. The sinner must say that I am wrong and rightfully going through this punishment. You are right, Lord, but I am wrong. Have mercy on m e and forgive me. Forgiveness can be obtained with very little effort. You should open your mouth and confess. Before the final moment, the thief acknowledged wrongdoing and confessed. Forgive me.

Luke 23:42 And he said unto Jesus, Lord, remember me when thou comest into thy kingdom.43 And Jesus said unto him, Verily I say unto thee, today shalt thou be with me in paradise.

That's all it takes, just confess. Long-suffering of God is to bring us to the place where we say, Lord, I confess I am a sinner. God will wipe away all sins, and you are free to go. Lord, remember me in your Kingdom. It is God's kingdom; a sinner cannot enter without repenting and receiving forgiveness for sins. His suffering on earth shows He loves us beyond our imagination. The Lord is merciful. Get rid of pride and say, please help me. I am a sinner.

I remembered the prophet caught in adultery. Instead of repenting, he started a religion where all could commit adultery and practice polygamy. He made it legal by not repenting. God urges us to repent, confess, and change our prideful ways instead of rebelling.

Long suffering has time.

Matthew 18:22 Jesus saith unto him, I say not unto thee, Until seven times: but, Until seventy times seven. You're disqualified if you surpass the limit set by God. God proclaims judgment on people if they do not change and offers excuses. Confession with repentance is what will solve our problems. The Lord is there to forgive instead of punish.

2 Peter 3:9 The Lord is not slack concerning his promise, as some men count slackness; but is long-suffering to us-ward, not willing that any should perish, but that all should come to repentance.

Many times, we voice our complaints to the Lord regarding those who do evil. Why is the Lord not taking revenge? Today, I pray to you, Lord, seeking vengeance against my enemy. Remember how you feel about all your children? You want your children to be saved—especially the ones at fault and living a sinful lifestyle. You pray since you are worried about them. Many pray and plead for them all their life. Just as an earthly parent who cares, your heavenly father watches over you, but with even greater attention. We who are His creation must remember that He has paid a greater price. If God can wait until one repents on the cross, on the deathbed, or at the last breath, then we should also wait. His long-suffering also has limits. If you do not show remorse, then He is done dealing with you. Keep forgiving, even if it exceeds seven times seventy.

2 Peter 3:15 And account that the long-suffering of our Lord is salvation; even as our beloved brother Paul also according to the wisdom given unto him hath written unto you;

Paul, viewed by the Lord as a Christian who committed murder, took many lives. Yet, as people persisted in praying and pleading for Paul, God encountered him on the road to Damascus and confronted him. Paul then repented and surrendered. Pray for the most notorious and rebellious individual. One day, someone's pleading will bring salvation to them. Be merciful, kind, and long-suffering.

Roman 2:4 Or 183 espises thou the riches of his goodness and forbearance and long-suffering; not knowing that the goodness of God leadeth thee to repentance?

We need to be long-suffering like God. Our long- suffering will bring someone to repentance.

The Israelites, who had endured severe slavery, quickly forgot their hardships. Despite their complaints, God remained incredibly patient with them. You say how silly of them; they forgot the beaten up and harsh slavery too. By His right hand, God brought freedom and inflicted plagues on the Egyptians. Still, murmurs and complaints were in their mouths. It demonstrates how quickly and easily we forget about God's goodness. If God is not long-suffering, we cannot last even a month.

Never take advantage of His long-suffering.

JUNE 22

Once settled in the promised land, God sent prophets like Jeremiah, Hosea, Joel, and others to correct and guide them. It shows that God does not react and act but warns and uses correcting rods, so we turn from wrongdoing.

In 1st Kings and 2nd Kings, God witnessed King Jeroboam-1 and many other kings, providing guidance to the northern kingdom. He soon saw them turn away from the living God to worship a calf, building idols and groves, and went whoring after the gods of the land, Baalim, Ashteroth, and all others. In the year 722 BC, God removed Judah from their land.

We are observing a repetition of the same circumstances today. We have the true prophets and teachers of the Lord that keep warning us to repent, repent and repent! The message should be something other than prosperity. If we turn to the Lord by amending our ways, He will bring prosperity.

The instruction from God is to seek His kingdom and righteousness, and in return, He will grant you all that you need. Hear! Seek religion, idols, or prosperity for a fulfilling life.

God will give all if we Love God with all heart, mind, soul, and strength. It takes time for the consequences of our wrongdoing to manifest. If you keep doing wrong, the Lord will have the day and time to enforce the judgment. Read the word of God and see God has a limit and will not put it off. Do not let Him find you sleeping.

Luke 21:34 And take heed to yourselves, lest at any time your hearts be overcharged with surfeiting, and drunkenness, and cares of this life, and so that day come upon you unawares.

Both you and I were included in the warning and correction mentioned in the Bible.

Psalms 94:13 That thou mayest give him rest from the days of adversity until the pit be dug for the wicked.

Moses pleaded for the stiff-necked, stubborn Israelites, and God forgave them. Your pleading will help God in His long suffering.

Your long-suffering with prayer can do mighty works.

In the end, if evil has gone too far and there is no repentance in the land, judgment comes! God loves and is patient with us, so we must be patient with others.

Noah built the Arc for maybe 60 to 70 years. Noah, the prophet of the righteous, kept preaching to the lost world to repent and take shelter in the ark to survive, but his word fell on deaf ears. We pray for the Lord's mercy and for him to open our ears and eyes. Lord, grant us leaders who will proclaim fasts like the city of Nineveh, resulting in the people turning from evil and receiving God's forgiveness.

Psalms 86:15 But thou, O Lord, art a God full of compassion, and gracious, long-suffering, and plenteous in mercy and truth.

LET US PRAY

Lord, we are blessed and thankful to have you as our God. We are dirt and will be back in the dirt. Have mercy, oh Lord. The Long-suffering of God shows us He is our real father. You have mercy on us. Grant us the wisdom to count our days with a grateful heart. Give us a thankful heart so we never lose our salvation. Teach us to be merciful and long- suffering toward others. We pray for others, especially those who have done wrong to us. Your long-suffering is the key for someone to find salvation, so help us have long-suffering so that our prayer for others can bring salvation to many in Jesus's name. Amen! God bless you!

JUNE 23

WHEN GOD SAYS NO, DEVIL SAYS YES!

The kingdom of God is in conflict with the devil. The devil falsely claims to have a kingdom with greater power. Lies and deceit are the operating principles of his kingdom. God discusses the concepts of eternal life and death, which are still unknown to men.

Genesis 2:17 But of the tree of the knowledge of good and evil, thou shalt not eat of it: for in the day that thou eatest thereof thou shalt surely die.

Genesis 3:4 And the serpent said unto the woman, Ye shall not surely die:

Eve fell for the devil's deception and believed his lies. There is no immediate judgment when you make a mistake. On the day of judgment, you will see eternal punishment in the lake of fire. When you see people who do what God said they don't do and are still alive, you wonder why? That is why people think it is okay to do what God doesn't allow. It is not Okay. Do not believe the devil, he is a liar.

John 8:44 Ye are of your father the devil, and the lusts of your father ye will do. He was a murderer from the beginning and abode not in the truth because there is no truth in him. When he speaketh a lie, he speaketh of his own: for he is a liar and the father of it.

The only one who remains faithful is the Lord. Follow the Lord! His word has the power to rescue you from eternal damnation.

John 14:6a Jesus saith unto him, I am the way, the truth.

There is one Spirit, and God is that Spirit. God is the Spirit of truth. Lord, tell us the truth. Please help us understand you are real.

God said thou should not make idols. The Spirit of God took on flesh in order to shed His Blood. Blood has life He gave His life for my life. Do not worship Mary or Jesus's Idols. The truth can set us free, not the serpent religion.

Leviticus 26:1 Ye shall make you no idols, nor graven image, neither rear you up a standing image, neither shall ye set up any image of stone in your land, to bow down unto it: for I am the LORD your God.

We see many idols called gods and goddesses. Even Catholics have idols. Making idols is not part of what we do. Those who create cannot find assistance through their creative work. Scripture is clear-cut. Despite God's command against idols, the devil would populate the land with nothing but idols. I am from India; they have many big idols. People believe in and worship artificial representations. The true God said, do not make idols. The devil will say, make all kinds and shapes of idols. The devil is a liar. Please do not believe it. See what happens when you set an idol on God's created earth. The effects are identical - homelessness, hunger, thirst, poverty, and absence of blessings.

God did not have to dress Adam and Eve when they were naked and innocent. Once they ate the forbidden fruit of good and evil, they couldn't stay naked. Now their senses were opened to perceive good and evil, and could no longer walk naked. Both Adam and Eve made an apron, which didn't cover their nakedness. Revealing flesh can arouse man's sinful sexual desire. If a baby is naked, that is okay. The child is unaware of what is right or wrong and remains innocent. Prior to consuming the forbidden fruit, we were innocent, resembling a child. However, as kids age, they need to dress appropriately as their understanding of right and wrong develops. The Lord made Adam and Eve a robe to cover their nakedness completely. Now, the devil designs the clothes to show more skin which causes adultery, fornication, child molesting, and rape. The devil says you are hot; you need to wear summer clothes and look sexy. The majority of people in our country don't dress modestly. Satan always opposes God's instruction. The devil uses a model for immodest dresses. I never shop in some stores; as a matter of fact, I shop in a specific store in winter only. I used to have my clothes tailored in India to cover my body. My body is for Jesus.

Look at Muslims, Jews, Amish, and Mennonites. They keep the commandment of the Lord. They have excellent teachers to enforce the laws of God. God is good and knows the best. The devil despises God's creation and acts in direct opposition. He hates you and entices you as he did to Eve. Please stay in the Word of God, and keep an open heart to obey. There was a time when everyone dressed modestly. May the Lord give us an ear to hear and an obedient heart.

The devil tried Lord Jesus, but the Lord came against the devil by using the Word of God. We must stand against the devil by using the word. I always stand on His Word. I am not repeating the same mistakes as Eve, Adam, and many who followed the devil. God is not a mocker; we must follow the Lord Jesus. The devil has the same tactic of forbidding.

The Lord overcame Satan by saying:

Matthew 4:4 It is written, Matthew 4:7 It is written again, Matthew 4:10 for it is written.

The Lord is good by giving us His written word. Do not let the word of God collect dust. Start reading it and utilize it as a weapon against the devil.

Remember, your adversary lies, but the Lord speaks the truth. Thank you, Lord. The word of God is the way. The Word of God is your sword to chop the plan of the enemy. Commandments, precepts, and laws of the Lord will pluck you out of the trap of Satan. The devil cannot do anything, but if you are ignorant, you will take advantage of it. So open the Bible, write it down in your heart and mind, and practice it when traveling anywhere. Reject all the devil's opportunities.

I had a little problem when I learned that a woman should not wear a man's clothes, which are pants. It was inconvenient since my job requires standing, bending, and walking. Sometimes people commented and

JUNE 23

laughed at my modest apparel. We know the devil uses people to bully us. I said to the devil; I love God, and I also love my modest ladies' clothes.

I prioritize God over churches, pastors, or organizations. We keep the Word of God in our hearts. My lifestyle remained unchanged, and the Lord helped me overcome. I'm not obligated to conform or abide by Hollywood designers.

The day I came to the United States, I searched for the Lord. I learned as I sought Him. The place I grew up in lacked any form of teaching or awareness about the Lord. My life took a transformative turn when I discovered the Word of God. I loved it; it was a challenge since I had heard many comments about it. Living for God is going against the flow of Satan's world. Obedience is the key to entering the Word of God. Please do not say I do not have to; or I am excused. I wouldn't die. We are not spiritual, but you will be if you do the Word. I love the Lord and understand that all He said is for my benefit.

Later on, many admired me as they came for prayer, Bible study, or counseling. They never have to ask me, are you, a Christian? Some even said I knew you were a Christian when I saw you. See, the devil is a liar.

In our country, adultery, fornication, makeup, revealing clothing, immodesty, and personal freedom are accepted. There are no guidelines. It has ruined and confused us more as individuals and as a nation. Right is wrong, or they will bully you, but do as the Lord says. May the Lord be merciful to us! The devil tries to bring what the Lord has forbidden, but I confront him and tell him to go away. You do not own but a hell. The word of God is ingrained in my heart. I go anywhere worldwide; I have no problem with hot, cold, or family gatherings. I want to be a Christian everywhere. The Holy Spirit must shine through you and me. I refuse to conform to the world's standards; instead, I am transformed by living according to God's word. There is no second chance. The Lord said, repent, change your image to His glory. Don't conform to the world's likes, actions, smells, or thoughts. There is no match for the blessing of God.

The devil has deceived many with material possessions, but they only found themselves in hell. The devil tries to hurt our Lord by making us appear confused, crazy, hurt, and cursed, leaving us wondering and sweating. If we had followed God's commandment, we would have received His blessings. He would have taken you to an expected end. Ask Daniel, Joseph, David, and many more how they overcame. Say NO to the devil and yes to the Lord.

LET US PRAY

Lord, you are our light and door. A righteous person knows the Word of God and does it. Oh, Lord God, there is none like you and none beside you. May the Lord give us an obedient heart to bless our descendants. We want the world to be livable, bearable, endurable, secured, and blessed for others. We say no to the devil but yes to the Lord, even if we have to stand alone. May our Lord find us in the world to chase us to bless us for keeping His Word in Jesus's Name. Amen! God bless you!

JUNE 24

MAJOR CHANGES IN END-TIME CHURCHES!

God's Word forewarns us about the Major Changes that will occur in the end time. There's a shift happening for churches known as "den build by thief not founded on rock." I am talking about true churches built on the revelation of Jesus called Church on the rock. Those who remain in the book of Acts are the ones resistant to change.

1 Timothy 4:1 Now the Spirit speaketh expressly(= meant clearly), that in the latter times some shall depart from the faith, giving heed to seducing spirits, and doctrines of devils;

2 Timothy 3:1 This know also, that in the last days, perilous times shall come.4 Traitors, heady, highminded, lovers of pleasures more than lovers of God; 5 Having a form of godliness but denying the power thereof: from such turn away.

We all acknowledge that we are living in the final days. We notice individuals engaged in deep sin, yet they continue to attend Church.

What has happened? The ones responsible for the changes are not the Lord, but the itching ears of teachers. We have a wide selection of teachers to choose from. People choose teachers who allow them to continue in a sinful lifestyle. We must change our lifestyle if we walk according to the Word of God. Keep following the Word of God since God is Word and Word is God.

Warren Buffett said: Price is what you pay. Value is what you get.

The cross was where the Lord paid an enormous price for both you and me. We, His bride and creation, cost him His life. The value He paid is His Blood, sinless blood has life. Each day, I show my appreciation to God for the priceless love I am blessed with. If I hold that much significance, then He holds the same significance to me. Obey His Word. If you do the work accordingly, his word has a miraculous effect.

Many have departed from the truth. It is their choice to drift away from the fact.

I am going to talk about fasting today. Fasting is essential in the life of a Christian. Let us see two or three examples of fasting to establish the doctrine of fasting. You are spending time with the Lord while fasting.

JUNE 24

Exodus 34:28 And he was there with the LORD forty days and forty nights; he did neither eat bread nor drink water. (Moses)

Deuteronomy 9:18 And I fell down before the Lord, as at first, forty days and forty nights: I did neither eat bread nor drink water, because of all your sins which ye sinned, in doing wickedly in the sight of the Lord, to provoke him to anger.

Fasting is without food, bread is food and no water. In the divine presence of God, you can survive without food and water. You need the attention of God to intervene in a particular matter.

Israelites practiced fasting by not eating and drinking.

Esther 4:16 Go, gather together all the Jews that are present in Shushan, and fast ye for me, and neither eat nor drink three days, night or day: I also and my maidens will fast likewise;

What is fasting? Fasting is not eating and drinking. If you are eating and drinking, that means you are not fasting. Does it make sense? Do not look for a shortcut. Prayer becomes more powerful with fasting. It allows them to fight the demonic world and draws God's attention. You must seek two or three scriptures supporting the subject to establish doctrine. We cannot develop biblical doctrine by using one scripture.

Matthew 18:16 But if he will not hear thee, then take with thee one or two more, that in the mouth of two or three witnesses, every word may be established.

2 Corinthians 13:1a In the mouth of two or three witnesses shall every word be established.

Two or three witnesses are needed to establish doctrine in the spiritual or secular realm.

Why is fasting essential to be a Christian?

Matthew 17:21 Howbeit this kind goeth not out but by prayer and fasting.

We are in the army of God. We wrestle not against flesh and blood but against Satan and his army, demons, and fallen angels. If you want spiritual power, then you must fast. Jesus fasted so He could work effectively against the spiritual world in the flesh. Fasting can win the temptation of the lust of eyes, the flesh, and the pride of life. Mortify the flesh to win the spiritual battle. The flesh has a strong desire, but when you fast, your spirit gets more potent than the flesh. We can't fight the devil in the flesh. The devil and your flesh are alike or twine.

Did heathen know how to fast correctly? Yes, and they accomplished it with perfection. Why? Their example was that of the Israelites, who were neighbors.

Jonah 3:5 So the people of Nineveh believed God and proclaimed a fast,7, And he caused it to be proclaimed and published through Nineveh by the decree of the king and his nobles, saying, Let neither man nor beast, herd nor flock, taste any thing: let them not feed, nor drink water:

Fasting means refraining from both food and water. The remarkable outcome of doing Biblical fasting and not doing it correctly has zero results. Without following God's fasting guidelines, the Church won't experience deliverance from demons or see any transformation in life. The only way to cure drugs, cigarettes, schizophrenia, bipolar, and other demonic operations is through fasting and prayer.

People are possessed and oppressed. Does Christianity make false claims by asserting deliverance? Churches are being infiltrated by false teachers and prophets, pretending to be ministers of light. By distorting the Word of God, they brought chaos through false teaching. And that's the explanation for why twisted words aren't successful.

Once, I fasted three days and nights. Again, the Lord asked me to fast three days and nights for a certain person. I started my second three-day and night fast. Now I only knew the fasting correctly: no food and water. On the second occasion, I chose to take a small sip of water after two days, just a tiny amount. I thought I had finished three days and nights, so having a small amount of water should be fine. As soon as I sipped, Lord said, you are too fast again for three days and nights. Just for a sip? Why didn't He stop me when I was trying to get the water? Once again, I went without food and water for three more days and nights. I went without eating or drinking for a full nine days. See what it cost me.

In later years, I heard the name "fasting" attributed to Daniel and wondered what it meant. It is the kosher diet that God spoke to Jews in Leviticus chapter 11. As a form of fasting, Satan has started following a kosher diet.

In the book Daniel 1:8 But Daniel purposed in his heart that he would not defile himself with the portion of the king's meat, nor with the wine which he drank: therefore he requested of the prince of the eunuchs that he might not defile himself.

Leviticus Ch 11 talks about what to eat and not to eat. Daniel lived in Babylon and could not eat unclean food.

He requested, *Daniel 1:12a I beseech thee, ten days; and let them give us pulse to eat, and water to drink.*

Daniel's daily diet consisted of this, but let's see what he ate when he fasted.

Daniel 10:2 In those days, Daniel was mourning three full weeks. 3 I ate no pleasant bread, neither came flesh nor wine in my mouth, neither did I anoint myself at all, till three whole weeks were fulfilled.

Now, what are you adding or subtracting? His diet was Jewish, called Kosher, but fasting was without a kosher diet. Why? reason was to get an answer from the Lord. The heavenly realm moves when you fast. The devil's kingdom sees fasting as a dangerous act. Let us see how Daniel won by continuing his fasting.

Daniel 10:12 Then said he unto me, Fear not, Daniel: from the first day that thou didst set thine heart to understand and to chasten thyself before thy God, thy words were heard, and I am come for thy words. 13 But the prince of the kingdom of Persia (That is Satan) withstood me one and twenty days: but, lo, Michael, one of the chief princes, came to help me; and I remained there with the kings of Persia. 14 Now I am come to make thee understand what shall befall thy people in the latter days: for yet the vision is for many days.

The plan of Satan was defeated by Lord Jesus through fasting. Significant changes come on earth by going on fasting with prayer.

JUNE 24

Matthew 4:2 And when he (Jesus) had fasted forty days and forty nights, he was afterward an hungred.

It's no surprise that you feel hungry when you neglect to eat or drink. Do you see the confusion, oppression, and possession in the world? Adding and subtracting from the word of God is a warning sign—Beware of false teachers and prophets.

2 Timothy 4:3 For the time will come when they will not endure sound doctrine; but after their lusts shall they heap to themselves teachers, having itching ears; 4 And they shall turn away their ears from the truth, and shall be turned unto fables.

LET US PRAY

Lord, we know the battle is against Satan's tactic used against us. We need your help; only the truth sets us free, so have mercy on us, Lord, that we can find this truth by doing as it says. We thank you for power through fasting without water and food. Lord, we know the Spiritual realm has much wickedness; it is not by might nor power but by the spirit. We must walk in spirit to destroy Satan, who kills, steals, and destroys. Lord, we appreciate you for the true teachers and prophets. Help us all the way fast correctly to win the battle, in Jesus's name. Amen! God bless you!

JUNE 25

DO YOU KNOW GOD OR KNOW OF GOD?!

Knowing someone and truly getting to know someone are two different things. People acknowledge God's existence, yet they often turn to alternative sources for assistance instead of trusting in His ability to heal. We receive an introduction to God from someone, and then we learn about God just as much as they do. Nevertheless, getting to know God is similar to having a one-on-one relationship with Him. Allowing Him to control your life makes it a personal experience. Being under God's control can be difficult for someone who is unfamiliar with the Lord. Testimony is a potent tool for introducing the Lord. When we bring God into our personal experiences, people often ask, "Can God actually do this?

In order to see the exceptional work of God, we need to give Him permission to work in every area. People's desire for money causes them to fall short in their commitment to God. Giving offerings or supporting laborers and missionaries is not a popular choice. You have to give the Lord the territory in order for Him to work. This scripture has been on my mind lately.

By His stripe, you are healed.

Isaiah 53:5 But he was wounded for our transgressions, he was bruised for our iniquities: the chastisement of our peace was upon him, and with his stripes, we are healed.

We have nothing to pay, He paid for it all. Thank you, Lord. Develop a deeper longing to discover what the Lord has to offer. By encountering Jesus, the man was delivered from a multitude of unclean demons. Jesus found him in the place where the tombs are located. No one can tame or chain him. We should have this kind of testimony.

Mark 5:5 And always, night and day, he was in the mountains, and in the tombs, crying, and cutting himself with stones.

Jesus asked all demons to leave. Per the demons' request to send them in swine, they drowned in water and were killed. The Devil's attempt to steal, kill, and destroy was unsuccessful as this man's deliverance served as a testament to God's power to make him whole. Many miracles occurred in Gadarenes due to the incredibly powerful and uplifting testimony.

JUNE 25

Mark 5:19 Howbeit Jesus suffered him not, but saith unto him, Go home to thy friends, and tell them how great things the Lord hath done for thee, and hath had compassion on thee.20 And he departed, and began to publish in Decapolis how great things Jesus had done for him: and all men marveled.

The sound of a man screaming, filled with violence and aggression, prevented anyone from going or passing through. Finally, he was in the right state of mind and paying attention. His testimony was beyond comprehension. Through our testimony, we can inspire others to have greater faith in the living God. It should be clear that, yes, the Lord is able. Not mix with some lies and mix with your medicine. Through your testimony, someone dares to touch the garment or the dead daughter to rise. What kind of God are you publishing? Advertise the one who can do all. Nothing is impossible, and all things are possible for God.

Luke 8:40 And it came to pass, that, when Jesus was returned, the people gladly received him: for they were all waiting for him.

Meanwhile, a 12-year-old girl was revived and a woman who had been suffering from a 12-year blood issue was cured by touching the clothing of Jesus. The way you share your testimony can either leave a good or bad impression of the Lord. You must know the Bible to testify that the Lord specializes in all impossible things. Connect with those who have a deep understanding of God. Know God and nothing else. It is the relationship you want to build by trusting Him. You know someone by spending time with them. Practice God's words by reading them to spend time with Him. It talks nothing but all about God. Like the characters in the Bible, find trust in the Lord. Testimony is just an open acknowledgment. You tell others and affirm that your experience of the Lord and how you experience God matters. My faith was built by hearing others' testimony. I started doing what they did, and God did the same for me. Your result depends on how you perceive God.

I remembered a lady testified, saying; she wanted God to send snow where she was on vacation, and He did. When I was visiting the East coast, I asked for the same. Lord, I want snow as you sent for my sister so and so. Snow was a rarity in my life, except for the mountain beside my house. Sure enough, He sent a lot of snow. I was glad to see snow while driving at night from Canada to New Jersey. The snow created a beautiful scene on the sides and trees. Driving under the blue sky on the long road from Canada to New Jersey was a delightful experience.

Seek God for healing, for your needs, or anything else, and witness how the Lord responds, provides, heals, delivers, and guides you. I met many godly people who knew God; they helped me to take it to a higher level. As I strive for healing, deliverance, or any situation, I turn to the Lord, and He faithfully heals, delivers, provides, and resolves every problem. You need to build a relationship with the savior. Please do not go on a route of religion; it is a time-wasting game without relation. You will never find God through the path of religion. You might experience it occasionally, but not to the level you should. The reason God chose 12 and then 70 disciples was to spread the word of the New Testament. If you avoid connecting with a demonizing serpent religion, everything will remain accessible. Religion is a stopper and blocker. Don't let your soul be harmed by joining religious institutions and losing hope, faith, and belief. You must allow God to minister to you. The church is embodied by you, not solely defined by a building label.

Acts 17:10 And the brethren immediately sent away Paul and Silas by night unto Berea: who coming thither went into the synagogue of the Jews. 11 These were more noble than those in Thessalonica, in that they received the word with all readiness of mind, and searched the scriptures daily, whether those things were so

Seek the word diligently and be prepared to receive it willingly. Search scriptures daily, not once in a while. May the Lord help us change our priorities. I've always had a longing to experience a deeper and more broad connection with God. You can have God as much as you want. You can have beyond, above, and overflowing. Ask to fill your cup with His power and gifts of the Spirit. Share with others and allow everyone to enjoy what you have. Allow your cup to declare His identity. Don't follow your religion, instead spread the mission of God's Kingdom. His mission involves healing the brokenhearted and sick, delivering the oppressed and possessed, casting out demons, and reclaiming what was lost in the garden of Eden. May the Lord come to our aid. Invite the Holy Spirit to be your guide and teacher, showing you the path to truth. All believers in Jesus have access to the door leading to abundant treasures. May the Lord be your shepherd, doctor, physician, provider, and protector. He has access to all the benefits you seek. May you call the Lord for the unseen to be seen. Let the supernatural become a part of the natural.

Jeremiah 33:3 Call unto me, and I will answer thee, and show thee great and mighty things, which thou knowest not.

Let God be your friend all the time. Accepting His ways comes from knowing Him. Through Jesus, it will guide you to the everlasting truth.

LET US PRAY

We are filled with gratitude to have you in our lives, Lord. You are our sovereign and guide, our divine authority and our uprightness. We need the robe of righteousness. We need your blood to cleanse every deepest sin and make us whiter than snow. Thank you, Lord, for your word promises us you will be our guide till eternity. Yes, Lord, we want you to be our guide for eternity. How wonderful it is that we can come any time without an appointment for your help. We long for our children and grandchildren to experience a greater connection with God and confidently declare His name, the name above all names, in the name of Jesus. Amen! God bless you!

JUNE 26

WE ARE THE REPRESENTATIVES OF GOD!

People are identified by their uniforms, company car, or actions. You recognize Army, navy, or marine service members by their dress. People identify the Police by their uniform or the car they use. Someone who wears a stethoscope is considered a doctor. Their profession is something we never need to inquire about.

2 Corinthians 3:1 Do we begin again to commend ourselves? Or need we, as some others, epistles of commendation to you, or letters of commendation from you? 2 Ye are our epistle written in our hearts, known and read of all men:3 Forasmuch as ye are manifestly declared to be the epistle of Christ ministered by us, written not with ink, but with the Spirit of the living God; not in tables of stone, but in fleshy tables of the heart.

A sign was given by the prophet to distinguish Jesus as God in human form. The incarnate God, Jesus, will heal the sick, restore sight to the blind, and free those who are captive. Seeing miracles, healing, and deliverance, people understood that Jesus was the Son of God, not Joseph's son but God incarnate. Only God can do all that Jesus did. If you can perceive with discernment, there is no question about Jesus being the Son of God. There are clear signs and characteristics that the Lord has provided to identify the Christian. First, they have love, joy, peace, and long-suffering. They are forgiving.

Instead of caring for God, the priests and high priests were focused on power, position, and money.

They recognized Peter and John: *Acts 4:13 Now when they saw the boldness of Peter and John and perceived that they were unlearned and ignorant men, they marveled; and they took knowledge of them, that they had been with Jesus.*

In order to reach out to other cities, Jesus chose 12 and later 70 Disciples as His representatives.

Matthew 10:1 And when he had called unto him his twelve disciples, he gave them power against unclean spirits, to cast them out, and to heal all manner of sickness and all manner of disease.

Jesus sent out disciples by giving them authority and power to exercise. Later, Jesus called 70 and sent them out.

Luke 10:1 After these things the Lord appointed other seventy also, and sent them two and two before his face into every city and place, whither he himself would come. 9 And heal the sick that are therein, and say unto them, The kingdom of God is come nigh unto you.

What are the signs of someone being sent by the Lord? Can you identify the familiar action?

Mark 16:17 And these signs shall follow them that believe; In my name shall they cast out devils; they shall speak with new tongues; 18 They shall take up serpents; and if they drink any deadly thing, it shall not hurt them; they shall lay hands on the sick, and they shall recover.

If you're employed as a mechanic but lack repair skills, will they consider calling you again? You will never be allowed to keep your job. Would you pay a surgeon who does not know how to operate? Will you allow him to operate on you? Regrettably, he is not going to be hired by anyone. Healing is a common topic among religious organizations, denominations, and non-denominations, despite their inability to perform healing or deliverance. Healing, deliverance, and speaking in tongues are often discussed and shouted about, but if signs don't accompany them, they are counterfeit. They are members of a religious organization. Their religious group has granted them authority, position, and an agenda. Their superiors must be followed in order to make the decision. We are aware that there is a wide range of denominations, churches, and organizations. To be part of their group, you must conform to their bylaw in your communication, behavior, and way of life. You have to abide by their rules and regulations.

Several denominations discredit the idea of speaking in tongues as a valid way to receive the Holy Spirit, attributing it to satanic influence. Discarding Jesus's teachings is necessary if you want to join false serpent churches. There's no alternative for you. When you refer to my church, you mean your church, not Jesus's. The denomination is what you represent, not Jesus. I've witnessed numerous denominations and organizations open and shut down already. Many have rewritten the Bible, revised their bylaws, and their followers must abide by them. Once someone becomes a follower of a religious organization, they must submit to the authorities, no exceptions. Nowadays, you find many denominations. Convert to Catholicism first, then consider Methodist, Baptist, or Mormon in the coming year.

People kept changing by the wind of the doctrines. Your identity within the organization would be based on its name, not your Christian name. To be called a follower or disciple of Jesus, you must follow Him. Believing in Jesus's teachings can lead to God's calling for your service. The Holy Spirit cannot work through you if you are a member of the Baptist, Catholic, or any religious organization. Speaking in tongues is only possible if the church believes in receiving the Holy Spirit. They will make sure you keep your mouth shut. You'll be misled by a false teacher who claims that speaking in tongues is not supported by the Bible.

The neighboring nations were aware of Jehovah and were afraid of Moses, Aron, and Joshua. The Mighty God employed them for miraculous signs. People saw the miracle, plagues, signs, and wonders done by them. People were scared of God when they saw thunder and Shekinah's glory. We now act as God's ambassador. Christians in every era have their own agenda or follow God's. Although people may have diverse concepts of God, God will only manifest Himself in a singular way. You have the choice to utter, "Lord, permit me to be of assistance to you," or utter "Lord, empower me to fulfill your service."

Followers of the Lord will pray, fast, expel demons, heal the sick, and serve people's needs. We must represent the Lord as 12, and then 70 disciples did. The moment you deviate from following the Lord, establish your own path, form an organization, and spread false teachings, Jesus's ministry reaches its conclusion. Responsibility for the decline of the one true church lies with the spirits of Jezebel and King Ahab. In this day and age, so-called churches are being influenced by the spirit of King Ahab and Jezebel, preaching prosperity and disorder. How can one have faith in this Jesus? It is not Jesus; it is Jezebel and King Ahab's ministry to turn your eyes away from Jesus and turn toward them. Money is their God.

We either represent Lord Jesus or something else. When we accurately represent the Lord, people will naturally be drawn to the Lord. If we complete our assignment, the Lord's work will persevere. When considering denominations, they are recognized as churches, with Methodist, Baptist, Mormon, and Jehovah's witnesses represented, while Jesus is not. The four gospels are key to representing Jesus. You can choose to base your actions on the Book of Acts, which is also referred to as the Acts of the Holy Spirit. People will see Jesus; People will turn to God. The Lord will be known through your life, actions, and work. Lord, guide us as we represent you! Our shadow has an obligation to work. The devil must run from us; the sick must recover; the broken-hearted must heal. The salvation of the whole world lies in our hands if we stay true to God's mission and live according to His ways. Represent Lord Jesus!

LET US PRAY

Lord, give us your knowledge to represent you. Give us that authority and power to cast the demon out and heal the sick. This world needs deliverance, hope, salvation, and truth. Only the truth is powerful and not any religion, denomination, or organization. Lord, give us the boldness and courage to stand for you, even if we are opposed by many religious groups. May the Lord give us the power of the Holy Spirit to turn the world upside down. Take us from city to city and from country to country to represent you and you alone. So, people may know Jesus Christ is a healer, deliverer, and savior of this world in Jesus's name, Amen! God bless you!

JUNE 27

ONLY HAPPENS IF GOD GRANTS!

There are many questions about why, what, and how to see God's judgment on people or earth.

God is just, righteous, and Holy. You will reach the expected end if you obey His commandment, laws, and precept. Lord, help us comprehend your divine ways! Avoid seeking fake teachers and prophets; God has already given us authentic ones. Do not make false religion because God does not change. God is the same yesterday, today, and forever. Look for the Lord to find blessings.

I came to the US in search of God. Seeking God has always been a priority for me.

There was a woman who admitted she wanted to go to the US and become white. Everyone has a different intention. Brown people don't magically become white anywhere. The way humans think can be quite crazy. It's true that everyone has their own motives for coming to the US. Wealth is the driving force behind America's attraction, offering superior and enhanced opportunities. Have you ever considered the underlying reason for America's prosperity? America is rich compared to many countries.

We must know the cause and who is behind it. Behind the United States of America lies the powerful hand of the Almighty. God kept showering blessings upon the US because they gave Him glory, sought His presence, and served Him. As they became materialistic, the nation turned their back on God and experienced a downfall. Their pursuit of money, wealth, and desire for worldly pleasures caused them to lose their blessings. Remember, God said I will take you to the expected ends.

Solomon's wealth and blessings came from his faithful service to God Jehovah. He died lost when his eyes turned from God to the woman and all worthless things. But he began his kingdom as the richest, wisest, and most prosperous king. Keep your eyes on Jesus; He got all.

King Saul, who was anointed by the prophet Samuel, made the same mistakes again. Despite his 40-year rule over Israel, his demise was tragic. God killed him, not Philistine; God used philistine to remove him from the land of the living. Revise your vocabulary selection. Imagine if God worked through me to achieve this and that. Never take the glory; the same token does not give glory to so-called gods and goddesses.

1 Chronicle 10:1 Now the Philistines fought against Israel, and the men of Israel fled from before the Philistines, and fell down slain in Mount Gilboa. 6 So Saul died, and his three sons and all his house died together.

JUNE 27

The philistine's killing of King Saul and his sons was sanctioned by God. Why did God allow King Saul to face judgment?

1 Chronicle 10:13 So Saul died for his transgression which he committed against the Lord, even against the word of the Lord, which he kept not, and also for asking counsel of one that had a familiar spirit, to enquire of it;14 And enquired not of the Lord: therefore he slew him, and turned the kingdom unto David, the son of Jesse.

Realize that the Lord's presence is evident in the deaths caused by sickness, suicide, or firearms. Disobeying God's commandment results in losing protection. Search your heart and repent. Make a change in your life to obtain forgiveness. Do not choose wrong; obey the Lord. If not, your end with your children will be disastrous and without a solution. May the Lord grant us humility, and may we seek forgiveness and salvation from the Lord. Locate the prophet or voice of God, unbothered by your sensitivities, committed to eliminating the sin that brings judgment upon you and future generations. Instead of judgment, I long for mercy.

Choose power wisely, avoiding harm to your sibling, friend, or in-laws, and refrain from teaching your children to harm your in-laws. Do not work against the Lord. Avoid showing favoritism, be fair to all, and act with righteousness. Walking on a dangerous road is the result of doing wrong. Your prospects are dim, as God is orchestrating someone to target you and your children with harmful intentions. Instead of honoring the heathen gods and goddesses, give glory to the true God, who instructed us to be holy like Him. God may employ idol worshippers to bring about your destruction if you refuse to acknowledge the true God and His commandments. Instead of focusing on your business, prioritize fearing God.

Do not deviate from the Word of God. The Bible is not a reading book but the book to observe. Do not let His word depart from your mouth. No individual can be blamed. It's not you that people are against, but rather your actions and refusal to obey. To find a perfect heart, the Lord's eyes are watchful and discerning. The judge, Lord Jesus, observes as individuals seek counsel from familiar spirits in underground night meetings. God is watching you. His judgment will hinder no more. Look around, tsunami, lava, earthquake. Is it possible for God to remove you from His earth without the involvement of a philistine? The owner of the planet is not delaying but waiting for you to repent and turn to God. He is watching you. God protected you from the gun, from sickness, and now you think I am rich and fine. Eventually, you will be caught by the Lord's arrows with no chance of escape. Many will not be going to see tomorrow, so do not boast, just check your heart and repent. God has a clear understanding of His actions. Prepared to encounter God through a transformed heart and life.

1 Chronicle 10:9 And when they had stripped him, they took his head, and his armor, and sent into the land of the Philistines round about, to carry tidings unto their idols, and to the people.10 And they put his armor in the house of their gods and fastened his head in the temple of Dagon.

According to the Philistines, their gods and goddesses were the ones who destroyed their enemies. The Bible, the Life manual, contains all the accurate information you need. God did all, and the heathen think it is their gods and goddesses. While in your best state, seek God and His Ways to obtain blessings. A large number of individuals look for a convenient religion and eliminate true teachers like Paul, Peter, and Jesus Christ, with the intention of starting a fake religious sect. Some, having itchy ears, look for false prophets and teachers to carry on their evil ways. But on the day of judgment, you will be shocked and surprised. Because God said, I change not. Daniel faithfully followed all the Laws and commandments of the living

God, unwavering even in Babylon. God protected Daniel from the Lion, but not his opponent who planned against him. It is God who does all. Yes, Daniel should not pray to his God for 30 days. Daniel said this was unacceptable. I choose God over my life.

Are you living in the US? Dress, drinking, adultery, and fornication are all permissible in a society that embraces freedom. You change since the nation does not condemn or prevent. Take a look around and explore. What becomes of them and their descendants? They cannot live half of their life span. They will be abducted and forced into sex trafficking. May the Lord give us some wisdom and understanding. Avoid accepting false prophets and teachers into your life. If they have departed from the truth, then run from them. Judgment is for King, Queen, pastors, prophets Eli, King Saul, and YOU. No one is excused. Be careful! Lord has given you much. Do not be conformed to this world by adopting Hollywood and Bollywood. Why don't you become role models like Queen Esther, Ruth from Moab, or Joseph from Egypt? May the Lord help us to set our eyes on Him. Disobeying leads to our ultimate judgment. Don't forget, no exceptions are made, not even for you. You cannot escape from His decision. But God helps those who reverence Him.

Daniel 6:22 My God hath sent his angel, and hath shut the lions 'mouths, that they have not hurt me: for as much as before him innocency was found in me; and also before thee, O king, have I done no hurt.

You are not offending anyone when you live for God among the heathen or in the US. He will secure you from the so-called priest, High priest, heathen, and all who oppose the Lord. The judgment against King Saul brought King David to the throne. Lord said, I have discovered David, the son of Jessie, who is passionately devoted to Jehovah God. He loved the Lord with all his heart, mind, and soul. Trust in God during the trial, and you will emerge stronger and more valuable, like gold. The only protection we have from the sword, fire, lions, and death is God. It can only happen if God permits it. In Jesus 'name, I pray the Lord grants you a wholesome fear of God. Amen!

LET US PRAY

Lord, you are the controller of the universe. There is nothing hidden from you. Anything that comes to us has to pass by you to get approval. The Lord gives us the knowledge of the truth and fear of the Lord, knowing He is a consuming fire. The Lord is the same all the time. His throne is in heaven, watching us all the time. Darkness cannot hide us from Him. He knows the motives and intentions of our hearts. Lord, Give us a clean heart for the right reasons. We want to be rich by the blessings of the Lord. May our Lord give wisdom and perception from above! All the treasures we have are in Him, in Jesus's name. Amen! God bless you!

JUNE 28

YOU OWN NOTHING!

The positive aspect is that you possess nothing, so avoid accumulating too much on this planet. Many individuals are working hard to achieve various goals on earth. Many individuals chase after money, degrees, business, power, position, wealth, and similar pursuits. A lot of people have two jobs. I know some people work 10 hours a day. The good news, one day, God will take it away. Upon the end of your temporary earthly abode, you take nothing along.

Luke 12:18 And he said, This will I do: I will pull down my barns, and build greater, and there will I bestow all my fruits and my goods. 19 And I will say to my soul, thou hast much goods laid up for many years; take thine ease, eat, drink, and be merry. 20 But God said unto him, Thou fool, this night thy soul shall be required of thee: then whose shall those things be, which thou hast provided? 21 So is he that layeth up treasure for himself, and is not rich toward God.

We do not live on earth forever. You cannot bring with you all that you accumulate. May we receive divine guidance in investing our time, life, and finances! The things you collect or gather are meant for someone! Someone will enjoy what you picked. Walk and think as if you were a flower or grass. Do not let your feet settle on earth. If you are wealthy but unable to utilize it, that is the sickness. There's a curse associated with your gathering. If you can't utilize it, you're accumulating wealth for someone else. They will find it enjoyable, but not you.

Hebrews 13:5a Let your conversation be without covetousness, and be content with such things as ye have:

There is a place where you should gather your wealth. The rich man had so much, and the poor man had nothing. The rich man left the world and was begging for a drop of water. In a waterless and undesirable location, Richman sought refuge. Friend, remember, you have time to change and learn to share. The den is full of thieves who will enchant you and steal your riches. I advise you to use it for the kingdom of God. I said God-given wealth invests in the poor, widow, orphan, and laborers of God. Put whatever you can into supporting His kingdom. You will be eternally rich in heaven.

I've witnessed the deaths of young individuals. The casino owner's son passed away, and he placed money in his hands. Does it show wisdom? Provide for those in need, as the Lord identifies them as impoverished, unclothed, hungry, and orphaned. A young millionaire died. They put a car, millions of dollars, and gold in his coffin. Sounds crazy! The place where they headed, they cannot use. The Bible says the earth belongs to God. All earth's treasure belongs to the Lord. God can give to whoever he wants to.

Have you read the *Psalm 24:1 A Psalm of David. The earth is the LORD'S, and the fulness thereof; the world, and they that dwell therein.*

It is in the possession of God, not you.

Deuteronomy 10:14 Behold, the heaven and the heaven of heavens is the LORD'S thy God, the earth also, with all that therein is.

The goodness of God is unquestionable. He shows generosity to those He chooses. It is under His ownership and He supplies. You may believe you possess something, but that's not entirely true. God has given us temporary ownership during our time on earth.

The key is to live on earth and enjoy every moment.

Psalms 37:4 Delight thyself also in the Lord: and he shall give thee the desires of thine heart.5 Commit thy way unto the Lord; trust also in him; and he shall bring it to pass.

The word delight means to be soft and pliable. Be flexible and workable in the hand of God; then, He will give you what you desire.

All that God gives you, eat, drink, and enjoy.

Ecclesiastes 6:1 There is an evil which I have seen under the sun. It is common among men: 2 A man to whom God hath given riches, wealth, and honor so that he wanteth nothing for his soul of all that he desireth, yet God giveth him not power to eat thereof, but a stranger eateth it: this is vanity, and it is an evil disease.

Proverb 11:24 There is that scattereth, and yet increaseth; and there is that withholdeth more than is meet, but it tendeth to poverty.

Where you spread matters more than getting more. Give to places where you receive many returns. I have heard some wealthy people have invested money where many will receive blessings continuously. How nice! Instead of giving everything to their children and grandchildren, they chose to give to those who were needy.

It's common for lotto winners and rich individuals to pass money down to their descendants. Consequently, they splurged on friends, drugs, and luxury. What happens next? You're feeling remorseful about it. Too late! You completely wreck their life. Allow me to explain how investing money can bring blessings from the Lord.

Matthew 25:34 Then shall the King say unto them on his right hand, Come, ye blessed of my Father, inherit the kingdom prepared for you from the foundation of the world: 35 For I was an hungred, and ye gave me meat: I was thirsty, and ye gave me drink: I was a stranger, and ye took me in:36 Naked, and ye clothed me: I was sick, and ye visited me: I was in prison, and ye came unto me. 37 Then shall the righteous answer him, saying, Lord, when saw we thee an hungred, and fed thee? Or thirsty, and gave thee drink? 38 When saw we thee a stranger, and took thee in? or naked, and clothed thee? 39 Or when saw we thee sick, or in

JUNE 28

prison, and came unto thee? 40 And the King shall answer and say unto them, Verily I say unto you, Inasmuch as ye have done it unto one of the least of these my brethren, ye have done it unto me.

Read repeatedly until you accomplish the correct tasks first. If God gives you generously, you also give generously. The Lord holds the good Samaritan in higher regard than the priest and Levite, who quickly fled from the person in need. It's yours, and mine's responsibility to help the needy. Be cautious about crossing over and avoiding helping those who require assistance. When you offer assistance, you will be rewarded in both heaven and on earth.

God gives on earth to prove you. He is watching how you are using your wealth. Is it me, myself, my children, and grandchildren, or are you thinking of others? I love reaching out to those who can never give me back. There will be some happiness if you provide them with shoes, shocks in winter, a glass of water, and groceries for their low-income family and children. Some widows and their children will eat if you give them some food.

Sometimes the rich boast about their waste and do not care for the poor. By helping the poor, beggar, naked, and orphan, we can receive more incredible blessings. I go to a convalescent home and carry clothes, a blanket, or whatever the need is. They take pleasure in declaring blessings upon me. They say God gives you more, so you give more to others. I am glad. They are unable to go to the store, I know. Some don't have children, and some children will not come to visit. So it is our responsibility to help. Always remember the Good Samaritan; God admired him. Acknowledge the attention God pays to those in need. Job, the wealthiest man on earth, said I own nothing on this earth,

Job 1:21 And said, Naked came I out of my mother's womb, and naked shall I return thither: the LORD gave, and the LORD hath taken away; blessed be the name of the LORD.

LET US PRAY

Lord, we thank you for your generosity. You have shared your wealth and treasure with us. Lord, please give us generous nature to do your work with love, not grudgingly. May the Lord help us spend our wealth with the sick, needy, poor, thirsty, widow, and orphan. Lord, you have given us all that we have. Wealth is our test, so help us, Lord. May our Lord provide us with knowledge and fear of God to be wise stewards of the wealth of God! All belong to you and not us. He has always used his wealth for the needy, poor, and widow. In the end, he received a double. His children do not need to beg. So, Lord, it is all yours. Show us how to use it for you to secure and multiply our blessings, in Jesus's name. Amen! God bless you!

JUNE 29

DO NOT PREACH, BUT TEACH BY EXAMPLE!

Have you ever noticed parents who never stop preaching to their kids? If you keep talking to them, it will not work. Some pastors, preachers, and saints do the same thing. Being a good preacher is important, but it's ineffective without the presence of power, signs, and wonders. Teaching someone the word of God is effective, but living by the word of God provides evidence of your preaching.

Jesus constantly taught. At different locations and times, such as the early morning, mountain, and seashore, he taught. Jesus was the greatest teacher. Children are influenced by your behavior, not your lectures. The life you live will be observed and followed by your children. You don't have to question who your parents are. You know, by their behavior. Fruit doesn't fall far from the tree. It is the saying you do not need to paint picklock babies. It has all its colors.

If we encounter a disciple of Jesus, we can be certain they were his followers. They performed the same acts as Jesus. Everyone is included, except for Judas. Isn't it true that every family has a black sheep?

Jesus delivered teachings on mountains, seashores, and in temples.

Matthew 5:2 And he (Lord Jesus) opened his mouth, and taught them, saying,

Matthew 7:29 For he taught them as one having authority, and not as the scribes. 28 And it came to pass when Jesus had ended these sayings, the people were astonished at his doctrine:(=teaching)

Mark 2:13 And he went forth again by the seaside, and all the multitude resorted unto him, and he taught them.

Jesus backed up his teachings with demonstrations of authority and power. If there are no signs and wonders accompanying your teaching, then it is just a word and not the Word of God.

Level up your faith by increasing your encounters with the Holy Spirit. Prepare your lecture, but reinforce it with the action of the Word of God. Through prayer and fasting, invite God into your teaching and preaching. Teaching is a constant part of my life, no matter where I am. The power of words is evident when they are obeyed and put into action.

JUNE 29

I had a conversation with a woman named Zila the other day, and she told me about her conversion. Before connecting with Lord Jesus, these women had nothing. Now, they have it all, and she wondered why. They have food, a motorbike, and are now building houses. She mentioned that she was acquainted with those women. I explained the key is the Word of God. I provided an explanation on how to open the treasure using the recorded instructions. God treats everyone equally.

Her wish is for everything except she needs guidance in understanding giving, offering, and mission. The other two ladies are consistently willing to offer. Especially one lady who has a faithful husband who gives generously. They both converted from worshiping idols to embracing the living God. Mrs. Lena and her Husband, Hemesh, are good Christians. They always share their testimony to give God glory. Mrs. Lena said I earn 12,000 Rs, and my husband makes 27000.00. We took 1200 from my pay and 2700 from my husband's pay and we gave it as tithes. Additionally, she will offer support to all visiting pastors. She mentioned that previously I would only purchase a few groceries, but now we own a motorcycle, a freezer, and have constructed a spacious house in the village with the land around it. Our house is filled with an abundance of food. She wondered what had taken place. Giving God opens up the window of heaven.

So as I was sharing this with lady Zila, she said I would provide 2,000.00 Rs for the ministry. By the end of the day, she received a refund of 1500. I said we blocked our treasure, do not block your blessings. Master the act of generosity. By following the word, you receive all blessings. Doing the Word of God is the Key. You have the power to lose your blessing. She understood very well. There are individuals who lack the ability to read or write. I clarify the Word of God, and they embrace it. If we teach people the truth, they will gain knowledge. They are ready to drive away the demon. Their testimony is exceptional. Why? Their learning of the word is happening through obedience. To be saved, you must follow the scriptural instructions for salvation.

During one of my days, I had a chat with a lady. She said we are the children of God; the devil cannot touch us. Did I state that we are protected from the devil's touch? Do not believe this false teaching. The devil has power, but we can defeat him by using the word of God like a sword. Without the devil as an opponent, the word, our sword, becomes unnecessary. Right? I asked how we could have victory without war. We have a triumph since we have nothing but the war.

By wearing the armor of God and holding the shield of faith, you can learn to battle. Day and night, the devil battles against God's kingdom. He opposes His saints, acknowledging us as God's army. Teach right. I taught her how to bind all the demons in that place and anoint with holy oil. Pray for the protection of yourself and all workers, covering them with the blood of Jesus. Keep going with the teachings of the Holy Scriptures. The difference will be apparent to you. Take your rightful position. Say, no weapon formed against me can prosper. By calling upon the name of Jesus, send Satan's weapon back to the enemy.

One of the new converts is a great follower of the Lord. She follows the word as it says. Mr. Mahesh, the woman's husband, learned that the man he assisted was conspiring against him. He went to bribe a manager to remove Mahesh and put him instead. Upon hearing this, Mahesh was filled with great disappointment. He obtained the word of God and continually declared, No weapon formed against me shall succeed. The Word of God brought peace, while the other person faced intense hatred for attempting to betray Mr. Mahesh.

Speaking is the key to unleashing the power of God's Word. It is for us and whoever believes. When you observe successful people, you guess they are doing things correctly. Do not doubt but believe. Remember, teaching must be supported by actual performance. I make sure to carry the holy oil, Bible, and prayer cloth in my car at all times. Through teaching and providing blessed oil and prayer clothes, I enable others to carry on the same practice.

The lady Lena got so much favor at work that people started believing in Jesus. Her supervisor has become very kind towards her. Before, he was always angry with her. A lot of her colleagues started attending prayer towers. According to her, she handed the Bible over to one coworker. With the Bible in hand, he reads whenever he can find the time. She began distributing Holy Oil. The children of their coworkers also started believing. Success comes from believing and putting it into practice. A Lady coworker named Madhavi said, her daughter-in-law tried to commit suicide. I prefer her not to become restless or annoyed while I minister. Madhavi said, I will take the Bible and oil, and she did. Her daughter-in-law listened and understood what her mother-in-law said.

My mission is to teach Lena, Zila, and as many others as possible about the word of God. Through living according to the teaching, they gain testimony. Testimony holds great significance. Please always prioritize teaching the truth. Preaching alone won't be effective.

May the Holy Spirit teach us all truth. It is necessary for me to give a testimony of God's word. Our God is faithful and mighty. The success of our testimony hinges on his word being upheld. God desires to find someone with an unblemished heart to showcase His authenticity, power, provision, care, healing, deliverance, and salvation.

This is God's Word, not man's. The word can be proven effective if you believe in it and take action, just like Abraham, Isaac, Israel, Daniel, David, Ruth, and Mary did. Hallelujah! Our God wants you to obey His word. His desire is for you to be blessed. By doing it yourself, you can teach the word to yourself. DIY. Do it yourself. You will be blessed.

A woman who converted claims that Christians not only drink alcohol but also face financial struggles and engage in wrongful acts by joining buildings under different organizations. They have been cursed. We make an effort to stay away from attending their religious services. I made it clear that I wouldn't accuse you. Seek out genuine teachers and prophets to discover the truth. My prayer is for God to raise up countless workers, trustworthy teachers, and genuine prophets during the end time. Breaking the harmful tradition that has affected the kingdom of God will require someone's intervention. Praying that God will raise up a multitude of people like Daniel, Shadrach, Meshach, and Abednego in the end to proclaim His word. Show the authenticity of the God of heaven by teaching the word through practical examples. May you receive true teachers and prophets, blessed by the Lord. In Jesus 'name. Amen!

LET US PRAY

Lord, as your word, is living if we obey. Lord, give us the faith of our father, Abraham. Lord, as we open the Bible, we open our hearts and minds to receive.

We know the Lord can do wonders if we do the word even today. We have many distracting obstacles in our way, but we can overcome them all by doing word. There is no person or era where the devil has not come against its tactic, so make us aware of it all. Make us wiser like a snake and harmless like a dove. Let our life teach as we obey the word of God whole heartily in Jesus's name. Amen! God bless you!

JUNE 30

AM NOT IMPRESSED WITH THE DEVIL'S IDEA!

God created the world with His power and genius mind. He created with His hand you and me with an extraordinary creative power to work and walk and communicate with Him. I have a profound appreciation for the notion of walking and talking with the solitary God. God, being super-powerful, creative, omnipresent, omniscient, and omnipotent, possesses knowledge of the future, presence, and past. He sees everything, there are no secrets. Darkness, whether above or below, cannot hide since everything was created by His power and purpose.

Daniel is considered less powerful and knowledgeable compared to the Devil, who is also known for being wiser.

Ezekiel 28:12 Son of man, take up a lamentation upon the king of Tyrus, and say unto him, Thus saith the Lord God; Thou sealest up the sum, full of wisdom, and perfect in beauty.13 Thou hast been in Eden the garden of God; every precious stone was thy covering, the sardius, topaz, and the diamond, the beryl, the onyx, and the jasper, the sapphire, the emerald, and the carbuncle, and gold: the workmanship of thy tabrets and of thy pipes was prepared in thee in the day that thou wast created.14 Thou art the anointed cherub that covereth; and I have set thee so: thou wast upon the holy mountain of God; thou hast walked up and down amid the stones of fire.

The Lord created Satan, a beautiful, wise, intelligent, and anointed cherub, not just a cherub. This spirit being is not ordinary; it is highly intelligent and extraordinarily designed for a significant purpose. All of us were created by the same One Spirit God. Different forms and multiple characteristics are found among birds, water creatures, fowl in the air, humans, and spiritual beings like angels and archangels. All creations were given power by God, but with certain limitations. The creator surpasses their creation in superiority. Man and woman were created by God's hand and blessed by Him. All of God's creations were placed in the hands of men, with authority over them.

On the other hand, Satan, we do not have any information about its fallen stage. However, Satan was present when the Lord revealed His plan to man, even though he couldn't be seen. Satan approaches and addresses at the time to Eve when the fruit comes in its season. By the way, it was not an apple. The Devil manipulates humans into turning their "NO" into a "YES" by talking them into it. The name he goes by is twister. Satan employs its evil plan and deceptive vocabulary to create devices that attract people. The Lord prohibits sexual immorality. Satan provides financial support to the fornicator. Provide financial assistance to each child if they have different fathers. Getting AIDS entitles you to free bus passes, cash, medical assistance, and more.

Let it be known that the Devil has failed to impress me. No matter how many millions, billions, or zillions he offers, it is nothing compared to the Lord's promises. Satan's plan entices suicide, mental illness, cancer, and disease.

You become an easy victim of the Devil's trap when you watch and listen to its enticing plan on TV and participate. Despite our limitations as humans, knowing our boundaries allows us to live a life filled with abundance and protection.

Devil is a divider, an evil architect, and plots traps and ditches for each person. He can say one thing at one moment and something completely different at another moment. Its dealings are never true, responsible, or pure. The only thing on Satan's mind is leading God's bride astray from His divine plan. We are part of God's divine plans, with an eternal home to gather and reside in forever. Along the same lines, God is obligated to establish hell and a lake of fire for Satan, fallen angels, and people who align with its scheme.

God has a plan to bless, protect, provide, and nurture you, whereas the Devil's plan is to curse you and remove you from God's protection to bring about your destruction. The Devil should not be a source of admiration for anyone on this earth. All this money, glamour, Hollywood, music, mansions, gold, diamond, fame, education, games, and glory he has created by creating a media platform is temporary.

Everything is illusionary. A quick look into their everyday life. It's nothing more than an empty husk. They have more problems than you can think of. The world has been burdened with an unimaginable number of problems caused by them. None of Satan's offers are for your soul to rescue from the eternal hellfire. Just so you know, he is fully aware of what he's doing, but as a liar, he wants to keep you in the dark about your destination. Following Satan's plan will lead you to eternal damnation in hell. And you responded to Satan's plan since you made your choice.

Keep your eyes on God, on His instruction, and it's a beautiful plan. Broaden the territorial scope. To win souls, we should make a plan that includes the nine gifts of the spirit, healing the sick, and delivering people from Satan's mouth and traps. Let's spread the word of God as He has instructed us. To prevent curses that will separate you, make sure to practice and refrain from trespassing forbidden areas. Repentance holds the key. Cleanse your sins by invoking the Name of Jesus through baptism and receive the power of the Holy Spirit for the rest of your journey.

One thing is sure, Satan is a drama, liar, father of the lie, an expert in deceiving, and a master planner to destroy all he can devour.

KJV dictionary says devour means to eat up; to eat with greediness; to eat ravenously, as a beast of prey, or as a hungry man.

Are you convinced that following Satan's plan is leading you to victory? Although you may be impressed by what the Devil offers, Satan's marketplace encompasses you, your children, your finances, and your talent. His strategy is effective because he manipulates your lustful desires, nothing more. Despite being

JUNE 30

unable to contribute anything, he urges you to work tirelessly in order to make the Devil wealthy by utilizing your mind, talent, hands, money, and so on. You serve as a slave to Satan, who is your master.

The key to avoiding its trap is finding the truth and the way to truth and life through Jesus Christ.

Power-hungry Eve, Adam, Solomon, King Saul, and others who rejected the plan of God, prophets, and teachers of God almighty. Genuine individuals who are devoted to God understand His word through their lifestyle, observation, and the results they display.

Satan's plan will ensnare you with demons, darkness, and destruction, leading to your ultimate destination in hell. Don't follow the Devil; it has a trap in giving the best that you think.

Despite visiting numerous places, Gospel is the one missing element. The Gospel is the good news that we must share with our city, county, neighboring states, and even the world. The great news is that those who believe in Jesus, get baptized, and receive the Holy Spirit will witness blind eyes opened, deaf ears hear, and sins forgiven. Verily, Lord said, born again, I say unto you believe in Lord Jesus Christ and His instruction and follow Him. His loyal disciple and prophet laid the foundation and just kept building on that foundation brick by brick. The gates of hell cannot conquer against that foundation. Please do not fool yourself by following different denominations, organizations, and nondenominational churches; they are building. You are the church. Again, do not let false doctrine, prophets, and teachers fool and trap you.

If there are no instances of deliverance, healing, or miracles, then take an additional step to seek, knock, and ask. This is how you can protect your soul from Satan's misleading plan. Begin with opening the Bible, praying, practicing the truth, and persistently seeking liberation from the trap. You will find an exciting restoration plan for you, your family, and others. It is a blessing from God that is enjoyable, authentic, and everlasting. You can extract all the benefits by embracing Jesus Christ's life-restoring plan. The Lord Jesus acknowledges your importance, whereas Satan's plan excludes you. Sin in human flesh is the nourishment Satan craves, as he roams like a famished lion. Don't hesitate to run if you notice the Devil attempting to deceive and trap you using its design, program, and methods. There is nothing positive about the Devil. Wise people find no allure or potential in any of Satan's plans. Observe those who are trapped. God requests that we spread the good news. Set people free from alcohol, depression, and cancer by laying hands and healing the sick. They are imprisoned by the Devil. He's using the people we care about to devour them. Avoid engaging, whether knowingly, unknowingly, or as part of its strategy. Your life, family, blessings, and privileges will be at stake.

Is it possible that despite investing time in education, working multiple jobs, and acquiring possessions, the end result is hell? The Devil possesses nothing but presents you with false glory, toxic relationships, illness, and devastation for you and your loved ones. Don't forget, you were redeemed by the blood of God Jesus. I know God is a Spirit, but He temporarily put on flesh to shed blood. Life is in the blood, and He sacrificed Himself for your sins, granting you life. His plan of salvation is easy; repent, baptize in Jesus 'name, and receive the Holy Spirit. Now you are born from above and can enter the kingdom of heaven if you continue in His word.

Amen!

LET US PRAY

Heavenly Father, we pray to keep us, guide us, and protect us from Satan's plan of destruction. Keep us hidden in your blood, in your shadow. Your name, Jesus, is our hiding place. It is a solid tower for those who trust the saving name of Jesus. The Lord is the keeper of our soul if we trust in Him. Our Lord has a plan for us as an individual. Lord, lead us to your plan so we find rest for our souls. With the power of Jesus's name, we overcome Satan's devices and find security. Amen! God bless you!

JULY

JULY 1

MAY I COME IN?

The Lord is seeking permission to reside in your heart. I have created you to be my sanctuary and you are my abode. May I come in, please? Have you built a house? Would you like to make it your home? You will say, Yes, I paid or prayed for it. It belongs to me. I possess the key and have the freedom to enter and exit. I have both documentation and financial expenditures. I have a document in my possession. I am the owner of this house. My home is where I currently reside. I've adorned my home and purchased lovely items for my house. It belongs to me. I have the power to do as I please. I can create a stunning garden, kitchen, flooring, ceiling, and painting.

I've put a lot of money into this house. Let me tell you, you have yet to invest your life in it. The Lord is saying I have invested my blood which has life for your life. You are both my sanctuary and my dwelling.

1 Corinthian 3:16 Know ye not that ye are the temple of God, and that the Spirit of God dwelleth in you?

God has designed you to be the dwelling place for Lord Jesus. Will you let Him? Welcome him. May the Lord help you to understand the purpose of having you as His building!

Hebrews 3:6a. But Christ as a son over his own house; whose house are we,

1 Corinthian 6:19 What? Know ye not that your body is the temple of the Holy Ghost which is in you, which ye have of God, and ye are not your own?

God desires to reside inside of you. Remove any evil things that don't belong in your life. Lord Jesus Said to repent, John the Baptist said Repent, 12 Disciples said to repent, and Peter said to repent and go in the water to wash away all your sins. Sin and God have no relationship. The disobedience of Adam and Eve resulted in a severed connection with God. In the past, we were without the blood of Jesus, the Lamb, during sinning, but presently we have it. The act of baptizing in Jesus's name represents the death of our old selves and the resurrection as a new creation. The Lord is constructing a new, yet initially impure dwelling, a corrupt abode that must be destroyed through baptism in the name of Jesus. The experience of coming up from a water burial can only be described by you. May you have a new story and give you a fresh, clean, holy building where the Holy Spirit can dwell!

Hallelujah! I've personally seen individuals regretful of their sins, cleansing them through underwater baptism in the Name of Jesus Christ. I thank him for His blood since I, my mom, my brother, and all I have seen going in the water came out with a clean conscience. It is called the born of water.

JULY 1

The blood of Jesus is greater than the blood of a bull, goat, or sheep. Animal blood cannot take away my sins. If your house, which is the body, is dirty, clean it up. Confess your sins. Confession of each sin has cleansing power. When you say, Lord, I am guilty of lying, cheating, pride, jealousy, arrogance, and haughtiness. Lord, I have transgressed your commandment. I am a sinner. Lord Jesus is faithful to forgive you. Then wash away all spots and wrinkles caused by sins calling the name of Jesus Christ. You will come out clean. The Lord will wash away your sins in the blood hidden behind the name of Jesus. May the Lord help us to obey His commandments. Please do not argue against His precious way! May the Lord help us to develop into spiritual and not religious, obedient and not disobedient! Please welcome the Lord to come to a clean house and sup with us in the name of Jesus!

John 14:18 I will not leave you comfortless: I will come to you.

When the Holy Spirit comes to you, it is Jesus. His spirit comes to dwell in you.

That is why Peter said,

Acts 2:38 Then Peter said unto them, Repent, and be baptized every one of you in the name of Jesus Christ for the remission of sins, and ye shall receive the gift of the Holy Ghost.

Please, allow God to come to you. Denounce the demon of vices such as smoking, drinking, drugs, infidelity, promiscuity, falsehood, deceit, avarice, and materialism, the source of all wickedness. The Lord is knocking. Let the door of your heart swing open. May He reside in His dwelling place. Learn from Eve and Adam's mistake, being fixated on one forbidden thing and rejecting all the blessings. Please do not repeat the history of failure. Staying in His condition will result in God's promised blessings. It is God's will to bless you; make His will your will.

2 Corinthians 7:1 Having therefore these promises, dearly beloved, let us cleanse ourselves from all filthiness of the flesh and spirit, perfecting holiness in the fear of God.

Prepare your heart. God created a habitable space for Himself, as He is the King and the Holy One.

Revelation 3:20 Behold, I stand at the door, and knock: if any man hear my voice, and open the door, I will come in to him and will sup with him, and he with me.

Purify the body thoroughly, leaving no trace of sin, for the Lord's entrance. By embracing false religion, many have closed the door on Jesus. Serpent religion is gaining acceptance among people, causing them to forsake the true teachings of Jesus for a more worldly path. Let us find the narrow road.

Matthew 7:14 Because strait is the gate, and narrow is the way, which leadeth unto life, and few there be that find it.

The gate's strait meant restriction. There existed only one fruit that was prohibited. Our persistent wrongdoing led to numerous conditions and regulations. Remember, staying within the restricted zone is safer to prevent any harm to your house. Your home needs maintenance; your house needs the touch of the Lord. Just say, Lord, touch me; my sin has brought me sickness. I acknowledge that I have sinned. May I touch your garment? I need the Word to receive healing, please send it to me. By thanking you, I find gratitude that completes me. I want my house, body, soul, and spirit to be whole, complete, and unbroken. I want you to come and stay in a beautiful home. There is no wrinkle, no spot, and no broken.

Romans 12:1 I beseech you therefore, brethren, by the mercies of God, that ye present your bodies a living sacrifice, holy, acceptable unto God, which is your reasonable service. 2 And be not conformed to this world: but be ye transformed by the renewing of your mind, that ye may prove what that good, and acceptable, and perfect, will of God is. 3 For I say, through the grace given unto me, to every man that is among you, not to think of himself more highly than he ought to think; but to think soberly, according to as God hath dealt with every man the measure of faith.

The Lord considers you important. When He was at Calvary, He was thinking of you. He wants you to purify His house and temple with His blood, a cleansing substance that surpasses any detergent. Jesus's blood can erase even the most serious sins and illnesses. May the Lord find us, wise steward, to keep His house worthy of His dwelling! May the Lord grant us the ability to perceive and eliminate all imperfections and weaknesses. He is knocking. Jesus is respectful and courteous. He comes and knocks. However, Satan, the thief, enters through the back door without consent. Secure the back door, unlock your home's entrance, and welcome the Lord to join you for a meal, in the name of Jesus, Amen!

LET US PRAY

Lord, I am your residence, temple, and house; please come in. Please stay with me. Please lead, guide, teach, and empower me. You are the master of your home. Thank you for coming to your house. It is at the mercy of God that you gave your blood to wash away our sins if we use your name 'Jesus 'in baptism. Help us never to reject your precious blood, which is hidden under the name of Jesus. I want my shadow to heal and deliver many since you live in me. It is not me but the Lord who lives in me and can do much. I am crucified with Christ. My desire with flesh and spirit is mortified so the Lord can live in me. Lord, come into your temple. My body is your house. I open my heart to welcome you in Jesus's name. Amen! God bless you!

JULY 2

PRAY FOR YOUR RULERS!

First, who are our rulers? The leaders in our nation go by various titles such as Prime Minister, President, King, Queen, Prince, Pharaoh, or emperor. The term for Priests in the Spiritual World is now pastors. Bishops or superintendents are the modern-day equivalent of high priests. In governmental offices, you will find sheriffs, police officers, judges, governors, and mayors. School college system, we have a principal or director of the Board.

I want to highlight who needs our prayers. The Bible states that individuals in positions of authority can be influenced by Satan to carry out its wicked plans. The devil needs people to carry on its agenda. All the devil plans to destroy God's agenda. May the Lord bless us with wisdom, a heart that obeys, and love for God and His kingdom! Always remember that mistakes should never be tolerated. It is absolutely not acceptable.

Galatians 5:9 A little leaven (= sin) leaveneth the whole lump.

The act of sin includes lying, cheating, pride, and transgression. Sin is not classified as big or small. A sin is always regarded as a sin. And the wages of sin is death (=eternal hellfire for your soul). Understanding, given by the Lord, is crucial. May the Lord empower us with bravery and fearlessness to do what is right! There is a government in heaven. Forever, His kingdom is established, and He will reign as king for all eternity.

Let's direct our prayers towards defeating satanic influence in nations and spiritual/religious authorities. Please keep them in your prayers.

What is the reason behind praying?

Ephesians 6:12 "For we wrestle not against flesh and blood, but against principalities, against powers, against the rulers of the darkness of this world, against spiritual wickedness in high places."

1 Timothy 2:1 I exhort therefore, that, first of all, supplications, prayers, intercessions, and giving of thanks, be made for all men; 2 For kings, and for all that are in authority; that we may lead a quiet and peaceable life in all godliness and honesty. 3 For this is good and acceptable in the sight of God our Saviour; 4 Who will have all men to be saved, and to come unto the knowledge of the truth.

On the land, we require a state of peace and quiet. Pay attention to the current situations in different countries. Fleeing from sword, famine, or war, numerous individuals are scattered across different countries. They should be located in a place where their languages are not spoken. This is the time we need to wake up and pray. We need a prayer garden, prayer tower, and prayer mountain where we can pray constantly. Our den, known by many names, is open once a week for midweek services. The duty of true prophets, teachers, and apostles is to train disciples to oppose their rulers 'evil agenda as part of God's army.

Esther, being a queen, knew how to prepare against the plan of Satan. The devil's evil plan through Haman the Agagite, the enemy of the Jew, was destroyed. The Haman carried out a highly deceptive secret scheme. But the prayer warrior put on the armor and started hammering the heaven. According to God, nothing is impossible. He heard from heaven to prevent Satan's plans. By fasting and crying out, the people of God overcame all weapons formed against them. Prayer was always making its way to heaven. You need to pray for nations. Numerous countries either have or are attempting to enact laws that target religious communities. Efforts are being made in India to eradicate Christianity. Christians and pastors were beaten up as Churches 'Bibles were openly burned. Who is responsible for this? An army of evil demons, Satan, and fallen angels are plotting to fight against the People of Living God. India and many other nations need Queen Esther of our time to declare a fast. Several nations, including Christian nations such as the US, UK, and Europe, Muslim nations like Egypt and Indonesia, as well as others like North Korea and various African countries, experience persecution. The only way is to pray and fast. The Prophet Alph Lukau urged all Christians to come together and pray with unity and agreement. Christians will face opposition from Hindus, Buddhists, Muslims, and satanists. It's important for all of us to gather and pray. The prophecy of Jesus concerning the end time is something we are familiar with.

Luke 21:34 And take heed to yourselves, lest your hearts be overcharged with surfeiting, drunkenness, and cares of this life, and so that day come upon you unawares. 35 For as a snare shall it come on all that dwell on the face of the whole earth. 36 Watch ye therefore, and always pray, that ye may be accounted worthy to escape all these things that shall come to pass and to stand before the son of man.

Hasn't this proven to be so accurate? Eating, drinking, and excessive indulgence in worldly matters are observed everywhere. It's acceptable to attend a building referred to as a church, but they have their limits. The agenda is not to follow Jesus. The subject has been neglected. May the Lord awaken us with a shake to encourage us to pray. In both the religious and secular realms, Athaliah and her mother Jezebel hold power. The Lord gave the throne to the seed of David, but someone brought the Athaliah as a queen from the northern kingdom of Israel to the Southern Kingdom. Be careful; your ruler can be dangerous.

2 King 11:1 And when Athaliah, the mother of Ahaziah, saw that her son was dead, she arose and destroyed all the seed royal.

Our prayer is for the Lord to provide us with a priest and High Priest who follows the righteousness of Jehoiada.

2 Kings 11:15 But Jehoiada, the priest commanded the captains of the hundreds, the officers of the host, and said unto them, Have her (Athaliah) forth without the ranges: and him that followeth her kill with the sword. For the priest had said, Let her not be slain in the house of the LORD.

JULY 2

It is crucial for both our spiritual and secular world leaders to be led by God almighty. May our leaders be awakened by the Lord's call to lead through fasting and prayer.

Remember to pray for those in authority!

Matthew 24:21 For then shall be great tribulation, such as was not since the beginning of the world to this time, no, nor ever shall be. 22 And except those days should be shortened, there should no flesh be saved: but for the elect's sake, those days shall be shortened.

Our Lord prayed before going through the most challenging trial on Calvary. Through prayer, he obtained help. God appeared in physical form and demonstrated the importance of prayer. Although he was self-sufficient, we all require strength and Jesus instructed us to seek divine assistance through prayer.

Luke 22:44 And being in an agony, he prayed more earnestly: and his sweat was as it were great drops of blood falling down to the ground.

Learning how to pray is necessary. Our prayer must be constant, without ceasing, and given priority.

Luke 22:43 And there appeared an angel unto him from heaven, strengthening him. 46: And said unto them, Why sleep ye? Rise and pray, lest ye enter into temptation.

My Lord, give us leaders like David, Daniel, high priests like Jehoiada, and Jesus Christ, the God in the flesh. Years ago, while living in California, my family and I encountered a challenging situation. The presence of a witch in your family through marriage causes disorder. Both of my siblings were going through some health struggles. My mom was praying day and night for them and all of us. My mom was a mighty prayer warrior. We won since she was a righteous prayer warrior. The woman who prays receives heavenly help in the face of the devil's attempts to harm her children and their progress. Thank God for my mom. She defeated the devil with the help of the mighty God. The witch's plan was consistently prevented by our prayers and fasting. Afterwards, the witch was plagued by serious diseases.

On one of my days off, I decided to visit the bookstore. I shop at a Christian Book store to buy books. My mom informed me that when she was in bed, she coughed and, as a result, her eyes opened. According to her, she witnessed a brilliant light resembling the sun inside the house, with an angel standing on her bed and the sun positioned behind it. Angel's hand reached out, hovering above me. She shut her eyes, and a few minutes afterward, she opened them. The Angel was seen leaning out of the window, with the sun streaming through the side window. Her day and night prayer resulted in an answer for both of her children. Our faith is grounded in the tangible presence of our God. He's willing to assist, but you must reach out for help. Would you mind praying for the future situation and taking your time? Watch and pray for yourself and others. In the name of Jesus, we can both escape and find a peaceful life. Amen!

LET US PRAY

Our heavenly Father, we humbly come before your mercy seat to find help from you. Our help cometh from our Lord. Overthrow the agenda and plan of the enemy to go against your people who are called by your name. Your warning for the end time is clear that we will face a bad time which was not before and will not be after. We ask for a prayer life like Daniel and King David to escape Satan's evil plan. Lord, give us the burden and desire to pray like never before. Let us unite worldwide and pray to overcome and overthrow the plan of Satan, in Jesus's name. Amen! God bless you!

JULY 3

PREPARATION FOR THE END TIME!

Lord, bestow upon us the understanding and commitment to prepare for our encounter with the maker! Our creator is the Lord. With a personal touch, he brought his bride into existence. Are you familiar with the matrimonial ad? The requirement specifies fair skin, good looks, proficiency in certain areas, a particular age, height, and background. I can't believe how many conditions there are! Through listening to others, I can discern the needs of the groom or bride. We can gain knowledge from engaging in family conversations. During a different epoch, the expectations, options, and necessities for an ideal life partner varied between men and women. The woman has an expectation for the spouse's salary. He ought to possess a house, vehicles, and an education.

The role of God is similar to that of a groom. God's vision for heaven excludes any form of chaos. According to God, my wife, my bride, must obey me, love me, and fulfill certain tasks. Let us check out His requirements. Possessing knowledge enables individuals to meet their expectations. Married individuals who are successful understand that their spouses treat them exceptionally well. It is important to understand the Lord's preferences and disapprovals. Once we concentrate on learning how to meet His need, it becomes easy.

Amos 4:11 I have overthrown some of you, as God overthrew Sodom and Gomorrah, and ye were as a firebrand plucked out of the burning: yet have ye not returned unto me, saith the Lord. 12 Therefore thus will I do unto thee, O Israel: and because I will do this unto thee, prepare to meet thy God, O Israel. 13 For, lo, he that formeth the mountains, and createth the wind, and declareth unto man what is his thought, that maketh the morning darkness, and treadeth upon the high places of the earth, The Lord, The God of hosts, is his name.

God is the ruler of this world. Gain knowledge about his choices by understanding the associated requirements and conditions. Carelessness is common among promiscuous individuals. The statement from God is that He does not change. If your goal is to meet God and have an everlasting connection, avoid searching for Him in the building called churches. Find the individual designated by the Lord, identified as a true prophet and teacher.

Mark 6:18 For John had said unto Herod, It is not lawful for thee to have thy brother's wife.

John the Baptist's purpose was to rectify the Jewish world, which had been corrupted by the envy, greed, and ambition of priests, levies, and high priests.

Leviticus 18:16 Thou shalt not uncover the nakedness of thy brother's wife: it is thy brother's nakedness.

According to Jesus, the born again church is his bride. His bride will be taken to Him when He comes. He seeks the individual who can bring happiness and pride to Jesus.

Proverb 12:4 A virtuous woman is a crown to her husband: but she that maketh ashamed is as rottenness in his bones.

The unfaithful wife will bring agony, but the virtuous one will bring delight and honor to Him. Isn't this a serious business? Find a wife, not a knife. Mother-in-law rejects a loose, rebellious, or wicked daughter-in-law. Mother-in-law is not looking for one who can sing well or is highly educated or beautiful. She possesses the qualities of sugar dissolving in water - virtuous and supportive of her family. The Lord is also looking for the virtuous to be with Him for eternity.

Lord, help us to prepare ourselves to be your bride! My work spans across countries as I serve God internationally. The Lord has chosen those who are illiterate, unattractive, uneducated, and lack communication, mobility, and style. However, their love for the Lord becomes evident when I talk to them. Their conversations revolve solely around the Lord. Their devotion to God is so strong that they are willing to abandon anyone and anything for Him, their future husband. May we be granted understanding by the Lord regarding the reasons why mothers may reject specific women as wives for their sons. In short, they are a major source of frustration! Her actions will go against her husband's family, specifically her mother-in-law and sister-in-law. All she brings is pain. Unhealthy, unpleasant, and jealous behaviors of subtle isolation are brought about by her presence. This type of bride is not desired by our God either.

A loving, sweet, and kind bride is what God longs for to be in His presence. I enjoy praying and particularly delight in hearing His voice. I've maintained a balanced line of communication with the Lord. I was surprised when he suddenly came up to me. The Lord will converse with me, provide explanations, and offer beautiful help. I hope you comprehend how Adam and Eve felt before they went down to temptation. The beauty of God's presence is beyond explanation. We should constantly engage in prayer, fasting, talking, and praising Him. How to meet the expectations of your future spouse? Once you meet Lord's requirement, you can embark on a journey with Jesus Christ, your groom. If you are promiscuous, rebellious, wicked, or disobedient, you won't understand this. The process begins with parents who exemplify excellence, raising children who are morally upright, clean, and righteous.

Proverb 31:10 Who can find a virtuous woman? For her price is far above rubies. 11 The heart of her husband doth safely trust in her so that he shall have no need of spoil.

May the Lord discover an admirable character within us, priceless and unique. There is a bride who is more precious than rubies. A Moabite Ruth was the ideal bride. The Lord and the people both praised and bestowed blessings upon her. She married Boaz, who was a wealthy nobleman. No wonder why the Lord is looking for the one who is a virtuous bride. If you find a terrible wife, then it will give a headache, pain, and sorrow to you and your family. Esau picked the woman of that land and was grievous to the family.

Genesis 27:46 And Rebekah said to Isaac, I am weary of my life because of the daughters of Heth: if Jacob takes a wife of the daughters of Heth, such as these which are of the daughters of the land, what good shall my life do me?

JULY 3

The Lord only accepts those who meet His standard. To be chosen, you must meet his standard. Prepare accordingly.

1 Timothy 2:8 I will therefore that men pray everywhere, lifting up holy hands, without wrath and doubting. 9 In like manner also, that women adorn themselves in modest apparel, with shamefacedness and sobriety; not with broided hair, gold, pearls, or costly array; 10 But (which becometh women professing godliness) with good works.

1 Peter 3:5 For after this manner in the old time the holy women also, who trusted in God, adorned themselves, being in subjection unto their husbands:

The Lord is looking for a woman with wisdom. They have oil-filled lamps, prepared to meet the bridegroom at any moment. It's necessary for us to get ready to meet the Lord. The Lord is coming, I do not know the time and hour, but He is at the door.

Matthew 25:6 And at midnight there was a cry made, Behold, the bridegroom cometh; go ye out to meet him. 7 Then all those virgins arose, and trimmed their lamps. 10 And while they went to buy, the bridegroom came; and they that were ready went in with him to the marriage: and the door was shut.

His bride should prepare themselves to meet Him! Cleanse yourself of sins through the act of being baptized in Jesus's name. Blemishes of sins will disappear. Furthermore, she will experience the blessing of a clean conscience and a renewed heart.

Ephesians 5:26 That he might sanctify and cleanse it with the washing of water by the word, 27 That he might present it to himself a glorious church, not having spot, or wrinkle, or any such thing; but that it should be holy and without blemish. In Jesus 'name! Amen!

LET US PRAY

Lord, thank you for paying the price for your bride. Thank you for coming in as the Holy Spirit to lead, guide, and teach. What an excellent Lord you are!

Let us fill our minds with your words so we think and act like you. Help us, Lord, as it is us who needs to change. Our gracious Lord went to prepare the place for His bride and was coming soon to receive her. Lord, you have given us everything without holding back. The Lord gives us a caring heart and life. You gave us life and abundance with future promises to live with you where you are. Help us keep our lamp ready to meet you, in Jesus's name. Amen! God bless you!

JULY 4

CARRY A BURDEN OF NATION!

We should feel a sense of responsibility for nations and commit to praying for a specific country. We have been assigned homework by God. We must intervene in prayer for one another. We have a responsibility to pray for those who are imprisoned within the nation, unaware of the path to freedom. I've been praying for North Korea for years. It is only through God that we can be released from our captivity.

Psalm 126:1 A Song of degrees. When the LORD turned again the captivity of Zion, we were like them that dream.

The people of God were held captive in Egypt, Babylon, and throughout the world. There's always a reason behind people becoming captive. Freedom can be attained through prayer, whether it's yours or someone else's. May the Lord burden us to pray for those trapped in their homeland, oppressed by darkness or someone. We have the responsibility and honor to call out to God and liberate them. God alone can set the captive free. You can be confined to your home, sick, or trapped in poverty. Captivity comes in various forms. Satan binds us, but God sets us free. If you reach out, scream, and plead for liberation against it. You are not obligated to embrace your circumstances. Remember, calling for help means help is on its way.

Luke 4:18 The Spirit of the Lord is upon me because he hath anointed me to preach the gospel to the poor; he hath sent me to heal the brokenhearted, to preach deliverance to the captives, and recovering of sight to the blind, to set at liberty them that are bruised.

Poverty was prevalent in South Korea before they discovered Jesus. Many missionaries went to South Korea and prayed on the mountain. At first, many missionaries lost their lives while preaching the Gospel in South Korea. Several ministers prayed for the heart of South Korea to be opened by God. Prosperity came to the nation when its people turned to the Lord. God has the power to change poverty into prosperity if you have faith. The Lord Jesus is the sole deity, no others! In Egypt, the Hebrews, who were enslaved and persecuted, cried out to the Lord Jehovah God.

Exodus 3:9 Now therefore, behold, the cry of the children of Israel is come unto me: and I have also seen the oppression wherewith the Egyptians oppress them.

Deuteronomy 26:7 And when we cried unto the LORD God of our fathers, the LORD heard our voice and looked on our affliction, and our labor, and our oppression:

JULY 4

Hebrews, enslaved and without power, are incapable of helping themselves, but the God in Heaven has the ability. We see many nations around us, we know the situation, bondages, without God, in darkness, poverty, illiteracy, and sicknesses. We are tasked with praying for these individuals. We must cry out to the Lord. Knowing that Jesus came to liberate the captive, we have to ask for the burden to pray for them. It is my Job to pray for all afflicted. I discovered the situation in North Korea, empathized with their hopelessness, and felt compelled to pray for them. It had them trapped in a manner beyond anyone's imagination. Situations that are separate or disconnected from others. Their position of authority hinders their understanding of other nations. No. Koreans have TV, Radio, or phones that are not connected to learn about another country. They cannot get out of the government. What information do they have? They do not have any. Whatever information their authorities provide, that is what they believe. When my Korean friend informed me about the nation's sickness, malnourishment, and poverty, I knew I had to reach out to the Lord. May we be given the burden by the Lord to pray for those who are unable to help themselves.

If they get caught running out of the nation, the army will bring them back to the country, and the military will shoot them and have the people clap. If they find out any family members speak against the government, it will kill them, or they will have to go to the labor camp with all family members for a few generations. The treatment and torture are horrible. I started gathering more and more information over time. Surprisingly, cataracts can affect children as well. Food is available to their military soldiers. Soldiers are very healthy, so they can fight for their nation to keep the country in bondage. Their knowledge of Jesus is nonexistent. Their leader claimed to be God. You cannot pass by their enormous statue without worshiping. Upon waking up in the morning, your initial action should be to pay homage to the leaders who assert their divinity. They hold the belief that the leaders of the country are deities, not ordinary humans. The leader authored numerous books and manipulated their minds.

Friends, consider this scenario and try to understand the mindset they are experiencing. Despite being free, my mind frequently dwells on these individuals and I say prayers for them. In today's tech world, I connect to the computer to observe, read, and watch what's happening. Due to its restricted status, I couldn't find any information on North Korea. At least we have a clear focus for our prayers, finding testimonies of escaped people from the land. Stepping on their soil is not advisable, as it would result in immediate arrest. There is no possibility of leaving that land. The fear that resides in the hearts of those who live there or plan to visit North Korea. Imagine the severity of the situation. As I dedicated years to praying for them, I started receiving countless great reports. Many chose to escape, but many also encountered the Lord Jesus. Jesus does not need a passport or visa to save them. Angels have the freedom to depart at their own will. In their wings, God can both touch and hide them. My prayers were for these people to experience supernatural provisions, protection, deliverance, and support. I know Jesus has the power to set the captive free. Then why not? God can bring them out with the wings of an eagle. God can keep them hidden from the border patrol soldiers. God can save them from the bullet, cold river. I prayed for their safety in other nations. When individuals escape from North Korea, other countries don't profit from the situation. The act of hiring someone and then using the threat of deportation instead of paying them is comparable to imminent danger. Always a sword hanging over them! I began researching and gathering knowledge to pray in that particular way. The Lord is merciful! If we cry out, God will hear our cry. But one has to cry for help.

A doctor who specializes in eyes went to assist. A cataract caused vision impairment for numerous individuals. Our goal is to have a vision that allows us to recognize our excellent leaders. Really? They are ignorant about other nations and their leaders. The Lord is merciful and gracious, always answering if we pray and cry out. If you hear someone's head being severed, you will not be able to sleep and will cry out to God. All night long, I will also be praying. I pray many nights for people I know or do not know. The situation they were in was so terrible that it stirred my heart with compassion. If the Lord hears my prayer, then why not? I am praying for God to send an angel to open the prison door and set the captive free. I have faith that one day, North Korea and other nations will become reachable by the Lord. If someone calls upon Him, the Lord is there, looking down and ready to offer assistance. Someone has to cry out. God said in His Word, I can only move as much as you allow me to. If you don't call, let, give, or hand it over, even God is helpless.

Investigate the country's needs, assess the situation, and seek the intervention of the God of heaven. Lord, the nations require your guidance. Often, carrying His burden is the solution to your problem. No wonder the world is so bound because we do not care enough to call on God. May you receive His mighty provision, deliverance, healing, and touch. Observe the impact it has. What is the reason behind the high numbers of individuals who are naked, suicidal, incarcerated, impoverished, ill, oppressed, or possessed? Our failure to carry His burden is the reason. May the Lord bless us with a burden to intercede for and adopt an individual, family, city, or country to pray for in the name of Jesus! Amen! God Bless You!

Job 42:10 And the Lord turned the captivity of Job when he prayed for his friends: also, the Lord gave Job twice as much as he had before.

LET US PRAY

Our heavenly Father, you came down to free us from sin, sickness, fear, demons, and many troubles and conditions. Help us, Lord, to carry the burden so we can use the power of the Holy Spirit and authority to use it for the needy. May the Lord give us the desire to pray for those who do not know who Jesus is. A nation ruled by the wicked, kept in iron bars, needs salvation. Let the Lord set these captives free! We pray for those who are bound by any kind of addiction, abuse, oppression, or. May our Lord meet everyone's needs and set them free in Jesus 'name. Amen! God bless you!

JULY 5

LIVE IN GOD'S BOUNDARY!

It will be a blessing if we live within God's given boundary. Enjoy the Lord and His blessings. Try not to go over. Just a reminder, it wouldn't make you exempt. Look at the world. What happened as a result? While the Lord grants blessings, it's important to remember the guidelines to stay in His favor. A lot of people are immersed in sin and are unaware of God's Laws, precepts, and commandments. Are you a goose?

Jeremiah 17:11 As the partridge sits on eggs, and hatches them not; so he that gets riches, and not by right, shall leave them amid his days, and at his end shall be a fool.

The Torah was given to the people when they left Egypt, where they had been surrounded by a polytheistic culture, in order to worship the one true God. Israelis were led by God to a land flowing with milk and honey. Avoid breaking God's laws. God created Adam and Eve, gave them one barrier, and they stepped over. Do not cross the God given boundary.

To continue receiving blessings, it is crucial to obey a specific verse. Every blessing comes with limits, rules, guidance, and instructions to follow. People who have experienced the world tend to be resistant to boundaries. People like to follow Hollywood, unrighteous friends, religious ways, and their lust.

It is your responsibility to educate your children about God's ways to ensure the continuation of blessings.

The responsibility of training and teaching children falls on parents, not pastors, teachers, or prophets. God has not changed and will never. Moses, under the guidance of his mother who also acted as his babysitter, devoted himself to Jehovah God.

You believe that God granted you the promised land for unrestricted living. God gave The Jewish people the Torah, which is His revealed teaching or guidance for all of humanity. We were called by God and given the Bible, which consists of 66 books. Why? He wants you to be aware of the dos and don'ts to maintain your blessings. People in the Garden of Eden were naked. Now make sure you cover the body for protection, meaning do not display your body. If not, your little girl will be molested, raped, and kidnaped for prostitution. Her little body needs to hide with clothes since the devil and demons are looking to use the little body to destroy. Don't place blame on the devil, as his purpose is to steal, kill, and destroy. Before the 80s, I lived in India, where they loved modesty. Parents had the sense to cover the little girl and little boy's bodies. When they step out of the shower, they wrap themselves in a towel. The presence of any exposed body part will make them feel shy. I never heard or thought anyone had done improperly to the kid's body.

According to reports, India has initiated a movement of removing clothes, which has negatively impacted the respect for women. Wow! Choosing modest clothing can help reduce the risk of harassment. The first lesson God taught after sin entered was to clothe the body.

God cautioned to be careful, while the devil's designer praised your attractiveness and suggested wearing comfortable attire. Really? Parents are to blame for their ignorance. A family member is sexually assaulting many little girls.

Live with the knowledge. Remain within the boundaries. Despite being attractive, my mom never walked naked. The devil enjoys manipulating our minds.

People who used to break the judicial or Halakha Law had some stripes at the most 39. Why? We abide by laws. We won't be stuck in eternal damnation. We do not want to be misguided by Satan, who is a liar. You may say I do not see the devil; I see my parents, family, or TV. Well, you are called to follow the creator. Choose to follow the creator and not the destructive devil.

The devil sent countless people to hell, making them rich, poor, healthy, sick, and heartbroken. Children endure challenges in various forms: incarceration, homelessness, or addiction. Our primary responsibility is to educate our children about the laws of the Lord, not the ways of the world. I don't own a TV and have no interest in observing a chaotic world. According to the serpent, eating the fruit will make you god-like. Life is short. Do not forget the oil in the lamp. The devil will rob you by misleading you.

If you disobey the Lord, blessings will become a thing of the past. The house, car, freedom, and abundance of food will disappear. Despite having the key to the house, the car, food in the pantry, and a shower, I neglected to follow the Word of God, resulting in losing them all. Prioritizing the Word of God was essential in life, not just praying and fasting.

Is your story similar to how I dressed modestly and avoided movies, alcohol, drugs, adultery, lies, deception, and stealing? A past activity that you no longer engage in. I currently face the challenge of finding food and water, with nowhere to rest. It's your present lifestyle that shapes your identity, not your past.

Remember, *Judge 2:19 And it came to pass, when the judge was dead, that they returned, and corrupted themselves more than their fathers, in following other gods to serve them, and to bow down unto them; they ceased not from their doings, nor from their stubborn way. 20 And the anger of the Lord was hot against Israel; and he said, Because that these people hath transgressed my covenant which I commanded their fathers, and have not hearkened unto my voice;*

God reserved one tree and commanded them to avoid eating its fruit, yet what action did they take? Ate it, of course. Keep your eyes on the word of God. You are blessed, all right. You are free, all right; now you are looking everywhere, adopting everything the devil introduces and thinking there will be no punishment or sentence. No judgment? There is no need to worry about being evicted from your home, job, land, or the earth. Go see for yourself, countless nations have been destroyed. Today, cities are being set on fire. I want to clarify that I am speaking about today specifically, not any other day. Reading history is not even necessary.

JULY 5

Do you realize that the Lord watched over you today? He waits with great patience for you to transform. Yet, that devil remains vigilant about your whereabouts, interests, and cravings. The wise understand the importance of living within limits and remaining wholehearted. Isn't it evident that we'll depart from here and eventually go to your selected destination? You determine your destiny, not God.

God said to Adam and Eve, *Genesis 2:17 But of the tree of the knowledge of good and evil, thou shalt not eat of it: for in the day that thou eatest thereof, thou shalt surely die. (eternal death in hell)*

Every sin is transgression; sin has a destiny, and you will pay the wages.

Roman 6:23a For the wages of sin is death; Death is eternal hell punishment without exit.

Let me advise you to keep your eyes on God's word, follow it, and exercise it. I'd rather suffer for walking holy and righteous than burning in hell.

1 Timothy 4:8 For bodily exercise profiteth little: but godliness is profitable unto all things, having promise of the life that now is, and of that which is to come. 9 This is a faithful saying and worthy of all acceptation. 10 For therefore we both labor and suffer reproach, because we trust in the living God, who is the Saviour of all men, especially of those that believe.

The reason why many don't understand is because they have built a circle of friends and churches that prioritize money over truth, avoid correcting them, and show indifference. Oh well. Are you paying for their luxurious lifestyle to send you to hell? Are you too clever? Open the Bible and read the word of God to avoid repeating past mistakes. Blessings are temporary and contingent upon certain conditions.

1 Corinthians 10:11 Now all these things happened unto them for ensamples: and they are written for our admonition, upon whom the ends of the world are come.

Romans 15:4 For whatsoever things were written afore time were written for our learning, that we through patience and comfort of the scriptures might have hope.

A college friend of mine asked if I read my college books. Because she always witnessed me reading the Bible. Oh, Well, not as much as the Bible! I prioritize instruction from God over my study book. My life is filled with blessings because I prioritize God. Amen!

LET US PRAY

Lord, we come before you in the name of Jesus. Our computer mind should be complete with your words.

May the Lord help us and give us hunger and thirst for the word! Our soul needs direction to heaven, so help us, Lord, to focus on you. Thank you for the blood. Wash our sins in the blood. What a wonderful Savior! We say Thank you, Lord, for your blood. Wash us in the blood to take away our sins, give us a clean heart, faithful teachers, and prophets to keep on the runway of heaven. Make us an excellent example of this dying world. Give us a wise soul, knowledge, and mind to remember our boundaries in Jesus's name. Amen! God Bless You!

JULY 6

WORKS OF DEMON!

There are many religious people who lack knowledge about the spirit realm. Satan, along with a multitude of demons and fallen angels, conspires for the kingdom of darkness.

Learn about your opponent. Ignorance about the kingdom of darkness can be used against you. Knowledge is power. People study, study, and study for that reason. They are seeking both more money and a higher job title. Those who recognize that true success comes from knowing God, not worldly knowledge, will prioritize studying the Bible.

Proverb 24:5 A wise man is strong; yea, a man of knowledge increaseth strength.

Isaiah 33:6 And wisdom and knowledge shall be the stability of thy times, and strength of salvation: the fear of the Lord is his treasure.

Psalm 119:66 Teach me good judgment and knowledge: for I have believed thy commandments

Understanding the divine realm of King Jesus, His Kingdom, Satan, and his dark forces. In every kingdom, you will find a range of roles, such as employees, helpers, ministers, administrators, and workers. In order to achieve their kingdom's goals or mission, the king or prince will assign tasks to their workers. The goal of God's kingdom is to bless, provide, and grant a life filled with beauty, prosperity, and success to His creation. The kingdom of darkness, which belongs to Satan, is focused on killing, stealing, and destroying. The devil operates through lies and deception. The Lord Jesus, the King of all kings and Lord of all Lords, is the best choice for you. It is our duty to keep our attention on the Lord. May the Lord bless us with wisdom in this short-lived life, similar to vapor and grass in contrast to eternity.

Learn the work of Satan, fallen, unholy angels, and all demons, which are the lost soul works for Satan. Each individual has distinct tasks, abilities, influence, and potential—without a doubt, they are all spiritual entities lacking of physical form. Jesus, the God almighty, knew how to war with them.

Mark 5:6 But when he saw Jesus afar off, he ran and worshipped him, 7 And cried with a loud voice, and said, What have I to do with thee, Jesus, thou Son of the highest God? I adjure thee by God that thou torments me not. 8 For he said unto him, Come out of the man, thou unclean spirit. 9 And he asked him, What is thy name? And he answered, saying, My name is Legion: for we are many.

JULY 6

Spirits were commanded by the Lord to come out from a far-off place. Once you grasp the power given to you by God, you have the ability to command the devil to leave. He said our time hadn't come, do not torment us. Demons haven't been thrown into the lake of fire yet. Their actions are dictated by Satan and the fallen angel. They have to operate according to the assignment given by Satan.

Understand the demons, fallen angels, and Satan to engage in the fight. During my time in India, I was unaware of the world of evil spirits. Although I've read the Bible, I've never seen religious churches partaking in casting demon out or replicating the actions of Jesus and His disciples. Isn't that a shame? The only thing I heard were stories, but there was no demonstration. The witch doctor or Muslim Imam is usually consulted by most individuals seeking spiritual aid. Lucifer is responsible for the creation of religious organizations, denominations, and non-denominations. Why don't you seek God? Seek out genuine prophets and teachers of the Lord Jesus through fasting and prayer. Lord, please bring us a man and woman filled with the Holy Spirit. Turn to those who can offer you help under the guidance of God, not under the influence of Satan.

In 1999, I faced a health battle and sought God's guidance. Prayer and fasting were reducing the pain, but my goal was to fully regain mobility without the wheelchair. I needed to handle my things. Previously, I handled everything alone but due to health issues, I did very little. I had complete faith to walk, but the timing becomes significant during times of testing. Even though I had great faith, trials are always intertwined with the Lord's timing. A lady in the prayer room received a message from the Lord, who revealed that sister Elizabeth Das is currently going through a trial but will come out of it like pure gold.

In this critical time, God has selected and empowered this prophet and healer to assist me. Several years later, the Lord brought me into contact with this God-fearing man. I went to him seeking healing and obtained healing. The recovery process is still ongoing and took a while to complete. Lord confidently declared, "I will definitely walk!"According to the Lord's promise, one day I will be able to run."

The timing is in the hands of the Lord. The story of the Lord healing me has reached many ears. This brother became the one they started coming to. He is gifted with an a supply of mighty powers, including healing and deliverance.

As individuals approached him, he claimed that numerous Indians were under demon possession. I stated that if we don't possess the Spirit of God, a different spirit will take its place. According to him, Indians were extremely private, whispering in your ear and pleading you not to share with anyone.

Let me advise you to expose the devil, confess, and get cleansed. No one will have a place to spread gossip. When the devil is found, it has to flee. Shed light on the matter by speaking to the appropriate person, as the devil despises the light. Once the devil is disclosed, it will run.

Once I was healed, numerous individuals also found healing and deliverance from evil spirits. My trial had a positive impact on people from various nationalities and religious backgrounds, bringing them healing and deliverance.
I have witnessed numerous people experiencing healing and deliverance.

I have a testimony I'd like to share.

One young Indian lady came to Bro. James 'shop. She was married for almost ten years. She had one son, maybe eight years old, and later miscarried many. She went without her period for almost four years. She always complained of stomach pain. Many doctors were consulted, medication was taken, and numerous diagnostic tests were performed. None was showing any problem. The report indicated she was normal.

While brother James examined her for any signs of spirits, her eyes turned glassy, and demons began to manifest. As he asked the devil the name, the demon monster gave the name. The lady arrived accompanied by her husband, who shared the tragic news that one of her friends had the same name and took her own life by setting herself on fire. She was her best friend, and this lady was right there while dying. As her life came out, she entered the friend's body.

So Brother James asked the demon what she was doing in her body. The demon said I was jealous of her and did not want her to be happy. I killed her baby, and I stopped her period.

The workers of Satan have the task of killing, stealing, and destroying, as per their boss's orders. After death, they are not family or friends. Through his authority, Brother Min ordered the demons to leave her body. You have no business with someone who is lost in sins and dies.

I've had countless encounters with deceased individuals, ranging from family to friends and more. Once they are gone, they are gone. Do not do any rituals like candlelight or other things for the dead person. Order their demon to leave and firmly state that it is not welcome, not even in your dreams, in the name of Jesus.

The day Brother James cast out the demon, the same night she started her period, and her stomach aches left. Despite her husband's job search struggles, they were blessed with good jobs by the Lord. Additionally, they bought a new car. The devil is a stopper, blocker, and hindrance to our progress. With her testimony, this strong lady gave all glory to God. If you don't give God glory, you'll face even more hardship. There are those who choose not to admit that demons departed from their bodies. We must know the works of Satan, fallen or unholy angels, and demons. We have the power to defeat and destroy them, just as Lord Jesus and His Spirit-filled disciples did. I am so glad He has given me the power to do the same. Do not trust those who lack knowledge of the Spirit world, including false teachers and prophets. Learn and defeat the kingdom of darkness working against us. In Jesus 'Name! Amen,! God Bless You!

LET US PRAY

With the Lord's knowledge, we become powerful and authoritative in the world. Lord Christianity deals only with truth. It is the most accurate word of God but deals only with your instruction in the Bible. We desire to have truth and nothing but the truth. It is our God who said He changes not. Lord, grant us victory in every battle through your word and the power of the Holy Spirit. Lord, Only you know all, so we ask you to help us obey what thus saith the word of God. May our Lord bless us with more light and power to come against all of Satan's work! We love the Lord our God. Train us for your army to work according to your ways, agenda, and direction to get all healing, deliverance, and victory in Jesus's Name. Amen! God bless you!

JULY 7

WHY IS CHRISTIANITY BECOME POWERLESS?

Have you ever questioned if Christianity truly reflects the teachings of the Bible? Do you ever wonder why Christianity has deviated from the path set by Jesus Christ and His disciples?

I'm not talking about preaching or teaching, but openly proclaiming the mighty power of God to perform miracles, healings, prophecies, and deliverances. The blind can see, the deaf can hear, and the crippled can walk again. Examine Christianity based on the claims made in the Bible. Christianity's power diminishes when Christians fail to stay connected with God.

Have you heard much prayer, much power? Then less prayer, less energy. That is right. Neither you nor I have the power to do supernatural things; only God has that capability. You are powerless if you do not connect with the one who does all.

I experienced a dream where I walked in darkness, with someone by my side. I sensed the Lord's presence as I walked, guided by the Spirit. I wonder if this signifies the storms of life or the difficulties we encounter. There were numerous Indians on foot that I observed. The Lord clarified, saying, "No, it's still early morning in New York on the east coast." He started saying Hinduism is coming to the East Coast since Hindus are consistent in idol worship. They are inherited and passed on from generation to generation. As I woke up, I started praying, Lord, I come against their consistency in worshipping idols.

God said, do not pray like this. I started praying that they would stay asleep and not wake up early to engage in idol worship. Lord said 'no'. I sought divine intervention to find a new approach to overcome this terrifying dream. The Lord kept denying me, saying no each time. I sought the Lord's help in understanding how to pray. He said to pray that the Lord put Love for Jesus in the Hindu's heart. I thought this was very simple. However, I also shared it with other individuals who pray fervently. One evening, we all started praying against this future agenda of Satan on the east coast. I kept it a secret from other women, how Jesus instructed me to pray. But one of the Lady prayed intensely as the Spirit of God came on her. We all were in deep prayer. One sister said, we just have to pray that the Lord puts the Love for Jesus in their hearts. I said, Yes, it is the Lord.

Ever since I have been praying, I also asked you to pray that the Lord put love for Jesus in Hindu's heart. Consistency is all-powerful; it is called omnipotent. You or Daniel, who prays three times a day, will experience the power of God in operation. We can see the superpower of God in operation if we pray without ceasing, pray three times.

Daniel 6:10 Now when Daniel knew that the writing was signed, he went into his house; and his windows being open in his chamber toward Jerusalem, he kneeled upon his knees three times a day, and prayed, and gave thanks before his God, as he did aforetime.

Despite hearing his life was in danger, Daniel never altered the prayer time. This is what consistency looks like. I mean, what a fearless man. He prayed by letting them know you are not changing me. You can try all you want, but I will never back down, devil. I am praying and ready for whatever you throw at me. We need this type of fearless people to pray to a living almighty God. The consistent worship of false gods and goddesses leads to the manifestation of their power. The true world is the spiritual realm. Engaging in prayers and performing rituals will activate their dark powers, causing harm. Imagine being connected to the one true God, known as omniscient, omnipotent, and omnipresent. He is the God of peace, provider, healer, creator, and savior. He is the eternal God, Jehovah Jai-rah, the great I am, and the comforter. If you tap into the light of the world by connecting with this almighty God, the potential is limitless.

In order to witness God's mighty works, we must follow the footsteps of the obedient who experienced His supernatural interventions. Most people do not take advantage of this great God. Do not want to connect with God, but a brief prayer at lunch or dinner. Some pray a little here and there.

Idol worshipers do not see the significant results but are taught to be constant. What happens if you forget to charge your phone? The phone serves no purpose. By attending a building known as the church and reading the little Bible, you too become powerless. Seek the place and pray constantly, connecting with the power of God and witness the results. Observe the endless strength found in prayer. Prayer is a connection with the Lord, who does the supernatural. He specializes in the impossible and does miracles. He will come on the show to do it all in no time to let the world know that 'I am that I am. I am the only God. The power of Christianity diminishes when people fail to establish a connection with the all-powerful God. Experience the power of God's work by connecting with the Lord, regardless of your location. Religion, denominations, and non-denominations made Christianity powerless by disconnecting you from the Lord Jesus. He alone can handle your situation with knowledge and wisdom. Today I urge you to take your business seriously, stop connecting with churches, organizations, positions, and other agendas, reconnect with the great God Jesus and see what the Lord does. Lord Jesus claimed that I haven't changed, so why have you changed? God Almighty has given us this privilege to connect with Him, and if you do not use it means you have fired the God almighty. His hand has been bound by you. You have rejected the Only God. Reconnect with Him and witness the transformation on earth. Earth, where you and I live, has nothing but problems. Since we are not connected, we are not calling the one who can do all.

Don't forget to include God in your biking, running, exercising, and driving. Please start praying for at least 1 hour a day and gradually increase. Read the Bible regularly. Please do not make God powerless. Witness how Esther and King David connected with God and witnessed His mighty work in action. If you permit His authority and power to operate, you'll observe the identical results. Connect with the Lord; water cannot bury, fire cannot burn, the lion will be powerless, and evil power bows before the Lord. Your decision to connect with God determines your significant role in His kingdom.

Similar to those who sought God's guidance during trouble, the enemy's plan was ultimately defeated. Worked valiantly and saw the deliverance. Would you please allow God? Reestablish the connection with

JULY 7

Him, restoring God to His rightful place. Put God first when considering the needs of the nation or community. Take it to Him and let God take care of it. Put prayer in your schedule and pray. Instead of relying on other sources, make Him the first priority and turn to prayer. Muslims, too, pray five times and exhibit remarkable discipline. Cry out for help against drugs, alcohol, divorces, and many problems in a home, also in our nations. Instead of scratching your head, bow your head and converse with the creator to witness Satan flee.

David said in Psalms 55:17 evening, and morning, and at noon, will I pray, and cry aloud: and he shall hear my voice.

If we pray, God can destroy all plagues, cancer, oppression, possession, sicknesses, diseases, drug, suicide, and alcohol. Your enemy is unseen and powerful, skilled, with many devices. You cannot, but the Lord can destroy the devil and his plan. Can you please pray? May the Lord give us praying pastors, evangelists, mothers, and fathers! I have great respect for pastors who constantly pray, showing the power of God in action. People travel to those churches seeking healing, deliverance, and a message from the Lord. Let's come together today and reaffirm our connection to the mighty God, demonstrating the true power of Christianity to the world.

LET US PRAY

Lord, we know that you have all the power to do anything and everything if we bring the matter to your altar. The Lord gives us the desire to pray. Give us the Spirit of prayer so that we can pray. Our Lord, if we pray, then the chaos will disappear. The cause of trouble, problem, anxiety, distress, diseases, illness, and darkness is that we are a prayerless generation. But today, we recommit ourselves to you. Nothing is possible without you. We enter with faith, giving all to you, knowing our savior will do wonders on earth. The Lord does beautiful things again, so the world can say that Jesus is the living God. He can do everything. Thank you, almighty God, for being so wonderful to us. Bless your people today; hear us today in Jesus's name. Amen! God bless you!

JULY 8

MAKE IT CONTAGIOUS!

Question the words of others as mere boasting, but Christianity is the divine discourse that is rational. Do what "thus saith the Lord." It is the Lord's talk to His creation. If His creation, the children of God, listen and follow His instructions, then the God of Christians can become highly infectious.. Christianity provides the solution for all problems, questions, troubles, situations, sicknesses, deliverance, supernatural occurrences, and impossibilities. The contagious knowledge or events happening in the world have the potential to be life-changing, mind-changing, heart-changing, and world-changing, just like the authority given by the Lord to His disciple. Diseases like coughs, colds, viruses, the flu, and others are airborne and easily transmitted. God possesses the power to heal and offer assistance. Through the demonstration of power in Egypt, we see that our God is impartial and carries the ability to heal, cure, deliver, protect, and more. The undeniable demonstrations of God's power, which affirm His truth and faithfulness, will surely draw people to Christianity. How large was the crowd that came to hear Jesus preach?

Luke 12:1a In the meantime, when there were gathered together an innumerable multitude of people, insomuch that they trode one upon another.

We read the miracle of fishes, healing, and deliverance around Lord Jesus. His preaching was so contagious that it quickly spread among the people, spanning from city to region.

I couldn't find the words to express the amazing and astonishing feeling of my water baptism in Jesus's name. I was filled with admiration for what had transpired to me. My tireless search for truth was transforming into an experience. The content I was reading had a personal connection to me. What made a difference was the quickening Word of God, not just any word. Once I started obeying, the words began to take on a life of their own. May we be blessed with the understanding and acceptance of the word exactly as it is, as granted by the Lord. The Word of God should not be watered down or altered. Keep it as it is, refrain from making any additions or subtractions. If you change then it will be ineffective and cause harm. When Jesus passed by, everyone was eager to see Him and reach out to touch Him. His shadow was just as effective.

Luke 6:19 And the whole multitude sought to touch him: for there went virtue out of him, and healed them all. When Peter passed by,

Act 5:15 Insomuch that they brought forth the sick into the streets, and laid them on beds and couches, that at the least the shadow of Peter passing by might overshadow some of them.

JULY 8

The contagiousness of Christianity intensifies when obedience is wholehearted and unconditional.

When Peter Baptized people in Jesus 'name.

Act 2:41 Then they that gladly received his word were baptized: and the same day there were added unto them about three thousand souls. 47 Praising God and having favor with all the people. And the Lord added to the church daily such as should save.

Act 4:4 Howbeit many of them which heard the word believed; and the number of the men was about five thousand.

Witness the remarkable influence of those who repented, were baptized in the name of Jesus, and received the Holy Spirit. Jesus and His followers spread their influence like a contagious force. People trust anything and everything. Let me update you on what's happening at this moment. Are people bringing sickness to the churches today? If you continue following Jesus, the Lord will use your body as His church to heal and deliver, and hell cannot prevail against it. Can you explain the process and reasons behind the drastic change? It is because of our adding and subtracting in the word of God. The one in leadership divides to deviate and stop teaching and following God, and then the word becomes non-effect. You killed Christianity with your false belief. False prophets and teachers have brought about the downfall of Christianity. It is a mass confusion and mass production of the non- contagious product of true Christianity.

True-name brands with false teachers and prophets will decrease the number of believers. I will only accept the truth and nothing false or misleading. I always believed it should work if you follow as it is commanded in the Bible. I always questioned. Jehovah's Witnesses and Seventh-day Adventist teachers were upset with me once. I asked a genuine question, and the false teachers did not know the answer and left my house, putting me down. They wanted me to follow the serpent doctrine. I know better that I have to follow Jesus. It is impossible to accomplish it differently. Refrain from following someone who is lost. They fool you with the service they provide. They will do whatever it takes to convince you and bring you into their building. But I am not looking for their help, services, and favor.

My help cometh from the Lord. I believe in the supernatural, in Angels, and in all that Jesus said. So do not bribe or manipulate me; it wouldn't work. May the Lord have mercy on those who compromise for the piece of bread and little 30 silver coins? Doesn't the Bible say bribes will blind the person? Yes, it does. They read the Bible and will exactly do the opposite. I can't understand them since the Lord said to seek, ask and knock. I've heard and said on multiple occasions that we don't like religious people who are like this. There is something they have adopted and removed to become ineffective and divided in the world. Keep in mind, following them will influence your actions, speech, and thoughts to resemble theirs. Hollywood, Bollywood, and many prominent characters have become influential and contagious in the world, country, and places. Since I found the truth, many have turned to the living God. I will never win souls for church or organizations, and I am asking you to stay away, or you will disappoint many. Work for the Kingdom by following as instructed by Jesus.

Ephesians 2:20 And are built upon the foundation of the apostiles' and prophets, Jesus Christ himself being the chief cornerstone;

Acts 2:42a And they continued steadfastly in the apostles 'doctrine

Paul, John, and Jesus warn, Galatians 1:8 But though we, or an angel from heaven, preach any other gospel unto you than that which we have preached unto you, let him be accursed.

Galatians 'beginning was great but was bewitched by the false teachers and prophets. Stay away from those influential in churches but deviate from the power that made God and His work non-effective. Accepting the part of the truth will not work. Please go find a seat and enjoy the show as spectators. You're valuable to their company, but not to God's kingdom.

John 4:1 Beloved, believe not every spirit, but try the spirits whether they are of God: because many false prophets are gone out into the world.

Attempting to sell fake religious merchandise will prove futile, leaving individuals feeling cheated and powerless.

Timothy 3:5 Having a form of godliness, but denying the power thereof: from such turn whenever

I preach the truth and people witness its impact. They questioned why we don't engage in and encounter the same things she does. False teachers and false prophets are the reason for your intoxication. Previously, I had doubts regarding the authenticity of Christianity. Christianity is true if you are following the Word of God and not religious groups of denominations and non-denominations. Interestingly, people always turn to me for deliverance healing or spiritual assistance, and it always works. When people need spiritual guidance, they contact me. Advertising is never necessary for me. They know where to find help. Christianity has the power to be infectious, as long as it remains faithful to its principles. Stay away from added, or subtracted brand religion.

During my mom's illness, she would always request me to pray. She insisted that there was no necessity to call anyone, just pray. Why? Because the truth was working through me. She always felt good when I prayed over her. Her hearing was also improved whe I prayed. My mom had faith. She always gave glory to God and was blessed. In religion, it is believed that people will attain glory. No, it is the Lord, and He alone can do all. Glory belongs to the Lord alone. Carry the truth within your body. I watched a Church in Africa; the man was anointed, and people wanted to touch his hand. Why? Because the man of God was preaching and teaching the truth. The church was full, and an ambulance began bringing patients for healing. Wow! Christianity is contagious. Continue to follow and uphold the truth.

LET US PRAY

Lord, we know you came to establish on earth the mighty contagious wonder-working power of God. We want the original, which you established in the N. Testament. It is the act of the Holy Spirit done by the Disciples. Let the book of Acts continue by us; we want to follow you and not any denomination. The devil is a liar and has made many changes in the word of God to make it non-effect. We want to be contagious by caring for the genuine product by submitting you and your word. Thank you to those who follow you. We testify it is still working and sets people free, healed, and finding direction. We thank you for the truth in Jesus's name! Amen! God bless you!

JULY 9

WHO IS RESPONSIBLE?

Taking responsibility is something nobody likes. Adam neglected to apologize or confess his sin when God charged him. The Forbidden Fruit was an evaluation of Adam and Eve's submission. Take note of their response to God, despite their wrongdoing. Be mindful of your responses to God or anyone.

Genesis 3:12 And the man said, The woman whom thou gavest to be with me, she gave me of the tree, and I did eat. Adam put all blame on Eve.13 And the Lord God said unto the woman, What is this that thou hast done? And the woman said, The serpent beguiled me, and I did eat.

All blame for the incident was placed on the serpent by Eve. Everyone avoided taking responsibility for the transgression. If it tells you to do or not, remember that you are responsible for your actions. No one but you! Do not blame anyone. Confession is a powerful solution for transgression. You are to blame, but you cannot perceive it as God does.

If you want eternal life, the Bible is your life manual.

Consider this as the instruction manual for my existence. It provides excellent guidance for achieving a life of abundance. It's essential to study and have knowledge of the Bible. It has all the information for all we face on earth. Whether you like it or not, God both created and governs the earth. If you desire an eternal, abundant, and successful life on earth, it's up to you to obey God. Knowing the consequences, many would have made different choices. The person does not see their ways, which are the wicked ways and outcomes of it. Following the Lord's plan will bring exceptional supernatural rewards. Observe the lives of certain family members who have made rebellious and regrettable choices. A life filled with disobedience is a life plagued by curses. God gave the option to either follow His instruction or go your own way. You are granted complete authority to inhabit earth, but you will be held accountable for your deeds.

Deuteronomy 30:19 I call heaven and earth to record this day against you, that I have set before you life and death, blessing and cursing: therefore choose life, that both thou and thy seed may live:

God keeps the earth and heaven as His witness.

Regardless of your reasoning, the blame falls on you in the end. None but you! May the Lord help us. Please open the Bible, yes, the Bible! Open and read the Bible to find what will make you most wealthy or by ignoring the poorest.

Genesis 13:2 And Abram was very rich in cattle, in silver, and gold.

Who was chargeable for that? Abraham's decisions were right.

James 2:23 And the scripture was fulfilled which says, Abraham believed God, and it was imputed unto him for righteousness: and he was called the Friend of God.

King Jehoram became king after His father, King Jehoshaphat. Jehoram's death was unusual.

2 Chronicles 21:19 And it came to pass, that in the process of time, after the end of two years, his (Jehoram) bowels fell out by reason of his sickness: so he died of sore diseases. And his people made no burning for him, like the burning of his fathers.

There must be some connection between this sickness and sin. Let us see why and what he did. Who should take responsibility for it?

2 Chronicles 21:12 And there came a writing to him from Elijah the prophet, saying, Thus saith the Lord God of David, thy father, Because thou hast not walked in the ways of Jehoshaphat, thy father, nor in the ways of Asa king of Judah, 13 But hast walked in the way of the kings of Israel, and hast made Judah and the inhabitants of Jerusalem to go a whoring, like to the whoredoms of the house of Ahab, and also hast slain thy brethren of thy father's house, which were better than thyself: 14 Behold, with a great plague, will the Lord smite thy people, and thy children, and thy wives, and all thy goods: 15 And thou shalt have great sickness by disease of thy bowels until thy bowels fall out by reason of the sickness day by day.

Heaven and earth have recorded his deeds. If you do not choose right, sickness will pop up in your body one after another. You may take medicine, but a cure comes from God. If you choose to take responsibility and sincerely ask for forgiveness, saying, "Lord, I am turning away from my wicked ways." Merciful God will forgive you. Don't forget, God is more powerful than you. Please choose right, fear God, and have wisdom. When I get sick, I always check my backpack. Is there any sin involved? The blind spot for anger, unforgiveness, lies, stealing, killing, disobeying, jealousy, and pride is often overlooked. Ignorance of sin can lead to numerous harmful illnesses. Take care of sin by confessing and turning from it. Your ailments will disappear. I have personally observed a multitude of individuals being baptized in Jesus's name, resulting in the forgiveness of their sins and receiving healing. They accepted responsibility for their actions and found a way to resolve the situation. Take responsibility for your doing or ignoring.

Haggai 1:6 Ye have sown much, and bring in little; ye eat, but ye have not enough; ye drink, but ye are not filled with drink; ye clothe you, but there is none warm, and he that earneth wages to put it into a bag with holes.

Who is responsible for their action? No one but them! Use the true prophets; He will confront you without fear. Allow the Word of God to speak to your heart as you read it. Give ear to the Holy Spirit's voice. It will guide you. There's a lot of assistance waiting for you if you are open to it.

Haggai 1:2 Thus speaketh the Lord of hosts, saying, these people say, The time is not come, the time that the Lord's house should be built. 3 Then came the word of the Lord by Haggai the prophet, saying, 4 Is it time for you, O ye, to dwell in your cieled houses, and this house lie waste? 5 Now therefore thus saith the Lord of hosts; Consider your ways.

JULY 9

When residing in a traditional country that has strong views on sin, respect their boundaries and live within their rules. However, this becomes an issue if you reside in a free country. Embrace the teachings of God in your life. Do not flow with Satan. Regardless of whether the country is unrestricted or restricted, the Lord granted you precepts, laws, and commandments. You have the option to obey or disobey, with potential gains or losses depending on your choice. You are responsible for all that you choose, do, ignore, or overlook. Let our hearts be filled with wisdom from the Lord. God did not grant any exceptions. King, priest, a high priest, Jesus as being the God in the flesh, poor, rich, free or bound; we all have equal responsibilities. We are responsible for our problems, sickness, trouble, or complications. Is it the one you see when you look in the mirror? Do you desire a life that is peaceful, blessed, and mentally, emotionally, and spiritually healthy? My mom was brave; she took responsibility in the home with her children. She was responsible, waking up early to prepare meals and making sure we had enough money for school and college, always staying committed. We are all grateful to her, but I am especially thankful. Through marriage, many people came and their children were blessed as a result of her bringing blessings. She never thought about what or how they would reward her. Fear not, the Lord showed great favor to her and rewarded her generously.

When I was visiting back in India, many said none of her sons or daughter-in-law kept her. I mentioned it, but only if you know how beautiful her life was until God took her to heaven. Honoring us is the Lord's responsibility, and He always remains faithful. Take responsibility for your doing. Regardless of your living conditions, job, and income, how are you doing and what are you doing with your life? Do not assume that God has blind spots, like you do. God is good! Remember to accept responsibility for your evil deeds and humbly seek forgiveness. You will receive your peace and blessings. Who should be held responsible for the deaths caused by illnesses? You alone are responsible for everything, not your spouse or neighbor. Become mature and take responsibility.

LET US PRAY

Our heavenly Father, thank you for the Bible. It is the most beautiful book we have. The Bible contains love, lights, food for the soul, and much more. We must dive deep into the word and learn to receive blessings. Help us read and digest in our daily diet. It is a life-giving and excellent book for everyone who believes and obeys, as your word says that on judgment day, the word will judge us. A book will be opened up to the judge. May Lord wipe out our sins and trespasses in His precious blood. We are in charge of taking care of our neighbors, children, and parents. We are responsible for the poor. Help us get mature and accountable in Jesus's name. Amen! God bless you!

JULY 10

THERE IS A RIGHTFUL FIGHT!

We all have to survive, so we must overcome all things that oppose, block, and resist. We all experience hardships and conflicts in our journey. Success belongs to those who actively seek and pursue it.

The devil will target anything that goes against the loving creator's human creation. Maintaining inner strength, courage, perseverance, and focus on a goal leads to success.

My mother was committed to providing education for her children and did whatever it took. She worked as a full-time nurse and a full-time mom. You know full-time mom is 24/7. She worked hard with many physical difficulties to pursue her goal. She diligently monitored her children's academics and personal affairs. I discussed my topic with her, and she was familiar with everything about me. She will work while I talk; she will hear and advise me. I can confirm that she did it for all her children. My mom had a goal for our future. She fought for it. Never back off or back down. May she receive the Lord's blessings!

God rewards those who earnestly seek Him.

Hebrews 11:6b and that he is a rewarder of them that diligently seek him.

1 Timothy 6:12 Fight the good fight of faith, lay hold on eternal life, whereunto thou art also called, and hast professed a good profession before many witnesses.

Anyone called by the Lord will go through the battle. I speak to many converted Christians. Seeing their commitment and made-up mind gives me more confidence for their future. If there is no fight in your life, then there is no future. Victory is only achieved through battle. If your goal is to become a leader or someone significant, then confront the enemy and its army. If you keep going and never quit, your dream will become a reality. Losing the goal is why cowards end up losing.

A letter was written by Paul addressed to Timothy and all of us. In Rome, he was executed by beheading for spreading the truth. Paul's teachings were rejected by the emperor due to his homosexuality. At last, his head was removed. Wow!

2 Timothy 4:7 I have fought a good fight, I have finished my course, I have kept the faith: 8 Henceforth there is laid up for me a crown of righteousness, which the Lord, the righteous judge, shall give me at that day: and not to me only, but unto all them also that love his appearing.

JULY 10

Paul can say that he achieved his goal.

2 Corinthians 5:8 We are confident, I say, and willing somewhat to be absent from the body, and to be present with the Lord

Paul said I long to see Jesus.

Paul gave a long list of his battles. He fought rightfully. Paul won in the end.

In 2 Corinthians 11:23, Are they ministers of Christ? (I speak as a fool) I am more; in labors more abundant, in stripes above measure, in prisons more frequent, in deaths oft. 24 Of the Jews five times received I forty stripes save one. 25 Thrice was I beaten with rods, once was I stoned, thrice I suffered shipwreck, a night and a day I have been in the deep; 26 In journeyings often, in perils of waters, in perils of robbers, in perils by mine own countrymen, in perils by the heathen, in perils in the city, in perils in the wilderness, in perils in the sea, in perils among false brethren; 27 In weariness and painfulness, in watchings often, in hunger and thirst, in fasting often, in cold and nakedness.

Once you've made up your mind, you won't budge. Heaven will provide assistance if your faith is based on a good reason and for God's purpose. You serve as a representative of God to demonstrate His power through living and practicing His teachings. Hebrew chapter 12 includes you as one of the characters in the cloud of witnesses.

David was involved in several battles, with God as a witness, resulting in the shedding of much blood. He was branded as the one who killed 10,000 people. His faith, submission, and trust in the Lord made David a great King of Israel during the monarchy. The Messiah descended from David's bloodline. A title cannot be achieved without going through a battle.

You win the battle on your knees by exercising the word of God. Winning against a righteous fighter is impossible, keep that in mind. God's got their back. King Saul, the Philistines, Amalek, Goliath, and numerous other nations had no chance against King David. The young shepherd boy fought bravely against anyone who threatened his sheep, his country Israel, or the name of God Jehovah, until he finally reached the throne.

Define the concept of a rightful fight. When you defend what's right and oppose anyone who goes against it.

Christian values of truth, kindness, generosity, compassion, and righteousness were evident in my mom's character. She stood up for all of us, including the underprivileged individuals at her job. Testimony regarding her was given by her superior. She was widely recognized as the most truthful and honest lady. What does it signify that she never engaged in any battles? Despite the many obstacles, she stood firmly on the truth and confronted the devil. She never made compromises when it came to falsehood or incorrectness. You can rely on the Lord God to support you. Mom commanded the devil to kneel. I would not. I am firmly rooted in the truth and sacred space.

Don't make deals with the devil or his followers, including King Soul, Caiaphas the high priest, Ananus, Herod the King, and all Jews. Despite the circumstances, Jesus did not back away, but chose to fight on the cross and bring us life. This fight is referred to as a righteous one.

Many paid the price of their lives to stay true to the truth. Nothing in life is easy, as you can see. There is a battle, but hold on to the Lord. He will see us through. May the Lord provide blessings and strength during these challenging times. The help of King Jesus is crucial for any battle to end in victory. You can never win without the support of the Lord Almighty. Your adversary comes as a roaring lion, but God can shut the mouth of that lion.

The result will be amazing. Goliath's head was given to the bird of the air by someone who stood up for their God. God removed King Saul as he wanted to do away with God's plan. God removed him as he tried to remove David. The end of the trial is critical because it feels like you're losing. You will die. The future promises will remain unseen, but wait. The battle is against your faith; no harm will come to you if you keep the faith.

Hebrew chapter 11 declares victory for the righteous. Read it over and over as a reminder. The fight worth fighting for is the only one that's just. Stay connected with the Lord as you fight your righteous battles in Jesus's name! Amen! God Bless you!

LET US PRAY

Lord, you love the righteous. Righteous children will never beg for bread. May we all have the breastplate of righteousness! Stand on the honest word of God on the battleground. Our nation can be blessed if we stand on the word of God, which is unshakable. Lord, let our country enforce the righteous laws of righteous God. Lord, give us courage and boldness like Daniel, David, and others who fought rightfully. We thank you, Lord, for your word. Teach us to be righteous. May the righteous Lord give our home, family, city, and nation His righteousness to prosper and bless in Jesus's name. Amen! God bless you.

JULY 11

SUCCESSFULLY DEVIL REMOVED THE BLOOD!

After the crucifixion of Jesus, the devil held a meeting with his fallen angels. He mentioned that the blood is now accessible, but questioned how to cease accessing the lamb's blood. If we fail to do so, the gates of hell will not overcome.

Matthew 16:15 He saith unto them, But whom say ye that I am? 16 And Simon Peter answered and said, Thou art the Christ, the Son of the living God.17 And Jesus answered and said unto him, Blessed art thou, Simon Barjona: for flesh and blood hath not revealed it unto thee, but my Father which is in heaven.18 And I say also unto thee, That thou art Peter, and upon this rock, I will build my church; and the gates of hell shall not prevail against it.19 And I will give unto thee the keys of the kingdom of heaven: and whatsoever thou shalt bind on earth shall be bound in heaven: and whatsoever thou shalt loose on earth shall be loosed in heaven.

The devil is aware of Jesus 'secret, which is only disclosed through revelation. The recognition of Jesus as the Messiah is known as the foundation of rock. Satan cannot prevail against the church if it is built on the grounds of Jesus 'revelation. By altering God's word, Satan created deceitful and manipulative idea. Let us raise many false teachers, prophets, and their followers. Make sure to never reveal Jesus 'true identity to anyone. Anyway, most believers originated from a polytheistic nation. Instead of being the only God, let's view Jesus as the second God. It will be a challenge for the devil to convince Jews, but it will be effortless with gentiles. By adding the Holy Ghost as the third God, we can establish a trinity and clarify its concept of being three in one.

Wow! Wonderfully removed the name of Jesus. Jesus is the name of a sacrificed lamb and the life giving blood is hidden under this NAME.

Acts 10:43 To him give all the prophets witness, that through his name whosoever believeth in him shall receive remission of sins.

Also, under the name "Jesus", God buried the remitting blood.

1 John 5:6 This is he that came by water and blood, even (which is) Jesus Christ; not by water only, but by water and blood. And it is the spirit that beareth witness because the spirit is truth.

In their conversation, Satan and the fallen angels determined that the exclusion of blood is essential in their plot to overthrow God's redeeming plan. The devil finds the blood of Jesus alive and terrifying. Blood has life. Through the blood of Jesus, their sins will be erased and they will have a renewed conscience, freeing them from the clutches of evil and the power of sin with memory. Jesus will come as the Holy Spirit in them; they will be powerful. Jesus will live in them. According to Satan, the book of Acts contains more than three scriptures supporting the doctrine of baptism in the name of Jesus. The doctrine can be established according to the Word of God using a rule that is known to everyone. Two or more scriptures are required to back up the doctrine you want to establish. So baptism is hard to replace with one scripture.

Matthew 28:19 Go ye therefore, and teach all nations, baptizing them in the name of the Father, and of the Son, and the Holy Ghost:

Who do you think will believe this? Jesus 'name of baptism is supported by more than three scriptures.

1st Acts 2:38a Then Peter said unto them, Repent, and be baptized every one of you in the name of Jesus Christ for the remission of sins.

2nd scripture Acts 10:48, And he commanded them to be baptized in the name of the Lord.

John's followers were baptized a second time in the name of Jesus.

Third encounter. Acts 19:5. When they heard this, they were baptized in the name of the Lord Jesus.

Acts 9:18 after converting to Jesus. Paul said,

Acts 22:16 And now why tarriest thou? Arise, and be baptized, and wash away thy sins, calling on the name of the Lord.

Satan was concerned about the most damaging scriptures for his realm of darkness. Satan struggles with this scripture. One follower of the devil said, but our kingdom's key is to divide and rule. The prophecy in Isaiah, concerning the one God incarnate sacrificing sinless blood for the world, is unknown to this converted heathen. By dividing one God, we represent Jehovah, Jesus, and the Holy Spirit as three separate gods. If we destroy the first commandment, then our job is well done.

Deuteronomy 6:4 Hear, O Israel: The Lord, our God, is one Lord:

At this moment, it has transitioned into a project. We are in need of a significant number of individuals to complete this task. Let the Alexandria apostasy be the starting point for the project of the antichrist. Excellent job! Take out or twist all references in the scriptures that establish Jesus as God incarnate.

The flesh is a manifestation of One God.

1 Timothy 3:16b God was manifest in the flesh,

Oh, also replace "God" with "he." Second, they do not have the revelation of Jesus, and our theological colleges will train the false teachers and prophets, missionaries, and evangelists. They will do good work. Offer them ample funds and persuasive arguments to oppose the truth. Our fallen angels and demons will

JULY 11

use scripture games as we did to Eve. Defeating the incarnation of Jesus Christ, the one God, will be effortless for us. The work of spreading Jesus 'revelation with His followers can be easily destroyed. We will allow false prophet and teachers to do whatever they want. They could exhibit traits of being deceitful, unfaithful, intoxicated, promiscuous, greedy, and the list goes on. It is fine! Simply don't educate on the truth. We ask them to use and confuse them by saying, Jesus said it.

Matthew 28:19 Go ye therefore, and teach all nations, baptizing them in the name of the Father, the Son, and the Holy Ghost:

Once they have no revelation of Jesus, it will be easy to follow the book of acts. Once the name of Jesus is removed, then the blood of Jesus is out. Without forgiveness of sins, there would be no deliverance from demons and sickness. The agenda of Satan is to create challenges for believers in God and Holy Ghost-filled churches, who have been baptized in Jesus 'name, through their religious leaders and followers. On Broadway, we will introduce the Devil's followers to the toxic doctrine of the Trinity, and they will willingly embrace it while rejecting the truth. Look at the success Satan achieved in Galatians. Paul stood firm in reality, while devil sent false teachers and prophets to corrupt. Paul was upset with the church in Galatians.

Galatians 3:1 O foolish Galatians, who hath bewitched you, that ye should not obey the truth, before whose eyes Jesus Christ hath been evidently set forth, crucified among you? 2 This only would I learn of you, Received ye the spirit by the works of the law, or by the hearing of faith? 3 Are ye so foolish? Having begun in the spirit, are ye now made perfect by the flesh?

Satan said, we need to start our project before the truth is revealed to everyone. Upon discovering our work in the churches of God, John, who held a special place in Jesus 'heart, delivered a warning to the followers of the truth.

1 John 4:1 Beloved, believe not every spirit, but try the spirits whether they are of God: because many false prophets are gone out into the world.2 Hereby know ye the Spirit of God: Every spirit that confesseth that Jesus Christ is come in the flesh is of God:3 And every spirit that confesseth not that Jesus Christ is come in the flesh is not of God: and this is that spirit of antichrist, whereof ye have heard that it should come; and even now already is it in the world.

Satan has a master plan to deceive many. In Los Angeles, Satan worshipers encountered a woman filled with the Holy Spirit who believed in one God and was baptized in Jesus 'name. According to a female follower of Satan, our church members are fasting, praying, and summoning demons to make pastors, preachers, and evangelists fall into financial adultery. During that time, a considerable number of preachers got caught up in affairs and became ensnared in money scandals. It's best if they don't engage in preaching, teaching, setting people free, delivering, and healing. People enter the church and leave as they were. We intend to make them infested with numerous demons, eliminating all chances of belief. According to the Devil, it has always been effective, even with Adam and Eve. To make it work, we need to be consistent in hypocrisy, lying, and cheating.

Currently, how many of our followers are affiliated with numerous denominations, organizations, and non-denominations? Satan claimed to have been in heaven, where there was only one throne and one God. He admitted to trembling, but revealed that his mission was to divide the one God into three and disrupt His plans for creation. By removing the name, we will successfully remove the blood that takes away their sins.

The name of the Father, Son, and Holy Spirit is not a priority for people, according to the Devil. If Jesus' name is removed, they won't have his blood and won't reach heaven.

If you're not a fan of organized religion, I advise you to pursue truth instead. Find the truth and unlock your freedom.

LET US PRAY

Our Father, which art in heaven Hallowed is thy name. The N.T. name of Jehovah God is Jesus.

It is the name above all previous names of Jehovah God. Every knee will bow, and every tongue confesses to the name of Jesus. All demons tremble before the name of Jesus. Sick, possessed, oppressed, healed in the name of Jesus. Our God Jehovah has taken the highest saving name, 'Jesus 'at the end of time. Where will we be named if they baptize us in this precious name? This name has authority in heaven, on earth, and below the earth. We bow before this name. Jesus meant "Jehovah's savior", our master, redeemer. Your name is beautiful; your name turns sorrow to gladness, beauty for ashes, and heals the broken in heart. Thank you, Lord, In Jesus's name! Amen! God bless you!

JULY 12

LOOK AT THE FRUITS!

The tree is identified by examining its fruits. The tree's name holds significance, just like its valuable fruits. Additionally, we possess both the fruits of the spirit and the flesh. Pride, jealousy, adultery, lies, drugs, and alcohol are all evil manifestations found in fleshly fruits. Similar to how no one would expect an apple to be on a thorn tree. Evil won't produce any products, so don't expect any. Those who walk in the spirit display their fruits.

Galatians 5:22 But the fruit of the spirit is love, joy, peace, longsuffering, gentleness, goodness, faith, 23 Meekness, temperance: against such, there is no law.

The act of repentance and baptism, in Jesus 'name cleanses sins with his blood. By calling upon the name of Jesus, they are filled with the Holy Spirit and begin to walk in the spirit. Those who are led by the spirit bear good fruits. Beautiful products come from good people. Good parents take time to train children well. They consistently lead righteous lives and speak God's word to the children.

Matthew 7:16 Ye shall know them by their fruits. Do men gather grapes of thorns or figs of thistles? 17, Even so, every good tree bringeth forth good fruit; but a corrupt tree bringeth forth evil fruit. 18 A good tree cannot bring forth evil fruit, neither can a corrupt tree bring forth good fruit. 19 Every tree that bringeth not forth good fruit is hewn down and cast into the fire. 20 Wherefore by their fruits ye shall know them.

Evil parents will give birth to evil products. Regardless of their level of education, their children cannot become good. If the mother is evil, her daughter will become a skilled and heartless individual. Do you ask the snake's offspring if they consider the rabbit to be their parents? You catch sight of them and immediately flee. The snake does not differentiate between God's children or Satan when it comes to biting. It is their nature; it is in their blood. Your children are a reflection of who you are. During our time in India, and later in America, my mom always emphasized the importance of being selective about who we spoke to. If there's anything wrong, she never fails to inform us about the person. When mom started saying awful things about the person, we chose to walk away. Companies with bad intentions can pollute our minds. My mom had a perceptive understanding of people. Reflect on the potential outcomes of having deceitful spouses. If the grandmother is a witch, her daughter will become one too and receive the same training. Evil parents cannot produce anything good.

Deuteronomy 7:3 Neither shalt thou make marriages with them; thy daughter thou shalt not give unto his son, nor his daughter shalt thou take unto thy son. 4 For they will turn away thy son from following me, that they may serve other gods: so will the anger of the Lord be kindled against you, and destroy thee.

Why shouldn't we mingle with the evil company? Our God is Holy, and we have to be Holy to serve the Holy God. If you marry a rebellious, wicked, jealous, ungodly spouse, you will become like one, and your children will also be like you. You produce your kind. God warned us to keep our distance from evil. If you want to contaminate the family, get women or men of that kind. They will infect not just their children but anyone in contact with them. I am cautious about my company, even if they are relatives. We do not have to mix or associate since there is no common ground. But pray for them.

The Bible warns us to be careful of false prophets and teachers. How do you know if it is inaccurate or accurate? Identify the fruits. They are no good if you see them talking well but living badly or thinking dirty. Run away from them.

Matthew 7:15 Beware of false prophets, which come to you in sheep's clothing, but inwardly they are ravening wolves. 16 Ye shall know them by their fruits. Do men gather grapes of thorns or figs of thistles? 17, Even so, every good tree bringeth forth good fruit; but a corrupt tree bringeth forth evil fruit.

How you produce good fruits.

Ephesians 5:9 (For the fruit of the spirit is in all goodness and righteousness and truth;)

Love, joy, peace, long-suffering, gentleness, goodness, meekness, faith, and temperance are the fruits that come from the combination of Goodness, Righteousness, and Truth. When you see this type of character, you can recognize that they are productions of God. Steer clear of individuals who are liars, deceivers, wicked, sinners, or unrighteous.

I was told by someone from my college that I have the ability to recognize the Christian in a crowd of thousands. So I asked her how? She remarked about seeing the light shining on their faces. Furthermore, she remarked that I have a Christian neighbor, and their kids have good discipline. Parents call and they immediately respond. Instead of saying later or in a minute, they always respond immediately.

I have great admiration for the missionaries. It was them who initiated the hostel in India. The ones who trained under the missionaries were well-regulated. Their lifestyle, eating, sleeping, and work habits serve as living examples. The missionaries sowed the seed of the Word of God in their hearts! The seed you plant in the heart will flourish. I often feel sorry for the children of the wicked; I believe the children are never wrong, but the hostile parents plant evil seeds. They corrupt their young spirits, shaping them to be just like themselves. The source of hindrance lies within us, not outside, but inside. A toxic relative will envy, deceive, and act maliciously towards you. Their sickness is a result of the cruelty they harbor. Be careful! Clean your heart which is the origns of the house. Strive for cleaning that meets God's standard.

2 Corinthians 7 Having, therefore, these promises, dearly beloved, let us cleanse ourselves from all filthiness of the flesh and spirit, perfecting holiness in fear of God.

Ruth Moabite received praise for her character and fruitful actions.

JULY 12

Ruth 3:11 And now, my daughter, fear not; I will do to thee all that thou requirest: for all the city of my people doth know that thou art a virtuous woman.

I am aware that the fruits cannot stay hidden. Whether you're wicked or virtuous, hiding is not an option. The only person who is blind is you? Deception will always uncover your true nature, regardless of how well you deceive and lie. You can't claim to be a fig while being a thorn in God's side. Turn your life around by repenting and confessing to the Lord. Confess your true self to God in detail, and He will grant you forgiveness. God will come and help you as the Holy Spirit. Transformation is possible if you allow the word of God to work in your life. Don't give in to Satan's lies, God has the ability to bring about change in you. He will make you a good fruitful tree. Many nations will be blessed because of you. Embrace peace by being in harmony with the Lord.

Ezekiel 47:12 And by the river upon the bank thereof, on this side and on that side, shall grow all trees for meat, whose leaf shall not fade, neither shall the fruit thereof be consumed: it shall bring forth new fruit according to his months because their waters they issued out of the sanctuary: and the fruit thereof shall be for meat and the leaf thereof for medicine.

LET US PRAY

Lord, we come before your altar to thank you. The word of God is a mirror; the word of God is a seed. Let it be planted in the good ground of our hearts. My Lord, we are grateful for your word, which we want to grow in our hearts. We are thankful for taking your time to give us your commandment and way of righteousness.

Your love is beyond. We try every day to be like you. We are grateful for the good God. He has all that we require to learn. You are the example of the manifestation of all fruits. We love you, Lord, for all you have done for us. Please give us your joy to be our strength. Encourage and strengthen us to bear the fruit of love and peace. We thank you, especially for giving us your peace in Jesus 'name. Amen! God bless you!

JULY 13

DO NOT STOP, PRESS THOUGH!

These are my observations over the past few decades. As a dictator emerges, religious authorities will stand by and observe. The program will include limited preaching, teaching, singing, and laying of hands, concluding with the end of the show and people leaving. The task is not properly executed but still requires completion. When you're working, you keep going until the job is done. The responsibility of raising children lasts until it's done. We don't give birth, leave children somewhere, and go home. Our responsibility is to complete the task when we serve Jesus. We do not see the fruits of deliverance, healing, and salvation anymore. I am not talking about what denominations and non-denominations say about salvation. Nothing is right, except for following Jesus. You should only follow Him, as you are the church and not the den created by the thief. You learn your new role by doing, practicing, and acting, not just sitting in the den on pew.

We consistently report the count of individuals baptized in the name of Jesus and those who have received the Holy Spirit.

Upon birth in the kingdom, individuals unknowingly become soldiers with no training. Rather than following Jesus, they must divert from their path and comply with the rules of the authorities. These babies don't have any parents. Taking care of and raising babies is not desired by anyone. Helpless newborn babies are being assaulted with no one to come to their aid.

The Lord shows us mercy. The purpose of Jesus coming to earth was to set an example. The Lord Jesus mentored disciples, offering encouragement, teaching, and ministering in every aspect. They were never out of His sight. These days, people simply go home once the church service is finished. People neglect their spiritual well-being and suffer from demonic torment. We respond to their tears by telling them to mature. We are operating under the assumption that they will be fine. The shepherds are occupied with their hobbies. Saying anything will lead to scrutiny, group hostility, and expulsion. Did Jesus cause a disturbance by overturning the table and accusing them of stealing?

I want to remind you that the devil has not changed. Satan is knowledgeable about how humans in their physical bodies experience lust, specifically the desire for material things and a sense of arrogance about their own lives. The devil has always sought to destroy and continuously devises new strategies to steal and kill what God has created.

JULY 13

I want to share my experience. Once in a worship service, the devil came over me like a tight dress. It came at me aggressively. The Devil and I were grappling with each other in a wrestling match. It seemed as though I was contending with a physical presence. If I hadn't wrestled and trampled it under my feet, he would have taken me down, and they would have called 911 and sent me to the hospital. The combination of my ongoing fasting, prayer, and teamwork with devoted disciples granted me both power and wisdom. I felt relieved when I successfully counter-attacked in the war zone and defeated the enemy. It exited the church building, and naturally, it first departed from my own body. When I left the church, it assaulted me right outside. I was in an awful wrestle with the devil that week. I learned and discovered that the devil waits outside to come against people.

What can happen to a new convert? Despite their lack of preparedness for battle, those who professed to be church authorities were still immersed in the water, baptizing people in Jesus 'name. It's regrettable that this gathering, consisting of a painting party, tea party, and luncheon, serves no purpose except to weaken and mislead the saints. Make new convert more ignorant about warfare. Jesus held onto His disciples and provided teachings on prayer, deliverance, and healing. The Lord provided disciples with diverse training in warfare. The world acknowledges the disciples of Jesus for their ability to revolutionize the world.

Acts 17:6 And when they found them not, they drew Jason and certain brethren unto the rulers of the city, crying, These that have turned the world upside down have come hither also;

During another instance, a newly converted individual brought her husband who was possessed. He dropped to the ground in front of me. I began the act of casting out demons. Despite the strong attack, I overcame it in the name of Jesus because my spiritual muscles were stronger than the devil's. As soon as they saw him on the floor, they called 911 and quickly transported him to the hospital. That statement is indeed accurate. Nobody had any idea of how to handle the situation. This was a non-denominational Pentecostal building or church. Can the doctor perform a casting out of the demon?

The individuals on the pulpit were unaware of the spiritual warfare. Watch out, the demon hasn't altered its doctrine, but we have. The devil's agenda is to kill, steal, and destroy. Nevertheless, we often choose to prioritize our own physical desires and ego, seeking to excel others. Despite going to church, nothing significant happens. You may be advised by organization leaders to seek medical help and be prescribed medication for dealing with demon oppression. Every battle is diabolical. Fallen angels command armies of demons in Satan's service.

Attend church, but refrain from mentioning subjects such as the devil, demons, fallen angels, fasting, and prayer. Going to hospitals, convalescent homes, jails, or prisons to reach out to the lost and sick, as Jesus did, wasn't included in the agenda. They sing a song, I got the Holy Ghost; I say for what? Only to jump, sway, and give the impression of being a fool. May the Lord have mercy on us. The name of my house is the house of dancing, jumping, tea parties, choir practice, collecting money, thievery, and entertainment. Instead we should have a house of prayer. However, den has business and only one hour, either monthly or weekly, for prayer or whatever.

Friends, seek those teachers and prophets who continue to pray and teach without ceasing even after you have been baptized in Jesus 'name and have received the Holy Spirit. However, it coaches you on warfare techniques and provides you with armor. Seek a mentor who can guide you in understanding the word as a sword, light, food, lamp, fasting, repentance, communion, and ultimate truth. Take the necessary steps to be ready for the field against the kingdom of darkness. The only truth has the power to set you free.

Can I suggest that you love your soul and refrain from following misguided shepherds, deceitful teachers, and false prophets?

God's command is to seek, meaning we should desire, ask, and knock. Refrain from remaining stagnant in the erroneous doctrines of religions that possess both truth and falsehood. They will tell you not to go church to church, that is called total control. You are welcome to attend their conferences, activities, and fellowship for both men and women, but not the locations where you seek deliverance. The devil said you belong to Paul; you do not need to hear Peter. The High Priest said do not listen to Jesus; he is crazy; He has a demon. Who possesses a demon, a spirit of murder against Jesus, greed, jealousy, and evil spirit? Can you provide me with the information? Put your faith solely in the Lord, not in anyone else. The title is misleading, so don't be fooled.

Ephesians 4:11 And he gave some, apostles; and some, prophets; and some, evangelists; and some, pastors and teachers;12 For the perfecting of the saints, for the work of the ministry, for the edifying of the body of Christ:

The title holds no significance. Examine the fruits carefully because many of them are deceptive. Find out how they spend their week and what they enjoy doing for fun. Be cautious and don't allow others to take advantage of you, lead you astray, or cast a spell on you.

Your responsibility is to destroy the killer, stealer, and destroyer by getting spiritual muscles. Learn how to use a Word, like sword, light, food, lamp, and hammer. There is nothing more important than the Bible. Seek understanding in the Word of God to know what the Lord says. Experience the transformative power of immersing yourself in the Word of God.

The day cannot be sustained with just a small word breakfast. Consume the word as if it were meat and quench your thirst with the Holy Spirit. Having the complete truth would be beneficial. I'm grateful that I avoided the same situation as the Hebrews who were trapped on Horeb. They spent numerous years in the desert. Modify your thinking, attitude, lifestyle, desires, and method of seeking God. There is a fight occurring between you and the unseen spirit World. The name of it is the kingdom of darkness.

Attending a den-like church building might hinder your growth unless you're in a place where supernatural signs and wonders are occurring.

The pastor and church are readying themselves, through prayer and fasting, to spread the Gospel in this world. Avoid being hindered, halted, or misled by your selection of religion or organization. What's the issue? The answer is in the mirror;go look. You will understand never to blame anyone but yourself. Let us seek the Lord's help to overcome the fire, iron walls, storm, water, trial, and trouble. Find your way solely through Jesus, there's no alternative. Religion is the giant stopper, blocker, and hindrance. Please do not believe it. My belief lies in repentance and baptism in Jesus's name, and I rely on the Holy Spirit to lead, guide, teach, and empower me. The idea that religious churches state there is nothing beyond this is difficult for me to accept.

Leaving those religious buildings, I discovered the powerful movement of God in an amazing way. I was caught off guard by the appearance and voice of the demon speaking through the person. Legs and arms stretched longer, and people were freed from demonic possession. The prophet provided details about the name, address, and phone number. He shattered the power of witchcraft. He revealed the identity of the

JULY 13

person involved in witchcraft. I can't believe I said wow, oh my God. The spiritual gifts of knowledge and wisdom reveal what is unseen. Seeing and hearing it opened my eyes. It felt like all my dreams had finally come true. I thank God; I did not let any religious authority bewitch me. I am guided by the Spirit of God to different locations. My desire for more keeps growing. In the name of Jesus, I will persist and push forward without giving up.

LET US PRAY

Lord, we thank you. We can do more significantly than you said. Please give us all nine spiritual gifts. We are the ambassadors of Jesus to let the world know that this God has the power to solve all and any of our problems. You only have to believe that God can and will. May you help us continue in His marvelous light to further the kingdom of God. We want to be the worker of the kingdom of God and make us the best, faithful, and true to you in Jesus's name! Amen! God bless you!

JULY 14

I CARRY YOUR BURDEN; YOU CARRY MINE!

We have been given work by God for His Kingdom. Being employed by the King brings both grace and joy. Your promotion is to the position right below the King. You will walk as royalty. People saluted Haman. They were favored highly, him and his family. We have been summoned by King Jesus to serve him. If God calls, one must complete the task with sincerity. We must be faithful to our King so His kingdom expands with the dynamic system. Is your work focused on serving the Lord Jesus or furthering the religious organization's goals? Our actions are driven solely by the organization's agenda and authority. As religious robots, we perform our tasks without seeking God's approval. Do we have to remember everything about our assignment? How many individuals pray but go against God's instructions? No wonder why the devil is winning. The worker God placed on earth is too intelligent, too prideful, and incapable of understanding God's will and ways.

Remember to act without hesitation once you establish a connection with God and understand His will. I kindly request that you avoid using the phrase "I will consider." Just do it. Many individuals reach out to me for counseling. I deliver God's message, yet some choose to go against it. Rise above hindrances, both external and internal, and pursue God's will.

People are unable to perceive God, His guidance, and wisdom. Disregarding God's counsel undermines the higher plan and its intended destination.

A woman named Lola called me, expressing distress over her decision. I expressed that this was not in accordance with God's intentions. She previously wanted to get rid of the business, but now she requires assistance. On her next call, she gave convincing excuses to carry on with the business. She stated that if she takes this action, she will have the means to do what you do. Since God called me, I've dedicated myself to missionary work. She made an excuse, saying she would work for Jesus only if she had stable finances. Sister Lola said, working for Jesus has always been my dream, but considering my condition? Lady Lola stated that she had experienced a similar situation before, and it led to serious trouble. God brought out miraculously from the enormous debt. Does that mean you repeat the same mistake? Is the point clear to you? She was financially burdened. Her thoughts were not focused on God's way. In contrast, she claimed that she was doing a favor for God. Reaching out to others will happen when my business is established. Despite their concerns about careers, money, and business, people offer bribes to God. It's not operational. God removed King Saul from power after his first and second errors concerning the Amalekites. God

JULY 14

mentioned that David would replace you. He will heed my words and fulfill my desires. It is our duty to carry the burden He has entrusted to us. What is the reason for the kingdom needing a worker? It is possible for the Lord's plan to be established on earth.

Luke 10:7 And in the same house remain, eating and drinking such things as they give: for the laborer is worthy of his hire. Go not from house to house.

God has no interest in King Saul's plan. King Saul proclaimed, "I will annihilate everything as instructed, but reserve a portion for sacrifice."

God has made it evident that He is not interested in your excuses. I desire someone to follow my commands precisely. If you serve God, He will ensure that your needs are met.

I had an encounter with a woman at the nursing home the other day. She requested prayers for her financial situation. Despite working three jobs, I still require financial assistance. I questioned if you rely on the Lord for financial support. Are you fulfilling the payment obligations as instructed by the Lord in the New Testament? Her refusal led to the curse on her money. A curse meant God sent His power to harm.

Malachi: 3:9 Ye are cursed with a curse: for ye have robbed me, even this whole nation. Verse 11 explains if you do not give what belongs to God, then He will not rebuke the devourer.

Ground, fruits, and fields will be destroyed by them. Is this something you desire? When you find God, it becomes essential to guide children in the proper way. If you are excessively occupied, what is the outcome? Your children will be raised by a babysitter or someone else. There are women who find the forbidden enticing. She loses her children and they are ultimately raised by one of her own kind. Are you open to hearing the Lord's message, or do you think your idea is better? I have the means to contribute more money to the church. God gave you a directive to carry out His task. He need someone who will pay attention and follow God's instructions. God is self-sufficient and doesn't require your aid. Obedient and submissive people can expand my kingdom. The supernatural plan of God will be disrupted by individuals who are hard of hearing. Why do we have so much chaos? Someone has come up with an idea that surpasses even God's. Avoid choosing rejection, following the examples of High Priest Eli, Eve-Adam, Esau, and more. An instruction from God has been given to you.

Genesis 18:19 For I know him, that he will command his children and his household after him, and they shall keep the way of the LORD, to do justice and judgment; that the LORD may bring upon Abraham that which he hath spoken of him.

Deuteronomy 6:7 And thou shalt teach them diligently unto thy children, and shalt talk of them when thou sittest in thine house, and when thou walkest by the way, and when thou liest down, and when thou risest up.

Keep reading these scriptures over and over until you can accurately observe them. Your children's responsibility falls on you, not on teachers or pastors. There are those who consider themselves wiser than God and are steering their children away from the Lord. If your children conform to the church's agenda, they will grow further away from the Lord. Open the Bible and not argue, debating, adding, or subtracting. Accept the word as it is.

Jesus said.

Matthew 11:28 Come unto me, all ye that labor and are heavy laden, and I will give you rest.29 Take my yoke upon you, and learn of me; for I am meek and lowly in heart: and ye shall find rest unto your souls.30 For my yoke is easy, and my burden is light.

What does He carry as a burden? What was the purpose of Jesus coming to earth? Was the purpose of collecting money to achieve a suitable house, cars, business, and financial freedom?

Let us see.

Luke 4:18 The Spirit of the Lord is upon me because he hath anointed me to preach the gospel to the poor; he hath sent me to heal the brokenhearted, to preach deliverance to the captives, and recovering of sight to the blind, to set at liberty them that are bruised,

What was Jesus 'request to His disciple?

Matthew 10:7 And as ye go, preach, saying, The kingdom of heaven is at hand. 8 Heal the sick, cleanse the lepers, raise the dead, cast out devils: freely ye have received, freely give.

Are you engaged in this activity? You can simply get up and do whatever you please. What is a common practice among new believers in the Lord Jesus?

Act 2:42 And they continued steadfastly in the apostles 'doctrine and fellowship, and in breaking of bread, and in prayers. 46 And they, continuing daily with one accord in the temple, and breaking bread from house to house, did eat their meat with gladness and singleness of heart,

From morning to evening, I pray, teach, minister to people, cast out the demon, heal the sick and visit the hospital and convalescent places. When I win a soul, I ask them to do what God said. I give them an oil Bible, pray with them, and teach them the word of God. They do the same and see the result. If you go Sunday after Sunday for decades until your lifetime, what is its use of it? Find the way of Jesus by studying His Word. A way of religion or denomination or following churches won't work. As God said, first pray, not drink coffee, watch TV, work like Satan's slave, and then stress. In the end, cancer, heart attack, and strokes. You can escape if you work on your assignment from God. Now read and obey the following scripture. This is your assignment with benefits.

Matthew 6:33 But seek ye first the kingdom of God, and his righteousness; and all these things shall be added unto you.

God made a promise to provide complete insurance coverage for everything and more. Practice humility, cease your actions, and reject your wicked ways, regardless of your justifications. The way is through Jesus. Hear His small voice.

LET US PRAY

Lord, we come before your altar, confessing our sins, disobedience, and rebellion. Forgive our sins. Today we turn from our wicked ways to carry your burden of the lost souls, sick and afflicted, possessed and

JULY 14

oppressed, to reach all lost. Lord, we desire our children and grandchildren to find the way if we walk in your path. Please help us find the way back to the Calvary. We rededicate ourselves and follow your plan in Jesus's name. Amen! God bless you!

JULY 15

GET VIOLENT IN THE SPIRIT AND NOT IN THE FLESH!

The presence of bloodshed and violence is widespread. The individual causing our harm is the one who needs to be eradicated. The Lord has instructed us to eliminate our enemy, Satan, along with its army. However, He manipulates us to create conflicts amongst ourselves. The facilities for inmates, including prisons, jails, and juvenile halls, are at maximum capacity. From homes to streets, cities, and across the world, violence is widespread. Why? The devil's strategies remain hidden from us due to our ignorance.

2 Corinthians 2:10 To whom ye forgive anything, I forgive also: for if I forgave anything, to whom I forgave it, for your sakes forgave I it in the person of Christ; 11 Lest Satan should get an advantage of us: for we are not ignorant of his devices.

Choosing forgiveness means refraining from using guns or knives to harm. Nations will refrain from bombing each other.

Through wealth, the devil bribes and implements a destructive master plan on earth. To have Jesus killed, he gave Judas 30 silver coins. You may think the devil did not kill, but the High Priest, Jews, Pharisees, and Sadducees did. Those who hold positions of influence and are seated in synagogues. Satan seats on high places. The individual in charge of upholding the sanctity of the temple, referred to as the church or in the language of Lord Jesus, traded their values for profit and unleashed violence upon the world.

Without proper instruction, you risk straying onto Satan's path. All who can negotiate with truth and serve the devil's kingdom are being purchased. I have been watching time slipping away. Babies are being killed by many. At night, families and cities are unable to rest due to fear. Can you explain what this chaos is? Choosing not to walk in the spirit is a mistake.

Action in the flesh causes tumult.

Galatians 5:19 Now the works of the flesh are manifest, which are these; Adultery, fornication, uncleanness, lasciviousness, 20 Idolatry, witchcraft, hatred, variance, emulations, wrath, strife, seditions, heresies, 21 Envyings, murders, drunkenness, revellings, and such like: of the which I tell you before, as I have also told you in time past, that they which do such things shall not inherit the kingdom of God.

JULY 15

God's spirit demands that we eliminate all lusts of the flesh, eyes, and pride from our lives. No, it's Satan, not God, who is at work in you. Nowadays, going to church doesn't require people to change. I mean, there is no change in their lifestyle. Why? Repenting is not something that anyone preaches. What is the definition of repent? It is the realization of the sin of the past, and you are sorry for it. You are turning 180 degrees from your previous sinful life. Here is the point: the spirit of repentance is a gift, which will be seen in the lifestyle of repentant sinners. Sinners are careless or have no regret for what they do. They are the hand, minds, and legs of Satan. It doesn't matter if you go to church or stand on the pulpit, king, or any person. Satan's program is to kill, steal, and destroy; you are the victim of his devices.

In our society, concepts like sin, saints, transgressors, good, bad, light, darkness, evil, holy, and unholy hold no significance. In this incorrect moment, individuals are falling prey to Satan. The nation is experiencing immense turmoil, confusion, and uproar. God said you mortify your flesh, then walk in the spirit. Eve might have chosen to move away from the tree. Choose to walk away instead of indulging in lustful desires. Who is in charge of overseeing divorces, gangs, family disorders, sicknesses, suicide, and governmental problems? We give in to our worldly longings, craving everything that God prohibits, while we choose to disobey. Some have already missed the opportunity to choose the right path.

God said if you walk in the spirit.

Galatians 5:22 But the fruit of the spirit is love, joy, peace, longsuffering, gentleness, goodness, faith, 23 Meekness, temperance: against such, there is no law. 24 And they that are Christ's have crucified the flesh with the affections and lusts. 25 If we live in the spirit, let us also walk in the spirit. 26 Let us not be desirous of vain glory, provoking and envying one another.

If you walk in the spirit, you will not fulfill the lust. You will overcome the devil's strategy.

My throat was giving me trouble and showing no signs of improvement. It crossed my mind that it might be my thyroid. While dining out, my friend brought up my thyroid problem. She directed my attention to the spot of the thyroid. According to her, you could be dealing with strep throat. The next time she inquired, she asked, "How are you doing?" I said I am praying for healing. She advised me to see any doctor and get tested. If not, your vocal cords may be damaged. For a moment, it shook me. But I have great faith, which I used as a shield against her statement, which came as a fiery dart. During my morning prayer, I placed my hand on my throat and prayed. I received a divine revelation: the Lord said to forcefully reclaim what was lost. You are healed 2000 years ago. I said hmmm, I will. I will smack the devil by the sword of the word.

Matthew 11:12 And from the days of John the Baptist until now the kingdom of heaven suffereth violence, and the violent take it by force.

The Word of God gave me the strength to fight the devil. I started binding the sickness in the name of Jesus. I commanded to get out of my throat. My body is the temple of Jehovah God, and not for you. No weapon formed against me can prosper. Enough is enough. Take your baggage and get out. Guess what? I was fine. May the Lord help us get violent and speak the right word of God with faith. The devil will make a run for it. Confidently using the word is your defense against the devil's harm. If you understand how to claim the Word, then you understand that all the promises belong to you. Ignorance can be seen as a form of illness. In the past, I experienced attempts by the devil to inflict various illnesses upon me, including cancer, paralysis, and multiple other ailments. I stand against you, oh devil, invoking the name of Jesus. I bind and whoop the devil out of the county; get out. You lost 2000 years ago, in Jesus 'name.

You are all self-proclaimed Christians, utilizing the Word of God, practicing shofar playing, anointing your home, and engaging in decisive warfare to defeat the enemy. The moment you bind the demon and speak the words "I break your power," it begins to operate. I experienced it once and heard terrifying screams as I bound the demon and broke its power when it jumped on my leg. Wow! I exclaimed. I wish our spiritual senses functioned like our physical senses, but they don't. So the devil fools us. Follow the instructions in the word of God without question. Just do it. Let us pray for divine assistance in our obedience.

I received a call from someone today, requesting prayers for her mother-in-law. I said, why don't you do it? You've been practicing Christianity for a few years! She said, I did, but got an attack on my chest. I said get violent with the devil; command it to get out. Open the door and inform them that they are not welcome, and do not touch me. Proclaimed that I am healed and whole by the stripe of Jesus.

It is not the drug dealer, the government, not your spouses, children, employed coworkers, or people, but the devil behind your pain. From every direction, I stand firm and command the devil to flee my life. I command the devil to leave my family alone. My matter is under the blood. I come against all curses, spells, witchcraft, sicknesses, poverty, drug, alcohol, rapists, murderer, abuser of humanity, and accusers of the brother; I destroy all your agenda of killing, stealing, and destroying in the name of Jesus.

Say, I release the army of angels of the living God. I use the blood of Jesus to cover everything. I come against depression, diabetes, HB, kidney, heart attack, the flu, cancer, and all disease in the name of Jesus. I release healing, miracle, salvation, and deliverance in the mighty name of Jesus. Familiarize yourself with how to use it. Avoid saying "the Lord knows" because He has the power and intention to act. Do as told, knock, and actively search for what is requested.

Luke 10:19 Behold, I give you power to tread on serpents and scorpions, and over all the power of the enemy: and nothing shall by any means hurt you.

Spiritual warfare can only be won by fasting, prayer, and with the word. Get ready, rather than enrolling in churches/den. Amen!

LET US PRAY

Lord, we are grateful for giving us the power over all disease, sickness, scorpion, and the serpent in your name. It cannot harm us if we walk in the spirit and mortify the flesh, which is the lust of eyes, lust of the flesh, and pride of life. May our Lord bless us with the truth since it is the key to defeating all daemonic forces and the kingdom of Satan. May our Lord put love for truth in our hearts! Our God has given His blood, which has life. We are grateful to you, Lord. May the Lord give us the desire and love for Jesus Christ to be our Lord and Savior! Our Lord has done all. Let us do what it takes to get it back. Lord, we get violent with the devil; we take it back in the mighty name of Jesus. Amen! God bless you!

JULY 16

A FALSE WITNESS WILL SUFFER PUNISHMENT!

Chaos is to be expected if there is a wicked individual in the family, on the pulpit, in the court system, police department, or government offices. The act of perjury, lying, or falsifying is being practiced. Their words will be unfair and harmful towards others.Exodus 20:16 Thou shalt not bear false witness against thy neighbor

God desires us to be honest, just like Himself. The Bible contains the ninth commandment given by God. Eventually, the liar will testify against you, causing the people of God to suffer. No need to be concerned! Can you recall the evil Jezebel? King Ahab desired Naboth's vineyard, but Naboth refused to give up his inheritance. The wife of King Ahab was wicked. She had intentions of ending Naboth's life. Do you have a daughter-in-law, wife, or anyone else in your house who is hostile? She will lie, and her daughter will be just like her. This wicked adulteress was a very religious woman. I specifically mentioned religious, not spiritual. With her understanding of God's laws, she ensnared the innocent. Two or more witnesses are necessary to testify and support the claim that you spoke against God and King in order to impose punishment. Two witnesses are enough for them to sentence you to death. This law goes by the name of the blasphemy law.

Chaos is inevitable if wicked individuals are present in your home, on the pulpit, in the court system, police department, or in government offices. May the Lord keep us safe from the evil Jezebel, the wicked king Ahab, and their malicious daughter Athaliah. A weak individual was King Ahab. He was responsible for bringing a lot of wickedness and bloodshed to Israel. Jezebel plotted a plan by the son of Belial (= dragon or Satan) to help witnesses. Her dirty goal was to kill an innocent man. She even declared a fast, can you believe it? Are religious people known to fast and pray as a means to justify lying? Can you trust their words? How did she intend to destroy Naboth?

Let us see.1 King 21:10 And set two men, sons of Belial before him, to bear witness against him, saying, Thou didst blaspheme God and the king. And then carry him out, and stone him, that he may die.11 And the men of his city, even the elders and the nobles who were the inhabitants in his city, did as Jezebel had sent unto them, and as it was written in the letters which she had sent unto them. 12 They proclaimed a fast and set Naboth on high among the people.14 Then they sent to Jezebel, saying Naboth is stoned and is dead.

Now This is what God said.

Exodus 23:1 Thou shalt not raise a false report: put not thine hand with the wicked to be an unrighteous witness.

Jezebel, being a wicked queen, thought she would get away from the judgment of God. Read this and think twice before plotting an evil plan. You are going against the all-powerful Lord. Expect possible judgment and a foolish demise. Recognize the standing of a true Prophet. They have been sent by the Lord to proclaim God's judgment. It is crucial to oppose evil rulers. Elijah was the prophet; he got a word from God and came to deliver it to King Ahab.

1 King 21:19 And thou shalt speak unto him, saying, Thus saith the Lord, Hast thou killed, and also taken possession? And thou shalt speak unto him, saying, Thus saith the Lord, In the place where dogs licked the blood of Naboth shall lick thy blood, even thine. 20 And Ahab said to Elijah, Hast thou found me, O mine enemy? And he answered I have found thee: because thou hast sold thyself to work evil in the sight of the Lord. 21 Behold, I will bring evil upon thee, and will take away thy posterity, and will cut off from Ahab him that pisseth against the wall, and him that is shut up and left in Israel, 22 And will make thine house like the house of Jeroboam the son of Nebat, and like the house of Baasha the son of Ahijah, for the provocation wherewith thou hast provoked me to anger, and made Israel to sin. 23 And of Jezebel also spake the Lord, saying, The dogs shall eat Jezebel by the wall of Jezreel. 24 Him that dieth of Ahab in the city the dogs shall eat; and him that dieth in the field shall the fowls of the air eat.

In battle, King Ahab met his demise without the safeguard of God, as stated in the Bible. God put Jehu as King instead, and they threw queen Jezebel from up high, and the dog licked the blood and ate her flesh. The dog licked King Ahab's blood. God is watching and will take revenge. False witnesses were brought by the Sanhedrin to condemn the innocent Jesus to death. Fearless in the face of false accusations. The combination of wicked spiritual and secular authorities, liars, and deceitful people creates the most dangerous time. They will govern in a corrupt manner. Observe the laws set by God.

Matthew 26:59 Now the chief priests, and elders, and all the council, sought false witness against Jesus, to put him to death;

Do not believe the religious leaders. They are dangerous if they are not walking in His commandments! The people will be corrupted as they misinterpret the law.

Matthew 26:63 But Jesus held his peace, And the high priest answered and said unto him, I adjure thee by the living God, that thou tell us whether thou be the Christ, the Son of God. 64 Jesus saith unto him, Thou hast said: nevertheless I say unto you, Hereafter shall ye see the son of man sitting on the right hand of power, and coming in the clouds of heaven. 65 Then the high priest rent his clothes, saying, He hath spoken blasphemy; what further need have we of witnesses? Behold, now ye have heard his blasphemy. 66 What think ye? They answered and said, He is guilty of death.

When we say "Son of God," we mean that God was embodied in human flesh. God has no Son, but

1 Timothy 3:16 says God manifests in the flesh to shed the blood for our sins. Jesus was not the son of Joseph but the only God walking among His people.

A Jew who believed in one God asked Jesus, "How can you claim to be God?"There is only one God," they affirmed. By declaring yourself the Son of God, you positioned yourself as God. The Jewish people were familiar with Torah, yet the absence of a relationship with God resulted in the Lord Jesus being sentenced to death. What are the consequences for the false witness?

Deuteronomy 19:18 And the judges shall make diligent inquisition: and, behold, if the witness is a false witness, and hath testified falsely against his brother; 19 Then shall ye do unto him, as he had thought to have done unto his brother: so shalt thou put the evil away from among you. 20 And those which remain shall hear, and fear, and shall henceforth commit no more any such evil among you.

When the false witnesses are punished, there is no need to feel sorry for them. Our God is real. I personally witnessed it firsthand. Judgment will be given to Wicked. God does not show favoritism towards people. May His people be blessed with courage and boldness from the Lord God! Never afraid of false witnesses. If you're righteous, you'll come out as the winner. You can count on God to support you. He is called the Man of War. He will fight for you. Be righteous, stay courageous, never give up, and never back down. Your Lord never slumbers or sleeps. You are constantly under His surveillance. Keep your head up high, for your redemption draweth near.

I prayed for a doctor last year who was wrongly accused. They stopped his promotion. His wife had a discussion with a nurse who is Christian. She reached out to me, and I said a prayer for him over the phone. The doctor's lack of success was a result of false accusations. As I spoke, his tone conveyed a sense of misery. I prayed to Jesus, the almighty God, on behalf of the suffering doctor. He is capable of saving the just from dishonest accusers. Later on, the doctor was promoted after winning the case. How wonderful!

Hallelujah! I bravely ignore accusers, liars, and alligators as I walk. The Lord keeps a watchful eye and blesses the righteous abundantly.

LET US PRAY

Our Great and merciful God who blesses 1,000 generations of righteousness. Protect us from all the wicked falsifiers. Your name is our strong tower, the righteous run-in for security. Hide us under your wings from all wicked and unrighteous. This is the end time; people have a form of godliness and no genuine godliness. They have no fear of God. But the Lord raises the standard of safeguard. May our Lord remind His people that He is the same yesterday, today, and forever! Let the Lord shine His face upon you and protect you and your loved ones from false witnesses. May the Lord reverse the judgment against the enemy today in Jesus's name. Amen! God bless you!

JULY 17

CURSES DO NOT WORK ON BLESSED PEOPLE!

The Lord's blessings provide protection against curses. By doing right and receiving the Lord's blessing, you can rest assured that your blessings are secured by God. Obeying God's commands is how you earn blessings. Doing what is forbidden leads to cursing, whereas blessing comes from doing what is permissible. Those whom God has blessed are immune to curses. Take responsibility for your actions and don't blame others for not receiving God's blessings. May the Lord direct us to receive blessings with ease. Blessings are gifts from God that He bestows upon us. The soothsayer Balaam was called by King Balak to curse Israel. Balak's attempt to curse Israel was a failure. All power on earth is subject to God's authority. With God's intervention, no enemy plot can prevail against you.

Numbers 22:6 Come now; therefore, I pray thee, curse me this people; for they are too mighty for me: peradventure I shall prevail, that we may smite them, and that I may drive them out of the land: for I wot that he whom thou blessest is blessed, and he whom thou cursest is cursed.

Instead of cursing, Balam could only give blessings. God, the creator of lips and tongue, possesses the ability to govern. What God has chosen cannot be cursed or harmed. If you ever seek, make sure it's for the Blessings. My desire is to be wealthy, but only through God's blessings.

Number 23:8 How shall I curse, whom God has not cursed? Or how shall I denounce, whom the LORD has not denounced?

May God's assistance guide us in bestowing blessings upon those already blessed by Him! We offer our blessings to those who are chosen by God. Those appointed by God for His services are blessed when they perform their duties with diligence and sincerity. Abraham believed in God. God's blessings are granted to those who believe in Him. Never think having lots of money in the bank means you are blessed. Money has wings.

Proverb 23:5 Wilt thou set thine eyes upon that which is not? For riches certainly make themselves wings; they fly away as an eagle toward heaven.

Abraham was chosen by God because he had faith in Him. Additionally, we possess a Bible. Read and believe by obeying to reconnect and access the abundant blessings of Abraham, Isaac, Israel, and additional ones. The book that wins is none other than the Bible. Trust, believe, and obey are necessary conditions. Shepherds can become kings, slaves can gain freedom, wealth can multiply, rocks can produce water, highways can exist in the ocean, and enemies can be submerged in water. If you desire more knowledge, open the Bible and read it on your own.

Genesis 12:1 Now the LORD had said unto Abram, Get thee out of thy country, and from thy kindred, and from thy father's house, unto a land that I will shew thee: 2 And I will make of thee a great nation, and I will bless thee, and make thy name great, and thou shalt be a blessing: 3 And I will bless them that bless thee, and curse him that curseth thee: and in thee shall all families of the earth be blessed.

Abraham's faith was unwavering. God rewards those who stay faithful with His abundant blessings.

Proverbs 28:20a A faithful man shall abound with blessings:

Explore the example of a successful character to understand how to defend against curses and attract blessings. God will bless you if you follow His commandments, precepts, laws, and statutes. You are the only one who can bring curses upon yourself by neglecting your responsibilities. We humbly ask for your mercy, Lord. The greatness of our Lord is truly remarkable! Each and every one of us has been called by the Lord. When God puts you on earth, you're not left without direction, instruction, or a life manual. The only downside is that we aren't robots. If that's the case, then we can hold someone responsible. We were created by God from dirt, with the freedom to make choices. If you're playing with your life, dirt is the riskiest game. May the Lord bless us with self-love and the guidance of the Spirit. The walk of the flesh and the spirit are contradictory. We often trick ourselves due to our inability to foresee the outcome. God is always aware of the good news, even when no one else knows or will know. He hears what you are saying in others 'ears and how you are playing the game. If you find yourself cursed, search for your backpack and investigate. Confess your faults and beseech the Lord for forgiveness and guidance. If you are blessed, then bless those who walk in righteousness.

Deuteronomy 11:26 Behold, I set before you this day a blessing and a curse; 27 A blessing, if ye obey the commandments of the Lord your God, which I command you this day: 28 And a curse, if ye will not obey the commandments of the Lord your God, but turn aside out of the way which I command you this day, to go after other gods, which ye have not known.

After achieving a promotion or receiving blessings, make sure to learn how to keep them. Lazarus was approached by the rich man, who requested water. Despite Lazarus 'poverty and affliction, the rich man paid no attention. When you have the opportunity to bless, don't hesitate to bless others. Be more generous, don't withhold mercy. My milliner's brothers have gone through divorce and one brother also experienced the loss of his wife, according to a true Christian friend I spoke with. The rich brothers never offered assistance when the Christian brother faced financial trouble. These two wealthy brothers criticized the lifestyle of the Christian brother. They asked why you're going around praying for others. Brothers were criticizing his children, wife, and mom. However, the Christian brother continued to fulfill his calling. Everything has been reversed by God; they are now without money, homeless, working tirelessly for their girlfriend, and have lost all their wealth and lavish homes. Their children are on drugs. However, the children of these Christian brothers are wonderful and hardworking. His grandchildren perform exceptionally well academically. If you do what is right in God's eyes, you will receive powerful blessings.

My mother was a truly virtuous woman. Despite facing numerous physical and financial trials, she remained steadfast in her pursuit of truth. Despite my mom's hardships, God, whom she faithfully served, transformed everything into blessings. Don't forget, patience is key. Get ready for payday. If you have everything but end up in hell, what's the purpose? Regardless of anything, stand unwaveringly on the word of God. The ground is truly a blessed and stable foundation. Your path will consistently lead you to the right. Keep your blessings intact. Self-righteousness holds no value in God's eyes. Take a look at the Bible and do what the Lord commands. Initially, King Saul, King Solomon, and multiple kings were on the right track but deviated later on. King David pleased the Lord throughout his entire life. He decided to go with the blessings. King David, a wise king, faced consequences for his actions but never wavered in his loyalty to God.

If we follow His commandments and statutes, and observe His laws, the chaos and commotion we see today will reverse. Blessings from the Lord will extend to our land, family, children, health, and country. May God show us mercy and bless us with genuine teachers and prophets who guide us to peaceful waters and nourish us in His abundant fields. May the Lord bless you with the wisdom to choose blessings today in the name of Jesus! Amen!

LET US PRAY

Heavenly Father, we humbly request your blessings for your chosen ones. We are encouraged by the Lord to make wise choices in order to be blessed. We hope to get the eternal blessing of salvation. Support us in guiding our children to follow your commandments, statutes, precepts, and laws, that they may be blessed by you. As your word says, who blesses Israel, God also will bless them. Israel, we bless you. May you bless all of your people, Lord, and shower us with your blessings. Providing for their needs and supporting them is what we bless them by. We bless you, Lord, for being our God and choosing us. It is a blessing for us to serve you. We thank you for protecting our blessings in Jesus's name! Amen! God bless you!

JULY 18

GOD WILL TRY YOU EVERY POINT!

Lord assigns a trial project to everyone He summons, regardless of their status. The position is only granted after successfully passing all tests. You will be replaced by the candidate who proves themselves most capable. God only hires those who are suitable for the job. When God summons, it signifies preparation for trial and examination. Remain attentive to His instructions, His circumstances, and the potential for promotion, failure, or being replaced in your role.

God Called Abraham to be the father of nations,

Genesis 17:4 As for me, behold, my covenant is with thee, and thou shalt be a father of many nations.5 Neither shall thy name anymore be called Abram, but thy name shall be Abraham; for a father of many nations have I made thee.

Before giving these promises, God called Abraham out of his native place. Later God asked him to sacrifice his only son to Mt. Moriah,

Genesis 22:1 And it came to pass after these things, that God did tempt Abraham, and said unto him, Abraham: and he said, Behold, here I am.

Abraham passed his test,

Genesis 22:10 And Abraham stretched forth his hand and took the knife to slay his son.11 And the angel of the Lord called unto him out of heaven, and said, Abraham, Abraham: and he said, Here am I.12 And he said, Lay not thine hand upon the lad, neither do thou anything unto him: for now I know that thou fearest God, seeing thou hast not withheld thy son, thine only son from me.

Abraham looked behind. One Ram was seen. He sacrificed there for the ultimate sacrifice. Jesus Christ was symbolized by Ram. The World was represented by Isaac.

Before aligning with the Pharaoh, Joseph's brother sold him into slavery. Afterwards, Joseph experienced harassment and false accusations from his master's wife. Joseph demonstrated unwavering dedication to God. Joseph knew breaking the laws, statutes, commandments, and precepts was a sin against the Lord. Is that something you do?

Genesis 39:9 There is none greater in this house than I; neither hath he kept back anything from me but thee, because thou art his wife: how then can I do this great wickedness and sin against God?

In prison, Joseph was blessed with favor from God. Enabled by God with the ability to interpret dreams, Joseph provided an explanation for Pharaoh's dream. He gained favor with Pharoh and was given a high-ranking position alongside the Pharaoh. Evil is deliberately employed for promotion within God's methods, specifically within the context of imprisonment.

Joseph was released from prison by God.

Genesis 41:39 And Pharaoh said unto Joseph, Forasmuch as God hath shewed thee all this, there is none so discreet and wise as thou art:40 Thou shalt be over my house, and according unto thy word shall all my people be ruled: only in the throne will I be greater than thou.41 And Pharaoh said unto Joseph, See, I have set thee over all the land of Egypt.

Joseph represents Jesus Christ symbolically. He rescued and preserved the people of God during times of famine. By being crucified at the same age, Lord Jesus saved us and redeemed humanity.

Following that, Mary showed up. She displayed great bravery. She was prepared to deliver Jesus. She submitted herself to the plan and will of God. In order to conceive, the Spirit God required a body. Despite the possibility of being stoned to death, she trusted in the Lord and disregarded the consequences.

At the appointed time, Gabriel came to Nazareth, where he found a virgin named Mary who was engaged to Joseph.

Luke 1: 28 And the angel came in unto her, and said, Hail, thou that art highly favored, the Lord is with thee: blessed art thou among women.30 And the angel said unto her, Fear not, Mary: for thou hast found favor with God.31 And, behold, thou shalt conceive in thy womb, and bring forth a son, and shalt call his name Jesus.32 He shall be great, and shall be called the son of the Highest: and the Lord God shall give unto him the throne of his father David: 33 And he shall reign over the house of Jacob forever, and of his kingdom, there shall be no end. 34 Then said Mary unto the angel, How shall this be, seeing I know not a man?

Mary would have been stoned to death according to Jewish law. Mary's courage was evident as she disregarded criticism.

She said, 38 And Mary said, Behold the handmaid of the Lord; be it unto me according to thy word. And the angel departed from her.

Your main concerns are people and criticism. Do not worry; surrender to God. Truth can put you in trouble but if you trust the Lord then it also bring you out of trouble. Every one of us must go through trials of various forms and shapes.

Job experienced complete loss before receiving double blessings. Throughout Job's life, God put him to the test.

JULY 18

Job 1:3 His substance also was seven thousand sheep, and three thousand camels, and five hundred yoke of oxen, and five hundred she asses, and a very great household; so that this man was the greatest of all the men of the east.

Job successfully completed his trial and was rewarded.

Job 42:12 So the LORD blessed the latter end of Job more than his beginning: for he had fourteen thousand sheep, and six thousand camels, and a thousand yoke of oxen, and a thousand she asses.13 He had also seven sons and three daughters. 15a And in all the land were no women found so fair as the daughters of job:

Notice how everything came back twice!

1 Peter 1:7 That the trial of your faith, being much more precious than of gold that perisheth, though it be tried with fire, might be found unto praise and honor and glory at the appearing of Jesus Christ:

Without trial, no one can reach the top. Athaliah, the daughter of Jezebel, used her clever strategy to attain a high-ranking position. Ultimately, it all comes down to judgment. God caused her death in a terrible manner. King Saul was unsuccessful in all of his trials, and when the time came, God announced, no more trials. Despite King Saul's attempt to kill him, David took over his position. God kept David safe. How wonderful! Your trial will make you and not break you. The trial is God's plan to test your ability to follow His highest order. Without adding or subtracting! God has the power to protect you from danger, whether it be from swords, lions, tigers, fire, or water. You are safe from harm as long as you are in God's plan.

During 1999, I endured a difficult test without knowing the result. I was left without a job and my health worsened. I was unaware of what He had planned for me. Since I only knew healing, I asked God if there was any sin preventing it. In the early morning, the Lord graciously visited this lady who was praying. Through divine revelation, it was revealed that sister Elizabeth Das is going through a fiery trial according to Lord. She will come out as a Gold. God specifically mentioned Elizabeth Das because there were three Elizabeths in church. As I asked, what did I do wrong to God? Why am I not getting healed? Although she did not know about my conversation with God, the lady stated that God also attested to your innocence. Lord also said I love her a lot which bothered the lady!? Isn't God so great and still cares for people like us? The long-awaited day has finally arrived. A Brother, blessed with the gift of healing, was sent by the Lord, and I experienced healing when he laid hands on me. What's more, many people came to him and were all given deliverance, healing, and release.

You have a divine plan from our God. He is just as alive as you are. Permit me to share with you, steer clear of repeating the mistakes. Learn to lean on God. He will renew your strength. If you pass the trial, he can guide you to your destination. Going higher doesn't require you to harm or crush anyone. Pass your test as if he throws one specifically for you. Your strength will be renewed, just like an eagle. May the Lord grant you strength to endure all trials, even the most challenging ones, in the name of Jesus!

LET US PRAY

Lord, thank you for being true and faithful. Lord, you went to Calvary and did it all. Satan will try at every point, but help us trust in you to come out victoriously. You achieved the name Jesus above all previous names. You are called the King of kings and the Lord of Lords. Please give us the strength to overcome all our trials. Please give us your wisdom, direction, and power to stand for what you have called for. Our God is faithful. Lord rewarded all who came out of their trial. You are a faithful God; make us faithful. We will be tired, but God knows how to bring us out of it. He will settle us on the immovable ground if we pass our trial. We thank you, Lord, for being with us in the test of our faith. You are good and faithful. We want to be like you in Jesus 'name. Amen! God bless you!

JULY 19

DREAM NEEDS INTERPRETATION AND KNOWLEDGE!

The dream that happens when you're asleep. Many have a dream in sleep, some have meaning, and some don't. Make sure to pay close attention to that dream. It's of utmost importance. I once dreamt of a snake on a Saturday night. On Sunday morning, I attended church. In case you were wondering, according to a preacher, a dream about a snake represents Satan. I recognized that his information about a snake was unrelated to his teaching, but instead a message from God.

As a vessel ready to receive, he conveyed the symbolism of the snake to the congregation. He had no knowledge of who had the dream. I perceived that I was receiving a message from God. Several dreams may fade, but the one sent by God will leave an indelible mark on your thoughts. The Bible discusses dreams and their interpretation.

Genesis 40:8 And they said unto him, We have dreamed a dream, and [there is] no interpreter of it. And Joseph said unto them, [Do] not interpretations [belong] to God? Tell me [them]; I pray you.

God is the interpreter of dreams for His people. When you dream, make sure to be attentive. Even individuals without knowledge of God have dreams. There are multiple ways in which God communicates with us. Dreams are one method. During one night, I dreamt of being in a car accident with my family. In my dream, I saw two snakes come out of the fence and try to come against us, but none of us were bitten. On that eventful night, we were in a collision, but thanks to a dream where God revealed His protection, we were unharmed despite the attempts of two drunk individuals to cause harm. Lord, thank you for exposing Satan's plan. The Bible is the reliable source of information given by God to His creation. Please pay attention when you have a dream. Some action is necessary. In numerous instances, the devil will give you a dream too.

Ecclesiastes 5:7 For in the multitude of dreams and many words [there are] also [divers] vanities: but fear thou, God.

Zechariah 10:2 For the idols have spoken vanity, and the diviners have seen a lie, and have told false dreams; they comfort in vain: therefore they went their way as a flock, they were troubled because there was no shepherd.

Seek for an authentic shepherd appointed by God. The title is also held by many false competitors. Don't let demons win - fight back if you have a multitude of dreams and nightmares. Blast the shofar and read the Bible with a loud voice. Apply anointing oil to yourself and everything around you. Keep in mind, you have the authority to bind, break, and cast out demons in the name of Jesus.

Don't forget to invite the Spirit of God to fill the place once you've expelled it. You might ask, "How is that possible?"

Extend an invitation to the Holy Spirit, warrior, protector, and ministering angels to dwell in your house. You consistently perform spiritual cleansing prayers at home. What you give place will be your guest. Keep in mind, the spiritual realm is what truly matters, not the physical one. Our actions, reactions, and production are of the spiritual world. God's presence is with you when you have a divine dream.

Genesis 28:12 And he dreamed, and behold a ladder set up on the earth, and the top of it reached to heaven: and behold the angels of God ascending and descending on it. 16 And Jacob awaked out of his sleep, and he said, Surely the LORD is in this place, and I knew it not.

It is the same dream when you dream twice about the same subject, even though differently still. God decides that this dream will happen.

Genesis 41:1a And it came to pass at the end of two full years, that Pharaoh dreamed: 5 And he slept and dreamed the second time:

Genesis 41:32 And for that the dream was doubled unto Pharaoh twice; it is because the thing is established by God, and God will shortly bring it to pass.

If you dream, consult a dream interpreter for interpretation. Joseph interpreted the dream of Pharaoh. Many times, God has granted people a dream and utilized those outside the faith to interpret it. God can utilize a donkey as a means of communication. There are no limitations on who the Lord can employ. God did not give Gideon a dream, but instead chose to reveal it to a pagan Midianite, and they comprehended its interpretation. Gideon heard the dream and interpretation. He found the bravery and conviction to engage in the battle against the Midian.

Judges 7:13 And when Gideon was come, behold, there was a man that told a dream unto his fellow, and said, Behold, I dreamed a dream, and, lo, a cake of barley bread tumbled into the host of Midian, and came unto a tent, and smote it that it fell, and overturned it, that the tent lay along. 14 And his fellow answered and said, This is nothing else save the sword of Gideon the son of Joash, a man of Israel: for into his hand hath God delivered Midian and all the host. 15 And it was so, when Gideon heard the telling of the dream, and the interpretation thereof, that he worshipped, and returned into the host of Israel, and said, Arise; for the Lord hath delivered into your hand the host of Midian.

God has always continued to communicate with His followers. Mary was espoused with Joseph and found with a child. Joseph, being a just man, tries to put her away privily. But the Lord's excellent plan was revealed to him in a dream.

JULY 19

Matthew 1: 20 But while he thought on these things, behold, the angel of the Lord appeared unto him in a dream, saying, Joseph, thou son of David, fear not to take unto thee Mary thy wife: for that which is conceived in her is of the Holy Ghost.

Following his worship and gift-giving to Jesus, a wise man received a warning from God in a dream. God asked them to return in a different way to overthrow the evil plan of King Herod.

Matthew 2:12 And being warned of God in a dream that they should not return to Herod, they departed into their own country another way.

God overthrew the plan of the enemy. Kings often turned to soothsayers, magicians, and astrologers in search of spiritual guidance. There is someone whom God has granted the ability to interpret our dreams and visions. Seek the living God for help with your spiritual journey.

It was prophesied by the, *Joel 2:28 And it shall come to pass afterward, that I will pour out my spirit upon all flesh; and your sons and your daughters shall prophesy, your old men shall dream dreams, your young men shall see visions: The Lord poured out Holy Spirit on the day of Pentecost.*

Peter interpreted the prophecy of Joel 2:28 saying this prophecy came true when people received the Holy Spirit.

Open your heart to the Holy Spirit and sincerely seek its presence. It could be something you're not familiar with, but rest assured, you'll receive an accurate answer. Place your trust in the Word of God through obedience. You need to acknowledge it. Prior to arriving in the USA, I had never heard anyone speaking in tongues. Despite rejection, I never stopped seeking God, for which I am grateful. I am still seeking God, allowing the Holy Spirit to lead rather than trying to lead the Holy Spirit. To interpret visions and dreams, you must receive the Spirit of God.

Peter said: Acts 2:14b be this known unto you, and hearken to my words: 15 For these are not drunken, as ye suppose, seeing it is but the third hour of the day. 16 But this is that which was spoken by the prophet Joel; Receive the power from above. Amen!

LET US PRAY

Heavenly Father, thank you for filling us with your spirit. Your spirit is the spirit of truth. It leads us to all truth and enables us to understand the dream. Your spirit knows all. We are grateful for the day of Pentecost when your spirit was sent, and we are able to receive it. We have a complete understanding of the proper methods for receiving the Holy Spirit. Speaking in the tongue is the only evidence we have of having your spirit. We thank you for the heavenly language. We thank you for your words that back up the importance of the dream. The Holy Spirit talks, warns, instructs, reveals, guides, and blesses us with a powerful special weapon to destroy the enemy. We thank you for your close relationship with your people, in Jesus's name. Amen! God bless you!

JULY 20

WHAT BRINGS LIGHT OR DARKNESS TO THE WORLD?

The Bible says my word is the light and lamp to your feet.

Psalm 119:105 Both light and lamp are to give light. By living and obeying, God brings light into our life. We feel happy, especially in the morning when the sun rises and the first light comes. We feel joyful and lively. We wake up and hear birds singing, flowers rejoice, and feel fabulous and joyous.

According to the Bible, Jesus is.*John 12:46 I am come a light into the world, that whosoever believeth on me should not abide in darkness.*

Living in accordance with the word of God generates light. When we follow Jesus, we are following light and becoming light ourselves. The absence of light can cause people to feel hopeless and depressed. The creation of heaven and earth was followed swiftly by God bringing light into being.

Genesis 1:2 And the earth was without form, and void, and darkness was upon the face of the deep. And the Spirit of God moved upon the face of the waters.3 And God said, Let there be light: and there was light.

God is light 1 John 1:5

How would you define darkness? Darkness exists when there is no light present. Each day, I offer my services as a minister to people residing in India. My prayer is honored by God. New converts face harassment from coworkers, family, and employers. They are clueless about what to say and express their dissatisfaction to me. I convey the message of the Word of God through my teachings. They follow my instructions and witness the outcome. I had a discussion with Lena earlier today. According to her, those who cause me problems are actually assisting me. Those who previously compelled me to consume food offered to idols and utter the names of their supposed deities are now attending spiritual services. I exclaimed, Praise be to our God! He is good!

According to sister Lena, once my coworkers learned about my fasting, they started bringing my sewing material to my machine. According to a coworker, I'll be fasting next Friday. Lena mentioned that people who used to taunt me had a change of heart and started going to prayer meetings after listening to my testimony. They began requesting me to pray for their family issues and difficulties. I mentioned that God

JULY 20

is reversing the situation. She told me today; we are the light if we live for Jesus and obey. I said Yes; it is true. We are the beacon of hope for those in darkness.

Matthew 5:16 Let your light so shine before men that they may see your good works, and glorify your father who is in heaven.

Lena is a selfless giver, constantly informing me about her Rs.500 donation and contributions of wheat and money to diverse ministries. She said I had no house; now I built a house. How? Only God! Lena said, my testimony and life are light to many.

Satan loves darkness. Being exposed is not something Satan appreciates. We must uncover Satan and bring it to light, then the devil wouldn't have a platform. Demon- possessed loves to be in darkness. In a dark room is where the demon feels most comfortable. Closing all curtains will invite the devil. Please open the window and the curtain to allow the light in.

One of my friends explained that if you pick up the rock on a bright sunny day, you will see the worm underneath. Why? Because the devil loves darkness. In the dark, the devil commits wrongful acts.

Ephesians 5:8 - For ye were sometimes darkness, but now [are ye] light in the Lord: walk as children of light:

For those in darkness, the Bible is a guiding light. By obeying, you can expect the precise outcome that God has declared and promised. Our God is real. Those who converted to Christianity used to worship nearly 33 million deaf, dumb men made idols. All of them possess something that will mislead you. Escaping rituals, caste, customs, and poverty systems is a challenge. Let the Lord bring light to the darkened nations. Jesus is the light. His living word can bring forth light in the world by working through us. I see the light in the Christians around me who faithfully follow God's word. Their faces become cloaked in darkness as they abandon the pursuit of truth. You can easily spot individuals who pray regularly due to the noticeable light surrounding them.

The following day, I went to work after receiving the Holy Spirit. Someone at work told me that you were filled with the Holy Spirit. I said yes. God filled me with the Holy Spirit yesterday. I wanted to know how you have that information. She said I see the light shining through you. I said, Wow! But how can you tell? Her comment was that she has been around this situation for an extended period and can clearly perceive the contrast.

Proverb 6:23 - For the commandment [is] a lamp; and the law [is] light; and reproofs of instruction [are] the way of life:

Moses's skin shone when he came in the presence of the almighty God.

Exodus 34;35a And the children of Israel saw the face of Moses, that the skin of Moses 'face shone:

Pray and experience the Lord's presence, illuminating you with His light. I witnessed my mom's face undergo a remarkable change and glow when she received the Holy Spirit in the emergency room. I couldn't make sense of it right then and there. Despite my efforts to pray over her, she couldn't speak her language after receiving the Holy Spirit. I was unable to comprehend her words. Later I realized and said, oh, Lord, you filled my mom with the Holy Spirit. Several years back, Pardeshi, an evangelist from South India, made his way to Gujarat State. He baptized her in the Name of Jesus. So mom was born of water and now the Holy Spirit.

Do not live under privileges; you submit to God's ways and word. The highway of light will guide you to become light yourself. The devil will run from you. The devil despises the light and will despise you. There's no need to paint a light bulb. When you become the light, you will find yourself needing nothing. The majority of individuals have either abandoned the idea of living for God or failed to remember His laws and commandments. Do you want to discard the Bible, attend prayer altar, and indulge in earthly pleasures? Filled with deceit, envy, arrogance, avarice, and malevolence. Don't you want to break free from the monotonous cycle of being sick and getting no real outcomes? Connect with God by living according to the truth. The Lord has called upon us to shine as His light. Live a holy and righteous life, following His commandments and laws, and watch as you make a difference in the world. The light is what the world is seeking. As you radiate for Jesus, darkness will fade away.

Matthew 4:16 The people which sat in darkness saw a great light, and to them which sat in the region and shadow of death light is sprung up.17 From that time, Jesus began to preach, and to say, Repent: for the kingdom of heaven is at hand.

Spread the Gospel and live according to its teachings. The people connected to you will experience a life-altering transformation. Even your worst enemy may seek your prayers during challenging times. I've witnessed people reaching out to me during their most difficult times. Whenever they need prayer, they seek me out. We are light, and our light should shine. Open the Bible and not only read it, but also follow His laws and commandments to bring light to the world in Jesus's name. The lack of light results in darkness. Embrace your role as the beacon of light in this world. Amen

LET US PRAY

Our father, you came on earth as light. You left the Gospel of life and light for us to preach. Help us repent and obey your commandment and laws. It is the lamp and light for us and others as you were in this world. God helps us to teach our children the Law and commandments of God. Help us teach them the word of God, so they never go through the dark time in their life. So They become the light for others. We thank you for giving us the Word of God. Let our work shine so this world gives our God glory, honor, and praise in Jesus's name. Amen! God bless you!

JULY 21
SIMPLE INSTRUCTION FOR DELIVERANCE!

How would you define the concept of deliverance? Deliverance meant to set free from the bondage of any type of evil spirits. It is to set at liberty or deliver from captivity. We disapprove of anyone knowing that we have or had an evil spirit within. Christians might struggle to comprehend that spirit can enter when there is an absence or emptiness in us. It's possible for us to remove the demons. You are empowered to command the evil spirit to depart from your body, home, place, or someone. The Evil Spirit has the ability to possess anyone's body just by opening their mouth.

I ended up getting sick from the sweets my friend gave me. I sought answers from God about the cause of my illness. God revealed to me the presence of a demon in sweets. It's likely that they made a food offering to idols. Well, I Got up and threw it away. Always pray over the food and drink you consume. Seek God's blessing and ask for its protection through the covering of blood.

Many religious people have an evil spirit in them in a distinctive form. I prayed for a woman who had asthma, and God made it clear to me that she was being attacked by a malevolent spirit causing the condition. While people may use medical terminology, Jesus would categorize it as a demonic assault. Jesus classified the act of a woman bending down as demonic.

Luke 13:11 And, behold, there was a woman which had a spirit of infirmity eighteen years, and was bowed together, and could in no wise lift up herself. 12 And when Jesus saw her, he called her to him, and said unto her, Woman, thou art loosed from thine infirmity. 13 And he laid his hands on her: and immediately she was made straight, and glorified God.

Can you perceive a demon in this case? But she had a demon of afflictions. What actions will the doctor take towards her? People are afraid of criticism if they find out you have a demon. Let me tell you, I cast out the demon from others, and I cast out from myself and my house. If you don't know, then you possess a lot within you. Everyone else knows, except for you. People go to church, where they are misguided by false teaching. The biggest demon is the demon of religion. Those churches provide a comfortable environment for demons. It will not manifest since most of them are possessed of evil spirits. A demon loves fellowshiping with one another!

2 Corinthians 7:1 Having, therefore, these promises, dearly beloved, let us cleanse ourselves from all filthiness of the flesh and spirit, perfecting holiness in the fear of God.

The Bible says you clean yourself from flesh and spirit. Spirit is air. Our bodies can come into contact with water, food, conversation, singing, watching disturbing content, and various other methods. Learn ti cast the demon out from yourself. This is mine and your job. Diseases like arthritis, high blood pressure, cancer, and others are viewed as demonic assaults on the body. They are classified differently in the field of medical science. Have mercy! Unless we expel them, we'll remain trapped. Lord is good! He claimed that I had been granted the power to cast them out after receiving the Holy Spirit.

Here's a straightforward solution: place your hand on the affected area and give a command to remove the demon, illness, or whatever it may be. Don't just do it once, twice, or thrice - keep going. Whenever I could, I would anoint my mom with oil and pray for her. During her stay with me, she experienced no joint pain. Keep doing it every day until you eliminate it completely. Read the powerful scriptures.

John 3:20 For everyone that doeth evil hateth the light, neither cometh to the light, lest his deeds should be reproved. 21 But he that doeth truth cometh to the light, that his deeds may be made manifest, that they are wrought in God.

Read Psalms 91 while anointing the house with Holy Oil. Speak with power and authority. The only way to fight Satan and its kingdom is with the word of God. Stay away from false pastors, bishops, or evangelists who are not in tune with the spirit. They will misguide you. To achieve deliverance, do as the word instructs. I'm being serious.

The lady and her mother used Holy Oil to anoint their house while reading Chapter 91. The demon of alcohol, drugs, and atheism broke off. May Lord make us a doer and not hearers. Place Holy Oil drops in water, food, and other substances. The word will be effective if you put in the work. Action is required to bring words to life, not just reading them. The power to cast out demons is given to all those who are filled with the Holy Spirit. The person will be free of the demon if you follow my instructions. God is wonderful. Never mess with going witch doctors, vizards, or a familiar spirit; it will destroy you. Religious Christians go to the witch doctor and soothsayer at night. If you confront them, they will fight you and bite you. Thinking they are invisible, they go about their business in the night, but God sees everything. An unseen spirit world is the source of the power of darkness. Say, I bind you, Satan, in the name of Jesus, and I break your power. Instead of the Holy Spirit, call upon warrior angels and ministering spirits. Cover yourself with the blood of Jesus.

Why do Christians have an evil spirit? Some have many since they reject the truth. They prefer religions. The spirit loves fellowshiping with the same demons.

John 8:31 Then said Jesus to those Jews which believed on him, If ye continue in my word, then are ye my disciples indeed; 32 And ye shall know the truth, and the truth shall make you accessible.

People who are religious tend to be uncomfortable with the idea that they may have demons such as greed, lying, adultery, alcohol, and various other types. They like familiar spirits. If you confront them, they will argue in the same way they did with Jesus previously.

JULY 21

John 8:33 They answered him, We be Abraham's seed and were never in bondage to any man: how sayest thou, Ye shall be made free? 34 Jesus answered them, Verily, verily, I say unto you, Whosoever committeth sin is the servant of sin.

If you sin, it means you possess the same kind of demon. The individuals who are possessed by demons are oblivious to the fact that they require deliverance. I first learned of Jesus's name, baptism, which I had never heard. Afterwards, I underwent baptism in the name of Jesus and experienced a newfound feeling of weightlessness. I no longer carried any sin, and I felt a lightness in my being. I had never experienced anything like that before.

I completed the entire Bible in 10th grade and kept reading. Until now, I had never seen baptism conducted exclusively in the name of Jesus. Satan has created multiple churches that actively oppose the use of Jesus' name in baptism. All demons will come out if you speak the name Jesus in the water. Numerous illnesses, alcoholic beverages, narcotics, deception, infidelity, and malevolent spirits surfaced upon being baptized in the name of Jesus. Quitting cigarettes, alcohol, and drugs was a breeze once anyone baptizes in Jesus's name, but dealing with the religious demon was a whole other battle.

I am grateful that God saved me from the religious spirit of the antichrist through His mercy. I am not religious anymore. Anoint yourself with consecrated oil and your family to see the result and power of the word. You are not the one doing the work, it's God. I carry out all the instructions given by the real prophet. I anoint my house and bury prayer clothes underground, while also placing prayer cloth on doors and windows. The ways of God will never be accepted by religion. Jesus faced, I faced, and you will face this antichrist spirit working through the religious group. Follow the voice of the Holy Spirit. It provides information that is unusual but within the realm of possibility. Obey His voice.

Acts 19:12 So that from his body were brought unto the sick handkerchiefs or aprons, and the diseases departed from them, and the evil spirits went out of them.

Anoint or hold sick people's clothes while praying. Before giving any gifts, anoint and pray over them. I always do. Even the shadow of anointed people works. Now, how crazy is this?

Acts 5:15 Insomuch that they brought the sick into the streets and laid them on beds and couches, that at the least the shadow of Peter passing by might overshadow some of them.

LET US PRAY

Lord, if we follow the instructions, everything revolves around you. We believe the word of God works wonders if it comes out of your mouth. It will show the world how wonderful our God is. He came to set the captive free. Deliverance is only in the name of Jesus. Let us take the name of Jesus in reverence. We have evidence from the past that those who dedicated their lives to you made it work. We dedicate our lives to you. Heavenly Father, we pray in Jesus's name for deliverance from all sickness and disease for those who are reading or listening. Amen! God bless you!

JULY 22

IT NEEDS TOTAL CONSECRATION!

Total consecration was followed by Daniel, David, Moses, and others, including Lord Jesus. If you want to be used mightily for God, you must consecrate unto the Lord. Everyone says I want to be like Jesus; or I want to be like so and so. What I'm hearing from you is that you want to follow the example of these exceptional individuals. If you want to, you can undergo the same trial as Daniel, David, and Moses, or any other trial you select. Are you prepared? When you say, I want to be like Joseph. That means you want to go through the trial of Joseph. Now tell me, do you want to be like Job? It is important for you to realize that what you are asking for requires the same level of dedication, trial, and test as Job.

Seeing their accomplishments and promotions, we tend to feel jealous and yearn to obtain that position. We have no desire to undergo the trial necessary to achieve what we want. We refuse all sorrows, dedication, and rough life of those people.

May the Lord grant us wisdom prior to our requests and wishes. It's easy to want, but paying the price is not well-liked. Cain longed for blessings, but he had to be more respectful of bringing the suitable sacrifice to the Lord. Cain decided to kill his brother instead of making the correct sacrifice. Don't take Abel's life. Jewish and Sanhedrin leaders gathered together against Jesus, the Savior of the World.

Are you ready for all the trials? Do you actually want to be known by what you are called? There's a special trial that has been made solely for you to receive blessings from God. In my prayers, I always asked the Lord to make me like Abraham, Joseph, Daniel, and others. According to the preacher, praying to be like someone else means taking on all the challenges they experience. Your prayers have been answered, and you will soon face all the challenges that remain ahead. Wicked individuals, like lions, will stand against you. Consider before questioning. You've forgotten what you requested. While you might say no, I specifically requested to be like Daniel. Daniel faced opposition, rejection, and even the Lion's den. So do not scream or cry; think about what you asked for. I have no interest in dealing with fire, raging water, lions, or the pain of rejection. I want to avoid harassment from my sibling and fellow countrymen. Make sure to request something with careful consideration. Before acknowledging someone's promotion, listen to their testimony. How is their lifestyle?

I saw Evangelist Benny Hin or my pastor Grant. I expressed my curiosity about their way of living. Their devotion to God is unwavering. The pastor, who has the ability to perceive and witness the spiritual realm, serves with nine spiritual gifts and lives a life like Jesus. All the time, they devote themselves to prayer and studying God's word. God uses them around the world. There was a time when Pastor Alph Lukau claimed

JULY 22

to have fasted for a whole year. He calls the church to fast for a week or 40 days. They Pray all the time and stay connected with God. God reveals the name, address, and birth date of the person he ministers to. I want what they have, and I'm not alone in feeling that way.

If you can't cast out demons or heal the sick, what good is it? Several weeks back, Sister Nile asked for prayers for an individual in a coma. I had a vision of a peaceful evening and gorgeous purple flowers while praying. While praying, I noticed Jesus standing right there. I shared with my dear sister Nile what I witnessed. I stated that her destination is her home. She is being promoted by God, and Jesus is eagerly waiting for her. A couple of days later, she sent me a text message saying that the lady I had prayed for had passed away. According to her, I passed along your vision to the granddaughter, who in turn shared it with her mom. Remembering the vision, Lady Nile recounted what I had witnessed while praying for this person. While at the funeral, the daughter turned to sister Nile and remarked, "Do you notice that there are only purple flowers?I wanted to know from Sister Nile when exactly the lady passed away. She said it was around 10 pm. While engaged in prayer, I reported witnessing a breathtaking evening brightness. I can't describe the splendid evening, but I loved what I saw. Lady Nile expressed her desire to understand your way of seeing things. Reflecting on what was desired, God emphasized the need for dedication. Keep me first in the season, out of season always. Depart and ignore everything for now. Make an offering that is acceptable in the sight of the Lord.

Individuals are overly occupied and desire to serve God on their own terms. That does not work. I wake up at 3:50 am or earlier to pray as part of my morning routine. Regular and prolonged fasting, abstaining from both food and water. Our prayers continue nonstop throughout the night. You might claim I'm committed, but this requires complete attention and dedication. My only desire is to be like Jesus, not anyone else. I want to cast out the demon, heal the sick, and preach the Gospel with signs and wonders. I am meant to be exactly what I am called.

Romans 12:1 I beseech you therefore, brethren, by the mercies of God, that ye present your bodies a living sacrifice, holy, acceptable unto God, which is your reasonable service.2 And be not conformed to this world: but be ye transformed by the renewing of your mind that ye may prove what that good, acceptable, and perfect will of God is.3 For I say, through the grace given unto me, to every man that is among you, not to think of himself more highly than he ought to think; but to think soberly, according as God hath dealt to every man the measure of faith.

During summer vacation, our cousins used to spend time with us when we were growing up. Their parents were told that aunty's children are exceptionally disciplined. You guys are not, as my aunt stated. She recounted to her children how they always respond with phrases like "wait mom," "coming mom," and "come after an hour" when she has called them countless times.

I remembered a true childhood story. Many warnings were given to the guy about standing by the door on the fast train. However, he still went ahead and did it. There was a time when we heard a guy die while riding a fast train. His head hit the column. Once people were notified, they instantly recognized the possible identity of the person. We can avoid many accidents, immature deaths, troubles, and trials if we learn to love God with all our hearts, mind, soul, and strength. Hear what He has to say and respond without delay.

Luke 11:28 But he said, Yea rather, blessed are they that hear the word of God, and keep it.

In the same way as in Heaven, God can assume the role of ruler, controller, and guide over the earth. You won't have to worry about jail, prison, suicide, lawyers, or the hospital. The chaos indicates that we are choosing to follow Eve and Adam rather than God. We are asking God to follow us. Are you helping God? Isn't it so sad? Is history repeating itself with King Saul, wise King Solomon, and Judas? Learn to surrender; God does not need your help; you just follow His plan. You were sent to earth with a divine purpose by God.

Jeremiah 29:11 For I know the thoughts that I think toward you, saith the Lord, thoughts of peace, not evil, to give you an expected end.

Are you interested in adopting a peaceful mindset and plan that will bring you to a desired result? It will prevent you from encountering evil, working tirelessly, and not attaining your goals. Listen to the small, still voice.

Jeremiah 29:12 Then shall ye call upon me, and ye shall go and pray unto me, and I will hearken unto you.

Peace, comfort, and an elevated lifestyle are what God desires for us. There are things that God has that are beyond anything your eyes have seen or your ears have heard. Having mercy on yourself would be the most beneficial. Make the choice to follow Him. Take the opportunity to consecrate your life today. May we be granted heavenly wisdom by the Lord! Isn't God so good? With the Lord's guidance, let us start from scratch. A life that pleases the Lord is a blessed one.

Matthew 6:33 But seek ye first the kingdom of God, and his righteousness; and all these things shall be added unto you. 34 Take therefore no thought for the morrow: for the morrow shall take thought for the things of itself. Sufficient unto the day is the evil thereof.

LET US PRAY

Lord, we bring our sacrifice of self-pleasing unto you. Your plan is what we tap into. We want you in our boat. Please take the reins of our life and govern it in your plan. Lord, we are grateful for choosing us. Be our master, who protects us from harm and danger and blesses us beyond. None like you have a better and greater plan for us. We dedicate our life, be the master of our life. Our heavenly Father, great is your mercy and goodness. We thank you for all you have done and will do in Jesus's name. Amen! God bless you!

JULY 23

IF THE FOUNDATIONS ARE DESTROYED!

Can you explain the concept of the foundation? Foundation is a base for building groundwork, support, or root. The word "foundation" has multiple definitions.

It pays attention to what you use it on.

Psalm 11:3 If the foundations are destroyed, what can the righteous do?

When the foundation is destroyed, even God cannot offer assistance. The Bible is the fundamental book that everything is built upon. The foundation's decay or destruction is possible if the word is manipulated through addition, subtraction, or twisting. Make certain to read the Word of God in its purest form. May we recognize that the Word of God is unalterable and no one possesses the right to change it.

1 Corinthian 3:11 For other foundation can no man lay than that is laid, which is Jesus Christ.

Now, who laid the foundation for the New Testament Church? We should consult the Bible for the answer. Not Jesus, since He came to shed the blood for our sins and set an example for us. Sinless blood has a life for all sinful people. Still, the question remains: who laid the foundation?

Ephesians 2:20 And are built upon the foundation of the apostles and prophets, Jesus Christ himself being the chief cornerstone;

The above scriptures show that the apostles and prophets laid the foundation. It's important that we work on the same foundation. Peter received the key to unlock the Kingdom of God after having a revelation of the Messiah. We cannot lay another foundation. If we do then we will have a new religion, which wouldn't work. It will go against the foundations that have already been set. Numerous individuals have set various foundations and created churches. Mormon, Jehovah's Witness, Methodist, Baptist, and other churches started with their title and have laid their foundation. It's not going to be effective.

Learn about the foundation laid by the prophet and apostle in the book of Acts on the day of Pentecost. We can build the church on the same foundation in Corinth, Galatian, colossi, India, or anywhere in the world. Baptizing individuals should be our initial action after they take the first step of repentance. It is important for people to realize and seek forgiveness for their sins. Repentance leads to baptism in the name of Jesus, erasing the marks of sin. Let us see how it works.

Act 2:38 Then Peter said unto them, Repent, and be baptized every one of you in the name of Jesus Christ for the remission of sins, and ye shall receive the gift of the Holy Ghost.

Understand the correct sequence of steps for foundation 1. Repent 2. Baptize in Jesus's name to wipe out your sins. 3. Receive the Holy Spirit.

Acts 2:41 Then they that gladly received his word were baptized: and the same day there were added unto them about three thousand souls.

3,000 Jewish individuals were included by repenting, being baptized in Jesus 'name, and receiving the Holy Spirit. The individuals responsible for Jesus 'death, as well as those who approved of it, mourned and had their sins fully forgiven.

Acts 8:12 But when they believed Philip preaching the things concerning the kingdom of God, and the name of Jesus Christ, they were baptized, both men and women.16 (For as yet he was fallen upon none of them: only they were baptized in the name of the Lord Jesus.)

The church in Samaria shared the same foundation of repentance, baptizing in Jesus's name, and receiving the Holy Spirit. Cornelius's home served as the starting point for the first Heathen Church, with a shared foundation. It is impossible for Peter or Paul to alter the foundation.

Acts 10:44 While Peter yet spake these words, the Holy Ghost fell on all them which heard the word. 48a And he commanded them to be baptized in the name of the Lord.

When they encountered the disciples of John the Baptist, who had been baptized by John the Baptist, let's find out if they modified the foundation. Paul encountered the followers of John the Baptist in Ephesus, who had previously received baptism for repentance. They also have to build the church on the Apostle and Prophets Foundation.

Acts 19:2 He said unto them, Have ye received the Holy Ghost since ye believed? And they said unto him, We have not so much as heard whether there be any Holy Ghost. 3 And he said unto them, Unto what then were ye baptized? And they said, Unto John's baptism.4 Then said Paul, John verily baptized with the baptism of repentance, saying unto the people, that they should believe on him which should come after him, that is, on Christ Jesus. 5 When they heard this, they were baptized in the name of the Lord Jesus. 6 And when Paul had laid his hands upon them, the Holy Ghost came on them, and they spake with tongues, and prophesied.

According to the Bible, the foundation can not change. Disciples of John Baptist were entering the grace era. They had to build their church on an established foundation of repentance, baptizing in the Name of Jesus, and infilling with the Holy Spirit.

 For my initial baptism, they sprinkled me and used the titles Father, Son, and Holy Spirit. Let me say it correctly. The action was not baptism, but rather a sprinkling, as baptism involved going underwater. Let us be awakened by the Lord. Salvation doesn't cost anything. The price was paid by Jesus.

Act 4:12 Nor is there salvation in any other, for there is no other name (Jesus) under heaven given among men by which we must be saved.

JULY 23

The foundation's essence must remain unchanged. Follow the instructions given by Peter in the book of Acts. Many have established different foundations because they haven't had a revelation of Jesus. It is not working since the Bible speaks not to lay other foundations. You may be in any nation, continent, or place still must repent, baptize in Jesus's name to wash away sins, and receive the Power of the Holy Spirit. Many antichrists, as warned by God, will demolish the foundation. It's already happened. Many church denominations are not continuing in the doctrine of apostles and prophets. A variety of organizations began with different foundations. The foundation of our physical body is provided by the skeleton. Alterations are possible for the nose, eyes, and skin, but the skeleton is unchangeable.

Paul confirms.1 Corinthian 3:11 For other foundation can no man lay than that is laid, which is Jesus Christ.

False teachers and prophets established a different foundation. That is why liars, drunkards, thieves, sick, and possessed have no deliverance or healing. May the Lord help them turn to the Rock of Jesus Christ. Take inspiration from Ephesians, Jews, Corinthians, and Galatians, who built the church on the foundation laid by apostles and prophets like Paul and Peter. If you have not been baptized to wash away your sins or any other way, repent and baptize in Jesus's name, which will not be the second or third time but the correct way to baptize, and receive the Holy Spirit's power. God Bless you,

Matthew 16:18 And I say also unto thee, That thou art Peter, and upon this rock, I will build my church, and the gates of hell shall not prevail against it.

LET US PRAY

We approach you, Heavenly Father, with the understanding that the word of God is constant. We cannot alter the foundation. Lord, we asked you to turn our hearts on a true foundation so we can be strong. Let all evil in us be washed away in Jesus's name. Fill us with the Holy Ghost to continue building on the correct foundation. Heavenly Father, please remove the power of religious demons from your people. Give us a humble heart so we do not lay another foundation, but we build correctly by baptizing in Jesus's name to wash away our sins in Jesus's name. Amen! God bless you!

JULY 24

MAKE UP YOUR MIND!

Nothing can stop the one who has made up their mind. The devil cannot touch or try the one who has decided. There are many other words for the made-up reason, decided, committed; purpose pursued, determined.

A man with a goal, determination, and purpose in their heart cannot easily be moved. You can't shake purposeful people. We have an enemy, the devil, and he has an army of fallen angels under them demons. Their job is to introduce you to many things, so be careful. We cannot bow to our will, lust, and pride by allowing the forbidden. They are to move us from the right path and way. We have helped with the lights and lamps called the Word of God to keep you on the right way.

Once you determine, no one will suggest or hinder. Your made-up mind has the inner strength to escape all coming against you.

The devil is a prince of the air. Once you decide to fast, pray, or read the word and preach, no one can stop you. When you are distracted by something, you know you are not determined or made up of mind.

James 1:8 A double-minded man is unstable in all his ways.

Discipline life or disciple has that kind of life. Anybody or anything will not distract them.

See how they live.

Luke 14:26 If any man come to me, and hate not his father, and mother, and wife, and children, and brethren, and sisters, yea, and his own life also, he cannot be my disciple. 27 And whosoever doth not bear his cross, and come after me, cannot be my disciple.

They concentrate on the project or calling they have. We all have a calling. Someone answers with determination, and someone wanders around. Once you answer, you will not look back, no matter what. You will follow the road even if it is rough, thorny, rocky, and full of trouble and trial.

Matthew 7:24 Therefore whosoever heareth these sayings of mine, and doeth them, I will liken him unto a wise man, which built his house upon a rock.

JULY 24

I have noticed in the church, children playing their games and even sitting next to the parents. Now think, how are the parents raising the children? Are they presented as soldiers for the kingdom of Jesus or raising them not to pay attention to the church? When I was little, our parents taught us not to make a noise while praying. We do not allow the children to play while praying. Life needs more attention and discipline when we are praying as a family. No matter what, this is the basic foundation to teach. When they grow up, they know how to focus.

Luke 9:62 And Jesus said unto him, No man, having put his hand to the plough, and looking back, is fit for the kingdom of God.

Children raised by wonderful parents have a disciplined life. These children will not have much trouble concentrating or focusing on their life.

Daniel, Moses, or Joshua had no problem going through the trial. They were determined to die or live, and nothing would shake or move them. They have decided to follow the plan of the Lord.

The Lord loves these kinds of people. They are dependable. God will position them where you may overwhelm and surprise. You will wonder how enslaved people are in this highest position, how this enslaved person is getting all the favors and benefits. The enslaved person has made up their mind with the right choices. A determination not to fear fire, water, hunger, thirst, or whatever comes their way. Once you are determined, the Lord will intervene in your matter. You will see the supernatural. Heavenly God does not want someone who thinks differently every day. They move by the jerk. Runs from the problems. Determined individuals know God. No need to cry seeing lions, fire, water, storm, and sword. Do as it pleases God, since you have made up your mind.

They will challenge the devil's move. Jesus came with a single mind on earth to sacrifice and give us life more abundantly. When you follow Jesus, you must focus on His plan rather than yours—no need to look around the world. The world has many catching nets, but you say no, devil, I do not need them; I am passing by. I have my mind made up, and no turning back. There is nothing in the world that can seduce me. Many have returned to the world, died of depression, suicide, and loss, and hell welcomed them.

I have heard the story of many who used to be great preachers, and worship singers, who lost out on women, money, power, and position. They died lost on the drug, never returning to Calvary. Once you follow the ways and footsteps of the Lord, you make sure you surrender to God and no turning back. You will achieve nothing but sorrow, suffering, curses, and burning hell.

As you know, the people following Jesus are not fearful; their mind is made up. Ready to war against the devil. They live a sacrificial life for the purpose they have chosen. May the Lord give us a made-up mind. It is the life of victory, the supernatural, and peace. May the Lord help us understand that trial and test are nothing for the one who has made up their mind.

No wind of doctrine can swing them. He is not waking up and thinking about what and how they will feel. It is the Lord who decides their future and plan. God takes them in His plan. God trusted Job, Abraham, and his descendants. Do you want God to trust you?

Confessing certain fears can cause problems when attempting to address them. Just to clarify, I want to make sure I understand what you meant by your previous statement that everything is okay. Money resides in the pocket, food rests on the table, and health is excellent. Marriage is a wonderful experience, and then everything falls into place.

May the Lord help us. Troubles are common to all, but it is the person who envisions a positive outcome that has made a deliberate choice.

Those who are uncertain will suffer a terrible fate, as they lack faith in the Lord and have no remedy. The Lord is present when you place your trust in Him. Trusting in the Lord offers an escape, assistance, deliverance, and healing. Enjoy the freedom and liberty in Jesus by claiming thousands of promises. Angels will come to minister, rescue, strengthen, and open the prison door for you. May Jesus help us overcome the instability in our minds and lives as we pray to the Lord. God bless you!

LET US PRAY

Gracious Father, we acknowledge and appreciate the lessons taught in Hebrew Chapter 11 through the stories of those who displayed unwavering faith. It was the determination of the mind, not the situation, that determined the outcome. Lord, enable us to be ready as we walk in the seasons ahead, following Jesus. By remaining steadfast, unwavering, and determined in the realm of God, we can fulfill our commitments. It is the constant and stable ground, the exclusive ground that ensures our safety. All others are sinking boats. So our heavenly father holds our hands as we keep our eyes on you. We rely on your guidance, as other paths are wide and lead us towards our downfall. Lord, grant us the determination and clarity to fulfill your perfect will. Thank you, In Jesus 'name. Amen! God bless you!

JULY 25

YOU ARE THE DESIGNER OF YOUR LIFE!

Make sure your choices and perseverance are guided by wisdom. Regardless of your words or the blame you place, ultimately, you are in control of shaping your own life. There's no pressure, but you can take on the role of your own designer. God is a skilled creator if you give Him permission. Many have planned their life precisely! They crafted their own destiny and received God's blessings. People often make the same mistakes repeatedly until they pass away. It seems they will never grasp the concept of learning. The all-powerful God has forewarned us of the outcomes, despite our free will. We can live a life without risks while still achieving all of our goals.

Samson received a divine calling from God and was granted supernatural abilities. The power had a hidden secret, but the man was not a wise designer. The conclusion of Samson's life story was marked by his decision to choose the prostitute. Throughout his life, Samson was not a skilled designer. The prostitute was offered 1,100 silver coins as a bribe to tempt Samson.

Judges 16:15 And she said unto him, How canst thou say, I love thee when thine heart is not with me? Thou hast mocked me these three times and hast not told me wherein thy great strength lieth. 16 And it came to pass, when she pressed him daily with her words, and urged him, so that his soul was vexed unto death; 17 That he told her all his heart, and said unto her, There hath not come a razor upon mine head; for I have been a Nazarite unto God from my mother's womb: if I be shaven, then my strength will go from me, and I shall become weak, and be like any other man.

Do not cultivate a connection with the enemy of your soul and your higher power. Understand Samson brought calamity and damage to himself. Take responsibility for your actions instead of blaming others. Your speaking, thinking, acting, choosing, and living will leave a lasting impact on your life. May the Lord assist you in becoming a proficient designer who receives recognition for a job well done.

Proverb 18:16 A man's gift maketh room for him and bringeth him before great men.

The Queen of Ethiopia brought many gifts to King Solomon.

1 Kings 10:10 And she gave the king a hundred and twenty talents of gold, and of spices very great store, and precious stones: there came no more such abundance of spices as these which the queen of Sheba gave to king Solomon. 13 And king Solomon gave unto the queen of Sheba all her desire, whatsoever she asked, beside that which Solomon gave her of his royal bounty. So she turned and went to her own country, she and her servants.

The Lord grants us wisdom to establish rightful and splendid positions in His divine realm. Ask God to provide you with knowledge; it is free. Life's journey only happens once. We must be cautious of the countless traps and obstacles that can hinder us. Ask the Lord to give you the wisdom to drive life gracefully.

Proverb 22:29 Seest thou a man diligent in his business? he shall stand before kings; he shall not stand before mean men.

Make it a habit to speak blessings from scriptures over your life every day. Say, I am highly favored; I am blessed beyond measure. I am first; I am head; I believe all things are possible. I am healthy and whole. I am the king's kid. Create the life you want, it's up to you and no one else. Take responsibility for your own mess and don't blame others. You're the reason for all the chaos. If God blesses them with talent, the faithful ones will make every effort to excel. Don't be afraid to showcase your talents, make use of them. Learn from King Solomon's example and don't let outlandish women destroy your life. Or Samson, who chased after a prostitute.

Exercise wisdom in your decisions and actions.

Matthew 25:21 His Lord said unto him, Well done, thou good and faithful servant: thou hast been faithful over a few things, I will make thee ruler over many things: enter thou into the joy of thy Lord. 22 He also that had received two talents came and said, Lord, thou deliveredst unto me two talents: behold, I have gained two other talents beside them. 23 His lord said unto him, Well done, good and faithful servant; thou hast been faithful over a few things, I will make thee ruler over many things: enter thou into the joy of thy Lord.

Our God has given us gifts and talent; if you do not have them, ask, and God will provide you abundantly.

Proverb 2:6 For the LORD giveth wisdom: out of his mouth cometh knowledge and understanding.

You have the ability to request wisdom for any area of your life. He will give you one. Don't you think it's amazing? There are numerous occasions when I am unsure how to proceed or respond. I immediately seek the Lord's help in knowing what to say or do without causing conflicts. God wastes no time in providing me with words. Additionally, I travel to different destinations. I have to discover what their personality is like. I seek God's help in finding the right words to be a blessing. Life offers us a single opportunity, and we must plan wisely to gain both earthly and heavenly rewards. A second life is not an option for anyone. Surrender your life to God every morning. Embrace God's design for your future and presence, and behold the masterpiece.

Wisdom should be the top priority.

James 1:5 If any of you lack wisdom, let him ask of God, that giveth to all men liberally, and upbraideth not; and it shall be given him.

Create a lifestyle that allows you to live like royalty. Daniel, the beloved man of wisdom, is highly regarded! What was his path to achieving this title?

JULY 25

Daniel 6:10 Now when Daniel knew that the writing was signed, he went into his house; and his windows being open in his chamber toward Jerusalem, he kneeled upon his knees three times a day, and prayed, and gave thanks before his God, as he did aforetime.

To design your life differently, try forming a connection with heaven.

Daniel 10:2 In those days, Daniel was mourning for three full weeks. 3 I ate no pleasant bread, neither came flesh nor wine in my mouth, neither did I anoint myself at all, till three whole weeks were fulfilled.

Daniel designed his life where the world saw the hand of God.

Daniel 6:26 make a decree, That in every dominion of my kingdom men tremble and fear before the God of Daniel: for he is the living God, and steadfast forever, and his kingdom that which shall not be destroyed, and his dominion shall be even unto the end.

You design your life with the skill of Jesus, with the wisdom of God, and make the best use of the talents given to you since you are the designer of your life. God bless you!

LET US PRAY

Our heavenly Father, thank you for being our precious God. Thank you for giving us all the power to continue this limited life on earth.

You have been good to us. We seek the ability to create our lives as masterpieces through wisdom and knowledge. When others witness our life and exclaim, wow, their God truly exists. Without a doubt, God exists. We thank you, Lord, for being such an extraordinary God. Enable us to faithfully follow and live out the divine plan intended for us in heaven, in the name of Jesus. Amen! God bless you!

JULY 26

GOD'S WAY IS EASY AND SUPERNATURAL!

The Bible says, who knows the way of God?

Roman 11:34 For who hath known the mind of the Lord? Or who hath been his counselor?

Isaiah 40:13 Who hath directed the Spirit of the LORD, or being his counselor hath taught him?

We have the option to wander from the hospital to the city, town, and country in pursuit of an answer. Keep in mind that the only accurate response comes from the Lord. Just because you can't see God doesn't mean He doesn't exist. May the Lord open our eyes to see all activity in the spiritual world. God exists as Spirit. Worship Him in Spirit and truth. Do not create idols in any form or shape whatsoever. God is Spirit; Jesus is the manifestation of Spirit God. Wherever you go, the Spirit of God will be there to support you. He is capable of doing everything without assistance. Many think when we pray, we should see or feel Him. Yes, many do. It is commonly said that I have the gift of seeing angels. The pastor, filled with the Holy Ghost, frequently witnesses the presence of angels around individuals. If your spiritual eyes are open, you can see.

Luke 22:43 And there appeared an angel unto him from heaven, strengthening him.

Despite being unseen, the Lord sends ministering angels to offer the help you require. Daniel was among those who relied on the supernatural ways of God.

Daniel 10:12 Then said he unto me, Fear not, Daniel: for from the first day that thou didst set thine heart to understand and to chasten thyself before thy God, thy words were heard, and I am come for thy words. 13 But the prince of the kingdom of Persia withstood me one and twenty days: but, lo, Michael, one of the chief princes, came to help me; and I remained there with the kings of Persia. 14 Now I am come to make thee understand what shall befall thy people in the latter days: for yet the vision is for many days.

When the vision came, Daniel was unaware of its meaning, but an angel was sent by the Lord to provide understanding. The Way of God is supernatural. I recently met someone who became a Christian. According to her, the demons I used to worship haunted me, but no psychiatrist could offer assistance. I provide counseling, prayer, and ministry to her. We once went on a sightseeing trip together in northern California. We were both staying in the same room that night. I was awakened by a noise in the middle of the night. As I opened my eyes, I saw a group of women sprinting towards her. The female demons possess multiple vertically moving hands that rotate counterclockwise. From what I observed, she was in a deep sleep. My

JULY 26

spiritual eyes were opened by God, revealing the activity of the spirit world surrounding her. She used to worship idols that were referred to as goddesses and had many hands.

Despite attending the holy churches, she was still unable to find deliverance.

The false teacher asserts that belief in Jesus prevents oppression or possession. On the following day, I told her and others about what I observed around her during the night. I included her in our meeting and drove out all evil spirits in the name of Jesus. She encountered a profound salvation. The purpose of God's visit was to release those in captivity. Make no mistake, this was imprisonment. The demon operates within individuals 'lives. In the name of Jesus, you engage in prayer, fasting, and deliverance from demons. Through the Holy Spirit, he bestowed upon you authority in Jesus 'name. God will use you to bring about deliverance from oppression and possession. Help is not available or possible from the mental institute. Think about the way of God! A lot of people become impatient and rush ahead of the Lord. Believe in the Supernatural ways of God. He promised to do it, so wait.

Genesis 18:11 Now Abraham and Sarah were old and well stricken in age, and it ceased to be with Sarah after the manner of women. 13 And the Lord said unto Abraham, Wherefore did Sarah laugh, saying, Shall I of a surety bear a child, which am old? 14a Is anything too hard for the Lord?

May God grant us understanding of His ways. It is simple and supernatural. Are you willing to wait and submit to God's will? Rely on God for physical ailments, life challenges, and your surroundings, and witness the impossible becoming possible.

God visits and sends help through His Angels.

Genesis 21:1 And the Lord visited Sarah as he had said, and the Lord did unto Sarah as he had spoken. 2 For Sarah conceived, and bare Abraham a son in his old age, at the set time of which God had spoken to him. 3 And Abraham called the name of his son that was born unto him, whom Sarah bare to him, Isaac.

Numerous people, including my friends, have had encounters with angels. On multiple occasions, I witnessed and heard Jesus speaking. I am aware of the spiritual world and its activities. He has spoken to me in my dream, as you know He does. God specializes in all impossible things. No need to get discouraged; instead, trust and wait—no need to reroute in the wrong direction. Stay on the route of prayer, fasting, and waiting on God. If He said or promised, you need to wait and believe until received. It is the assurance of the Lord. It is solely up to you to put an end to your promises by rejecting them. When you wait on God, it brings pleasure to the Lord. Seek Him through prayer and fasting.

Acts 10:1b Caesarea called Cornelius, a centurion of the band called the Italian band, 2 A devout man, and one that feared God with all his house, which gave much alms to the people and prayed to God always. 3 He saw in a vision evidently about the ninth hour of the day an angel of God coming into him, and saying unto him, Cornelius. 4 And when he looked on him, he was afraid, and said, What is it, Lord? And he said unto him, Thy prayers and thine alms are come up for a memorial before God.

The angel provided Peter with directions and an address for the place, along with instructions on how to be saved. God will answer if you seek. Don't be impatient with God. Stay in the direction of most high. Our religious mode is the worst thing in our life.

We believe we know everything and see God as distant, putting our faith solely in ourselves. I believe I need direction from the Holy Spirit to avoid feeling lost. Walking in peace is a beautiful life when He is directing us. Joy is found in a life of victory under the Lord's leadership. All that comes into our view is the Lord actively moving, doing, and enabling possibilities. A visitation from heaven also comes to Peter. Thank you, Lord. Peter heard Cornelius 'report:

Acts 10:30 And Cornelius said, Four days ago I was fasting until this hour, and at the ninth hour I prayed in my house, and, behold, a man stood before me in bright clothing,

That's truly inspiring! It is possible for individuals to pray, fast, and patiently wait for God. You can pray, pray, and pray, but also learn to wait on Him. He will show you the path to the supernatural realm. No one but God! Heaven will open just for you to direct, guide, protect, and for provision. It's easy to follow God's supernatural way.

LET US PRAY

Lord, we thank you. You are real and true. We will see the supernatural in our life and path if we wait on you. Our God makes all the impossible possible.

Our Lord is Spirit and has the ability to perceive the spirit realm. Fasting, praying, and waiting cause movement in the world. We pray and fast to see all that we need to know in our direction. Our heavenly Father, our precious Lord, is our supernatural guide and instructor. Our life could be much more peaceful and joyful if we learn to wait till we get directions from you. We love and bless you for all you are doing, even though we do not see with our physical eyes. Dear Lord, in advance, we say thank you In Jesus's name. Amen! God bless you!

JULY 27

WHISPERERS CREATE CHAOS!

Always be careful! People of God will speak openly, but Satan will whisper in the ear. My family did not have this experience much since nothing stayed hidden from my mom. But they are meeting some people, who are quiet in a group like they do not know how to talk. They only speak in the ear since they always speak evil. If you have this kind of person living in your house, as a friend or coworker, make sure you are extra careful. This kind of person has a jealous nature and an evil motive. Whisperers use everyone's mouth and will use you by whispering in your ear.

Proverb 16:28 A froward man soweth strife: and a whisperer separateth chief friends.

If you see this kind of person, you write it down; there will be a division in the family or wherever they go. Keep your ear protected from this wicked whisperer. I have seen this kind of person. One mother told her daughter that she was evil. As soon as she enters, expect chaos. She will speak in every ear, and harmony will be out the door.

Let me advise you, why are you so ignorant, foolish, or unintelligent to allow your mouth for Satan's agenda? Tell them to do it themselves. In every family, there will be a wicked whisperer. They will come with a wrong motive, and if you are not wise, they will take advantage of your mouth while acting innocent and playing the role of Satan.

Ecclesiastes 5:14 Be not called a whisperer, and lie not in wait with thy tongue: for a foul shame is upon the thief and an evil condemnation upon the double tongue.

Stay away from the tattler. They need an ear, and your ear should not be the victim. I have noticed around certain people, and things will change right away. We question what happened. All was well when this sudden tornado came. Yes, the one who stays quiet and sweet uses the ear and mouth of the one who is carnal. Whisperer uses the one who has a big mouth and is emotionally immature. Never worry about those people. They are very unsuccessful in their wickedness. But be careful if you have a wife or husband who whispers and stays sweet but uses your mouth for their evil agenda. Say no, stay away from my ear. Watch them; they blow the air in your ear and act like all is well.

If you must meet since they are family, pray that the Lord reverses their plan back against them. Some use their children's mouths by blowing evil air.

Proverb 26:20 Where no wood is, there the fire goeth out: so where there is no talebearer (whisperer), the strife ceaseth.

If you have a family member like this, do not expect peace. Learn how to keep them away from your ear. It is your job to stay away from this evil character. Remember, snakes blow air before stinging. Whisperer is precisely that way. No need for their favor. They will use honey-dripping language but run from them. Stand for the truth.

I know whisperers come and get hold of the weak vessel. The one easily influenced, who likes the sweet word. For example, they use words like, oh, you are the best, brilliant, you are better than your sister, or so and so. Tell the devil who asks your opinion. I understand your agenda. I need no comparison with my family. I am no better than anyone. But whisperers will use this tactic. Stay away if you have a spouse, mom, friend, family, or any XYZ. They will divide and rule.

Proverb 18:8 The words of a talebearer (whisperer) are as wounds, and they go down into the innermost parts of the belly.

Please think twice before letting them speak in your ear. They run from me. I punch back. I perceive these people since I have the Holy Spirit. They are the most dangerous, like a nuclear bomb. They will not be suitable to anyone but also dangerous to themselves, their family, and who become their victim. Pray for them, say Jesus; what they speak in the ear makes it null and void. Reverse back to them all that they say. Return to the senders. No weapon formed against us can ever prosper in Jesus 'name.

Do not be a victim of a whisperer. Whisperers need someone's ear. Someone who loves gossip. Some have no sound judgment, perception, or discernment. Whisperers separate friends and family. They will be punished.

Most of the separation of friends, breaking of families, and putting people's lives in jeopardy results from the talebearer, a whisperer called a gossiper.

Keep them away. They separate families and friends and cause deep wounds. They are the children of Satan.

Remember What Lord says.

Matthew 5:9 Blessed are the peacemakers: for they shall be called the children of God.

Roman 14:19 Let us, therefore, follow after the things which make for peace, and things wherewith one may edify another.

If you have a spouse or family member like this, please pray for them and do not support their whispering. Remember, you can stop it by not responding to the tactic or plan of the enemy. They will need the hand of God to see the miracle in them. No matter what you say, the disease they carry is worse than cancer. Damaging families and quickly spreading like a virus.

Wise people always react after collecting accurate information with a sound mind. But more than that, they also know where the lie, allegation, and story came from. It is the same who has the personality of the snake and the fruits of Satan.

JULY 27

We all have this experience. Thank God for my mom; she was wise and perceiving. She warned us of this type of conniving people. Even after years, I always remembered her advice. If I see those gossipers, I will get away or not respond to the phone call. You can reply to this wildfire from far away. Do not put yourself to burn since no one can hold fire without getting burnt.

This happened to one of my college friends, and I had to get involved. There was an unsolved marital problem. They sought counsel from religious leaders, friends, and family for years. Once I sat next to her husband, who was not ready to take my friend after being married for years. I used the same tactic as an allegation he used against his wife. I made him believe he was characterless and immoral since that is what the whisperer spoke in his ear about his wife. Guess what? It worked. I think the Holy Spirit used me mightily. Since the word affected the whole matter, he brought his wife home, and they are still together.

They used the weapon of gossiping against my friend's husband's ear. I used the same against him. In my college years, we had a mutual friend, and she wanted to have this particular friend for her brother. It did not happen, so this wicked friend put a nasty allegation in her friend's husband's ear. And the husband said I have nothing to do with my wife. I am glad I was bold enough to tear down the separation wall.

Now they have a good marriage, a wise son, and a wonderful daughter-in-law. She is still thankful. One good thing about the Hindus, they are very grateful. Even today, she remembers me. Not just her, but all family treats me like I am one of their family. I am not afraid of the whisperer. I pray and say return to the senders. May Lord use their word against them, in Jesus 'name. Amen!

LET US PRAY

Heavenly Father, we come before your altar. Lord, bring in our home peacemaker. Peacemakers bring peace, harmony, and unity to our family.

Lord, we shut our door tight against every whisperer. Keep them away from our family and us. Please keep our family surrounded by true peacemakers. We know the whisperer will be a stink in the family. Unknowingly, they damage themselves more than others or the ones they have targeted. Give us perception and discernment to stay away in Jesus's name. Amen! God bless you!

JULY 28

YOU WILL WANDER IN THE WILDERNESS!

When one wanders in the wilderness, they experience no progress, find themselves going nowhere, and endure a desert of time with no future. What is the reason for the Lord allowing them to wander despite having over 5,000 promises? May the Lord bless you with the ability to read and comprehend the Bible. Learn from the Bible to ensure history doesn't repeat itself. Nothing comes to you freely. If it's true, then there's no need to get out of bed. Expect the arrival of coffee. Stay in the house; you will reach your destiny. What is your opinion on the matter? Are you a robot? It's impossible to anticipate human actions. Happy when all is well, complaining in little trouble.

In California, I received assistance from a woman named Elizabeth when I was unwell. We were both members of the same church. There was a time when she came over to clean and her voice conveyed sadness and depression. I wanted to know why she was feeling sad, so I asked her. She said my cat was sick; I prayed, and God did not heal. She continued to express her grievances about her belief in God. Her words revealed her unhappiness towards God. Do you no longer trust God because of what happened to your cat? Really? I was unwell, constantly fainting, and on the brink of losing my job. I suffered from insomnia for days, and when I did manage to sleep, it was only for a short while. My hand would become numb if there was no blood flow. It caused me to stay awake all night, unable to sleep. Due to my inability to walk, I had to rely on a wheelchair. The pain caused me to lose my memory. There was no relief to be found in my body.

The Lord made a promise to heal me. I couldn't understand why I wasn't getting cured even after waiting for years. Recognizing that God knows our hearts, I approached the Lord for His promise. I inquired God one night about the reason behind my lack of healing. The following morning, Lord approached Elizabeth in the church while she was praying. Later that day, lady Elizabeth came to clean my house. Elizabeth had a strong prayer life, but struggled with faith. Jesus told Elizabeth that Sister Elizabeth Das was going through a fiery trial. This trial is going to be a lengthy process. Furthermore, God declared his intense love for me. She has done nothing wrong, and she will come out of trial as gold. Elizabeth said I was jealous when the Lord said; I love her a lot. In that church, we had three Elizabeth, which is why the Lord mentioned my last name. Elizabeth told me she was jealous when the Lord said; I love sister Elizabeth Das a lot. When the cat was not getting healed, that upset her. She also confesses I do not want to believe in God since He didn't heal her cat. Can you think she wants the benefit without meeting the prerequisite? Here she saw my trial, how hard it was for me to go around and couldn't do my daily routines.

JULY 28

Another time she got mad since I couldn't work. She said my back hurts, but despite that, I work. Wow! Now I was paying her for her work; she was not working for free. She was not charging me less; I was paying her good money.

Elizabeth wanted to hear the words like a good and faithful servant, greatly beloved, a friend of God. Something He has used for David, Abraham, or Daniel. Now, do you see the personality of Cain, Esau, and King Saul? Do people need to get what they desire to receive? You are the only one who can provide the answer. Our Lord is not a respecter of people or biased. The Lord does not see the color of your skin, relation, your money, or the way you look at the world. In the midst of a trial, God observes your heart, attitude, and how you react. Hebrews wandered 40 years in the wilderness after coming out of the slavery of Egypt. Let us see some words they spoke. It's easy to forget about trials when you are blessed and no longer suffer from sickness, poverty, troubles, and slavery.

Exodus 14:11 And they said unto Moses Because there were no graves in Egypt, hast thou taken us away to die in the wilderness? Wherefore hast thou dealt thus with us, to carry us forth out of Egypt? 12 Is not this the word that we did tell thee in Egypt, saying, Let us alone, that we may serve the Egyptians? For it had been better for us to serve the Egyptians than that we should die in the wilderness.

Despite witnessing numerous miracles and provisions, they continue to complain.

Exodus 15:23 And when they came to Marah, they could not drink of the waters of Marah, for they were bitter: therefore the name of it was called Marah. 24 And the people murmured against Moses, saying, What shall we drink?

Exodus 16:2 And the whole congregation of the children of Israel murmured against Moses and Aaron in the wilderness:3, And the children of Israel said unto them, Would to God we had died by the hand of the Lord in the land of Egypt, when we sat by the flesh pots, and when we did eat bread to the full; for ye have brought us forth into this wilderness, to kill this whole assembly with hunger.

After seeing many miracles, again, no water at Rephidim: witness their reaction.

Exodus 17:3 And the people thirsted there for water; and the people murmured against Moses, and said, Wherefore is this that thou hast brought us up out of Egypt, to kill us and our children and our cattle with thirst? 4 And Moses cried unto the Lord, saying, What shall I do unto this people? They are almost ready to stone me.

Moses, the leader of the Hebrews, found himself in trouble because of his people's insane behavior. God despises the act of complaining and murmuring. Rejection and punishment await those who engage in such behavior and they will lose their promises. Trust in God, the Almighty who can do everything.

Numbers 11:1 And when the people complained, it displeased the LORD: and the LORD heard it, and his anger was kindled, and the fire of the LORD burnt among them and consumed them that were in the uttermost parts of the camp.

God knows how to count.

Numbers 14:22 Because all those men which have seen my glory, and my miracles, which I did in Egypt and the wilderness, and have tempted me now these ten times, and have not hearkened to my voice;

God's patience is boundless, but it runs out after seven times 70. Wait for the punishment. You've surpassed the limit.

Numbers 14:27 How long shall I bear with this evil congregation, which murmur against me? I have heard the murmurings of the children of Israel, which they murmur against me.

Words have power; choose your words wisely. His goodness is something you must learn and never forget, regardless of the circumstances. He is real. Your promises are conditional and need your positive participation. Your words speak your character. Be careful of choosing words. You will reveal your identity. God remains God, regardless of your belief.

Number 14:26 And the Lord spake unto Moses and unto Aaron, saying, 27 How long shall I bear with this evil congregation, which murmur against me? I have heard the murmurings of the children of Israel, which they murmur against me. 28 Say unto them, As truly as I live, saith the Lord, as ye have spoken in mine ears, so will I do to you: 29 Your carcasses shall fall in this wilderness; and all that were numbered of you, according to your whole number, from twenty years old and upward which have murmured against me.

I have something to tell you. Can you guess what it is? Your word determines whether you remain lost in the wilderness or find a way out.

LET US PRAY

Heavenly Father, help us always be thankful. We will never forget your blessings. Grant us the wisdom to perceive and the ability to witness your merciful guidance upon our family and ourselves. We are here on earth because of your constant, renewing mercy and love. Give us eyes to see and ears to hear. A thankful heart is what we need. We thank you in good and evil as well. We give the sacrifice of praise unto you, knowing trial is to make us and not break us. Our faith will be tried and will provide us with powerful muscles. May our Lord grant us believing hearts in all trials! We all have to go through the test and will come out as gold if we keep the faith, so the Lord sealed our faith in Jesus's name. Amen! God bless you!

JULY 29

WHY DON'T WE SEE SUPERNATURAL?

When the light cannot work, we verify all the connections. For the light to function correctly, we need to connect the wires accurately. It is common knowledge that God is the Supplier of spirit. The spirit can do miracles, healing, and mighty works if we connect with God's condition.

Zechariah 4:6b Not by might, nor by power, but by my spirit, saith the LORD of hosts.

When the Spirit of God came on David, David danced. David also killed many in the war. Samson destroyed many Philistines. When you pray, you will experience the presence of the Holy Spirit.

Acts 1:14a These all continued with one accord in prayer and supplication.

Acts 2:4a And they were all filled with the Holy Ghost.

If you get connected with SPIRIT, then you can do mighty work. Those who did mighty works, including Paul and Peter, were linked to God. If you don't see miracles in the building, search with whom they have connected. An open invitation is extended to anyone ready to work with the Lord. You might say yes, I pray, but what type of prayer do you mean? The strength of our connection will demonstrate the presence of divine anointing, the Holy Spirit, and God's power in action.

There was a time when I was sick. During that time, I prayed day and night since I couldn't sleep. I recall when the Lord requested me to come forward to the altar. I slowly made my way to Alter. Despite the difficulties, I obeyed the Lord's call. Every time, I would lay down on the last pew. As I made my way towards the altar, I observed people gleefully sleighing in the spirit. Despite my lack of understanding, I continued to ponder the events that transpired. Afterwards, a woman informed me that despite attending church for years, I had never encountered the Spirit of God. When you walked by, I felt the presence of God. She mentioned that I had never encountered the Holy Spirit before. I recalled that specific day. Connecting to the throne room is a result of my continuous prayer life. I was walking very close to the Lord. I was always praying! It felt like I was constantly in God's throne room.

During that time, I was also using the neck pillow for relief. While praying, I kept my hand on it. After my healing, I traveled to India with my pillow. While returning, I needed to remember my pillow. The lady who had my pillow used that night to sleep with. Well, she had pounding noises and pain in her head that disappeared. She said I had seen you using the pillow while praying. I said Yes; it was an anointing that broke the head pain.

As I was passing by, people were sleighing in the spirit. Why? When I was ill, I sought spiritual strength through daily fasting and prayer, anointing myself. It's a blessing that we can now watch live services in different countries. Prosperity preaching is not their focus. Day and night, they pray in order to establish a connection with God. Prayer is a regular practice for the pastor and their congregation. Weeks and months of praying and fasting! Miracles, signs, and wonders are every day. We can see a mighty move of the Spirit, Deliverance, and healing like never seen before. The key is to pray and establish a connection with God once more. Those connected to God witness signs and miracles.

Prayer serves to connect with God. Channelize Yourself with the Lord through prayer. Do you want to see what the early church did? Start praying and fasting. Attending the prayerless and powerless building is a waste of time. No need to waste time. You will not see blind eyes; deaf ears open. Pray day and night and witness miracles: the lame will walk, demons will be expelled, and darkness will be defeated. The Lord wants to do all; it is the mission He left on us. Connect with the Lord again. Pray and pray! I used to be religious, but I always allowed the Holy Spirit to lead and guide me. By connecting with God in prayer, we can witness greater glory in this end-time.

Connect with the Lord on your knees, for you are the church. The church is a separate entity from the building. God is all it requires. He said I would not give my glory to anyone. No religious denomination or organization can receive the glory, whether Baptist, Methodist, Alliance, or Catholic. Jesus is the way. How did Peter manage to escape from prison and avoid being killed? Supernatural power comes from above only.

Acts 12:5 Peter, therefore, was kept in prison: but prayer was made without ceasing the church unto God for him.

To eliminate the chaos on earth, connect with God. Find the place where you meet God. Go to that mountain to pray where you find the God of Abraham, Isaac, and Jacob. It is not too late. I hope the Lord guides you in finding your way back. Seek out the supernatural on your own; no one will guide you there. Praying was a regular part of my day. My brother often whispers "Amen" in my ear. Every time I see her, he says that I am praying. My friends often ask me, "When do you find time to read?" Due to being enrolled in a science college, I had to prioritize studying, yet I made sure to pray fervently as well. I did not worry about the exam, but prayer. Teaching our children about prayer is essential. Our prayer life must be first and foremost. All flesh must connect with God.

Acts 4:31 And when they had prayed, the place was shaken where they were assembled; and they were all filled with the Holy Ghost, and they spake the word of God with boldness.

Only through prayer can you bring the dead back to life. Only God can do supernatural things, and no one can . Take back your weapon of prayer and empower yourself. It would be best if you never put it down. First of all, pray and never stop. What can you do without prayer?

God makes Himself known through signs and wonders in this time, leading to a high number of prisons filled with divorce, drugs, and suicide. Pastors, preachers, saints, apostles, prophets, and teachers hold no power over the devil's fearlessness. I think the demons laugh at them. Satan assures the demons that there

JULY 29

is no cause for concern, as he has ownership over these churches. I rendered them without prayer or power, and now they belong to me.

Acts 9:40 But Peter put them all forth, and kneeled down, and prayed; and turning him to the body said, Tabitha, arise. And she opened her eyes, and when she saw Peter, she sat up.

To dismantle false religions, denominations, and organizations, align yourself with the one who possesses extraordinary power. The falsehoods tied to the Bible will be exposed and torn down by God. Establish a relationship with God.

Acts 16:25 And at midnight Paul and Silas prayed, and sang praises unto God: and the prisoners heard them. 26 And suddenly there was a great earthquake so that the foundations of the prison were shaken: and immediately all the doors were opened, and everyone's bands were loosed.

May the Lord transform us during prayer, reveal the places, and give us the street names, phone numbers, and addresses. Assist us in experiencing spiritual travel. I dedicate my prayer life to the early morning and late-night hours.

I had an experience where I prayed for a woman who identified as Muslim. I saw all the Hindu gods, and I started rebuking those demons. She mentioned that she used to be a Brahmin before I converted to Islam and abandoned the gods I used to worship. I did not know her; I met her at someone's house. If you want to work for God; you must connect with Super God to do Supernatural, or you are wasting time. Religion is not the path to God or heaven. By showing exorcisms, healing the sick, and performing all the supernatural miracles mentioned in the Bible, illustrate the message of the Gospel. Kneeling down is how you connect with God. May you receive the Lord's wisdom and be freed from the grasp of religious fanaticism.

LET US PRAY

Our heavenly father, we would like to be like you. Just like the word of God states, we have the potential to achieve greater things than you. We believe and desire to do so. Lord, bless us with truth; deliver us from the power of darkness. We want our shadow and handkerchief to work against the devil. Our hand becomes yours. Let the fire come out of our hands to burn the sicknesses and diseases. There is a greater level of power available because of the blood of Christ. Your blood speaks for us, and we thank you for the blood. We love your power of the Holy Spirit living in us to show the World you are original, true, and only God in Jesus's name! Amen! God bless you!

JULY 30

WISDOM IS PEACEABLE!

What is wisdom? Wisdom is common sense, intelligence, prudence, or judgment. Wisdom is necessary when handling any circumstance.

Wisdom or common sense is necessary for a parent, officer, or ordinary employee to work effectively. Wisdom is an essential requirement for living in this world. King Solomon sought divine wisdom to rule over God's people. He was generously granted by God. What could have transpired if he had requested wisdom to oversee his personal life? Learn from King Solomon and ask for wisdom for all matters concerning you.

1 King 10:23 So king Solomon exceeded all the kings of the earth for riches and for wisdom.

Wisdom is necessary when facing different situations. When I went shopping, I prayed to God for sensing. Take control of my lips and steer them with expertise. I've consistently sought wisdom to excel in everything I do. Lord, please grant me the strength to complete a job. If we ask, the Lord is capable of doing new things. Isn't that what He said? Lord makes sure that each day brings something unique. Always remember that God generously bestows wisdom.

Tap into the new day and new mercy by simply asking Him.

James 3:17 But the wisdom that is from above is first pure, then peaceable, gentle, and easy to be intreated, full of mercy and good fruits, without partiality, and without hypocrisy.

God's instructions for His creation are found in the Bible, serving as a manual. Our brief lifespan is at risk of destruction without a guiding principle from our creator. May the Lord help us receive the wisdom from above to receive wealth, treasure, success, and blessing. Anyone can access knowledge by simply asking for it. Your business will be handled by God's divine sense or judgment. God is generous in giving wisdom to all who desire and ask for it. The goodness of our God is undeniable.

Proverb 4:7 Wisdom is the principal thing; therefore, get wisdom: with all thy getting get understanding.

There are many who can attend to their business. There are those who rely on God's wisdom to manage their lives. Pray for divine knowledge to carry out your responsibilities.

JULY 30

James 1:5 If any of you lack wisdom, let him ask of God, that giveth to all [men] liberally, and upbraideth not; and it shall be given him.

At every step, King David faced trials before ascending to the throne. God made a promise to David and anointed him to be on the throne. It's clear now why Lord chose to anoint David when he was young. Prior to attaining the throne he was promised, he endured a prolonged conflict with King Saul and Israel. May the Lord bless us with wisdom prior to receiving our promise. It happens from time to time that we receive what was promised to us without any hassle or fuss. As we pursue the promises, the devil will try to hinder, block, and stop our progress. During trial and battle, we must act and react discreetly. What are your thoughts on the idea of working for your enemy, especially if they hold a position of power like being the King or supreme ruler? You might say, Lord, have mercy. Lord, bestow upon me the wisdom needed to navigate my business dealings. Yes, I would too. The problem lies in our need to request it. We mistakenly perceive ourselves as mature, which is the problem. It is customary for us to follow every person. If you are under divine protection, your enemy will notice it and be filled with fear. If not, as a king, he can take away, substitute, end your life, and imprison you. Let us seek the Lord's help and wisdom in all our interactions.

1 Samuel 18:12 And Saul was afraid of David, because the LORD was with him, and was departed from Saul. 13 Therefore Saul removed him from him, and made him his captain over a thousand; and he went out and came in before the people. 14 And David behaved himself wisely in all his ways; and the LORD was with him. 15 Wherefore, when Saul saw that he behaved himself very wisely, he was afraid of him. 16 But all Israel and Judah loved David because he went out and came in before them.

David was called the man after God's own heart. The Lord is good. He sought someone who could obey His commandments, unlike King Saul. Obey and follow God's instructions when He calls. Direct your attention and request for strength. Amen! Revelation 5:12 and 7:12 says God has wisdom, so He can give you to take care of His business.

God's wisdom surpasses all others. I always ask for wisdom in every little or big matter. Rather than relying on your own knowledge, invite God to show you the way. New ideas will be seen when it comes to managing the same business. As you know, the world is advancing. Why? Someone asks for the wisdom to view it from a different perspective. May the Lord give all of us His wisdom to deal with our business, so we see miracles every day. It is His promise. In Strong's Greek concordance, wisdom is a skill, intelligence, cleverness, and learning. All our wishes can be granted. Simply ask, believe, and trust. There are numerous distinct ways in which God can show and teach us. While dealing with people, some are wise and some conniving. By relying on God, you will always rise above and emerge victorious against all schemes and tactics of evil.

Proverb 21:12 The righteous man wisely considereth the house of the wicked: but God overthroweth the wicked for their wickedness.

Be patient and observe how God intervenes against those who oppose you. If you want to conquer your enemy, embrace the teachings of God. Satan is called wiser than Daniel. Daniel was wise. Nevertheless, the devil has the intelligence to cause destruction. If there's someone in your family who behaves like a devil, have faith and wait for God's guidance. Satan's plan against you will be overthrown by God.

Daniel 28:3 Behold, thou (Satan) art wiser than Daniel; there is no secret that they can hide from thee:

Don't forget, the devil has spent centuries scheming to undermine God's plan. If we practice waiting and faithfully follow God's instructions, we can avoid stumbling, becoming ensnared, or being overcome. Due to people's failure to do God's work as commanded, the devil was able to prevail against God's creation. So the only way to defy Satan, the wise serpent, is by doing exactly as God has asked. The only solution is to conquer the devil using God's clever methods. I am asking for divine intervention to keep our family safe from evil spirits. Through prayer and fasting, I seek the Lord's intervention in defeating the enemy. Take it to God; He will consume it. May God bless you with wisdom. May the Lord provide His wisdom to overcome every strategy of Satan and foil its plans.

LET US PRAY

Heavenly Father, we need an obedient heart to defeat Satan's agenda. While the devil may be wise, your wisdom surpasses theirs. We ask for the wisdom from above to follow your statutes, laws, and commandment to be known as intelligent people on earth. Your word says, The fear of the LORD is the beginning of wisdom: a good understanding has all those that do his commandments: his praise endureth forever. We want a healthy fear of God. Give more knowledge than our enemy to defeat all the schemes of the enemy. We love you and bless you for a generous supply of wisdom. In Jesus 'name. Amen! God bless you!

JULY 31

SURRENDER TO JESUS!

God's promises were bestowed upon Abraham, Isaac, and Joseph, the Fathers of the Nations, who humbly submitted to His divine plan. Jesus said, not my will, but thy will be done.

The divine took on a physical body to show us the way. He made the ultimate sacrifice by offering himself on the cross, even facing death. Isaac, Joseph, and Jesus were all the same age when they stood up to rescue. Isaac was a representation of the world, and Abraham, known as the Father of faith, tested his obedience by sacrificing his son. The lamb in the wood did not replace Jesus, as he himself was the lamb.

All submitted, and Joseph's surrender led to the Lord's ultimate plan for him. Isaac, who was 30 years old, surrendered. Jesus was crucified when he was around that age.

The most challenging and first lesson is to surrender. I really do mean it. There will come a time when God seeks to bless you. He is looking for someone who is willing to say, "I surrender to you."

May God's will be achieved first and foremost in and through you. You can expect him to deliver everything you want and crave. The Lord sees and knows everyone, and there is no escape. Those who do not surrender will be regarded as losers, just like Priest Eli, Judas, and numerous others who arrogantly believed they were superior to God.

Knowing and surrendering to God's will is more important than going to church. Why do we witness a proliferation of churches without achieving the expected outcome? In India, I didn't have any interest in making friends who were Christian. I made a point to never get too close to them. I encountered various falsehoods, deceit, and shallow religious acts under the guise of Christianity.

It's the same scenario no matter where you go. The discrepancy lies in the board of denomination containing lies and deception in the tongue.

God wants you; you are His bride. The purpose of earth's creation was for you to have a place to live. The day He created you, He bestowed His blessings upon you. May you be blessed, prosperous, wise, and find favor wherever you go, as it is God's will. However, your initial lesson is to surrender. I know some people; who never learn to surrender, and their life is a mess. Finding a husband, good friend, or blessings from God is a challenge for many of them. Their refusal to surrender is the cause. Just like Cain, they are filled with envy towards their siblings. Their actions resemble Joseph's brother, destructive and unrepentant. The

Bible instructs my people, who are called by my name, to humble themselves. Eliminating pride is the initial step. If Lucifer had shown humility, the story would have taken a different path.

People who belong to God will experience the same outcome, unlike those who belong to the world, who have a different outcome. It's unexpected that individuals who go church to pray and listen to teachings that suit their way of life. Don't you find that surprising? Is the word of God something to pick and choose from, or to fully comprehend and internalize? People are experiencing a spiritual deficit. They do not take the word of God for instruction, perfection, guidance, and correction. Their belief that everything is wrong stems from their misguided refusal to surrender to God. If Priest Eli had surrendered and observed, what would have happened to him? All his descendants would have escaped the curses of having dim eyes, dying young age, begging for the morsel of bread, and painful days on earth! All would have been granted to Eli and his descendants by God.

This generation is called self-righteous adulterers, stoning the true prophets and teachers. Why? This generation cannot submit to God. John Baptist and Jesus would have been stoned, crucified, or destroyed by this generation. Nobody is as dangerous as the rebellious, unsubmissive, so-called Christian. Be humble and surrender, as God has commanded. Do not teach my people the wrong religion and don't make rebellions like you.

The Lord promises healing for you and your land if you surrender to Him. What is the cost of not surrendering? A lot, right? We have the ability to manipulate scripture to make Jesus appear unfavorable. The Torah experts, priests, Levites, High Priests, scribes, and Pharisees all did the same thing. The generation of wipers raised by the false prophet and teachers. These people, filled with pride, arrogance, religion, and rebellion, can only bring about destruction and death. God cannot receive glory because He cannot walk among them. I make sure to anoint my house with holy oil and command any religious demons to leave whenever they visit. Home destruction can occur when religious visitors bring demons with them.

Some individuals use the Bible as a shield for their rebellious and disobedient lifestyles.

Matthew 16:24 Then said Jesus unto his disciples, If any man will come after me, let him deny himself, and take up his cross, and follow me. 25 For whosoever will save his life shall lose it: and whosoever will lose his life for my sake shall find it. 26 For what does a man profit if he shall gain the entire world and lose his own soul? Or what shall a man give in exchange for his soul? 27 For the Son of man shall come in the glory of his Father with his angels, and then he shall reward every man according to his works.

The work we do matters. Jesus seeks nothing from you except your surrender. He has the ability to lead you to the desired outcome. God cannot harm His children, it's impossible. Your heavenly Father knows how to bless you. In order to receive more blessings, trust and surrender are essential. It's important to learn from your mistakes and avoid repeating them. Keep in mind that by surrendering, you will receive strength comparable to that of an eagle. You'll be able to run without feeling exhausted. Our God knows how to grant what you desire and expect.

We see many divorces, people behind bars, troubled, falling into the same ditches, and entangled in the net. Why don't you surrender and have your testimony like Abraham, who surrenders all the way even to sacrifice his only son? God had not lost His mind when He asked to sacrifice His son. If He asked you to sacrifice something, what would your answer be?

JULY 31

Without trust and surrender to God's will, nothing can be achieved. We all like to start by seeing the result first. The key to seeing the result is to first surrender and successfully navigate the tests and trials. To see the result, surrender first and complete all the tests and trials.

James 4:8 Draw nigh to God, and he will draw nigh to you. Cleanse your hands, ye sinners, and purify your hearts, ye double-minded.

If you surrender with your will and desire, God will do great and mighty, which you have never heard and imagined. Only surrender; all fear will leave you, and peace will over take. May the Lord give you the determination to believe and trust.

Proverb 3:5 Trust in the Lord with all thine heart; lean not unto thine own understanding. 6 In all thy ways acknowledge him, and he shall direct thy paths. Amen!

LET US PRAY

Lord, as your word says, For I know the thoughts that I think toward you, saith the Lord, thoughts of peace, not evil, to give you an expected end. This can only be possible if we surrender. It is the first step of faith. So help us, Lord, to submit. We believe all who surrender the will of God will see a significant result. Thank you for giving us the privilege to choose. Lord, give us the wisdom to do it under your guidance and protection. We can bring great blessings to ourselves, our families, and this world. Lord, you are a birth father, the shepherd who will keep us in your shadow if we surrender. We surrender to you, our family. Let your name be the solid tower for hide and save in Jesus's name. Amen! God bless you!

AUGUST

AUGUST 1

WHY IS THE WORK OF GOD NOT DONE?

What is the work of God? Do you know?

Jesus said. Mark 16:15 And he said unto them, Go ye into all the world, and preach the gospel to every creature. 17 And these signs shall follow them that believe; In my name shall they cast out devils; they shall speak with new tongues 18 They shall take up serpents; and if they drink any deadly thing, it shall not hurt them; they shall lay hands on the sick, and they shall recover.

Satan is spreading a deceptive doctrine, discouraging people from following in Jesus' footsteps. The Bible is a book where the Lord wrote work instructions in black and white for humanity to read and understand. Why did Jesus come in flesh? What did He accomplish on earth and what tasks did He assign to you?

1 Timothy 1:15 This is a faithful saying, and worthy of all acceptation, that Christ Jesus came into the world to save sinners; of whom I am chief.

John 10:10b I am come that they might have life and that they might have it more abundantly.

John 9:39 And Jesus said, For judgment, I am come into this world, that they which see not might see; and that they which see might be made blind.

His purpose on earth is to release people from the bondage of disease, sickness, and sin. The devil has managed to keep God's creation under his influence. The Lord performed healing, deliverance, and taught. By granting them power and authority in His name "Jesus", He trained the 12, then 7o to do the same. Send equipped saints out into the world to heal and deliver God's creation. Now you understand where I am going. There are people who think that being saved means you can't get sick. That is a deceitful statement from Satan. Jesus is the physician who provides insurance if you're sick. He suffered 39 stripes for your sake, for your healing. God has given you the power to cast out all demons, diseases, and sicknesses. Have confidence in yourself and realize that you, not the sinners, have the power to do all the work. What is missing? Faith! It's surprising to see the blind leading the blind and causing confusion. Get away from false teachers and prophets; they will misguide you.

That is why Jesus said.

Matthew 10:16 Behold, I send you forth as sheep in the midst of wolves: be ye therefore wise as serpents, and harmless as doves.

As a preacher, you will come face to face with wolves, serpents, and scorpions. You will face opposition from them. Those individuals are deceitful teachers and prophets.

Luke 10:2 Therefore said he unto them, The harvest truly is great, but the laborers are few: pray ye, therefore, the Lord of the harvest, that he would send forth laborers into his harvest.

Lord Jesus, while ascending after the resurrection, instructed to go make disciples of truth. He mentioned that I would provide you with power. I'll ensure you have everything you need to succeed in your work. According to the Bible, the spirit of the antichrist was active during the time of the disciples. Nevertheless, this spirit is presently operating at greater magnitudes and larger quantities. The antichrist Spirit was always warned against by John the beloved, Paul, and another disciple. Jesus mentioned that my work could go on with the help of laborers. What is a laborer? A working man and woman who are also workers in spreading God's word.

Where are those laborers? Where are they working? Think why such chaos is everywhere. What is the reason behind people being bound? The Good News is not being shared due to a lack of people going out into the world. Why do bars tend to have a high population of alcoholics? Where is the worker of God? Why haven't they shown up for work? God said I hired them. Where are they? Religious figures are golfing, vacationing, fishing, hunting, and mistreating their followers. Everyone is having a great time using your money. They patiently awaited their messiah, only to criticize my prolonged absence.

Make fasting easier for the body by distorting the scripture. Both prayer and reading of the Bible can be uninteresting. They enjoy preaching, but avoid making any personal changes. They go around the bushes, leaving the matter that God is interested in. Churches are established by denominations, organizations, and pastors to gain followers for themselves rather than for Jesus. They got addicted to hobbies; they have become a follower but not of Jesus. What is happening on the earth? They have been called by God, but they desire what is forbidden. Has it crossed your mind why divorces, drug addiction, evil, nastiness, killings, shootings, and looting occur so frequently? The person who was supposed to work hasn't shown up yet.

Let us be faithful and good through the Lord's blessings. Pray and ask for the laborers. Each day, I request for the coming of true prophets and genuine teachers, similar to those who ministered in Corinth, Galatia, Ephesus, and various other locations. After being trained by Lord Jesus, disciples were called apostles and carried out their assigned duties. They persist in teaching the correct principles and making an impact on the world. I am doing the exact same job. To cast out the demons and heal the sick in the name of Jesus. Do not explain the gospel. We cannot explain away it, but if you are following Jesus's footsteps, then you will demonstrate the Gospels.

I attended some services where I saw true prophets demonstrating the gospel. I was looking for the same thing. Currently, the Bible has transformed into a multimillion-dollar enterprise. Wake up, follow Jesus, and do not follow so-called churches, denominations, and organizations. If the Holy Spirit's work is not evident, it indicates false teachings, denominations, churches, and prophets. That falsehood from Satan doesn't interest me at all. Accept the truth. I went to the building known as the church and observed Christians who were sick, oppressed, possessed, and afflicted by curses. If you work for Jesus, drugs, bars,

AUGUST 2

alcohol, or many other Satan's businesses will shut down. Get the truth by receiving the Holy Spirit to continue the book of Acts. One of the signs is they will speak in tongues. The disciple received the sign from Jesus. In the absence of speaking in tongues, healing the sick, or casting out demons, they turn to their religions and organizations. You are not a follower of Jesus, but rather of the religions and denominations associated with Satan. Moreover, individuals attending their churches are afflicted with illness and demonic possession.

Many Christians have been freed from demonic influence through my use of Jesus 'name. Many individuals possess a familiar spirit that they greatly enjoy. Please stay away from them; they will fight and come against you. You haven't fully embraced the doctrine of the apostles and prophets. By embracing various religions and false philosophies, you have terminated the progress of the book of Acts. The book of Acts is acts of Disciples who followed Jesus. John the Baptist discovered that Jesus was the one to be followed.

His work, John 11:3b Go and shew John again those things which ye do hear and see: 5 The blind receive their sight, and the lame walk, the lepers are cleansed, and the deaf hear, the dead are raised up, and the poor have the gospel preached to them.

Now We can also be a disciple if we are doing the same that John the Baptist heard of Jesus doing. Jesus did not become a theologian or emphasize the importance of preaching, teaching, and writing books. Through his performance, he demonstrated the power of the gospel. Prior to departing from Earth, the resurrected Jesus proclaimed that you would witness the identical sign that was previously seen.

Mark 16:15 to the last verse, then you believe they are working for me. If you don't see, then run from them.

Why do we see the chaos? The book of Deuteronomy discusses oppressed individuals, possessed individuals, sicknesses, illnesses, cancer, and heart attacks. Satan has a revival among the people of God! Satan successfully recruited more followers, created multiple denominations and organizations, and convinced many to help carry out his mission of stealing, killing, and destroying. Open your eyes. Go work in the world, which is the field of the Lord. Many need you; Jesus will work with you by confirming His power to recover the lost world. Amen!

LET US PRAY

Our heavenly Father, open our eyes and ears. You came not to have a good time, but to work for your creation. To heal the brokenhearted, set the captives of Satan free from diseases, drugs, curses, and spiritual blindness. Lord, you ask us to do the same by giving us power over Satan and his work. Lord, we ask for forgiveness since we have not followed you, but temples and Satan made religion. Help us follow you as written in the word of God. You have given us the power to help your creation and not to start many denominations and religions to keep the creation blind, sick, and demon- possessed. Lord, we repent and pray to do your perfect will as many disciples followed and did. So the word set free from all darkness. We are the light if we follow you alone. Our heavenly Father, we want to bring your mission to earth, so help us, Lord, in Jesus 'name. Amen! God bless you!

AUGUST 2

POWER OF TRUTH!

What is the Truth? Truth is reality, actuality, correctness, truth to the fact, or straightforwardness. What is the opposite of truth? It is lies, falsehood, fiction, or dishonesty. The Bible says Jesus is the way of all truth. Jesus is the key to finding the truth and attaining freedom.

John 8:31 Then said Jesus to those Jews which believed on him, If ye continue in my word, then are ye my disciples indeed; 32 And ye shall know the truth, and the truth shall make you free.

What is the truth? The WORD of God is the truth. Freedom from bondage, sickness, diseases, addiction, and the power of Satan is possible if you strictly follow the instructions. Every Bible verse holds the key to unlocking the treasure. You'll see results if you have the courage to follow their instructions.

John 17:17 Sanctify them through thy truth: thy word is truth.

Psalm 119:160a Thy word is true from the beginning:

If you learn to love the truth, life on earth and eternal life after death will be good. You can be rescued from hell by embracing the truth. Speaking the truth will result in God rescuing you from hellfire and brimstone. There will be no hearing for the liar in front of Judge Jesus. Yes, you heard me right; the liar has no hearing, so speak the truth. Avoid distorting God's word by claiming the Lord loves and forgives. It's not true that He is unable to send His creation to hell. Let us read the scripture.

Revelation 21:8 But the fearful, and unbelieving, and the abominable, and murderers, and whoremongers, and sorcerers, and idolaters, and all liars, shall have their part in the lake which burneth with fire and brimstone: which is the second death.

Truthful individuals were intended to inhabit heaven by the Lord. The correction officer on earth can correct you, and later you will face judgment. Abiding by the scripture results in truth, deliverance, and healing. May the Lord guide us to embrace the truth wholeheartedly. Discover the truth and nothing else. Obeying the truth, as stated in the word of God, will grant you freedom. I read and apply scriptures to learn them. As stated in the word of God, baptize in Jesus's name to experience the washing away of your sins.

Acts 22:16 And now why tarriest thou? Arise, be baptized, and wash away thy sins, calling on the name of the Lord.

AUGUST 2

My sins were washed away when I was baptized in the name of Jesus. I came out of the water with a brand-new consciousness. My sins were washed away, leaving me feeling as light as a feather. I thought I could walk on water.

I've never had this experience of water being sprinkled with titles before. The titles of Father, Son, and Holy Spirit all pertain to One God. Satan has established multiple religions, denominations, and churches, offering a multitude of possibilities. They don't scare me because the religious demon can bring you down if you don't give in to them. The Bible teaches that freedom comes from obeying the truth. All religions claim to possess godliness, yet reject the power of truth. How? You deny the truth, which is the only potent weapon. There is no doubt that God's word is true, and our word/sword is the only weapon for offense. The devil represents the complete opposite of truth. He is known as a liar and will instruct you to lie. But watch out,

John 8:44 Ye are of your father the devil, and the lusts of your father ye will do. He was a murderer from the beginning and abode not in the truth because there is no truth in him.

When he speaketh a lie, he speaketh of his own: for he is a liar and the father of it.

The devil is against anything that God is in favor of. Have you come across someone like this before? A liar will contradict you when you speak the truth. If you try to discipline the children, they may become your adversaries. There are those who oppose the truth. They are followers of darkness, children of Satan, who will continuously deceive and lie. The devil gives advice without any truth.

The devil said to Eve, eat the fruit. You will not die. Lost the blessing and kicked out of the Garden to toil and sweat with all curses attached. The clarity of a blessing is as distinct as black and white. Do as it says. Nevertheless, the curses will haunt you once you move away from the truth. Please do not listen to the false teachers and prophets; they are the misleaders. Love yourself and believe in the Lord's instruction. I love the truth. In accordance with the Bible, one is commanded to cast out demons and cure the sick. Devilish offers medicine and advice, but discourages them from laying hands, anointing with oil, and fasting to cast out demons. They will provide an excuse; I cannot fast. It's not a simple thing to do. Can God make requests that are difficult to comprehend?

No, never, He fasted days. Paul frequently fasts, so it is not unusual. In fact, he once fasted for three days straight without consuming any food or water. Moses abstained from eating and drinking for 40 days and nights, not once but twice. Esther and all Jews did it for three days and nights without food and water. The neighboring county, Nineveh, also observed the correct fasting. How do they know not to drink and eat when they fast? They learned from the Jews; they were a neighboring country. If you come across any doctrine, verify its credibility by finding support in two or three scriptures.

According to the Bible, doctrine must be supported by at least two or three scriptures. Lord, grant us a love for the truth. The only power that can liberate us from hellfire, sickness, diseases, the devil, and his lies is the truth. May the Lord grant us the ability to obey His truth, finding sanctification and freedom from all bondage in Jesus's name.

I had a friend in India. She worshipped idols. Her father was an author. I always witnessed them about Jesus. Once, her father said, I find peace when I read the Bible. The Word of God states that peace can only be found in Jesus, and no one else. A woman who had converted went to pray for her relative's house, as her husband had passed away. The widow was left to raise her children on her own after her husband passed away. She was overwhelmed by an enormous weight. A Christian who had converted paid a visit to the widow and prayed for her. The widow specifically requested a Christian lady who had embraced the faith to visit and offer prayers. The widow lady said I feel peace when she prays for me. I grant you my peace, as stated in the Bible. I have His peace. Wherever I go, I pass it on to others because I have it. My friend's mother was communicating with others while reading Hindu religious books. She was in search of peace. By laying my hand on her and praying, she found peace. She experienced the peace of Jesus for the first time. She requested I stay with her while I was touring India.

Visitors to your home bring chaos and unwanted demons with them. I noticed a mess when someone visited me. The demon will manifest, things will break, and you will encounter the killer, stealer, and destroyer. The Bible is an accurate record of God to us. Refrain from maintaining any connections with evil and devilish individuals. Have a love for the truth; if not, then word says:

2 Thessalonians 2:11 And for this cause God shall send them strong delusion, that they should believe a lie:12 That they all might be damned who believed not the truth, but had pleasure in unrighteousness.

Strong delusion means errors, misinterpretation, or disbelief. The devil will represent a lie, and God will allow you to believe if you don't receive the truth. And you will be damned. What is damned? An endless punishment in hell! Why do people follow a religion? God will send false teachers and prophets if you don't have a love for truth.

1 John 2:21 I have not written unto you because ye know not the truth, but because ye know it, and that no lie is of the truth.

Love the truth and be free from hellfire. Love the truth to be free from illnesses and disease and Satan, in Jesus's name. Amen!

LET US PRAY

Lord, we want the love for truth in our hearts. Jesus is the way of truth. Our enemy, Satan, is a liar. Lord frees us from evil, helps us love the truth, to be free from the devil, his tactics, devices, and hell. It's your word that we need in our hearts. Our heart is where the origin of life is. The Bible is the only source of the truth. Help us use, read, meditate, obey, and love the truth. God gives us freedom from all evil. Help us to love and obey the truth. It sets free anyone who loves the truth. It is universal if you believe, receive, and love the truth to be set free. Yes, we want to free others by your truth in Jesus's name. Amen! God bless you!

AUGUST 3

DOUBLE FOR THE TROUBLE!

Stay alert when Satan brings trouble and tries to shake our faith. You will receive double blessings from God. Despite facing allegations, the righteous will remain steadfast.

A double blessing will be given by God to replace the loss.

Isaiah 61:7 For your shame ye shall have double; and for confusion, they shall rejoice in their portion: therefore in their land they shall possess the double: everlasting joy shall be unto them.

The agenda of Satan is to bring trouble upon you by accusing and shifting blame onto other believers.

Revelation 12:10c, which accused them before our God day and night.

Do you wonder and question, I did nothing, and why are all coming against me? Satan's end is near when your enemy persistently accuses and falsely charges you. Double blessings await those unjustly accused.

Zechariah 9:12 Turn you to the strong hold, ye prisoners of hope: even today do I declare that I will render double unto thee;

I am thankful for those who have experienced God's blessings after going through a trial. They were tried and came out as gold. Job stands as our prime example.

God said,

Job 1:1 There was a man in the land of Uz, whose name was Job; and that man was perfect and upright, and one that feared God, and eschewed evil. 8 And the LORD said unto Satan, Hast thou considered my servant Job, that there is none like him in the earth, a perfect and an upright man, one that feareth God, and eschewed evil?

Understand how the devil represents Job? Armed with arguments and eyes for evidence, the devil seeks to challenge Job.

Job 1:9 Then Satan answered the Lord, and said, Doth Job fear God for nought? 11 But put forth thine hand now, and touch all that he hath, and he will curse thee to thy face.

The devil cannot be trusted because he is a liar. He disputed the claim made by God. The devil has artistic skills in creating a terrible depiction of you, but the Lord has the power to defeat him. Your heart is known by God. Our Lord allowed all trouble recognizing Job as a sincere and righteous man.

Job 23:10 But he knoweth the way that I take: when he hath tried me, I shall come forth as gold.

I was going through the trial, which started in the year 1999. When I walked, the Lord gave me the same scripture. God has the ability to defend us. It turned out that all of my assumptions were incorrect. During the physical sickness, I lost my job. I never thought I would be able to afford a new house without a job. If I maintain my house, it will be good enough. I was on the verge of losing my car, so buying a new one is out of the question. Afterwards, I was healed by God and received a bigger house and new car as a blessing.

While going through a trial, thinking you are alone and see no bright future. God is there to overturn the tables and bless you with double the blessings. I left my old furniture behind and got all the new furniture for myself. I was instructed by God to give everything to him. God is in the blessing business if you allow Him to.

Let us see what job lost. Job 1:3 His substance also was seven thousand sheep, three thousand camels, five hundred yokes of oxen, and five hundred she asses, and a very great household; this man was the greatest of all the men of the east.

Job 42:12 So the LORD blessed the latter end of Job more than his beginning: for he had fourteen thousand sheep, and six thousand camels, and a thousand yoke of oxen, and a thousand she asses.

If you're wrongly accused and face consequences, God will make sure you're rewarded twice as much. The wonder of God is truly remarkable. He is capable of doing for you what He did for others. Daniel achieved the top position, and his enemy vanished from his sight forever. The Egyptians handed over all their valuable possessions to the Hebrews and eventually submerged into the ocean. Joseph attained the highest position, despite facing false allegations from the woman. Fueled by envy, his brothers plotted to end his life. The enemy is simply pushing you to a promotion for double blessings and testimony. May the Lord grant you strength, courage, and endurance through trials!

Job 8:7 Though thy beginning was small, yet thy latter end should significantly increase.

Hallelujah! May the Lord give you double for the trouble! The enemy's plan is no match for the Lord, who can elevate you to a higher position. God knows our hearts, but the devil portrays you as opposed to what you are. The source of false accusations and allegations is Satan. Pray that the senders receive it back as the Lord intervenes. Be joyful and glad because your outcome will be the greatest.

My righteous mother faced numerous financial, family, and health challenges while working hard. But she lived till 98 and saw her grandchildren and great-grandchildren. Despite facing numerous trials in her life, she was well looked after and her righteousness resulted in abundant blessings. The Lord knows how to bless us. He bestows blessings upon us, even in the presence of our enemies.

Psalm 23:5 Thou preparest a table before me in the presence of mine enemies: thou anointest my head with oil; my cup runneth over.

AUGUST 3

May the Lord give you endurance while going through the trial. I'm grateful that we worship a living God who can deliver us from trials and bless us abundantly.

Psalm 40:2 He brought me up also out of an horrible pit, out of the miry clay, and set my feet upon a rock, and established my goings. 3 And he hath put a new song in my mouth, even praise unto our God: many shall see it, and fear, and shall trust in the Lord. 4 Blessed is that man that maketh the Lord his trust, and respecteth not the proud, nor such as turn aside to lies.

All glory to God. Keep going through the trial; it will be behind you. The math is in God's hands, and He will bestow double blessings. You do not have to keep an account of your loss and gain. What God removes, He replaces with twice as much. The Lord knows how to seek vengeance on your enemy and make them disappear from your sight forever. Isn't that great? When we go through trial and trouble, we question, where is God? Maybe you are complaining and crying, but cry no more. He has the power to make your enemy cry, save you from your enemies 'plans, and elevate you to a higher position. Think about a promotion and double blessings, and thank God for your enemy. If you do not have an enemy, you do not have blessings. Amen. May the Lord bless you abundantly for all your hardships in the name of Jesus. Amen!

LET US PRAY

Lord, we see how faithful you are. You have blessed our little life. Lord, rescue us from false accusations and recover our life from the enemy. Our heavenly father, we pray for those facing the trial of fraudulent charges and allegations. Give them strength. Prepare the table before the enemy and rescue them with double blessings. Let the enemy fall, removed and gone, for giving trouble to the righteous. May the Lord prove to be faithful. He knows how to bless and rescue His creation that loves the Lord with all hearts, minds, souls, and strengths! We thank you. You have always kept yours in Jesus 'name. Amen! God bless you!

AUGUST 4.

MATURE CHRISTIAN!

Maturity is achieved by going through various stages. They say maturity comes with age, but it's not always true, as age doesn't define maturity. A specific season is when fruits reach maturity. Following training, a person progresses to a stage called maturity, earning the title of a mature man or woman. Similar to Christianity, individuals who follow God are considered mature after enduring trials and tests for a specific period of time. A responsible individual who has reached full maturity can handle the task. According to Cambridge, maturity is the process of mental and emotional development, accompanied by responsible behavior or the encouragement of such behavior.

When reaching the end stage, a person is fully equipped, advanced, and prepared to take on responsibility. You have reached the point where you can respond appropriately.

Trained individuals were sent out by Jesus in the Kingdom of God. He taught them how to work in His field. They were called because they demonstrated maturity and fulfilled their purpose.

Ephesians 4:11 And he gave some, apostles; and some, prophets; and some, evangelists; and some, pastors and teachers; 12 For the perfecting of the saints, for the work of the ministry, for the edifying of the body of Christ: 13 Till we all come in the unity of the faith, and of the knowledge of the Son of God, unto a perfect man, unto the measure of the stature of the fulness of Christ: 14 That we [henceforth] be no more children, tossed to and fro, and carried about with every wind of doctrine, by the sleight of men, [and] cunning craftiness, whereby they lie in wait to deceive;

To attain enlightenment, seek out legitimate apostles, prophets, evangelists, pastors, and teachers to assist us in deepening our relationship with God. Let's not be led astray by false doctrines. Despite being Jehovah's God in flesh, Jesus went unrecognized as such during His time on earth. The misrepresentation of the truth led to the establishment of a religion. Our duty is to do what the Lord requires from us.

Experience the power of Christianity in action!

James 1:22 But be ye doers of the word, and not hearers only, deceiving your own selves.

It's the first milestone towards becoming mature. It will take us to complete development in our walk. Although a man may be considered mature at 18, brain development continues until 25. There is a specific

AUGUST 4

time when the fruit becomes ripe. The maturity of a prophecy is time-dependent. Each thing grows at its designated time to fulfill its purpose and reason for existing.

Galatians 4:4 But when the fulness of the time was come, God sent forth his Son, made of a woman, made under the law.

Jesus was about to be born, but time was the limiting factor. Stay patient until the creator's designated time arrives. The promised Spirit of God came at its appointed time. Before the Lord sets the time and season, nothing can take place. If you try to hurry and rush before the time and season, it won't be effective. With proper development and ripening, an apple can become tasty. Planting and harvesting must wait for the right time.

Acts 2:1 And when the day of Pentecost was fully come, they were all with one accord in one place. 2 And suddenly there came a sound from heaven as of a rushing mighty wind, and it filled all the house where they were sitting.

It is important to remember that inexperienced and untrained individuals should not be tasked with God's work. They will destroy the work of God. What occurs when the company, God, or the country opens up employment or leadership roles to anyone or everyone? It will be a significant disorder, disarray, and confusion. Saul, later called Paul, killed Christians. He was named as a chosen vessel. But time was not mature since Saul needed some correction in his thinking. His brain was filled with inaccurate information and understanding. It is like giving a loaded gun to a baby, like providing a car to children not tall enough to see or drive. Before being sent to the field, Paul was called but appointed to go to Arabia for training.

Galatians 1:17 Neither went I up to Jerusalem to them which were apostles before me, but I went into Arabia and returned unto Damascus. Paul Accepted by Apostles and Others 18 Then after three years I went up to Jerusalem to see Peter, and abode with him fifteen days.

Paul was a chosen vessel.

Acts 9:15 But the Lord said unto him, Go thy way: for he is a chosen vessel unto me, to bear my name before the Gentiles, and kings, and the children of Israel:

Paul was required to grow in maturity to meet the requirements of his field.

The Bible says. Galatians 1:23 But they had heard only, That he which persecuted us in times past now preacheth the faith which once he destroyed.

Saul, the Christian killer, needs to receive training, instruction, and preparation before being sent on a mission.

Surgery on the patient is only permitted for those who have received training as a surgeon. Christianity is plagued by numerous accidents, misunderstandings, and confusion. Several divisions and religious leaders have assumed the titles of apostles, teachers, prophets, pastors, and evangelists, even though they are not mature in truth, knowledgeable, experienced, or ready for such positions. The primary sign of the gospel is not just to explain or teach, but also to demonstrate. In spiritual warfare, you need an experienced soldier. May the Lord give us a mighty spiritual warrior with visions, dreams, and active spiritual senses! Proper teaching and training from the right individuals enable work to be completed. The trainer must be called and chosen by the Lord. The chosen will practice, study, and try to be skilled in calling. All successful, mature saints will bear the fruit. They must preach the gospel with signs following. They will cast out the demon, heal the sick, open blind eyes, and open the deaf ear. God is only working with mature Christians, not all who say I am Christian.

Remember, we are in a war with Satan and its cohort. A mature, trained soldier can go into a battle. In the event of their failure, Satan will overcome them by defeating and crippling them. Immature soldiers can be detrimental to others due to their lack of knowledge, wisdom, skill, and understanding of the Word of God.

2 Timothy 2:15 Study to shew thyself approved unto God, a workman that needeth not to be ashamed, rightly dividing the word of truth.

Let us pray that the Lord assists us in developing our faith, in Jesus 'name. Amen!

LET US PRAY

Our Father, we need your spirit to teach the word. Help us practice Word to reach maturity. Lord, we know Jesus is true and living God. Give us more laborers who have the revelation of Jesus. Let the Lord send us true laborers to continue the mission of setting captives free. Use us in healing and delivering. Our God breaks every yoke from the shoulder. We speak freedom over the people of God. No more yoke, chain, the burden of religion, and ignorance. May Lord bless and help us reach our maturity in Jesus 'name. Amen! God bless you!

AUGUST 5

HAVE PASSION TO ACHIEVE A MEDAL!

How would you define passion? Passion means blind rage, a strong and barely controllable emotion. Love, desire, affection, zealousness, obsession, craze, or crucifixion. Passion is essential for achieving success. Success can be seen on TV, computers, games, in real life, as a scientist, or in any field. Success is only achieved by those with an uncontainable passion. Those who are passionate don't pay attention to anything that tries to disrupt or hinder them, including obstacles, resistance, and internal or external forces. They will overcome any obstacle, hindrance, or difficulty in achieving their goal. May our hearts be set ablaze with a passion for Jesus Christ and may we faithfully follow His path.

Saul of Tarsus, the murderer, had an unwavering dedication to his one God. Later on, he demonstrated this by sacrificing his life for the Lord Jesus in Rome. His passion for Jesus Christ was evident through the revelation of the Messiah. A monotheistic believer named Paul couldn't grasp why people would so quickly turn to Jesus. Jesus and the God Saul of Tarsus worshipped was one and the same. The dispute centered on Paul's lack of knowledge regarding Jehovah's manifestation as Jesus in human form. Spirit God Jehovah manifested in the flesh as Jesus Christ, called Son of God, Messiah, only savior. Saul of Tarsus had passion for the Spirit God. Paul was killing because he thought Jews turned away from the first commandment.

Deuteronomy 6:4 Hear, O Israel: The Lord our God is one Lord: But the Torah expert Saul of Tarsus found out that this is the one he also was waiting for, see how he changed.

Act 26:7 Unto which promise our twelve tribes, instantly serving God Day and night, hope to come. For which hope's sake, king Agrippa, I am accused of the Jews.

Not knowing the truth is called ignorance, a common misconception. Paul is the leading example of it. May the Lord give us an understanding of Him, so we walk in harmony! But let me also remind you; that you need a passion for the truth. It will lead you on a transformative journey, like the road to Damascus, where you can find correction from your maker. Many either follow the church or live without a passion for it. Jesus fulfilled His role as a savior because of His deep love for His creation. Unless one has passion, they cannot do what Jesus did for His creation. Nevertheless, Paul boasts about his passion for Christ.

He has written,

2 Corinthians 11:21 I speak as concerning reproach, as though we had been weak. Howbeit wheresoever any is bold, (I speak foolishly,) I am bold also. 23 Are they ministers of Christ? (I speak as a fool) I am more; in labours more abundant, in stripes above measure, in prisons more frequent, in deaths oft. 24 Of the Jews five times received I forty stripes save one. 25 Thrice was I beaten with rods, once was I stoned, thrice I suffered shipwreck, a night and a day I have been in the deep; 26 In journeyings often, in perils of waters, in perils of robbers, in perils by mine own countrymen, in perils by the heathen, in perils in the city, in perils in the wilderness, in perils in the sea, in perils among false brethren; 27 In weariness and painfulness, in watchings often, in hunger and thirst, in fastings often, in cold and nakedness 28 Beside those things that are without, that which cometh upon me daily, the care of all the churches. 29 Who is weak, and I am not weak? who is offended, and I burn not? 32 In Damascus the governor under Aretas the king kept the city of the damascenes with a garrison, desirous to apprehend me: 33 And through a window in a basket was I let down by the wall and escaped his hands.

Saul from Tarsus underwent a transformation and became Paul. The ability to hear and see the life of a changed man and be inspired by him is truly amazing, isn't it? Only those who are passionate receive the medal and highest admiration from God.

Paul, Peter, John, Daniel, King David, Moses and many great people we see in the Bible had a great passion for God.

Hebrew 12:1 Wherefore seeing we also are compassed about with so great a cloud of witnesses, let us lay aside every weight, and the sin which doth so easily beset us, and let us run with patience the race that is set before us.

The way they play the game in sports is truly amazing to us. How? The game is something they are absolutely passionate about and won't compromise on.

It wasn't as simple as waking up one morning and deciding to play the game. Their lives have been devoted to reaching a place that leaves spectators breathless. Singers, dancers, players, actors, and actresses were elevated by their passion and unwavering dedication. Nobody reaches their goals without an unwavering passion for what they want. Frequently, we encounter a segment and react by exclaiming wow! By learning about the time, effort, sacrifice, and history of their achievement, we can develop a deep respect for them. I say wow Lord! Achieving, establishing, or receiving anything is impossible without pain. Some individuals, like brainwashers or jealous people, enjoy stealing credit for our work production to gain recognition. Acknowledge the person who deserves credit. May the Lord ignite a deep passion within us for Jesus. We do the best purpose of insignificant life granted to us. The world should long for the same level of passion that is expected. Our life is sustained by the legacy we create. Courage, boldness, fearlessness, and passion are essential for advancing.

I've visited destinations that left me wondering how I managed to get there. It is my Love and passion that took me to the uttermost part of the world. While I may not always fulfill my plans, my unwavering passion for God's Spirit and truth makes me unstoppable. I am determined to fix my gaze on the cross, witnessing the miraculous path unfold. I stumble upon a fresh highway, roads, and a separating ocean, but I persist in sailing towards my destination. Without passion, life is like a sailor lost at sea. Instead of aiming for the medal, people focus on their passion.

Let us pray for unwavering determination and unwavering focus as we pursue our passions for the Lord. It will leave a legacy of success to someone who has a similar passion. The Lord exempted no one from hurting, suffering, and losing life for their passion.

AUGUST 5

Jesus said, Matthew 16:25 For whosoever will save his life shall lose it: and whosoever will lose his life for my sake shall find it. 26 For what is a man profited, if he shall gain the whole world, and lose his own soul? or what shall a man give in exchange for his soul?

May the Lord give us a passion for our calling! Keep in mind that it is for the glory of King Jesus. Many individuals will reap the benefits. I have an immense and unwavering passion for Jesus, no matter what. Everything revolves around Him, not around me. May the Lord grant you a passionate heart for His creation, similar to that of Jesus! It shows on the cross every stripe He took and all the work He did with significant opposition. May the Lord bless you and fill you with a fervent passion for Him.

LET US PRAY

Our Father, we need your spirit to teach the word. Help us practice the Word of God to reach maturity. Lord, we know Jesus is the true and living God. Give us more laborers who have the revelation of Jesus. Let the Lord send us faithful laborers to continue setting captives free. Use us in healing and delivering. Our God breaks every yoke from the shoulder. We speak freedom over the people of God. No more yoke, chain, the burden of religion, and ignorance. May Lord bless and help us reach our maturity in Jesus 'name. Amen! God bless you!

AUGUST 6

BLESSING AND CURSING RESULTS FROM YOUR ACTIONS!

Life's result shows whether you are obedient or rebellious. The consequences of your actions can either bring curses or blessings to your life and the world. By submitting to the word of God, you will receive rain, security, provisions, health, and supernatural help from the creator for both you and the land. The creator of our world gave us permission to inhabit His planet, known as Earth. Live on planet earth complying with the conditions of God and not yours. If you miss, then you will be wiped out little by little. God dealt with the sin of the nations Hittites, Girgashites, Amorites, Canaanites, Perizzites, and the Hivites. The owner of earth asked His creation (humanity) to do right in the sight of God. You should always follow the owner's instructions. Choose a different route to prevent eviction. If you deviate from serving the living God and prioritize pleasing the flesh, the Lord applies the same rules and regulations to individuals, groups, and nations.

Deuteronomy 7:1 When the Lord thy God shall bring thee into the land whither thou goest to possess it, and hath cast out many nations before thee, the Hittites, and the Girgashites, and the Amorites, and the Canaanites, and the Perizzites, and the Hivites, and the Jebusites, seven nations greater and mightier than thou;

Exodus 23:30 By little and little I will drive them out from before thee, until thou be increased, and inherit the land

Heaven takes note of all your actions and reactions.

Revelation 20:12 And I saw the dead, small and great, stand before God; and the books were opened: and another book was opened, which is the book of life: and the dead were judged out of those things which were written in the books, according to their works.

Daniel 7:10 A fiery stream issued and came forth from before him: thousand ministered unto him, and ten thousand times ten thousand stood before him: the judgment was set, and the books were opened.

The Lord sees everything; nothing can be hidden from Him. Be cautious, as there's a possibility that someone observed your actions. It's already been seen by God!

AUGUST 6

Hebrew 4:13 Neither is there any creature that is not manifest in his sight: but all things are naked and opened unto the eyes of him with whom we have to do.

Luke 8:17 For nothing is secret, that shall not be made manifest; neither anything hid, that shall not be known and come abroad.

Allow the teachings of God to correct any hidden motives. Or else you live in an imaginary world. Get a grip on reality. All deceptive, secret ways are labeled as hypocrisy or deception. You and children after you must be taught the way of God, the creator of the earth. It is common knowledge that there are no planets where you can live.

Psalm 115:15 Ye are blessed of the LORD which made heaven and earth. 16 The heaven, even the heavens, are the Lord's: but the earth hath he given to the children of men.

Visit the cemetery and see at what age people die nowadays. In recent times, there has been a significant increase in the deaths of young people. Once they hit their twenties, they no longer exist.

Psalm 55:23 But thou, O God, shalt bring them down into the pit of destruction: bloody and deceitful men shall not live out half their days; but I will trust in thee.

Moses lived to the age of 120. David lived a long life. *1 Chronicle 29:28a And he died in a good old age, full of days, riches, and honor*

Psalms 37:11 But the meek shall inherit the earth; and shall delight themselves in the abundance of peace.

Avoid seeking a quick path through religion, deceitful instructors, and prophets. They will mess you up. Have love, fear, and reverence for the owner and creator of the earth.

There's nothing quite like receiving favor, protection, and blessings. Your best way is Jesus. No one but Jesus!

Deuteronomy 29:9 Keep therefore the words of this covenant, and do them, that ye may prosper in all that ye do.

It is easy once you overcome the lust of the eyes, the lust of the flesh, and the pride of life to receive blessings. Only if your performance is according to God's command, laws, precepts, and statutes, then,

Deuteronomy 30:9 And the LORD thy God will make thee plenteous in every work of thine hand, in the fruit of thy body, and in the fruit of thy cattle, and the fruit of thy land, for good: for the LORD, will again rejoice over thee for good, as he rejoiced over thy fathers:

When people have an abundance of food, possessions, and everything they desire, they tend to forget about God. God's importance decreases. People should pay more attention to hearing the Lord's voice. It's essential for individuals to handle their actions and reactions correctly, regardless of who they are. May the Lord guide and preserve us as we obey His laws and commandments!

Remember, it is essential to keep God's commandments and statutes and to teach the next generation to continue the benefits. Your destiny is largely influenced by your actions. It is your choices, not God, that determine your destiny. God always blesses.

Number 32:13 And the LORD'S anger was kindled against Israel, and he made them wander in the wilderness forty years until all the generation that had done evil in the sight of the LORD was consumed.

The destruction of the land, including lava, earthquakes, tsunamis, and plagues, results from the people's actions and a sign of judgement. Righteous judgment is determined through actions.

Leviticus 18:28 That the land spue not you out also, when ye defile it, as it spued out the nations that were before you.

God's condition has remained unchanged since the beginning.

Revelation 3:16 So then because thou art lukewarm, and neither cold nor hot, I will spue thee out of my mouth.

What role do you play in terms of responsibility? Do not get busy with the church program. Do not buy God with your tithes, offerings, or by sacrificing meat, coke, or anything. It's your responsibility to continue God's blessings. Your careless actions, disregarding laws, commandments, and God's precepts are not tolerated by Earth. May we receive sincere prophets and teachers from the Lord, who will help us stay on the right path. Our responsibility is to pursue truth and remain steadfast in our quest. Do not ignore God, since it is a serious matter. It is a matter of even losing the land. To rectify your action today. Mend your ways and love your maker. The Lord has taught us how to act if we want to be blessed.

LET US PRAY

Heavenly Father, we thank you. You will never keep us in the dark. Thank you for giving us your word as a lamp and light to find the road to heaven.

The way of Jesus has the life expectancy and establishment for you and the next generation. Help us, Lord, to keep the Word with all diligence. We know the Holy Spirit is the most significant help and comfort to live right. Thank you for the Holy Spirit. May the Lord give us the wisdom of Daniel, David, and Moses to call us as one of those good and faithful! One of them whom God said I give this land to inherit for you and your children. May the Lord give us that desire to carry on in fear of the highest God in whom there is no variance! We check our ways and hearts to find God and His ways to be blessed in Jesus 'name. Amen! God bless you!

AUGUST 7

HOW DOES DISPENSATION END?

What is Dispensation? The divine ordering of the affairs of the world. An appointment, arrangement, or favor, as by God. a divinely appointed order or age: the old Mosaic, or Jewish, dispensation; the new gospel, or Christian dispensation.

From htttps://www.dictionary.com/browse/dispensation

There are three dispensations reckoned, the Patriarchal, the Mosaic or Jewish, and the Christian. (Taken from Bible Study tools) Dispensation means management, system, or arrangement. God governs earth from heaven with His laws, commandment, precepts, and statutes for specific times and eras. The benefits may be yours if you decide to follow. In the dispensation of innocence, God governed the earth with just one commandment. Refrain from eating the fruit of the tree that is forbidden. Is it really that easy?

Genesis 2:17 But of the tree of the knowledge of good and evil, thou shalt not eat of it: for in the day that thou eatest thereof, thou shalt surely die.

What does death mean? The death mentioned here, pertaining to Adam and Eve, is not physical but rather the eternal death of your soul.

Once the forbidden fruit was eaten,

Genesis 3:7 And the eyes of them both were opened, and they knew that they were naked, and they sewed fig leaves together and made themselves aprons.

Now, they have to clothe and drive out to the ground. They had no knowledge of tilling land, sweating, experiencing the agony of childbirth, and consuming the fruits of their labor. Wow! Breaking the order, the dispensation of innocence ended. Human disobedience is a result of transgressing God's command and is inherited in their flesh. Without the commandment of God governing the flesh, you will drift apart from God. Breaking the commandment of God led to great strife. The dispensation of innocence ended, and after that, a dispensation of knowledge of good and evil started.

The second dispensation was called the dispensation of conscience. The human government began after the earth was destroyed by a flood. Noah and his family established an agreement to safeguard against future floods and granted permission to consume meat, employing rainbows as a symbolic reminder to spare human lives from being taken by floods.

Genesis 6:11 The earth was also corrupt before God, and the world was violent. 12 And God looked upon the earth, and, behold; it was corrupt; for all flesh had corrupted his way upon the earth. 13 And God said unto Noah, The end of all flesh is come before me; for the world is filled with violence through them; and, behold, I will destroy them with the earth.

He then started a dispensation of promise to Abraham, who believed the Lord. The trial demonstrated Abraham's faith. He received the assurances of sons and nations. He received a blessing for his descendant. God promised Abraham; I will bless who blesses you and curse who curses you. Circumcision was the symbol of the covenant. The dispensation of law, known as the fifth dispensation, ended prior to Jesus' crucifixion. By giving the Israelites laws, Jehovah God demonstrated that following His commandments leads to earthly blessings. Keep the Law.

Deuteronomy 4:40 Thou shalt keep therefore his statutes, and his commandments, which I command thee this day, that it may go well with thee, and with thy children after thee, and that thou mayest prolong thy days upon the earth, which the LORD thy God giveth thee, forever.

Deuteronomy 28:1 And it shall come to pass, if thou shalt hearken diligently unto the voice of the LORD thy God, to observe and to do all his commandments which I command thee this day, that the LORD thy God will set thee on high above all nations of the earth:

Man's disobedience to God's commandments and statutes brought an end to this dispensation.

Malachi 2:11 Judah hath dealt treacherously, and an abomination is committed in Israel and Jerusalem; for Judah hath profaned the holiness of the Lord which he loved, and hath married the daughter of a strange god. 3:5 And I will come near to you to judgment. I will witness against the sorcerers, and against the adulterers, and false swearers, and against those that oppress the hireling in his wages, the widow, and the fatherless, and that turn aside the stranger from his right and fear, not me, saith the Lord of hosts.

Remember, God means what He says and says what He means. It is beautiful to practice and remind yourself of the dos and don't since there is no other way but the Lord. Historical evidence demonstrates that grace always prevails over different past dispensations. Instead of animals, we possess the blood of the savior. May the Lord grant us the wisdom to avoid repeating history. Open your heart, eyes, and ears as you wake up and read your Bible. God has compared the end time with the time of Noah, Lot, and the coming of Christ. We know the sixth dispensation as the dispensation of grace, gospel, or God.

Ephesians 3:2 If ye have heard of the dispensation of the grace of God which is given me to you-ward:

Colossians 1:25 Whereof I am made a minister, according to the dispensation of God which is given to me for you, to fulfill the word of God;

1 Corinthian 9:17 For if I do this thing willingly, I have a reward: but if against my will, a dispensation of the gospel is committed unto me.

It has been prophesied in the Bible that this will conclude when the people of God stray from the truth.

AUGUST 7

Signs indicating the end of Grace or God's dispensation.

1 Timothy 4:1 Now the Spirit speaketh expressly, that in the latter times, some shall depart from the faith, giving heed to seducing spirits, and doctrines of devils; 2 Speaking lies in hypocrisy; having their conscience seared with a hot iron;

The repetition of our behavior. Keep in mind the teachings of the Lord. I will judge. I haven't changed. Do you think it is okay since it's taken too long? Engaging in activities similar to those during Noah's time - eating, drinking, and more. May the Lord bless us with the ability to discern between right and wrong. We must continue in the word of God, watch, and pray more. We must obey what God says. The Lord always provided an escape for the righteous in every era. There has to be an ark for righteousness for this dispensation. Ready yourself for baptism in the name of Jesus. This is the ark for the current era.

1 Peter 3:20 Which sometime were disobedient when once the longsuffering of God waited in the days of Noah, while the ark was a preparing, wherein few, that is, eight souls, were saved by water. 21 The like figure whereunto even baptism doth also now save us (not the putting away of the filth of the flesh, but the answer of a good conscience toward God) by the resurrection of Jesus Christ:

LET US PRAY

Our heavenly Father, we come before you; please be merciful. We are responsible for judgment and ending each dispensation. We ask for a sincere heart that will faithfully follow your commandments and uphold your word. Our responsibility is to do our part, and we will never fail ourselves and others. We know and believe that God never changes, but we do. Make us more like you to do your perfect will. All your words are valid, and we must keep them, no matter what. Help to Keep yourself first by obeying the word of God. This is the best time since the savior shed his blood for us. Thank you for your blood in Jesus 'name. Amen! God bless you!

AUGUST 8

WHAT IS RELIGION, DENOMINATION, AND ORGANIZATIONS?

Explain the meanings of religion, denomination, and organizations.

After retiring or taking over from God, present your religion. I, me, and not God are what it is. Satan's kingdom greatly benefits from religion. Helping establish a denomination or organization becomes the norm for the follower. When you join and fully dedicate yourself, you assist in the establishment of a religion.

The majority of religious individuals attend church and observe to convenient rules. People contribute tithes and offerings to ensure the continuation of their churches/religion. Once you meet their condition, you will receive a warm welcome. A religious leader will dismiss you if you decide to follow Jesus. Harassment, both direct and indirect, will be part of your experience. As Satan assumes the pulpit, the organization slowly but surely replaces God. There are many cults spread across the world, each with its own name.

In the past, I came across a newsletter from Satan's high priestess that claimed we must convert Christians to establish Satan's kingdom. Since the beginning, Satan has employed the most deceptive approach. Religion is a deviation from the truth. Following Jesus is what matters in Christianity, not denominations or non-denomination. The most conspire way of representing the Word of God. Satan twists and misrepresents God's commandment, precepts, laws, and statutes to destroy God's entire plan.
Satan is wiser than Daniel.

Ezekiel 28:2 Son of man, say unto the prince of Tyrus, Thus saith the Lord GOD; Because thine heart is lifted up, and thou hast said, I am a God, I sit in the seat of God, amid the seas; yet thou art a man, and not God, though thou set thine heart as the heart of God: 3 Behold, thou art wiser than Daniel; there is no secret that they can hide from thee: 4 With thy wisdom and with thine understanding thou hast gotten thee riches, and hast gotten gold and silver into thy treasures:

It becomes clear that dealing with the devil is a grave concern. Those who are not spiritually grounded can easily be led astray by the devil. The flesh is filled with lust, pride, and desires of the eyes. A person is walking in the flesh; a devil will ride on them. The devil eats dirt and depends on dirt; remember, God made you of dirt. Sin serves as a meal for Satan if one indulges in it.

AUGUST 8

Once upon a time, the Devil was thriving in heaven. He had access till the day Archangel Michael kicked him out of heaven. He had the experience of having the truth, walking, and obeying God. Satan knows our power by connecting with God's throne room. Having access to God means having everything. By obeying God's voice, you can still tap into the Power of the throne room. This is most dangerous for Satan. It was his argument.

Job 1:10 Hast, not thou made a hedge about him, and about his house, and about all that he hath on every side? Thou hast blessed the work of his hands, and his substance is increased in the land.

Satan planned to get rid of the hedge and have access to steal, kill, and destroy Job.

The sole method to cause their downfall is by diverting them from God's commandments and precepts. It's not a direct assault, but a means of calming by offering something. The devil never convinces us not to believe in God but twists God's Word. Find the new deceptive way rewording of His spoken Word. Many Bible translations, except KJV, are deviations from the truth.

The Bible cautions against adding or removing the Word of God. There is a significant consequence to paying. Owning a book known as the Bible, which consists of 66 books, implies a substantial obligation to continually seek, live out, obey, and surrender to God. The religious authority considers themselves above God. Religion, organization, and denomination will force you into their preaching and teaching. If you don't, then face persecution.

You are better off getting hold of God by reading the Bible and obeying it. Only God's power has the ability to eradicate the influence of religion, manifesting through those who have turned away from Jesus and embraced the devil. Do you have a desire to learn about the Bible? Then do as it says. Lay a hand on the sick, cast out demons, heal the afflicted, help the destitute and needy, visit widows and orphans, and open blind eyes and deaf ears.

You know the way of Eve, Adam, and King Saul. Corruption and violence, just like what we experience now, were prevalent during Noah's time. Crosses and churches of different denominations and organizations mean nothing. It's acceptable as long as you obey them, but if not, you'll experience persecution and being singled out. The denominational people will throw the disciple of truth out.

Be careful. Once you discard the truth, then part of the truth has no value. The Bible instructs us not to add or subtract. May we receive the bravery of David, the courage of Joshua, and the humbleness of Moses from the Lord. It is crucial to have it during this time, season, and age. People of God will be compelled by religious leaders to believe falsehood. Be prepared to be targeted and subjected to harassment and accusations. Who will trust your word when accusations come from the priest, high priest, and all religious leaders? May the Lord accompany and converse with you, reminding you that He is the true God, surpassing any church, authority, denomination, or organization. Religion is a beautiful way of saying I believe in God but obey the one who has replaced God.

The prayer connects us with God. They get attacked whenever I invite people to pray, or the religious leader and their wife will invite them to play a game. They permanently moved prayer warriors away from me. Do not connect with God. Let's have fun. When we connect with God, then Satan is in big trouble. Prayer is talking to God. Prayer is the relationship with God. Once disconnected, you are in a zone without Wi-Fi for connection to the heavenly realm. Satan is called the wisest. Many religious leaders have replaced God and made millions of unbelievers. Instead of carrying on God's commandments, laws, and precepts, they carry on the devil's agenda—initially, only two human beings and one tactic to thrust them out. Now, for our time takes many tactics, religions, organizations, and church denominations to replace the truth. We have a form of godliness. Churches have the most harmonious orchestra and programs to deceive saints. The church is a money-making firm on earth. God's mission is to set the captive free; beauty for ashes; heal the broken in heart; sick to be healed and lose the captive and break the yoke is gone out the door. No one is digging, seeking, asking, or knocking because the leaders are fallen. The practice of Christians seeking a quiet place to pray and commune with God has been lost over time. Contact God and discover His divine plan. Truth is exchanged for the tea party, luncheon, and fishing. The biggest problem is that shopping, eating, drinking, and working are essential. The leaders want all the tithes and offering to have fun, vacationing, hunting, golfing, nice cars, and all the best. How did it happen? Jesus of Nazareth departed this world, leaving us with the responsibility to proclaim the Gospel with signs and wonders as evidence. In the present day, due to the devil's new teachings, if you're unwell, you must book a doctor's appointment, take medicine, and use your finances.

No worry, once you're brainwashed, it is easy to pass the next generation to overlook what it is all about. Especially do not let them pray, so they have no connections with God. The word is God and God is the word. Knowing the word is crucial to knowing God. Knowing God is the true essence of studying the Word, as only then can one understand the message of the Lord. Always say my pastor, my church, or my denomination; it is me and me. What happened to Jesus? We retire Lord Jesus. This is called Satan's sophisticated business, religion, denominations, organizations, or churches. Open the Bible, read, and pray.

LET US PRAY

Our heavenly Father, we come to your altar in the name of Jesus. We asked humbly to help, lead in all your truth, and not to religion. We know the power is in the truth, and your word is true. Teach us how to say, 'it is written 'when an enemy comes as religion to deviate us from the truth. May Lord give us His Word, which is the only offensive weapon to get the devil's plan destroyed. May our Lord help us and put the green and red light signal to know to proceed or stop by seeing the danger! Our God has practically shown us the way of truth and life. Thank you for the living word of God to quicken us, in Jesus 'name. Amen! God bless you!

AUGUST 9

LORD, MAKE ME HUMBLE!

Another word for Humble is meek. What is humility? Humble meant Meek, submissive. The opposite is proud and arrogant! For God to rule on earth as in heaven, there must be someone obedient to Him and His commandment. Can I request that you humbly listen to and obey His voice? It is God's will to bless, guide, and protect His creation. Is there anyone humble enough to execute God's plan? God is sought by those who are humble. Humble is the chosen one to express the voice of God.

Numbers 12:3 (Now the man Moses was very meek, above all the men which were upon the face of the earth.)

Moses was exalted by God in the presence of Pharaoh and the people of Egypt because of his humility. You're aware that God has the power to lift you up and then humble you if you become arrogant. As you go high, be careful, stay humble, and not be so proud of it will thrust you out like King Saul and High Priest Eli. No matter how high your position, always remember that before the mighty God, you are nobody. There is a project and plan from God that needs to be heard and carried out on earth.

God once spoke to me, asking me to visit my neighbor's house. During my trip to India, I brought a small present for an elderly neighbour. I knocked, and she promptly opened the door, allowing me inside. I offered her a gift, and she revealed the tragic news of her husband's death a few days prior. I was so glad that I heard God asking me to visit her. She was sad and crying. I provided comfort and offered prayers. Let us be instruments of the Lord's comfort and prayer for His people. The devil won't be able to take advantage of situations if we act accordingly. If we are humble and open to God's guidance, we can avoid regret.

There have been numerous occasions where we've believed that God isn't fair. We wonder why a kind and loving God would permit all the bad things. Our pride and arrogance, not God's lack, is the issue. God has not made us robots, but has given us free will. Give heed to God, look after yourself, and have confidence that the Lord will safeguard and supply.

God appointed Moses to undertake the extensive projects of guiding the enslaved people to the promised land. Due to God being the director, he successfully guides this multitude through the desert. Moses, being humble, God engaged him to bring various plagues to Egypt. Egypt and the rest of the world discovered the true and living God of Abraham, Isaac, and Israel. The earth belongs to God. He rules the universe. He remains unchanged. May the Lord God grant us the virtue of humility. Hear Him, so He can show the world that He is a living, loving, and caring God. You can change the myth of God into reality.

Daniel allowed God, not fearing the sentence of Lion's Den. It is true that sometimes, standing on the word of God, you will walk contrary to the world's authority, power, and flow. Hear and fear no one but the Lord. God cannot use you If you listen, spouse, the lust of the flesh, lust of the eye, pride, or anyone but God. God uses who hears and obeys. The Lord designed the holy life of Jews with commandments, statutes, precepts, holy laws, and a kosher diet. It is for the humble to accept and obey to be blessed. God wants to bless you, but are you humble enough to let Him? One who rejects God or acts rebelliously or disobediently cannot be used by Him. It is all God and nothing of you; then the Lord will be done on earth.

Proverb 22:4 By humility and the fear of the Lord are riches, honor, and life.

1 Peter 5:6 Humble yourselves therefore under the mighty hand of God, that he may exalt you in due time.

Moses was considered humble because he obeyed God's instructions without hesitation.

Exodus 11:3b Moreover, the man Moses was very significant in the land of Egypt, the sight of Pharaoh's servants and the people's sight.

While Moses was next to Pharaoh, his love for God surpassed power and glory. He had no interest in the world's treasure. May the Lord bless us with wisdom. Earth will be burned. We are here for a reason and a season. Your actions and reactions to the word of God determine your success on earth.

Act 7:22 And Moses was learned in all the wisdom of the Egyptians, and was mighty in words and in deeds.

The almighty God desires to bless His creation above all else. The Lord is deciding who will be His forever wife. May the Lord give us a sense of responsibility.

The humble acts we perform now will benefit future generations to come.

Receiving blessings often leads people to become filled with pride. It's important for them to recall both the how and the who of the giver. Where do the blessings originate? Where did it come from? Our first responsibilities are if we want to continue in our blessings, we must fear the Lord and teach our children and grandchildren the commandments and precepts of God almighty. The first step is to educate them about the Word of God, prayer, and reverence for our God.

Matthew 18:4 Whosoever, therefore, shall humble himself as this little child, the same is greatest in the kingdom of heaven.

We should not ask why or fear when God calls us to act. Yes, sir, is the word we should use.

Matthew 23:12 And whosoever shall exalt himself shall be abased, and he that shall humble himself shall be exalted.

Numerous individuals attained positions of authority, but neglected to uphold God's blessings. The primary focus should be on humility and avoiding a downward slide.

AUGUST 9

The moment people embrace pride, haughtiness, and arrogance, they start to go downhill. Recall the Lord, who stands as an exceptional model of humbleness. Jesus was God in the flesh. Spirit, God walked in the flesh.

Philippians 2:5 Let this mind be in you, which was also in Christ Jesus:6 Who, being in the form of God, thought it not robbery to be equal with God: 7 But made himself of no reputation, and took upon him the form of a servant, and was made in the likeness of men:8 And being found in fashion as a man, he humbled himself and became obedient unto death, even the death of the cross. 9 Wherefore God also hath highly exalted him and given him a name which is above every name:10 That at the name of Jesus every knee should bow, of things in heaven, and things in earth, and things under the earth; 11 And that every tongue should confess that Jesus Christ is Lord, to the glory of God the Father.

The nature of our God is humble. Despite facing numerous unbearable punishments, mocking stripes, and insults, He humbly persevered and triumphed. Lord Jesus said it is finished! May we receive from the Lord a heart that is humble. Humble won't attempt to prove or even consider proving. He believes God will handle His duties. It is God who takes you high if you are humble. Be humble.

LET US PRAY

Thank you, Heavenly Father, for becoming human and sacrificing yourself so that I may have eternal life. It is the mighty God who suffered and did not protect himself. May the Lord our God give us a humble heart. He exalts the humble one. We submit ourselves to the will of God and not ours. Thine will be done. We know that, Lord; we need to be humble to fulfill your will. The Lord gives us a humble heart. Lord, I want your plan to be established and the devil's agenda destroyed. Help me do what you want me to, in Jesus 'name. Amen! God bless you!

AUGUST 10

REMEMBER, GOD COMES FIRST!

God is always the first and foremost, regardless of anything. Don't seek Him only when you have spare time or are in awful crisis. Many people keep God as a side dish. God will always be first, never second. He is always the number one priority in our lives. It is common for us to set Him aside and only remember Him when we need Him. What does He need in order to come in first place? Keeping Him first requires your full dedication.

The question came from Ascribe, an expert in the Word or Torah, directed towards Jesus. What is the first thing we should keep in our heart, life, and mind?

Mark 12:29 And Jesus answered him, the first of all the commandments is, Hear, O Israel; The Lord our God is one Lord: 30 And thou shalt love the Lord thy God with all thy heart, and with all thy soul, and with all thy mind, and with all thy strength: this is the first commandment. 31 And the second is like, namely this, thou shalt love thy neighbour as thyself. There is none other commandment greater than these.

The guidance of God helps us determine our life's priorities. It is important for us to be in accordance with the Lord's order.

Before you encounter trials and troubles, make sure to have a conversation with Him in the morning. Do you typically shower, drink coffee, or brush your teeth in the afternoon? No, you do the first thing first. Start your day by seeking the Lord's guidance to overcome the enemy's plan. May you receive God's blessing early in the morning to guide your day. Give priority to the Lord and step into His presence. Who moved away from God? You did. Do not stray from the Lord's presence. If you speak to Him, He will attend to you while sitting on the throne.

1 Timothy 2:1 I exhort therefore, that, first of all, supplications, prayers, intercessions, and giving of thanks, be made for all men.

Before anything else, this is what we need to do. Remember to pray for your family, the government, and those around you. The wicked ruler of nations often occupies positions of power, so please pray against all evil deeds. Religious leaders occupy prominent positions. Not following them will lead to your complete downfall. The path to following Jesus is prayer, and it should not be ignored. According to what you asked, the movement takes place on earth.

AUGUST 10

The Bible says in.

Proverbs 16:3 Commit thy works unto the LORD, and thy thoughts shall be established.

Give your thought to God in the beginning, not later when you lose. Surrender your thoughts to God and let Him guide you towards elevation. Lord, help us understand His ways. If we make Him our priority, he will give us everything we need. Recognize His power, wisdom to take us to the expected end. Let's make sure we commit our work early, not just when we mess up.

Matthew 6:32 (For after all these things do the Gentiles seek for your heavenly Father knoweth that ye have need of all these things. 33 But seek ye first the kingdom of God, and his righteousness; and all these things shall be added unto you. 34 Take therefore no thought for the morrow: for the morrow shall take thought for the things of itself. Sufficient unto the day is the evil thereof.

When you keep God as your priority, your needs will be taken care of. Your life will be different from the heathen, who constantly struggles and perspires. The nonbeliever goes to great lengths to attain their desires. Christians will be the first to receive the best, effortlessly. God is expressing Himself through different parables. He did not just say parables, but also demonstrated by using two fishes and multiplying.

I remembered someone shared the true story of a widow. A preacher came to her house to visit. She said, I would like to cook food for you. Well, when she turned around, she remembered that there was no oil to fry her food. Not knowing what to do next, she felt disturbed. As she watched, oil started to fill up in the bottle before her very eyes. Can't we attribute everything to God's influence? Our God is not a beggar, but a provider. We do not give food to God; He gives us.

Keeping God as your top priority extends beyond material things like oil or flour. It involves your body, soul, spirit, children, government, nation, and all your possessions. He will do good, since God is good. What is the meaning of keeping God first? It means keeping His commandments, statutes, and laws. To be called blessed, the nation must meet a specific requirement.

Exodus 19:5 Now therefore, if ye will obey my voice indeed, and keep my covenant, then ye shall be a peculiar treasure unto me above all people: for all the earth is mine: 6 And ye shall be unto me a kingdom of priests, and an holy nation. These are the words which thou shalt speak unto the children of Israel.

If you prioritize God, you can receive all your desires and more. Your priorities are completely out of order.

I heard the testimony of the visitor preacher. He said he was poor while growing up. When he got home from school, he requested food. His mother instructed him to seek God's provision. This family was deeply committed to Christianity. The young boy acted without hesitation. He went and offered prayers at the family altar. As he was praying, he heard a loud explosion. He began searching his surroundings. Upon entering the backyard, he noticed the large fish was in motion. The big fish slipped out of the bird's beak. With the ocean nearby, the bird flew with a fish in its mouth and accidentally dropped it in his yard. He received the food. How good our God is? Our God is wonderful. Keep Him first. He will take care of everything you need if you turn to Him.

I am mentoring a young brahmin man. He is actively seeking a relationship with Jesus. He refers to Jesus as my father. In some way, he discovered God, or God discovered him. He was conversing with a fellow

Hindu who had been unemployed. The brahmin guy said, pray to my father; he will give you the job. The Hindu guy said, no, I will not. A brahmin young man said, if you do not then I will talk to my father. He will give you a job within thirty days. The man got a job and said I would like to meet your father. Now the Lord listens to those who keep Him first.

Would you keep God first and see what happens? The examples of individuals like Daniel, Moses, Enoch, Noah, and Abraham show God can accomplish the impossible when He is given first place. May our Lord give us the courage to step into the water, so we see the miracle of parting of the ocean! We witness mountains moving, the dead coming back to life, and paths being created out of nothing. May every crooked way straighten up and fountains of blessing breakthrough in your life! We would not need the jail, prison, security systems, police department, or judges. The concerns about health, finance, provision, and sickness will fade away. May we receive divine wisdom to prioritize the Lord and find joy in earthly existence. May the Lord bless us with discernment to prioritize and witness supernatural provisions. Hallelujah! Keep God first in your life, in Jesus' name. Amen!

LET US PRAY:

Lord, help us act on your word without question. Our God said nothing is impossible; all things are possible if you believe. Our job is to let the world and self-know that God almighty needs someone to believe in Him. Follow in the footsteps of Esther, Mary, Elizabeth, Daniel, Jabez, and other remarkable figures who trusted the Word of God and pursued acting. God kept them as peculiar, blessed people above all nations. Many inherited the blessing of Abraham, Isaac, and Israel by keeping God first. We face challenges in this world. Many crises, but today we decide to put all things aside and bring God first to let the world know that God has not changed. We found toys and kept ourselves engaged. Our actions have been tainted by wickedness, but we are now humbling ourselves and seeking redemption in Jesus 'name. Amen! God bless you!

AUGUST 11

FRUIT BEARING WORD!

God's word is like a seed. If you sow it in your heart, it has the ability to revolutionize your life. The fruit will become visible once the tree starts to grow. It is the Lord who will show us how to use the word as a seed. Do you have faith that it is a seed? God is capable of everything, but requires a suitable foundation. It is us who are that ground. Let us welcome the Word into our hearts and seek it through prayer. The tree will provide shelter for many birds. Being made of dirt means that we are grounded.

Matthew 13:1 The same day, went Jesus out of the house and sat by the sea side. 2 And great multitudes were gathered together unto him, so that he went into a ship, and sat, and the whole multitude stood on the shore.3 And he spake many things unto them in parables, saying, Behold, a sower went forth to sow; 4 And when he sowed, some seeds fell by the way side, and the fowls came and devoured them up: 5 Some fell upon stony places, where they had not much earth: and forthwith they sprung up, because they had no deepness of earth: 6 And when the sun was up, they were scorched; and because they had no root, they withered away. 7 And some fell among thorns, and the thorns sprung up and choked them: 8 But other fell into good ground and brought forth fruit, some a hundredfold, some sixtyfold, some thirtyfold. 9 Who hath ears to hear, let him hear.

How the seed is influenced by the ground.

All the ground is not the same. There are many kinds of ground. Make sure to remove any debris to prepare the ground. Prepare the ground through prayer and fasting to be receptive to the word. Blame falls on the receiver, not the sower. There are four grounds declared by God.

- Wayside
- Stony Places
- Thorny places and
- Good ground.

God is referring to our way of living. The word of God produces different outcomes depending on the soil it falls on. It's important to pray before you start reading the Bible. I pray that your Word will penetrate my heart and shape my life. Quicken me through your Word. Let your word become my lamp, light, and food.

It's not just about the word being a seed, but what actions people take with that seed. Lord, may we be open to receiving your Word and may it bear fruit in Jesus 'name. The effectiveness of God's word depends on receiving it on good ground. Receive the Word with the right motive and attitude. Our hearts need to be cleansed of lies, jealousy, wickedness, deceitfulness, and evil.

Wayside seed refers to those who have knowledge of the Word but never truly understood it. It is a must that you find excellent teachers and pastors to explain the Word of God. If not, then the devil will come and mess you up.

Stony Places responds to the word, but when trouble and trial come, they get hurt, wounded, angry, and turn away from the truth. They get back, fight, angry and resentful. These individuals are not yielding any results. They are like a thorn in the side. They will fight, argue, and get angry and bitter about their situation.

Worldly individuals who prioritize the world are represented by the thorny ground. When your time is consumed after the world, money, riches, lust of the eyes, flesh, and the pride of life that will choke the word of God within them. The busy lifestyle of these individuals prevents the Word of God from taking root in them. Trying to keep up with others and constantly striving for more makes life chaotic. These individuals are unable to produce fruits because they prioritize other things over God.

When the ground is good

23 But he that received seed into the good ground is he that heareth the word and hit; which also beareth fruit, and bringeth forth, some a hundredfold, some sixty, some thirty.

Applying it provides a great explanation for how the ground receives the Word of God and its impact on life. When you listen to the Word, apply it in your life. It will bear fruits. This is the precise revelation from God. Not just the hearer but also the doer! By following the word of God, you will put the word into action. No worry about forgetting. It will give spiritual muscles. People who meditate on the word of God day and night are the ones who have the hope of bearing fruit. They are called trees planted by the river. Think about the Word manifested in the flesh, Jesus Christ. How much He bears the fruits? Healing, deliverance, eye and ear opening, raising the dead, and curing leprosy were all manifested. Similar fruits can be observed in the people of God who have good ground. Countless individuals who have recently converted experience spiritual growth as they passionately love God and are eager to obey His commands. God seeks those who will forsake the world and turn to Him. We are made by the Lord to produce fruit.

Changes in a person can be seen through their behavior and lifestyle choices. Old things have passed away, and all have become new. No interest in anything related to the world. Their topic and subject are God and God alone. They may not be a theologian, but they are a laborer of the Word. The Word is working in and through them. The fruit bearer showcases the word instead of explaining it. The testimony they hold is about healing and deliverance. They believe that if others receive the Word, they will experience the same results. The fruit bearer speaks the ground type. You cannot testify without bearing the fruit. I do not see how the preacher turns blue, red, and purple. It doesn't have anything to do with your proficiency in Greek and Hebrew. How much experience or what degree do you have? It is about the fruit. The fruits of Christians will show that they follow Jesus. The proof of the Followers of Jesus lies in their actions, not just in quoting scripture. The Bible consistently says the fruit is a sign. What sign do you see on an apple tree? Apples, right? The Lord Jesus asked John Baptist's disciples to see the fruits. What kind of work and fruit he was producing,

AUGUST 11

Matthew 11:2 Now when John had heard in the prison the works of Christ, he sent two of his disciples, 3 And said unto him, Art thou he that should come, or do we look for another? 4 Jesus answered and said unto them, Go and shew John again those things which ye do hear and see: 5 The blind receive their sight, and the lame walk, the lepers are cleansed, and the deaf hear, the dead are raised, and the poor have the gospel preached to them. 6 And blessed is he, whosoever shall not be offended in me.

Do you have good ground? Are you bearing the same fruits as what Jesus gave to John the Baptist? You follow the one who bears these fruits. If not, they are the thorny wayside and the stony ground where the seed has fallen with no hope of producing fruits. May the Lord give us a divine understanding of His Word to find hidden truth in the Book called the Bible! Life-changing Word has world-changing power. Operate and allow the word to grow on good ground, in Jesus' name.

LET US PRAY

our word works wonders if we allow it. It is the power of the ground and the power of the Word. We ask for soil to be fruit-bearing for the Word of God, so we bear good, godly fruit in the name of Jesus. Lord, we pray against the stony, thorny, and bad ground to be gone and produce the good ground. Word is ready to receive on good ground. Our ground is delightful to grow and bear fruit. We significantly affect the world and not just the Word on us. My Lord, your word is good, but if we are good and grateful for the Word to grow, to change others. God's word needs the ground. Let us be that ground, so we bear thirty, sixty, and hundredfold fruits, in Jesus's name. Amen! God bless you!

AUGUST 12

IT IS THAT EASY!

If God says it's easy, don't assume it's difficult. It gets more difficult when you depart from God's way and seek an alternative path. God's way is the only, best, and straightforward way. God's arrival on earth involved teaching and proving. The first thing He said was to repent. You must change your ways and forsake your sins. God and sin have no shared platform. God is not on the platform of sin, and the devil is not on the platform of righteousness. The two are opposite roles: one works in light and the other with darkness. Our God works with light. Even when it makes little sense, you must not rationalize but obey. It is not your job to think. It is His thought for you, and you have to carry on. The supernatural God engages in supernatural thinking and performs extraordinary actions that surpass what natural humans can comprehend.

Psalm 18:30 As for God, his way is perfect: the word of the Lord is tried: he is a buckler to all those that trust in him. 31 For who is God save the Lord? Or who is a rock save our God? 32 It is God that girdeth me with strength and maketh my way perfect. 33 He maketh my feet like hinds' feet, and setteth me upon my high places. 34 He teacheth my hands to war so that a bow of steel is broken by mine arms. 35 Thou hast also given me the shield of thy salvation: thy right hand hath holden me up, and thy gentleness hath made me great. 36 Thou hast enlarged my steps under me that my feet did not slip.

Moses was instructed by God to enter Egypt and lead the descendants of Abraham, who were enslaved, out. Moses did God's command, as you see how God worked mightily against the mighty country of Egypt. The Hebrews experienced the brutal force and power of the Pharaoh. But the Lord fought against Satan's power to free the Hebrews. Hebrew can only achieve freedom if God ensures their accessibility. A natural human being cannot comprehend any of God's productions. Obey and witness the change in yourself.

John 8:36 If the Son, therefore, shall make you free, ye shall be free indeed.

When a man loses the path of God, he is walking in complete darkness. They are under the control of another power, the power of darkness. To release the captive, you require a higher power than Satan, Jesus Christ. On other days, I talked to a young man in India; he was afraid of a heathen around his house. Hindus wanted to put the idol on his property. Fear got hold of his heart. His freedom was achieved through my prayer. To liberate individuals, we must understand God's teachings. Before I pray for people, I use oil to anoint them. If the person is bound by sickness or disease, they will be free. It is that easy!

AUGUST 12

Sensations of lightness, tiredness, or dizziness indicate the liberation from the Lord. The anointing has the power to break chains and yokes. Follow the instructions given in the Word of God. Satan is not an easy opponent, don't underestimate him. Defeating him is only possible if you have the way of God. Open the Bible and faithfully carry out its teachings. Lord asked the man to go to a pool to wash His eyes. Upon his obedience, his eyes were able to see again. Is that hard?

John 9:7 And said unto him, Go, wash in the pool of Siloam, (which is by interpretation, Sent.) He went his way, therefore, and washed and came seeing.

Don't just listen, take action as well. Do exactly as it says. Every time I follow the Word of God or the prophet's instructions, I see a significant outcome. I simply do it without arguing, no explanation necessary. I produce numerous prayer garments and distribute them for free. On one occasion, the prophet instructed me to do it. I anointed and prayed over a piece of material, then made 2x2 inch pieces and put them in the ground. It relieved me of the torment Satan had put me through. That is simple! The easy way out.

The Bible is not the book for debate; it is the book of a duty. He said to pray without ceasing. Then would you just pray? The replacement of God's truth is evident through the prevalence of kidnapping, gang violence, suicide, and the disintegration of both the city and the country. And who went away from God? You and me? There seems to be an issue with the report.

The woman visitor was seated inside the church. As the worship began, the demon inside her was unable to withstand God's power. She went under the pew, moving like a snake. Upon being asked, I willingly went under the pew. Seeing it was a new and terrifying experience for me. I kept my eyes on her and asked her to say the blood of Jesus.

It seemed as if she was not in her right mind. Her long, terrifying nails gripped my hand tightly. Despite her initial struggle, the woman eventually managed to utter the phrase "the blood of Jesus."

While I continued to bind the demon and expel it, she uttered the phrase "the blood of Jesus."
She finally found freedom from her inner demons. When I told her to worship Jesus, she was filled with the Holy Spirit. God filled her with Spirit by evidence of her speaking in their tongue. It is that easy.

In 2015, I was in India, and at a meeting in Naroda; I put a hand on a man to pray, and he fell. I later discovered that the man was saved from alcohol by the Lord. For twenty years, he battled with alcohol addiction. It is that easy. How did it happen because I flew from US?

I observe the Bible's guidance precisely, praying and fasting in accordance with its instructions.

I once made a phone call to India to check on a sick woman. Her family is an idol worshiper, so many demons attacked her. When I prayed over her on the phone, the demon left her, and she was healed. See, it is easy. God is the one who does that. You do not worship the work of your hand. Worship one true God; his saving name in this dispensation is Jesus.

The lady came to my house one day with her granddaughter. She engaged in self-harm and made multiple suicide attempts. I began ministering and prayed for her on three occasions. She started feeling fine. It is that easy. This kind comes out through prayer and fasting. Do Biblical fasting and prayer. Regularly anoint and pray over your children and grandchildren, placing your hand on them. Through the Holy Spirit, the Lord has granted you power and authority in the name of "Jesus."

A lady named Brandy had all her sons without a job. Her sons moved in with their wife and children at Mrs Brandy's home. Her sons were on drugs and other addictions. Praying resulted in a miracle where all the boys found jobs. The righteous prayer availeth much. What is the righteousness of God? It is to follow the word of God. Jesus is the highest name of Jehovah God in the flesh. The name of God is mighty. No other name. Trust the name, Jesus. I remembered working among Asians; many came to me asking for prayer. Just with my prayers, they are able to recover. If there's a problem, the Lord will provide a solution. It is that easy.

When praying for a new convert, I first provide two or three scriptures that back up my actions. In order to establish the doctrine, the Bible mandates the presence of two or more witnesses. When they are ready to wash away sins and change their life, then they go under the water and baptize in the name of Jesus. The Bible only recognizes baptism in Jesus 'name, don't forget. Reputation is important; that is God's way. When they come out of the water, they are newborn as new creatures, purifying hidden sins with blood. They also recover from their sickness and addiction to drugs and alcohol. It is that easy. Truth is powerful and very easy.

Accept the word of God as it is and put it into action. Trusting and obeying are the keys to accessing God's power, regardless of famine, enemies, or sickness. Do as the Word of God says, and you will see salvation. Salvation meant healing, deliverance, and salvation. How beautiful! God's way is easy and successful. To cast out the demon is a piece of cake if you are fasting, praying, and walking righteously. May the Lord help us follow God; you get a simple life like a garden in Eden before sins. No hard work, perspiration, risk, curses—only peace, provisions, deliverance, and blessings. God's way is simple if you follow them all the way. It is that easy! God bless you!

LET US PRAY

Lord, our ways have made this world without God. In our ways, we toil day and night. We have no rest, and our ways have much hardship, curses, sicknesses, oppression, and possession of demons. Your word, Lord, assures us that it is simple to follow you because you are always there to guide, support, and shower us with blessings. We know history has proven, and even today, your word is as powerful as before. There is no debate about it, but we require submission to it. It is the easiest route you have prepared for us. May the Lord give us obedience to God's voice, which is God's word. Our God's way is higher and more accessible, so please help us believe and obey. Give us an eye of an eagle, a passion like David, Samson's strength, and Daniel's determination to tap into the way of God. It is the best way to let the world know it is easy. God is a superpower and supernatural. Do not think it is beyond. Lord, help us do as you have said in Jesus 'name. Amen! God bless you!

AUGUST 13

FOR YOUR SAKE, DO NOT TOUCH RIGHTEOUS!

Zechariah 2:8 For thus saith the Lord of hosts; After the glory hath he sent me unto the nations which spoiled you: for he that toucheth you toucheth the apple of his eye.

To protect yourself, refrain from going against those who are righteous. God will fight the battle for the righteous. His right hand does powerful work. Right hand means 'power'. So if you want judgment to fall against you, then come against the righteous, but if you desire mercy, grace, and blessings, never touch the righteous.

My mom saw anyone who came against her unjustly suddenly perish. They were doing fine and suddenly died. See, God is for the righteous. Those who judge, scheme, or spread rumors against the righteous will be ridiculed by God. Warning: Eye-rolling or finger-pointing will lead to your downfall. Remember, promotion cometh from the Lord.

Those who fought by my side experienced demotion, harm, unemployment, or the destruction of their families. One time I prayed very hard because someone came against my family. Next week, their family member committed suicide. We were unjustifiably harassed by a woman who was abruptly killed and died. She tragically lost many family members who took their own lives, not just one. Stay away from the cursed family. Do not marry or, if you are divorced, then get rid of the connection from a cursed family. May the Lord disconnect your soul tie from cursed people! Sad, isn't it? Your desire for them stems from the fact that your soul is linked to those people through marriage or a similar bond. But I disconnect your soul from the cursed people in Jesus' name.

The Babylonians observed, experienced, and took note of the mighty deeds carried out by the Hebrew God. The God of the Hebrews was acknowledged by the Babylonians. The story they had was about Daniel, who was saved by God from lions, while his enemy's plot against him backfired.

They heard the rescue report of Shadrach, Meshach, and Abednego from a fiery furnace. But people who touched them burned in the fiery furnace. Return to the senders. Do not dig for God's people; you will fall into it. In Babylon, the Jehovah God stood against the Prince of Babylon. In Babylon, Prince Satan appointed his principality to target the Jewish community. The God of Hebrew fought against every enemy.

Babylonians failed, were destroyed, and demoted. So remember, when you see the plan of Satan against you, then rejoice; God will destroy those wicked. God said to take the revenge is mine.

Make sure when the person is Christian, I am not talking about nominal religious, but truly God-fearing, righteous, then do not touch them.

Who can save you from this great God? God can use tsunamis, lava, earthquake, fire, hail, and many more weapons to remove you from positions and even from earth. Wicked lives like they are living in hell. Sicknesses caused by their sins, no peace, no health, and many internal and external problems make their life miserable.

Haman, the ruler next to the king of Babylon, was warned by his wife Zeresh not to challenge Jewish Mordecai.

Esther 6:13 And Haman told Zeresh, his wife, and all his friends everything that had befallen him. Then said his wise men and Zeresh his wife unto him, If Mordecai be of the seed of the Jews, before whom thou hast begun to fall, thou shalt not prevail against him, but shalt surely fall before him.

Haman had a prominent position in Babylon, but God overthrew him. The promotion comes from God. If you receive a promotion, then be righteous and stay humble. You are done if you touch God's people, and if they cry out, pray, and fast.

Later Haman, who tried to destroy all Jewish in Babylon, and wanted to destroy Mordechai, was hanged on the Gallow he built for Mordechai. Hallelujah! May your adversary stumble today, you righteous ones.

In order to safeguard yourself, avoid interfering with the righteous. Righteous knows how to call on God, pray, fast, and cry out. God will judge you. They will replace you, and you will eventually turn to dust.

I have personally observed the divine vengeance upon my adversary. God takes revenge. Working in India or the US, everything is the same. It is one or all, a family or an outsider. The Lord possesses a weapon that can eradicate anyone, whether they are a king, queen, or commoner.

May the Lord encourage you to be righteous. Do not discourage when you see wicked liars and unrighteous plotting, planning, and digging. They are harming themselves. No weapon formed against the righteous can prosper. To find the report of Daniel, David, Joseph, Moses, and the people of Egypt. God knows how to overthrow your enemy. May the Lord give us a prayer and fasting life to connect with Him. Bringing the problem to the throne room will resolve the issue. The enemy will be overcome by the supreme judge. The judgment of God protects the righteous from their enemies.

Remember, the Egyptians followed with chariots to take over the Hebrew slaves. God buried them in water. Everlasting judgment! You will see your enemy no more.

Christians were opposed by Hindu Indians a few years ago. Christians were specifically targeted and subjected to persecution. May I remind you that our Lord is the same yesterday, today, and forever? In response to persecution, people began praying and fasting. An earthquake was sent by God to punish those who attacked Christians. Those who fought against His people were taken out by God. To take revenge is

AUGUST 13

the Lord. Then, they disappeared completely. God can be found in India, America, or even inside a fish saving Jonah.

Make sure to do it the right way, regardless of the circumstances. Pray for the people of God. Learn to cry out to God.

Psalms 34:4 I sought the LORD, and he heard me and delivered me from all my fears. 17 The righteous cry, and the LORD heareth, and delivereth them out of all their troubles.

O ye righteous, do not worry, even you fall. It is just to elevate you. God is the supreme power. When you see the king, your bosses, family, nations, and enemy rising against you, God will judge them. They will vanish away. God has the last word to say, not your enemies. The enemy can plot, whisper, dig, and build gallows to hang you. May the Lord reverse it back to them in Jesus' name.

Those who do evil, deceive, and speak the words of Satan, be prepared for God's judgment. God is against you, and He will find you. You cannot go unnoticed in darkness. You cannot run away from judgment. God will find and destroy you. Have a healthy fear of the Lord.

I pray for all the unrighteous. The Lord gives the fear of Him. May the Lord bless you with a sound mind, deliver you from unrighteousness, and save you. To protect yourself, refrain from ever touching the Righteous. Amen!

LET US PRAY

Heavenly Father, as you said, forgive those who despitefully use you. We forgive our enemy.

To take revenge is yours. So, Lord, we forgive our enemy; we bring our problems, enemy, and enemy of the cross to your altar. Please help us, Lord. We cry out and pray with fasting for the situation rising against the righteous. Your people are persecuted, killed, and destroyed everywhere. Lord, we bring our petitions to you. God of Abraham, Isaac, and Israel, rise to rescue, deliver, and help your people. So send help from above to rescue the righteous to bless them. We depend on you. You were the same yesterday, today, and forever. We trust you for all matters, situations, and trouble. Please, Almighty God, help us overthrow our enemy with their evil plan in Jesus 'name. Amen! God bless you!

AUGUST 14

RESPONSE TO THE WORD OF GOD!

What is your reaction, behavior, thought process, and response when you encounter the Word of God? Your action and response are essential when the word of God comes to you. The Lord loves to send the anointed people to help with the plan concerning you; special help to you. You have the role of receiving and making changes. It is suitable for you. There was no other option for John the Baptist but to correct the king, queen, people, priest, Levi, and lost people, as directed by God. The wicked woman, Herodias, ended the life of John Baptist because she didn't want to be corrected. The prophet of God was killed as a result of the correction she received in her flesh from him. A woman who commits adultery poses a threat to the righteous followers of God. She practices her power to destroy the work of God on earth. The people who killed the Lord Jesus heard Peter and pricked their hearts. They changed their actions by repenting.

Acts 2:36 Therefore let all the house of Israel know assuredly, that God hath made that same Jesus, whom ye have crucified, both Lord and Christ. 37 Now when they heard this, they were pricked in their heart, and said unto Peter and to the rest of the apostles, Men, and brethren, what shall we do? 38 Then Peter said unto them, Repent, and be baptized every one of you in the name of Jesus Christ for the remission of sins, and ye shall receive the gift of the Holy Ghost.

David, who held the title of king, committed the acts of adultery and murder against Uriah Hittite. God sent the prophet Nathan to confront David. As a spiritual and God-fearing king, David heard Nathan and repented. He thought that Prophet Nathan was not singling him out or harboring any ill will towards him. Since God loves King David and understands his heart, the message is from Him. Do not get upset if it is from God. Get humble, kneel, and ask God to forgive you.

2 Samuel 11:4 And David sent messengers, and took her, and she came in unto him, and he lay with her; for she was purified from her uncleanness: and she returned unto her house.15 And he wrote in the letter, saying, Set ye Uriah in the forefront of the hottest battle, and retire ye from him, that he may be smitten, and die.

Confronting your sin is to let you know God is not bios. There is no variance in Him. God gives position; stay on the right track.

13 And David said unto Nathan, I have sinned against the Lord. And Nathan said unto David, The Lord also hath put away thy sin; thou shalt not die.

AUGUST 14

There are two types of receivers; one receives with flesh. The nature of flesh resembles that of Satan. Adultery, fornication, lies, jealousy, wickedness, disobedience, rebelliousness. The message from the prophet is not accessible to those who are fleshly. Do not see the Man of God as ordinary, but fear the man of God. He must verbalize the words that God desires you to listen to.

2. Receive by the spirit. The truth is seen, known, and heard by spiritual individuals. They will both receive and act upon it. Or seek the righteousness of God. The voice you're hearing is that of the Lord, not a human being. When God calls for His kingdom, He will train you to fit in for the calling. Respect God's correction. We need inner change. It is only possible if you work together with God. Get ready to listen to the true teachers and prophets, ready to receive God's message and ignore all others. Whose possession are you? Is it Jesus or Satan? Remember that God has a vested interest in making you heaven-ready. He has appointed authority to correct you. In what way did Jesus interact with people, and how did they respond?

Matthew 12:23 And all the people were amazed, and said, Is not this the son of David? 24 But when the Pharisees heard it, they said, This fellow doth not cast out devils but by Beelzebub, the prince of the devils.

Jesus, being God, did a mighty work, and His assigned authority said something like this? Jesus reveals their true nature to them. 34a O generation of vipers,

Lord, address Matthew 23 to the Scribes, and Pharisees, who were Hypocrites. Jesus told the truth. Build your church brand if you love lies and are a hypocrite, since He is the true God who builds the church on truth. Jesus will use the same word He used for the priest, high priest-scribe, Pharisees, and people in authority. Do not expect this word.

Matthew 25:21 His lord said unto him, Well done, thou good and faithful servant: thou hast been faithful over a few things, I will make thee ruler over many things: enter thou into the joy of thy lord.

The Lord is helping you, accepting your spirit. Your success and failure are how and what you do when you receive the message from God.

Romans 8:5 For they that are after the flesh does mind the things of the flesh; but they that are after the spirit the things of the spirit. 8 So then they that are in the flesh cannot please God.

The beginning and eternity are known by God. He granted us the freedom to choose. The decisions we make are under our control, not God's. We are not robots; that is why He corrects us. God is aware of the existence of both heaven and hell. He tries his best to correct us so we do not end up in hell. May the Lord help you love yourself! God can help, but you are not helping yourself if you choose wrong. Do not look for the churches where the sinner is on the pulpit. Someone who is a wimp or coward isn't capable of teaching you. He is not strong enough to live right. It is necessary to control the desires of the flesh.

Isaiah 46:9 Remember the former things of old: for I am God, and there is none else; I am God, and there is none like me, 10 Declaring the end from the beginning, and from ancient times the things that are not yet done, saying, My counsel shall stand, and I will do all my pleasure:

God is not a dictator; He is a father. Find a genuine prophet, pastor, teacher, and man of God who is free from bias, prejudice, sin, and wickedness. Choose to go where the man of God receives direct communication from God and presents it without personal explanation. May the Lord grant you the ability to receive the Word! Nobody desires your descent into hell, but are you even interested in your own self-care? Do you love your soul, and can you say, Please help me, Lord? Living a sinful life won't be of any help. Approach the altar of God with confidence.

Hebrews 4:16 Let us, therefore, come boldly unto the throne of grace, that we may obtain mercy, and find grace to help in time of need.

Embracing the Word with a sound mind has the power to revolutionize you. Changing is necessary if we want to reach heaven.

LET US PRAY

Lord, we come before your altar and ask you to give us the true prophet, teachers, and pastors. We want the anointed man and woman of God to help us grow. We want the Word of God to be the two-edged sword that cuts evil off in the area where we need surgery. Let your word work and mighty change come within. As we are your disciples, I want to follow in your footsteps. Transform us so we make it to heaven. We thank you. You are the father, and you care for your creation. Give us love for the Word. Let it fall in heart and grow, bring all impurity out, and make us pure, righteous, and holy to serve the righteous and Holy God in Jesus 'name. Amen! God bless you.

AUGUST 15

SUPPLY COMES WHEN YOU WORK!

Just as you receive a paycheck for working, if you go out and work like Jesus, God will provide all your needs. What actions does God demand from us or what aspects do we need to prioritize in our fieldwork?

Mark 16:20 And they went forth and preached everywhere, the Lord working with them, and confirming the word with signs following. Amen!

So as you go, cast out demons, heal the sick and preach the Gospel, then Jesus will work with and through you. Through your hand, Jesus will perform miracles by healing the sick and driving out demons. God is working and providing knowledge with wisdom. God grants the word of knowledge for locating addresses. Word of wisdom on how to survive at the time of famine.

1 Kings 17:8 And the word of the Lord came unto him, saying, 9 Arise, get thee to Zarephath, which belongeth to Zidon, and dwell there: behold, I have commanded a widow woman there to sustain thee. As reaching that address, Elijah met a widow. Elijah said. 11 And as she was going to fetch it, he called to her, and said, Bring me, I pray thee, a morsel of bread in thine hand.13 And Elijah said unto her, Fear not; go and do as thou hast said: but make me thereof a little cake first, and bring it unto me, and after make for thee and thy son.14 For thus saith the Lord God of Israel, The barrel of meal shall not waste, neither shall the cruse of oil fail, until the day that the Lord sendeth rain upon the earth.

God commanded Elijah, and the supply came. God only gives commandments, not suggestions. Can you go out and witness the outcome of obeying His command? We have filled hell and not the devil. Visiting those in jail, sick, possessed, oppressed, widows, and needy is not something we do. No one cares for the widow; she cannot give since she is poor. The mentality of most religious leaders is to seek people who are financially well-off. Our provider is Jehovah Jireh, but only if you follow His instructions. Our God gave us information about Peter to go to Cornelius's house. He went with the information provided above. The Church welcomed its first gentile as a result. If you move, the supply will follow. The work we need, along with His provision, knowledge, and wisdom, will arrive.

A brave woman decided to seek out Jesus.

Matthew 9:20 And, behold, a woman, which was diseased with an issue of blood twelve years, came behind him, and touched the hem of his garment: 21 For she said within herself, If I may but touch his garment, I shall be whole. 22 But Jesus turned him about, and when he saw her, he said, Daughter, be of good comfort; thy faith hath made thee whole. And the woman was made whole from that hour.

God will grant healing to those who touch the hem of His garment. Receive your necessity as you work the work of faith. The church in Colossi, Galatian, Corinth, Ephesus, and Asia grew as Paul and Peter preached to the people there. Go out; the Lord will supply people with supernatural provisions. The goodness of our God is evident. His platform is absolutely outstanding. The Lord is skilled in making and providing things that are considered impossible. The key is to act on the Word once you have read and studied it.

Matthew 15:22 And, behold, a woman of Canaan came out of the same coasts, and cried unto him, saying, Have mercy on me, O Lord, thou son of David; my daughter is grievously vexed with a devil.

Against His wishes, she was able to convince the Lord. Her unwavering determination resulted in her daughter's deliverance.

28 Then Jesus answered and said unto her, O woman, great is thy faith: be it unto thee even as thou wilt. And her daughter was made whole from that very hour.

Isn't God doing all? You must do whatever is necessary.

This morning, I engaged in a discussion with a young Hindu Brahmin individual. He stated he heard his father, who is the voice of Jesus. The Bible has brought me peace through my reading. He was absolutely thrilled! The brahmin man expressed his desire for the Holy Spirit and to be baptized in the name of Jesus for the cleansing of sins. His residence is in India. I am always open to teaching and spreading my message wherever I go. How did God bring him into my life? A Brahmin man was instructed by God to go to a specific church where the lady standing outside was acquainted with me. She attended to his needs and shared my phone number with him. That's the story of our connection. He was instructed by God to go to a specific area, and he followed through and ended up connecting with me in the U.S. May the Lord give us faith to follow His instruction.

Once, someone gave me the gift of a veggie bullet. It was missing small gadgets attachments. It needed a different cut for the veggie. A year later, God asked me to go to a particular store I did not care for. While I was there, I realized that the small gadgets were surprisingly cheap. God supplies all our needs. Obey God's commands and listen to His voice. To bring about change, salvation, healing, and freedom for the world, follow the example set in the book of Acts. The goodness of God is undeniable. Everything will go well if you make the effort.

Luke 10:1 After these things the Lord appointed other seventy also, and sent them two and two before his face into every city and place, whither he himself would come. 17 And the seventy returned again with joy, saying, Lord, even the devils are subject unto us through thy name.

As they went and worked, a supply of healing and deliverance followed. I visited the hospital with a lady to offer prayers for a sick man. Prior to that, I had a dream. The writing was faded and fuzzy, except for the word LIVER, which was clear. I had a dream where I said "kidney" instead of "liver" and the words disappeared. But once more, the writing reappeared and I spelled a word liver in my dream.

AUGUST 15

We visited many hospitals in the following weeks, praying for those who were ill. I questioned the lady regarding the individual's sickness. Her response was, "I don't know." When I reached the hospital, I asked him to help me understand my dream about the liver. He said Yes; it is my liver. Twice, God sent me to this man whom I had no previous knowledge of. Since I don't go to that church, I have no way of knowing about his illnesses. However, there is another woman at the church who asked me to join her in praying for this man. Just how amazing is it? While on my way, I had both knowledge and the miraculous healing power of God. When I touched him, the Lord Jesus and my obedience completed the work. Later on, I learned that God miraculously healed his liver, and he's now attending church again.

Our outings include shopping, vacationing, attending church, and going to places we want to visit. How about we obey Jesus 'command and engage in demon-casting, healing the sick, visiting widows and orphans, and teaching and preaching? As individuals encounter God's supernatural power, they will embrace Cornelius, Galatians, Colossians, Corinthians, and additional texts. People will approach us to touch our clothes. Waiting for our shadow to pass over them; the dead will rise, leprosy will cleanse, sicknesses will flee, and God will supply all your need. God's power is supernatural, providing healing, deliverance, and help to individuals.

The young Brahmin informed me I would travel worldwide and proclaim Jesus as the true God if my father grants me knowledge and the Holy Spirit. According to him, he possesses experience but feels the urge to share it with others. He is ready to go. It appears that God is furnishing individuals to aid him. Just Go as you work; God will provide all that you need. May you be blessed by God.

LET US PRAY

Lord, your word says there will be no lack, poverty, or sicknesses in our camp if we work for you. We want to work for you. We understand you have not called us to attend the church but to preach the Gospel by demonstrating the power of God! May the Lord see us as meriting the opportunity to perform miracles, bringing healing and solace to those in need. Lord, we want you to send many laborers to go out and work so people see that, yes, you still supply our health, healing, and provisions. As you said, the laborer is worthy of His reward. We believe you will provide all our needs. We will need something as we go places to take your word. It is the God who supplies reach, knowledge, miracle, prophecy, discernment, and all our daily needs. Thank you, Lord. The disciples needed more since they went out and worked for the Lord. We trust you for our needs as we also go out in Jesus 'name. Amen! God bless you!

AUGUST 16

LIFE PLANNING IS MUST!

Live your life within the boundaries of the Word of God to protect yourself from the devil's tricks.

The word of God affirms that His plan is superior to yours. That's correct, he does. If we plan in accordance with God's will, we can read, implement, and experience prosperity. If you receive instructions to complete certain tasks, make sure you have a plan in place to accomplish them. The problem lies in our desire for benefits without giving importance to the highest priority plan. The problem arises when one plans to go against God's plan. Israel abandoned God's wonderful plan, resulting in their desire for a King. The Lord proclaimed that I would be your King, with no man above me.

1 Samuel 8:4 Then all the elders of Israel gathered themselves together, and came to Samuel unto Ramah, 5 And said unto him, Behold, thou art old. Thy sons walk not in thy ways: now make us a king to judge us like all the nations. 6 But the thing displeased Samuel when they said, Give us a king to judge us. And Samuel prayed unto the LORD.

God led Abraham away from his homeland. He had faith that God would fulfill the roles of their leader, guide, father, and God. However, the multitude that descended from Him was different from Abraham. God's promises and mercy were of such magnitude that the Lord upheld and bestowed them. Despite the Torah, priest, high priest, and Levi continuously devising plans against God's plan. Israel brought pollution to the Holy God and His name. The destructive nature of humanity is evident as we make our own plans instead of following God's plan. Are you superior, more knowledgeable, or smarter than God?

7 And the LORD said unto Samuel, Hearken unto the voice of the people in all that they say unto thee: for they have not rejected thee, but they have rejected me, that I should not reign over them. 8 According to all the works which they have done since the day that I brought them up out of Egypt even unto this day, wherewith they have forsaken me, and served other gods, so do they also unto thee. 9 Now, therefore, hearken unto their voice: howbeit yet protest solemnly unto them, and shew them the manner of the King that shall reign over them.

Be mindful of the Lord's plan and adapt your actions accordingly.

Let's say you're chosen for a kingdom project, similar to Moses, and then learn to follow orders without personal thoughts. Show yourself love and stay open to God's leading. Just because you have free will doesn't mean you can make mistakes without consequences. The freedom I offered included heaven,

AUGUST 16

blessings, and provisions, all within God's boundaries. God granted you the gift of free will. Decide on your preference, but be prepared to confront the aftermath.

Esther was selected by God to become a queen. She demonstrated prudence, knowledge, and comprehension of God's intentions. With determination, she worked to dismantle Satan's plan. Is it possible for us to precisely coordinate our efforts in undertaking God's project? There are no barriers preventing us from proceeding. When the Lord is in the boat, sailing will be possible.

The Babylonians' plan to destroy the people of God caused immense agony for the Jewish community. Choosing fun and planning over God's plan would have resulted in the death of Esther's people. Never think I excused you. Make sure to have goals and be prepared to move in the right direction for your benefit and the benefit of future generations.

Esther 4:14 For if thou altogether holdest thy peace at this time, then shall there enlargement and deliverance arise to the Jews from another place; but thou and thy father's house shall be destroyed: and who knoweth whether thou art come to the kingdom for such a time as this?

Esther had a plan to ensure she completed it properly. People make plans without considering the consequences. We know that our God came with a specific plan. Without a goal, aim, motive, or intent, we cannot simply wake up and sleep. Creation often involves a variety of requirements. Not some, but all! The first priority is prayer. This is God's way of reconnecting with us and keeping us informed of His plan. Being aware of His authority requires us to be caring and sensitive.

Get out there and engage in interviews with different individuals. Their possible response could be, "I am not acquainted with God." It is not like Paul; the Lord struck him down and spoke. Hey, wait, you are playing against me, Jehovah God. Now re-plan in the right direction. Our God has the last word; our God is real and knows how to help, provide and care.

Esther protected the line of the Messiah to keep them from perishing. Joseph's actions and life were guided by God's plan to keep the Hebrews alive.

I have a memory of when God gifted me with this truth. I did a great job working on God's plan.

2 Timothy 2:15 Study to shew thyself approved unto God, a workman that needeth not to be ashamed, rightly dividing the word of truth.

While specific planning is not mandatory, making wise choices for your soul is crucial. If you lack intelligence and fail to plan your life carefully, your soul's destiny may be compromised.

God's purpose for creating hell was to punish the Devil and his angels. Their only destination is hell; they can't plan to go anywhere else.

Matthew 25:41 Then shall he say also unto them on the left hand, Depart from me, ye cursed, into everlasting fire, prepared for the devil and his angels:

What we do has the power to determine where we end up. There is a continuation of life beyond the mortal realm. Life of the flesh is like all born to die physically. Dust returns to dust. By following God's plan, both your soul and the destiny of others can be altered. As stated in the word of God. By doing what God asks, we can prevent countless souls from burning forever. May we be awakened by the Lord. It's important that we realign our lives with God's plan. In order to prevent getting lost, hurt, or damaged, we need redirection. God assists us in gaining wisdom.

The Holy Spirit was given by God to assist us in planning our lives.

John 16:13 Howbeit when he, the Spirit of truth, is come, he will guide you into all truth: for he shall not speak of himself; but whatsoever he shall hear, that shall he speak: and he will shew you things to come.

There is still a need for the Lord to safeguard and direct us. The creator desires to provide us with the assistance and strength to lead a peaceful life.

Several individuals, including Paul, Peter, Thomas, James, and the Lord Jesus, lost their lives. Understanding God's intention to leave the world in pursuit of truth. Courageous and bold individuals with unwavering conviction are necessary to execute God's plan. It's a wise decision to create a plan for achieving wealth and pursuing careers as a doctor and engineer. Nevertheless, the best option is to plan your life with eternity in mind. My friend, don't forget the importance of life planning, as the soul's ultimate plan brings eternal blessings. Amen.

LET US PRAY

Lord, do not let us sail our life in the jungle of this world. We lost the world since we forgot to meet our maker for help in designing life. God already made our master plan before we were born. Lord Abraham, Isaac, and Israel planned life in the will and plan of God. They saw, and also their generation, later on, found the promises of God. It is our desire since it says whosoever believes in the Lord and plans in God's will, commandments, precepts, and laws will have great success on earth and for eternity. Life depends on our choices. Give us a wise heart, ear to hear, and sound mind to make our life plan in the will of God, in Jesus 'name. Amen! God bless you!

AUGUST 17

TOUCH, NOT MY GLORY!

Are you being used by God? Many people are used by God to do something for someone. Let's give all the glory to God, as He is the one who uses us. May we seek the Lord's guidance in learning humility. Satan's personality and quality are extremely ill.

Being overly self-assured will have a negative impact on you. The act of robbing others of their honour is a trait of Satan and will ultimately cast you out. With this kind of mentality, you'll be doomed to failure regardless of your hard work. Have you ever seen someone always boast? They constantly brag about their accomplishments. According to them, it's because of them. It was their idea; I centered people. The focus of the talk is on glorifying them, rather than giving glory to God. May the Lord shut them, so they do not get hurt further. Everyone in the world assists someone. If you love to brag about yourself, then listen up to this.

Isaiah 42:8 I am the LORD: that is my name: and my glory will I not give to another, neither my praise to graven images.

Isaiah 48:11 For mine own sake, even for mine own sake, will I do it: for how should my name be polluted? And I will not give my glory unto another.

I hear the talk of a true Christian saying it is God; he healed me, He provided, He gave me; and I am grateful to God for His mercy. It is all God, God, and God gets the glory. Whenever I go somewhere, I let people know that I am a vessel of God, and He uses me for His glory through prayer, prophesy, and deliverance. Our mission is to assist and bring relief to the sick, afflicted, poor, orphaned, possessed, and oppressed. I hope that God in heaven grants our prayers. May I say He does more than we pray, ask, and think? Acting as the hand or mouth of our God brings blessings to us. No one with sound judgment would claim the glory.

At my workplace, there was a man who had a drinking problem. He was the boyfriend of a girl I used to know. I decided to cut off our friendship once I found out about their unholy relationship. But before I do, I thought, I must speak to them since I heard about their immoral lifestyle. I have the duty to make them aware that God is not pleased with their sinful lifestyle. I made several attempts to invite her to church in the past, but she always turned me down, citing her boyfriend's unwillingness to attend. I said ok. Before ending the relationship, I decided to discuss Jesus with her. I witnessed her for two hours. It convicted her of her immoral lifestyle. Upon her request, I came and conducted the Bible study. Eventually, her boyfriend was rescued from an evil way of living. They both got married and began living virtuous lives.

However, I noticed that when the husband thanks God for using me to guide them, it upsets the wife. Her boyfriend was drinking, drugging, and had many bad habits. He was delivered after I started giving them the Bible study. When he mentions my name for his new life, it will upset his wife and she will question why he doesn't give her the same level of recognition. I had no issue because I always gave glory to Lord Jesus. It is beyond my capabilities to deliver, heal, or save others. However, this woman desired the recognition. Seeking help, her husband attended numerous religious churches. By some means, our paths intersected, and God listened to my plea and fasted to save this man.

Can I declare that this is God's doing and not mine? I am willing to serve as a conduit for whatever needs to flow through me. This duty was left for us by the Lord. If you are mentally prepared, you can affirm, "Yes, this is my assignment, and I am responsible for completing it."

The Bible emphasizes that we have limited abilities, but God has granted us authority. The purpose of the authority and power granted to us is to bring glory to Him, not ourselves. Our gratitude goes out to everyone who lends a hand. In return, we bless or reward them with our gratitude. The greatest gift one can possess is a heart full of thankfulness. It is entirely inappropriate for someone to use the promise of credit as a means of blackmail or bribery. Then I tell them to hit the road and get moving.

The Bible says; If you do not give God glory, the rock will cry out. If the donkey can speak thanks to God, why can't we when we already possess the gift of speech through our mouths? Keep in mind that some people hold positions in the church, such as churchgoer, prayer warrior, pastor, evangelist, or missionary, but don't give due recognition to the greatness of God. When I received the Holy Spirit, I realized my insignificance. I had a sense of insignificance, feeling as small as a dot. The individuals who possess understanding of God, accompany God, and hold reverence for God are the ones who perceive his might, authority, magnificence, compassion, and love. Those who fulfilled the role of powerful men and women of God understood that it was God who was responsible, not themselves. Give a round of applause to God, not to yourself.

Exodus 15:3 The LORD is a man of war: the LORD is his name.

Lord told Joshua.

Joshua 1:5 There shall not any man be able to stand before thee all the days of thy life: as I was with Moses, so I will be with thee: I will not fail thee, nor forsake thee.

I encourage you to read the scripture below. Do you see your name? All glory goes to God. If God has ever chosen to use you, celebrate and express gratitude towards Him. Give God glory and Him alone.

Ephesians 3:20 Now unto him that is able to do exceeding abundantly above all that we ask or think, according to the power that worketh in us, 21 Unto him be glory in the church by Christ Jesus throughout all ages, world without end. Amen!

I go out to places and pray over people, pray on the phone, visiting the hospital, homes, countries, and villages. I assist numerous individuals in need. I am an individual that remains unseen by many. So who connects me to these needy people? It is the hand of God that reaches those needy. Thinking about myself is something I don't do and will never do. God is reaching out through me to fulfill the need.If I give Him glory, then God will.

AUGUST 17

Psalms 33:13 The Lord looketh from heaven; he beholdeth all the sons of men. 14 From the place of his habitation he looketh upon all the inhabitants of the earth. 15 He fashioneth their hearts alike; he considereth all their works. 16 There is no king saved by the multitude of a host: a mighty man is not delivered by much strength. 17 An horse is a vain thing for safety: neither shall he deliver any by his great strength. 18 Behold, the eye of the Lord is upon them that fear him, upon them that hope in his mercy; 19 To deliver their soul from death, and to keep them alive in famine. 20 Our soul waiteth for the Lord: he is our help and our shield. 21 For our heart shall rejoice in him, because we have trusted in his holy name. 22 Let thy mercy, O Lord, be upon us, according as we hope in thee.

Always remember to give glory to God. God is the one behind it all, but He has empowered us through His Spirit. He works through us; we are not making the miracle, healing, help, provisions, or feeding, so give God glory. Amen! God Bless you!

LET US PRAY

Lord, we thank you that the Glory of God comes down as we worship and honor by recognizing your might and power. The creator of heaven and earth deserves praise, honor, and Glory. We are your vessels and laborers to let this world know that, Lord, you are good and are doing all alone. We are your mouthpiece, hand, and feet to proclaim your power and glory. Use us, take us where people find and know this great God. Our God has created us in His image to give Him glory. Lord, be merciful and help us bring glory. You said touch, not my glory, so we give you the glory and no one else. We are grateful that our God is Holy, righteous, all-powerful, and wonder-working to receive the Glory forever and ever in Jesus 'name. Amen God bless you.

AUGUST 18

JESUS HAS ALL AUTHORITY!

All supernatural miracles, healings, and deliverances were carried out by the Lord's will and power. The Lord went against every religious authority. Religious fanaticism is the greatest threat; obey or face execution. This applies to all religions, whether Christian, Hindu, Muslim, or others. Jesus is the supreme power. Approval from others is not required by Lord Jesus. The Lord Jesus is not subject to anyone's commands or restrictions. His power holds the utmost significance compared to any other power. He had the capacity to both grant power and strip it away from those of his choosing. By the power of His Word, God walked upon the earth He created. He holds the highest level of control over what He has created.

Luke 13:11 And, behold, there was a woman who had a spirit of infirmity eighteen years, bowed together, and could in no wise lift up herself.

Lord Jesus did a healing on the Sabbath day, so the hypocritical leaders of the synagogue went crazy. Does this scenario of authorities discourage people from seeking healing on the Sabbath day sound familiar to you? If you are in the presence of God, how can you possibly be sick? If the building does not have Jesus, then yes, you will also be sitting sick for 18 years. Sad story! May the Lord assist you in understanding that the church building or title is not what's important. You are a church. Embrace the divine flow of God's Spirit within you. The devil also assumes the roles of pastor, apostle, prophet, teacher, evangelist, missionary, and saint of God. The devil is incapable of offering healing, deliverance, or liberation to anyone.

On a daily basis, I interact with many people who are engaged in a battle of the spirit. Even now, a woman contacted me to complain about her toes or feet being pulled by someone. She stated that she had encountered an unseen attack. Since her husband's passing a few years ago, she has been experiencing discomfort in her legs and toes. This precious lady, her niece, and her granddaughter all went through the same situation. Additionally, she stated that I had excruciating pain from my neck downwards.

I told her you to have the authority to use it. In a puzzled tone, she asked, "Authority? What's the deal with that?" I said, you command that devil to get out in Jesus 'name. "I never realized I had the ability to do that," she admitted. If I have the ability, so do you. After praying a few times, the pain disappeared. According to her, I attend church every Sunday, but I'm losing faith. The devil's doctrine aims to erode our faith and create a generation without faith. Further she said, many things are breaking into the house and having many problems. I used prayer and commanding to cast out the demons, leading to a state of peace in the house.

AUGUST 18

I taught her about the power of the Holy Spirit, the work of demons, fallen angels, and Satan. She understood it was a fallen angel since the spirit could not do that pulling-pushing. A demon, which is an evil spirit, needs a body. A demon is a lost soul that inhabits the body of a living person.

The lady had a bent posture for 18 years.

Jesus said.

Luke 13:12 And when Jesus saw her, he called her to him, and said unto her, Woman, thou art loosed from thine infirmity. 13 And he laid his hands on her: and immediately she was made straight, and glorified God.

Jesus arrived to set His creation free. He gave us the authority to enforce the power in the world to destroy the work of the enemy. If you are attending an organization, denomination, or non-denomination and don't see supernatural work, then pack up and leave. Do not look back. Follow Jesus, start going out, and do the work of what the Lord asked you to do. The Holy Spirit will train, teach, guide, and empower you. Don't be a hypocrite and do not deceive yourself. Satan manipulates you by employing actors and actresses who pretend to be genuine saints.

If judges, police, and authority fail to utilize their power to prevent crimes, apprehend offenders, and prosecute them, what could occur? Look around; what do you see? All we witness are crimes, murders, and shootings. Someone is not performing the job properly.

Similarly, Satan has placed individuals in pulpits, organizations, churches, and denominations where they are forbidden from utilizing God's power. Their lack of ability is evident. Their instruction will be for you to go back home. Today is Sunday, the Sabbath day. You cannot be healed by us. We should feel ashamed if we fall for Satan's deception. Seeking a doctor or medication when you're sick means you're being deceived by a hypocrite. These individuals are known as Satan's actors. I am healed by His stripes.

John 5:16 And therefore did the Jews persecute Jesus, and sought to slay him, because he had done these things on the sabbath day. 17 But Jesus answered them, My Father worketh hitherto, and I work.18 Therefore, the Jews sought the more to kill him, because he not only had broken the sabbath, but said also that God was his Father, making himself equal with God.

'Son of God" essentially meant that God was manifest in bodily form. Jews were waiting for the Messiah, but they never knew the mystery of the birth of Jesus. There is a multitude of mysteries waiting to be discovered. By doing so, we will avoid becoming enemies of the Cross. We must avoid using power inappropriately when granting names and positions. The title meant nothing. The title doesn't appeal to me. I have the power to move mountains when I work for Jesus.

On a different day, I visited the hospital in Plano, TX. A lady had been there for quite some time. The surgical procedure her mom referred to was meant to be a two-day stay, but she ended up being there for a few weeks. I prayed, and now she's back at home. I'd rather not receive any of your rules and regulations. My only authority is Jesus Christ. I am led and educated by the Holy Spirit, His divine presence. I have no need for a hypocrite's instructions on what is right and wrong. Only walk in Jesus 'footsteps.

God has complete control over everything. Don't be concerned about a fabricated plan. Master the use of the authority bestowed upon you by God and find the one meant for you. Follow the Bible. The devil will claim that you don't need healing or that you're not even sick. Please do not listen to him. The devil has already been conquered. Tell him to sit down. What is the reason for the high number of individuals struggling with drug addiction, suicidal thoughts, divorce, hospitalization, cancer, and illness? Why did the Lord choose to give you the Holy Spirit? So you can show off by speaking in the tongue? The Holy Spirit is the power given to us to work on earth. Satan's deception only succeeds when you believe a hypocritical actor is performing from the pulpit.

Beware of false teachers and prophets who may deceive you.

Luke 10:19 Behold, I give unto you the power to tread on serpents and scorpions, and over all the power of the enemy: and nothing shall by any means hurt you.

According to the Bible, power should be employed to heal, rescue, and emancipate captives. It's meant for both of us to receive. Avoid associating yourself with any religion or organization. Study the Bible and surrender yourself to God.

James 4:7 Submit yourselves therefore to God. Resist the devil, and he will flee from you.

Jesus has authority; submit to Jesus. He will give you power. He desires to utilize us according to His will. He desires for you to incorporate references in order to produce better work. Just give Him all, and He will use you. Following the lost will only lead to being misguided. It will obstruct not only your faith but also others. I am certain of this because my daily work is for Jesus. The Lord has never changed, but Satan calls for building a church. People will misguide you, but not God.

Matthew 28:18 And Jesus came and spake unto them, saying, All power is given unto me in heaven and on the earth.19a Go ye therefore and teach all nations, 20 Teaching them to observe all things whatsoever I have commanded you: and, lo, I am with you always, even unto the end of the world. Amen.

LET US PRAY

Lord, we come before your altar knowing we have all the power if we believe. We believe and follow as disciples follow you. Our God is lovely and has done incredible work. We want to do the same so sick, oppressed, and possessed people in the world to be free and delivered. Our Lord gave all authority in His precious name. Thank you for giving us the Spirit of God, which is the Holy Spirit, to do the mighty work of healing and deliverance. It is my job to set the captive free, lame walk, blind see, deaf hear, since you have given me authority. The Lord is doing and will continue if we submit to the will of God and not the will of religion. Our God has paid an enormous price, and we must do the same if we want to continue His work. Thank you for giving us authority in your precious name, Jesus. Amen! God Bless You!

AUGUST 19

WISDOM IS A MUST FOR CHRISTIANS.

Play sensibly and not as a fool. You will play like a fool walking in flesh, pride, and lust. Living in the boundary of the laws of God will save you from many heartaches and headaches. The wisdom of the Lord helps. Do not look in the world for an answer. Worldly wisdom or thinking makes a fool out of you. Do your children a favor, and give your children wisdom through the WORD of GOD! Our God's life manual, the Bible, is full of wisdom. Life cannot be repeated. Life will not come back in some other form. Once it is over and done and now wait for the judgment. There is no incarnation, for sure. So teach your children the Word of God by being a good observant and follower of Christ. If you follow the word of God and observe it with all your heart, then you will be a light to your children and not a stumbling block. Wise parents teach wisdom through their lifestyle. Since children learn and follow their parents.

What is wisdom? According to Strong's concordance, it is insight, skill (human or divine) intelligence. Wisdom is the application of knowledge. King Solomon was a wise king. He had divine wisdom given by God since He asked for it. You can ask for wisdom as well. I ask for it in every situation.

Like a king over Israel, he had a case to figure out of two harlots. King Solomon needed to find the actual mother. One harlot lost the baby by crushing it under her bosom. But being a wise king, he used the foresight given from above to find who was the legitimate mother. The matter needed wisdom or divine help to apply to the situation to provide correct justice to the case. A problem or concern can be solved if it is obvious, but if not, then you need wisdom from the Supreme.

1 Corinthian 12:8 For to one is given by the spirit the word of wisdom; to another the word of knowledge by the same spirit;

These two gifts work together. It is God's given gift. Verses 4, 5, and 6 say the same Lord, same spirit, and Same God since there is one God who has three manifestations for different purposes in a different dispensation. It is only ONE GOD. Do not ever divide ONE into THREE. It will create much confusion about religion, organization, denomination, and churches. None of them will work. The wisdom of God comes from above.

James 3:17 But the wisdom that is from above is first pure, then peaceable, gentle, and easy to be intreated, full of mercy and good fruits, without partiality, and hypocrisy.

Opposite to wisdom is stupidity or folly. Act wisely means do not rush in making decisions. Give a thought to the matter. Do not jump into the case to make hasty decisions. Have you seen people who jump into every opportunity they get? These people repeat the mistake. Some advice all but their life says that they have no wisdom. Be careful, do not advise if you are not wise. When you face a situation beyond you, go to someone intelligent. Get advice from them. The matter is often beyond, and we all find a need to make a decision. I always pray for wisdom, and I take it to God if I have a problem. He has all the knowledge and help.

Proverb 2:6 For the Lord giveth wisdom: out of his mouth cometh knowledge and understanding. 7 He layeth up sound wisdom for the righteous: he is a buckler to them that walk uprightly. 8 He keepeth the paths of judgment and preserveth the way of his saints.

Do you know you can ask for wisdom for the project you have taken? Ask for the knowledge to be wonderful parents, teachers, or any task you have taken. Life gets easier.

James 1:5 If any of you lack wisdom, let him ask of God, that giveth to all men liberally, and upbraideth not; and it shall be given him.

King Solomon was tender in age. He knew, being a king, he would need the wisdom to operate God's given kingdom. He asked the wise God, Jehovah, to grant His wisdom.

2 Chronicles 1:11 And God said to Solomon, Because this was in thine heart, and thou hast not asked riches, wealth, or honor, nor the life of thine enemies, neither hast asked long life. Still, hast asked wisdom and knowledge for thyself, that thou mayest judge my people, over whom I have made thee king: 12 Wisdom and knowledge is granted unto thee; and I will give thee riches, and wealth and honor, such as none of the kings have had that have been before thee, neither shall after that thee have the like.

Before I face my day, I always ask God to give me mighty wisdom and knowledge to minister to every phone call that comes to me. It is God's ministry, and I have to work wisely. It is His ministry, and by His wisdom, I work. Life has great meaning if we apply God's wisdom to every question situation and before making every decision. Not after making a mess, but before making decisions! I have many aged friends; as you know, they are not afraid to tell you the truth. My mom was like my friend. She was a wise lady. You know the children raised by wise women are primarily good. I mainly said since sometimes you have exceptions. But the foolish woman raises devastating pain giving children. If they come as the spouse to your sons and daughter, Lord have mercy. Seems like they enforce their stupidity on their children.

Please pray for them without ceasing and continually. Break that spirit. My elderly friends are still alive and still talk to me. Still, give me advice. Isn't that nice? I have noticed that wise people's life is an open book, but for stupid people, their life is a hush. They will do their folly act behind the door, hiding everything. They do not want any advice, but they will come to you in their mess. Well, some never learn. Continue repetition. Jesus has all the wisdom to run heaven. God created the earth and us for His grand plan with His understanding. We need that wisdom to carry on His agenda. The world can run beautifully if we have wise people over the nation, state, city, school, and judicial system. Wise brings peace and safety to the land. It brings prosperity to the nations! Our outcome of an action is a greater witness than what you try to speak about yourself. So, would you ask God to give you wisdom?

Proverbs 24:3a Through wisdom is a house built; Wisdom is a principal thing.

AUGUST 19

So always run your life, family, your business with wisdom. You will be blessed and established. May the Lord grant us His Wisdom in Jesus' name.

LET US PRAY

Lord, we know the wisdom that comes from above is pure, then peaceable, gentle, and easy to be entreated, full of mercy and good fruits. We desire your understanding. Give us wisdom. Not in one area, but in all our matters, we need knowledge. We also pray for our nation to have a wise ruler. We need wisdom for all who have to do with us. Who is connected with us in any way? Knowledge is more precious than rubies and gold. Our life is once. To live on earth in your plan, we desire your wisdom. It is free if we ask for it. You promised, ask, and you will give it. Let us build our home on your shared wisdom in Jesus 'name. Amen! God bless you!

AUGUST 20

HAVE YOU RECEIVED THE HOLY SPIRIT?

What is the reason for the Bible's mention of the Holy Spirit? The Bible instructs how to receive the Holy Spirit. There is much discussion, arguments, and misunderstanding about receiving the Holy Spirit. You must accept the Holy Spirit to enter the Kingdom of God. Lord Jesus explains to the master of Israel. The Master must understand to teach others. He questioned how to enter the Kingdom of heaven.

John 3:3 Jesus answered and said unto him, Verily, verily, I say unto thee, Except a man be born again, he cannot see the kingdom of God.

Nicodemus and other first-time hearers must understand the significance of being born again. It means born from above.

5 Jesus answered, Verily, verily, I say unto thee, except a man be born of water and of the spirit, he cannot enter the kingdom of God. 6 That which is born of the flesh is flesh, and that which is born of the spirit is a spirit.

The prophets of God, including Joel, Ezekiel, and others, foretold the outpouring of the Holy Spirit. Everyone had been waiting for it for a while.

Joel 2:28 And it shall come to pass afterward, that I will pour out my spirit upon all flesh; and your sons and your daughters shall prophesy, your old men shall dream dreams, your young men shall see visions: 29 And also upon the servants and upon the handmaids in those days will I pour out my spirit.

The time we live in is characterized by God's abundant pouring out of His spirit onto us. It is the duty of believers to spread the teachings so that others can also be born again. Many will discourage you from receiving the Spirit of God because they themselves do not possess it. I did not know what I was privileged to have. His Spirit came to lead, guide, teach, and empower me. Since the Holy Spirit is the Spirit of God, it empowers us.

Acts 1:8 But ye shall receive power, after that the Holy Ghost is come upon you: and ye shall be witnesses unto me both in Jerusalem, and in all Judaea, and Samaria, and unto the uttermost part of the earth.

There is only one spirit, and it is God.

AUGUST 20

Ephesians 4:4a There is one body, and one spirit, God is Spirit.

John 4:24 God is a Spirit:

The Spirit of God dwells in you as you receive the Holy Spirit.

John 14:16 And I will pray the Father, and he shall give you another Comforter, that he may abide with you forever;

The comforter is the Holy Spirit. Yes, forever. Not a few days, but it will not be taken away from you.

John 16:13 Howbeit when he, the spirit of truth, is come, he will guide you into all truth: for he shall not speak of himself; but whatsoever he shall hear, that shall he speak: and he will shew you things to come.

God prophesied through Ezekiel 37:14 And shall put my spirit in you, and ye shall live, and I shall place you in your own land: then shall ye know that I the Lord have spoken it, and performed it, saith the Lord.

Satan's constant battle is to stop the work of God. He will misguide, explain away, and wouldn't allow the powerful God to come and dwell within you. I also did not believe in speaking in tongues as evidence of receiving the Holy Spirit. I attended religious churches where they preached against it. But thank God, what I rejected ignorantly came to me. Our thinking must often be changed by putting correct information about the Word of God. Our God wants to live within us. Do not reject it. The only sign of receiving the Holy Spirit is to speak in tongues. It is your prayer language.

Acts 2:1 And when the day of Pentecost was fully come, they were all with one accord in one place. 4 And they were all filled with the Holy Ghost and began to speak with other tongues, as the spirit gave them utterance.

Then Peter preached the first message at the birth of a new church on the day of Pentecost. All who crucified Jesus were amazed and repented.

Acts 2:38 Then Peter said unto them, Repent, and be baptized every one of you in the name of Jesus Christ for the remission of sins, and ye shall receive the gift of the Holy Ghost. 39 For the promise is unto you, and to your children, and all that are afar off, even as many as the Lord our God shall call.

Promises of the Holy Spirit for all who are added to the church of God. Now do not settle for less. If they baptized you in Jesus 'name, you need the Holy Spirit. Samaritans heard the message and received Jesus, then baptized in Jesus 'name. But the Holy Spirit had not fallen on them yet.

Acts 8:14 Now when the apostles which were at Jerusalem heard that Samaria had received the word of God, they sent unto them Peter and John: 15 Who, when they were come down, prayed for them, that they might receive the Holy Ghost: 16 (For as yet he was fallen upon none of them: only they were baptized in the name of the Lord Jesus.) 17 Then laid they their hands on them, and they received the Holy Ghost.

Acts 10:44 While Peter yet spake these words, the Holy Ghost fell on all them which heard the word. 45 And they of the circumcision which believed were astonished, as many as came with Peter, because that on the Gentiles also was poured out the gift of the Holy Ghost. 46 For they heard them speak with tongues and magnify God.

Gentiles were baptized in Jesus 'name and received the Holy Spirit when they spoke in tongues. The disciples of John Baptist were not familiar with the Holy Spirit and were re-baptized properly, in the name of Jesus.

Acts 19:2 He said unto them, Have ye received the Holy Ghost since ye believed? And they said unto him, We have not so much as heard whether there be any Holy Ghost. 5 When they heard this, they were baptized in the name of the Lord Jesus. 6 And when Paul had laid his hands upon them, the Holy Ghost came on them; and they spake with tongues, and prophesied.

I do not want you to miss this powerful experience. Speaking in tongues is one of the signs that Jesus mentioned for his followers. Is it possible for Jesus to lead astray? He wouldn't, but false teachers, prophets, churches, pastors, and organizations will.

Mark 16:17a And these signs shall follow them that believe; 17c they shall speak with new tongues;

Ensure that they baptize you in the name of Jesus and that you receive the Holy Spirit through speaking in tongues. This is the sole approach to achieve a new birth. The gates of hell won't overcome the Church if it's founded on the revelation of Jesus Christ. Amen!

Look for someone who can perform a baptism in Jesus 'name to cleanse you of your sins. Speaking in tongues is the evidence of receiving the Holy Spirit. Separate yourself from those who do not possess the Holy Spirit and refuse to believe in the truth. They are called false teachers and false prophets by God. I've personally witnessed how those churches function. An antichrist spirit is present in dead churches. You have no business there. Have you received the Holy Spirit? If not, then you need the Holy Spirit! Don't forget that you represent the church, not the physical structure.

LET US PRAY

Heavenly Father, thank you for your word. Your word is the witness. We thank you for the history in the book of Acts. According to Ephesians 2:20, we build our churches upon the foundation of the apostles and prophets. Jesus Christ is the chief cornerstone. Lord, we thank you for permanently giving us the comforter, guide, and teacher. Thank you for the power to witness. Thank you, Holy Spirit, for giving us the power to cast out demons, heal the sick, and power to witness. The Holy Spirit is not talking in tongue but is the sign of receiving the Holy Spirit. Without the Holy Spirit, we cannot enter Heaven. It is God living in us. Thank you for giving us the Holy Spirit in Jesus 'name. Amen! God bless you!

AUGUST 21

YOUR LEADERS WILL MAKE YOU JUST LIKE THEM!

Choose leaders wisely. Your lifestyle reflects whether you have a good or bad leader. I always kept morally smart and disciplined friends. If you agree or not, we all follow someone. As a learner, I surround myself with exceptional teachers. I enjoy being in the presence of someone who can provide valuable teachings. Whenever I have lunch with my friend, she shows me the ropes of eating food from around the world. I learned a lot from her since she is an experienced teacher.

Due to Abraham's strong leadership, his sons Isaac and Jacob grew up as God-fearing individuals. The lifestyle of followers of good leaders reflects their character. The followers of Lord Jesus demonstrated their greatness through their actions. Whether something becomes extraordinary or horrible depends on the leader, not the individual.

Jezebel had a daughter named Athalia. She was evil, wicked, religious, and murdered like her. The mother, who is a fierce leader, will reproduce her species. The mother's role is more important than the father's, since she stays in her children ear. When we observe the children or grandchildren of someone, we often say "like father, like son" or "like mother, like daughter."

In our childhood, our options are limited, but as we mature, we have the ability to make choices. Please stay away from wicked family heads, do not attach to them.

Moses and Joshua are being trained for battle under the divine leadership of God. The people of God were raised through God's ways and instructions.

The instructor or leader should possess integrity, ethics, and a commitment to truth. Do not follow evil, treacherous and corrupt leaders. It will be chaos. Life is going to be a complete mess. Only leaders and followers are responsible for the blame.

Matthew 15:14 Let them alone: they be blind leaders of the blind. And if the blind lead the blind, both shall fall into the ditch.

Throughout my life, I've surrounded myself with great friends and gained knowledge from observing their lifestyles. I've noticed that if they are not good, your life will have a negative impact. During my time in school, I had a friend who was Muslim, and I was deeply impressed by her lifestyle. She was always on top of her assignment. Through watching and adopting her habits and lifestyle, I emerged as the top performer in a class study. Her study plan, which I adopted, led to me getting a good grade. We need good guidance from a successful leader. God is good. I even imitated her methods of serving my God. I began reading the Bible and praying because she was always committed to her prayers and never missed them for anyone. Avoid keeping friends who lack discipline. I've begun dedicating more time to praying, reading the Bible, and living according to God's teachings.

Judges 2:7 And the people served the LORD all the days of Joshua, and all the days of the elders that outlived Joshua, who had seen all the great works of the LORD, that he did for Israel. 8 And Joshua the son of Nun, the servant of the LORD, died, being a hundred and ten years old.

The leaders and elders of Israel, who were good, have now died. Israel got lost and found themselves downhill. At first, we had individuals who prayed and fasted with us, but now we have a completely new set of people. Some individuals have drifted off to sleep! Why? They started following the ones who did not have their priority in order.

First, pray; connection with God is essential. If you do that, victory is guaranteed. People are encountering the devil without God's covering and protection. Their confusion lies in deciding whom to follow. If your leaders do not pray, your parents do not pray; then you forget all about the priority of prayer. You are following someone who doesn't prioritize God. Be careful; get away from them.

Judges 2:17 And yet they would not hearken unto their judges, but they went a whoring after other Gods and bowed themselves unto them: they turned quickly out of the way which their fathers walked in, obeying the commandments of the LORD; but they did not do so.

Unfold the pages of the Bible, read attentively, examine closely, contemplate deeply, and obey the teachings. Is it time to give up all events and start following Jesus? Since the Bible says so, why not?

Luke 9:23 And he said to them all, If any man will come after me, let him deny himself, and take up his cross daily, and follow me.

Keep in mind that Jesus, as God, took on human form, shed his blood, and provided us with a model to follow.

Peter 2:21 For even hereunto were ye called: because Christ also suffered for us, leaving us an example, that ye should follow his steps:

Make Jesus your leader. He prayed, and you should also pray. God manifested in human form and both prayed and granted the prayer. He prayed to serve as a model, so we pray. Jesus proclaimed the Gospel, drove out demons, cured the sick, restored sight to the blind, comforted the brokenhearted, and brought the dead back to life. Let's continue with His missions now. After being baptized by John the Baptist, Jesus started his mission. Baptism in the name of Jesus is necessary for the forgiveness of sins. The name is Jesus, since we know there is one name. The term "Father, Son, and Holy Spirit" represents the roles of One God. Find the word or study the plan of salvation given in the book of Acts. Please study the Bible, since there are many false teachers and false prophets who deceive people. They are called antichrists and will misguide you.

AUGUST 21

Peter 2:1 But there were false prophets also among the people, even as there shall be false teachers among you, who privily shall bring in damnable heresies, even denying the Lord that bought them, and bring upon themselves swift destruction. 2 And many shall follow their pernicious ways; by reason of whom the way of truth shall be evil spoken of.

If you don't want to be tricked, it's best to avoid attending their Bible study or their so-called church building. You, being a church, follow Jesus. Follow true prophets, teachers, pastors, and apostles who do what Jesus did. However, if not, then it's best to distance yourself from them. Apostle John warned when he was old. He knew Satan was working to deceive people. You know the devil is a liar, deceiver, and twister of the Word of God. Many like to follow that easy broadway. John, the sole surviving apostle, warned both them and us in the first century.

1 John 4:2 Hereby know ye the Spirit of God: Every spirit that confesseth that Jesus Christ is come in the flesh is of God:3 And every spirit that confesseth not that Jesus Christ is come in the flesh is not of God: and this is that spirit of antichrist, whereof ye have heard that it should come; and even now already is it in the world.

Even if it means traveling long distances, make sure to find the right leaders. It is the life and death of your soul.

LET US PRAY

Our heavenly Father, we thank you for giving us apostles, evangelists, prophets, teachers, and pastors. Please also give us the perception to know the true and righteous. Keep the false and deceiver out of our life. We love you and ourselves, so your plan was never destroyed. Many destroyed the plan of God's salvation by being led by false leaders. You were out there on a mission, and we also want to pursue your mission. We want wise, righteous, and Holy leaders who are not afraid to follow you. We can turn the world upside down if we have leaders who are following the Lord. Lord, we need you to be our leaders. Thank you for the Holy Spirit, a helper, teacher, and guide to all truth. It is the biggest help to continue on the right path in Jesus 'name! Amen! God bless you!

AUGUST 22

WHAT IS THE BLASPHEME?

Blasphemy involves speaking disrespectfully or negatively about the Holy Spirit, who is God. Irreverent words or speech against God are blasphemy. These laws are shared by both Muslims and the Israelites.

Leviticus 24:16 And he that blasphemeth the name of the Lord, he shall surely be put to death, and all the congregation shall certainly stone him: as well the stranger, as he that is born in the land when he blasphemeth the name of the Lord, shall be put to death.

Blasphemy involves the Holy God. This law allows any nation to carry out capital punishment with the evidence of two or three witnesses. Two or three witnesses are required for the death penalty. One witness is insufficient for it to work.

Many liars have falsely accused innocent individuals by misusing the Blasphemy law.

Luke 12:10 And whosoever shall speak a word against the Son of man, it shall be forgiven him: but unto him that blasphemeth against the Holy Ghost it shall not be forgiven.

Remember, in the end, God will punish you and send you straight to hell. Blasphemers will not be given a chance for a hearing.

Remember, the highest authority is God. If you're unsure, have faith in God and wait for answers. Do not, in any way, associate with the false teachers and prophets. Even those who perform miracles and cast out demons will end up in hell. Be careful!

The Bible says that the name of Jesus is Holy, reverenced the name in Baptism.

James 2:7 Do not they blaspheme that worthy name by the which ye are called?

Under this law, many people have been subjected to stoning. According to a Law expert or Torah master, it is blasphemous for Jesus to forgive sins. Sin can only be forgiven by God. Who has a problem? The one who proclaims mastery in Torah commands great authority in Israel. Jesus healed the man with palsy brought through the roof and spoke.

AUGUST 22

Luke 5:20c Man, thy sins are forgiven thee. 21 And the scribes and the Pharisees began to reason, saying, Who is this which speaketh blasphemies? Who can forgive sins but God alone?

Yes, He was God in the flesh, but the teacher of the Torah knew Torah but not the God of the Torah. Today we lack; we know the Bible and believe, but not the Holy Spirit. Why? We seek out deceitful pastors, preachers, bishops, and evangelists. Do not speak against the Holy Spirit; it is real. God will never grant forgiveness for the sin of blasphemy.

Naboth resisted surrendering his vineyard because he considered it a sacred inheritance from God.

1 Kings 21:2a And Ahab spake unto Naboth, saying, Give me thy vineyard.

The religious man and woman use the blasphemy law dishonestly for their own advantage. Jezebel, along with many false, unrighteous, and unholy individuals, will engage in the same behavior.

1 King 21:9 And she wrote in the letters, saying, Proclaim a fast, and set Naboth on high among the people:10 And set two men, sons of Belial, before him, to bear witness against him, saying, Thou didst blaspheme God and the king. And then carry him out, and stone him, that he may die.

The cycle of history continues. A man's mind can be criminal. Life is given by God, while Satan kills, steals, and destroys. When God introduces a better plan to rescue His creation, the devil will oppose Him with an anti-plan. God took on human form to sacrifice His blood for our lives. Removing the name of Jesus nullifies the plan and abolishes the strength of the lamb's remitting blood. Satan employs false teachers and prophets to alter, twist, and eliminate the word of God. There is a lack of awareness and knowledge among many of them. It's best if you refrain from reading the corrupted Bible. Use the King James Version, the untainted edition of the Bible. The Holy Spirit will be felt as you engage in reading.

Genuine instructors communicate in a tongue that signifies their possession of the Holy Spirit. Also, it should be led by the Spirit. The Helper gifted by God. The Holy Spirit serves as a guide and an educator, providing the necessary empowerment to help you uncover all truths. Don't allow false teachers and prophets to explain it away by the words of those who say you have it without speaking in tongues.

What was the reason for Peter and John coming and placing a hand? (Acts 8:17) Why did Peter say they received the Holy Spirit? (Acts 2:38) You do not see Spirit, but hear them speaking in tongues. Why did Paul lay hands on John's baptist disciples? (Acts 19:6) Why did Cornelius and his family speak in the tongue when they received the Holy Spirit? Acts 10:46). What caused the Holy Spirit to descend upon 120 individuals and enable them to speak in different tongues? Watch out for teachers who lack knowledge.

There is talk of the Holy Spirit being cursed by the devil's teachers. I attended churches of the same kind, yet I persisted in seeking. Be open to God. Wait on God; He will give you His Spirit. It's both free and incredibly powerful. There's nothing else like it. Believe me; I was glad when I received it. The Spirit speaks through me in multiple languages, revealing its many tongues.

God instructed His disciple to wait. I say to you, tarry, you will receive the Holy Spirit by evidence of speaking in tongue.

It's disheartening to see that the people in authority within organizations, denominations, and non-denominations are often the worst kind of individuals. Their interest in donations is driven by a lack of knowledge.

Hebrew 6: 4 For it is impossible for those who were once enlightened, and have tasted of the heavenly gift, and were made partakers of the Holy Ghost,5 And have tasted the good word of God, and the powers of the world to come,6 If they shall fall away, to renew them again unto repentance; seeing they crucify to themselves the Son of God afresh, and put him to an open shame.8 But that which beareth thorns and briers is rejected and is nigh unto cursing; whose end is to be burned.

God has made efforts to rescue us, yet humans refuse His help. Jehovah came as Jesus in the flesh and accepted the blame in this end-time. His flesh was crucified as a result of the blasphemy law. He assumed responsibility, even though it should have been us. Under the blasphemy law, He took it upon Himself to bear our sins. Despite Jesus being blameless and free of sin, the ignorant priest, high priest, and their followers crucified him. It's just repeating itself. Following ignorant teachers, preachers, and pastors causes us to turn away from the gift of the Holy Spirit. May your mercy be upon us, Lord. Rather than engaging in waiting, searching, asking, and knocking, we decide to find a place where we can fit in and be validated by the false authority. Follow the Bible and the teaching of the apostles and prophets in the New Testament; Jesus is the chief cornerstone.

Matthew 26:64 Jesus saith unto him, Thou hast said: nevertheless I say unto you, Hereafter shall ye see the Son of man sitting on the right hand of power, and coming in the clouds of heaven.65 Then the high priest rent his clothes, saying, He hath spoken blasphemy; what further need have we of witnesses? Behold, now ye have heard his blasphemy.66 What think ye? They answered and said, He is guilty of death.

The application of the law of blasphemy resulted in the death penalty for Lord Jesus. Did you witness it? Approach with caution when choosing to follow Jesus and His Word. Open your heart and mind to the teachings of the Spirit of truth. Avoid falling into God's grasp at all costs. The blasphemy law is quite frightening. You will suffer eternal punishment in hell. Pray to Lord Jesus for His help, invoking His name. Amen!

LET US PRAY

Lord, our history says we failed God continuously. Help us, so we do not repeat history. We need your help. Send your true teachers, filled and led by the Spirit. We desire to bring the truth. God gave the Gospel to me to preach to the lost world. Help us so we lead them to eternity in heaven by teaching the truth. Open the new door to witness. Put hunger, thirst, and love into you. We want everyone to be a partaker of the Holy Spirit. It is like water to drink. No one will be thirsty after they receive the Spirit. Many have compromised, disappointed, or given up. Lord, fill them with your Spirit, refresh them. Our generous God loves to come in and knocks on the door of our hearts. Please come to the Lord and abide in us forever, in Jesus 'name. Amen! God bless you!

AUGUST 23

BEAUTY!

According to Google, beauty can be defined by shape, size, or color. Beauty has many definitions. Beauty is humility, a sense of humor, self-confidence, intelligence, or many ways you see the beauty in a person. The most beautiful woman I've ever seen was riding the morning bus on Wilshire Blvd in LA. When I arrived in the US, I made use of the bus to get to my workplace. I caught a glimpse of some beautiful girls while riding the bus. When I observed, I was amazed by the beauty of these girls. Beauty is a must in this end. I observed a woman who is adept at dressing, applying makeup, and managing her hair. Each day, the ladies appeared absolutely gorgeous. This is the proper way to present yourself. Beauty is a natural gift for some. Admiration should be given to the beauty that originates from God.

In the present era, possessing a TV and using makeup, dermatology treatments, cosmetics, and various other elements, including dressing up, enhance one's beauty. Yet God places importance on inner beauty. Education, intelligence, shape, height, weight, and talent are all mandatory in our beauty pageant.

Does God place any importance on this beauty? It's important to examine the concept of beauty and its significance in God's teachings.

Proverb 31:30 Favour is deceitful, and beauty is vain: but a woman that feareth the Lord, she shall be praised.

Women who fear God lead righteous and holy lives in God's presence. People often believe that being right in society's eyes is important. Mary, a woman who feared God, was unbothered by the news that she would conceive the Lord while unmarried. She had no fear of the Law of being stoned to death, criticism, or rejection from Joseph. Marriage had not yet happened to her. But she feared God and said so to be it. God expects us to possess this type of inner beauty.

While searching for a new king to replace King Saul in the Old Testament, Samuel encountered a handsome man that caught his attention.

1 Samuel 16:7 But the Lord said unto Samuel, Look not on his countenance, or on the height of his stature; because I have refused him: for the Lord seeth not as man seeth; for man looketh on the outward appearance, but the Lord looketh on the heart.

I've met women who obsessively analyze their own image, purchasing excessive amounts of dresses to escape their perceived appearance in the mirror. Believe in your own appearance. Stay grounded in the Word of God.

Eccles 3:11a He hath made everything beautiful in his time:

Trees possess an undeniable beauty during certain times and seasons. According to my friends, she really liked the tree with no leaves. I couldn't believe what she said. Do you know why? Beauty is in the beholder's eye, according to the English dictionary. I experienced driving on California freeways. Every day, the mountains presented a new but breathtaking beauty. Despite spending twenty years there, the hill's appearance always changed. Summer, rain, winter, fog, or even during a fire, it remains stunning. I appreciate and thank God for the stunning views of nature while driving on the freeway and admiring the mountains. I marveled at the beauty of the mountain, saying, "God, your craftsmanship is remarkable." They are gorgeous. Lord, your painting is absolutely breathtaking!

Psalm 96:9 O worship the Lord in the beauty of holiness: fear before him, all the earth.

My camera fails to capture the beauty. Its brilliance cannot be justified.

Worldly beauty is not admired or desired by God.

Psalm 149:4 For the LORD taketh pleasure in his people: he will beautify the meek with salvation.

Meek individuals listen to the Lord and obey His will and path. Our God can make obedience shine with the beauty of salvation. Have you come across someone who is simultaneously dealing with substance abuse, battling cancer, and consistently engaging in harmful actions? It seems like they are burdened, mistreated, unattractive, and under some kind of possession. They appear extremely unattractive. If God heals them from sicknesses and diseases, these people can undergo transformation. The liberation from addictions like drugs, alcohol, cigarettes, and cancer results in a physical transformation. Back when I lived in India, a prophet would regularly come to see my family. His appearance was displeasing. His testimony stated that he embraced God after reading a paper that flew into his path. The police had a terrible time dealing with him. People had grown tired and fed up with him. He was a drunkard, a lawbreaker, and anything else you can think of. Nevertheless, the piece of paper that came flying towards him turned out to be a page from the Bible. As he began reading, the word leapt off the page, touched his heart, and brought about a transformation.

I moved to the US and then flew back to India for a visit. During my visit to a church, I noticed a book store stand selling Christian books. On the hunt for Christian books for my mom following church. The bookstore owner, while observing the books, said, "Allow her to purchase as many as she desires." This bookstore belongs to her, which means it belongs to me. I thought I did not own any bookstore in India. I was unable to identify this person. He came to me and said, sister, my name is Brother Daniel. I was in disbelief because his outward appearance had completely altered. The distinction was clear, similar to black and white, or day and night. I'm amazed at how much your appearance has changed. It's hard to believe.

At the Apostolic Church, I often saw individuals emerge from the water, looking completely changed after being baptized in Jesus 'name. Tell me, what took place beneath the water? Does this water have the power to make them beautiful? Water performed a remarkable surgery, transforming not only the mind but also

AUGUST 23

the appearance. Your physical appearance undergoes a change as your sins are washed away, and you are liberated from illnesses and demonic influences.

The Lord grants salvation to those who are meek and humble. Salvation was derived from the word saved. The Greek word is Sozo which is healing, deliverance, and redemption.

The devil employs tactics to make you seem unattractive and impure, but the Lord purifies us with His blood. The blood of Jesus is life-giving. It is under His name when you get baptized using the name of Jesus. Instead of worldly beauty, God grants us true beauty. Although you are capable of performing facial surgery, face lifting, and makeup, make an effort to immerse yourself in water while invoking the name of Jesus. Your first step is to repent. Repenting involves making a change in one's lifestyle. You will undergo a transformation in your appearance. The Lord is the ultimate authority in dermatology and beauty treatments.

Isaiah 61:3 To appoint unto them that mourn in Zion, to give unto them beauty for ashes, the oil of joy for mourning, the garment of praise for the spirit of heaviness; that they might be called trees of righteousness, the planting of the Lord, that he might be glorified.

Are you in search of beauty? Look for inner beauty. Your face shines with inner beauty that will be admired by many. Experiencing happiness, peace, and joy will cause a noticeable change in your face. Your face is the reflection of your heart's mirror. If your heart is clean, full of joy, peace, love, long-suffering, gentleness, kindness, and goodness, then you will look beautiful.

I have noticed that a woman full of jealousy, pride, and envy looks ugly. Apologies, but she definitely does. All evil is evident on their face.

Proverb 14:30 A sound heart is the life of the flesh: but envy the rottenness of the bones.

Envy gives some kind of darkness, and their bones deteriorate. The way it looks and its shape also shift as a result.

May we be blessed by the Lord with inner beauty.

1 Timothy says 2:9 In like manner also, that women adorn themselves in modest apparel, with shamefacedness and sobriety; not with broided hair, or gold, or pearls, or costly array; 10 But (which becometh women professing godliness) with good works.

LET US PRAY

Our Lord, we desire and strive for inner beauty. Inner beauty brings outer beauty, which you admire. We can be most beautiful if we have the salvation of God. Delivering us from sins causes illnesses, diseases, and demon oppression. We will look the most gorgeous. Thank you for Holy beauty. It is not what people strive for, but we strive to look clean, pure, and holy to have you in our life. You shine through our faces. The Lord gives His peace, love, and Joy which shines through our faces. Thank you for giving beauty to ashes. We desire the meekness of the heart, so you can beautify us. The people of God have the beauty that the world is looking for. We thank you again for beautifying us in Jesus 'name. Amen God bless you.

AUGUST 24

MARY PONDERED IN HER HEART!

What did Mary ponder in her heart? Mary concealed the divine dialogue within her heart. She shared with those who needed to hear. She kept it to herself and didn't tell her family. However, Elizabeth, her cousin, was aware as she was one of the selected by the Almighty, everlasting Father and Prince of Peace. She was the mother of a forerunner of God. Elijah's spirit was conceived and born by her, and she named him John the Baptist. It unveiled the plan to the right people and kept it hidden from the wrong ones. Hallelujah! God is aware of those whose hearts are transparent and sincere.

Standing in the priest's office was a man named Zechariah. In the temple, he held the position of High Priest. Does it hold any meaning? Without belief in the heavenly message, it holds no value. A response is needed to believe in the impossible and supernatural heavenly matter. In order to carry out God's plan, belief in God is necessary, as he chooses them.

Mary and Elizabeth, who are remarkable and courageous, are distinct from average Jewish women. Both women were loyal and had a profound understanding of God. The reaction to an experience is more important than the experience itself. Our God wants someone to believe and submit to His plan. Yes, God only needs someone to believe, obey, and submit. Would you believe, obey, and submit?

Let me tell you, when Joseph learned about the conception of the child in Mary's womb, he did not know how it happened. Thinking naturally, Joseph, a man, believed she had made an error. Mary didn't disclose how she got pregnant. The Lord gave Joseph a dream since he was planing to hide her from the judgment of adultery. Adultery is punishable by death through stoning.

Yet, the Lord communicated His plan through a dream, and Joseph immediately embraced it. In heaven, God recognized Joseph as a righteous man. How do you think your reputation is viewed in heaven? Daniel was called the beloved of God. He was more than just a prayer warrior; he was a fervent worrier for the mighty God. A courageous and wise act of standing alone and declaring, "So be it." No worry about laws, consequences, trouble, and trial. Believing in God means obeying and submitting to Him, knowing that nothing is impossible. The plan and way of God are supernatural, not human. Let's examine the mindset of people during Mary's pregnancy with Jesus. They were known by God as the generation of vipers!

Who was responsible for the generation of wipers? The leaders who were in power during that time. The religious leaders were much interested in the tradition developed by scholars. Be careful of tradition; it is the most dangerous. We should be watchful of tradition, as Lord Jesus advises us.

AUGUST 24

Mark 7:13 Making the word of God of none effect through your tradition, which ye have delivered: and many such like things do ye.

During that time, Paul walked on the earth and spoke.

Galatians 1:14 And profited in the Jews 'religion above many my equals in mine own nation, being more exceedingly zealous of the traditions of my fathers.

The current situation is identical to before. Scholars have accepted tradition to make the word of God non-effect. Baptism was not practiced by them, as per.

Matthew 28:19. The Father, Son, and Holy Spirit are introduced as three roles of the same God. In the baptism formula, the name was used in its singular form. Jesus is the name of the one God for the new dispensation. According to the Bible, two or three witnesses are necessary to establish the doctrine.

Today, we're facing the same issue. We place our trust in the deceiving teachers and prophets. Open your Bible and explore the particular subject in depth. Identify a couple of scriptures that provide support for the doctrine. Otherwise, you are continuing a tradition set by deceitful instructors and prophets.

John 11:45 Then many of the Jews which came to Mary, and had seen the things which Jesus did, believed on him. 46 But some of them went their ways to the Pharisees and told them what things Jesus had done. 47 Then gathered the chief priests and the Pharisees a council, and said, What do we? For this man doeth many miracles. 48 If we let him thus alone, all men will believe in him: and the Romans shall come and take away both our place and nation.

These people, can you believe them? Oh my goodness! Instead of focusing on your sickness, healing, and deliverance, religious leaders and scholars are concerned about income, power, and position. Why? God knows them in heaven as a generation of Wiper. Your work record is stored in heaven under your name.

John 19:15 But they cried out, Away with him, away with him, crucify him. Pilate saith unto them, Shall I crucify your King? The chief priests answered. We have no king but Caesar.

This is the situation surrounding the birth of Jesus by Mary. No one was ready to believe in God, but the expert in the Torah used it for personal benefit and gain. The tradition was brought to make you feel good about yourself. Read and obey the Word of God. We are facing the same mentality today. Truth doesn't interest them; they prefer tradition, false prophets, and teachers. Today's false teachers and prophets are responsible for crucifying Jesus and distorting His truth. Initially, Eve was the sole monopoly holder, followed by Jewish individuals, and now gentiles have joined in. Only some people will have faith in and follow God's plan. There's no need to fear if they kick you out of their building. They say church to the building, but remember; in this dispensation, you are a church, not a building.

During this time, God will use ladies like Mary and Elizabeth, the wife of Zechariah, since the generation of wipers never walked with God but with the tradition of the priest, elders, Pharisees, and scribes. The God almighty had been removed by them. God cannot be replaced. A believer like Daniel, Joseph, Queen Esther, and Ruth will rise up on earth. A bold man and woman in harmony with God, rejecting traditional practices. The Lord is in search of someone who is obedient and submissive. Thank you, Lord.

By the same token, Zechariah, the priest, did not believe. Do you have this kind of individual as a religious leader who will not believe the word of God and has established their kingdom?

God has cursed their tongue; they will not speak the truth. Elizabeth was a believer but not her husband, who was a High priest. He heard the Angel Gabriel give the news of John the Baptist coming through and coming through his wife. He said how I am old and my wife too.

Luke 1:20 And, behold, thou shalt be dumb, and not able to speak, until the day that these things shall be performed, because thou believest not my words, which shall be fulfilled in their season.

Religious leaders are actively working against God's plan. They forgot to keep and ponder what they must. No need to announce to those people who have no importance to God's plan. God is speaking to those who have an ear to hear. Those who can meditate on the things of God will be blessed with abundant good news from heaven today. However, there's no reason to share it with the fool. May the Lord empower countless brave souls to confront these dictators without fear.

LET US PRAY

Lord, we know in our time, a dispensation of grace is coming to an end. As history repeats, it is repeating in our time. Lord, we know God's complete mission has shifted. In this time and day, no one goes to organizations, denominations, and non-denomination buildings to get healed or delivered, for prophecy or miracle. It has come to our end as just a religious routine. Our God is good and will talk to the one who connects and believes. Our God knows how to publish salvation and whom to use. Let our God find us faithful believers and submissive wise servants. Lord, you brought salvation by picking intelligent, courageous, and bold ladies like Mary and Elizabeth. Lord, let us be one of them for this end-time, in Jesus' name. Amen! God bless you!

AUGUST 25

TRUTH REQUIRES SACRIFICE!

The problem that Satan, the Prince of the earth, has is with truth. The Prince of the Earth seeks to have countless divisions, religions, gods, and goddesses. Various misleading religious paths, including atheism, can lead you to hell.

Paul was a man bound with tradition and needed deliverance from tradition. Religion acts as chains, preventing us from truly following Lord Jesus. The enslavement of humanity is achieved through religion by Satan. It serves as both a blocker and stopper. No matter what you say, it is crucial when sailing your boat and not knowing which way to go. The person in charge of your boat or their assistant is lost in the sea. It was chaos when Paul was leading many to destruction, thinking the disciples of Jesus were wrong. While the goal and aim were on point, tradition became a hindrance and enslavement. Escape the clutches of tradition, religion, churches, organizations, and the power of control in the realm of lost authority in the religious world. A strong foundation is essential for starting a business or pursuing spiritual matters. Starting your doctrine demands a combination of perfect knowledge and absolute dedication. Recognizing God as all-powerful, supernatural, almighty, and omniscient enables you to overcome any problem, situation, or trouble. Demonstrate that nothing is beyond reach by proving it.

Your talk is not well-received, yet people are curious to see the evidence. If you claim he heals, delivers, and sets captives free, why are so many sick, many in hospitals, possessed, oppressed, and lost people in the world? Satan has managed to manipulate numerous minds, leading them astray by preaching without any evidence of miracles or wonders, based on new doctrine of simple faith and belief. Religion is what it's called, and Satan established the boundary. Keeping Bible in hand, knowing few scriptures, and justifying that I do nothing wrong, I am a good Christian.

Once you are misguided and bewitched, it becomes harder to change. To encounter you on your Damascus road, one needs the power of God almighty. Moreover, you require something to ignite your enthusiasm for the word of God. You need someone to put a drop of blood mingled with the Holy Spirit in your ears and eyes, so you can see and hear. You find yourself lost in a massive religious wilderness, ensnared by lies and manipulation. The world of religion, denomination, and organization is like a dark, tangled jungle. Open yourself to the Holy Spirit's instruction, guidance, and empowerment to overcome this falsehood.

God is unable to utilize you. I am not saying your organization, denomination, or churches, but God cannot. Without acknowledging Jesus 'true identity, you'll find yourself in the same lost state as Saul.

Peter claimed that I had knowledge of Jesus 'identity. It is clear to me that you are not Joseph's biological child. You are the Messiah we have been waiting for. I am certain that you are the one mentioned in Isaiah's prophecy. Although you are Mary's son, you are the Son of God sent to save His creation. I know the Torah talks about God coming and taking revenge in Isaiah 35.

Isaiah 6:9 is you; I know One God is supposed to come on earth to deliver, heal, save, and rescue us from the death of hell. I know I am walking with Him since He is doing all, and I am seeing all signs and wondering what Lord wrote in the word.

Isaiah 61:1 The Spirit of the Lord God is upon me; because the Lord hath anointed me to preach good tidings unto the meek; he hath sent me to bind up the brokenhearted, to proclaim liberty to the captives, and the opening of the prison to them that are bound; 2 To proclaim the acceptable year of the Lord, and the day of vengeance of our God; to comfort all that mourn;

The prophecy from the Old Testament is fulfilled in the New Testament. I observe the embodiment of God as a person, known as the Word. God, you came with the purpose of bringing healing, deliverance, and salvation. I witness Jehovah God walking by my side, clothed in human form. I know who you are. You are the Messiah, the anointed one, the Prince of peace, the mighty God, the savior of the world, and great I am. I am privileged to be one of your followers. I am ready to die. Peter was crucified upside down as he chose to give up his life for the truth. The truth is that God came to earth in the flesh.

Saul, another individual chosen like the rest, was anticipating my arrival without realizing I was Jesus. Nevertheless, it has no knowledge of its completion. The opportunity to meet and eat with the Lord slipped through his fingers. However, he cherishes the traditions of his ancestors. Saul displayed unwavering devotion. He devoted his heart, mind, soul, and strength to loving God. Devotion can be both beneficial and risky if you are unaware of the object of your devotion, your idols, and the person you are following. Your devotion needs some brush-up, and your knowledge needs some explanation and understanding of the Diviner. Jehovah God requested a rearrangement of your customs, introducing Jesus Christ as the new way. I must train and communicate with you because your enthusiasm stood out to me. Carrying my name and spreading my word needs all of you, but you must meet me face-to-face. I met Moses and Isaiah. For more than thirty years, I walked on earth, training and teaching. I granted them power, commandments, instruction, and extensive training. Sending you Paul won't work because you love your tradition and don't know me. You were trained by the best lawyer, Torah expert Gamaliel, who is the leading authority of Sanhedrin. It is important for you to understand who I am. Without knowing me, it's not possible to talk about me.

Do you know about those who constantly talk about us without realizing it, especially those who follow tradition and religion? I used to be trapped by religions and traditions, unable to see or hear. Showed no willingness to yield or have faith in others. Oh God, have compassion for my lack of understanding. What makes you trust those false teachers, pastors, and prophets? Please show mercy to your soul. On the day of judgment, your soul will hold you responsible for sending it to hell. By the time you say sorry to your soul, it will be too late. It will be forever consumed and grieved.

Paul, the chosen one, possesses bravery, courage, and profound knowledge, but is unable to be dispatched for God's work in the world. Changing and resolving his confusion about Jesus is necessary for him to teach, heal, and deliver. Are you believing those who are very wrong, despite their large number? You are causing Jesus to be killed and crucified again. You are unaware of Jesus and unwilling to support His

AUGUST 25

mission of salvation, healing, deliverance, and redemption. Please, allow God to have the space to work. You have discovered a path that transforms denominations, non-denominations, and organizations. Refuse to comply with the authorities just to please them. Pray for those who do not have revelations of Jesus and avoid following them. They do have faith in God, but doubt that Jesus was the Jehovah God who came to fix Adam and Eve's mess.

Are you falling into the same traps as Adam and Eve? God proclaimed that upon eating the fruit, death would be inevitable. What did he mean by the die? It meant destruction of their soul in hell. They had a long lifespan and a large number of offspring. Are you also doing the same? Why? You will lose your soul and the legacy of your successors. The punishment is eternal hellfire. May the Lord give you the courage and boldness to stand for the truth. May lord Jesus deliver you from the power of lust of eyes and flesh. Your soul is at risk when you let pride take over. Take the sip of humility and humbleness, and take the rejection of false people in authority. Take the road of Damascus; take the instruction, training of trial made, and tribulation training for you. So you learn to divide the word of truth accurately. May the Lord help you understand there is a price to pay. The things that come at no cost hold little value, while those with a high price are valued. It will mean much to you if it costs you your pride and lust for flesh and eyes. May the Lord bless you.

LET US PRAY

Our sacrifice is so little compared to yours. Our God is great and mighty to know the road He is taking us. We know the Word of God is the highest authority, and learning through the Holy Spirit is the best way. So teach the Holy Spirit what you meant by each scripture with each subject. Your word is the last authority, not anyone, churches, teachers, or pastors. Lord, talk to us; we listen and submit to you. We want to be one who does not care about life and die for the truth. They sacrifice their lives to bring and keep the truth on this earth. We will have the battle, but we know the truth sets us free. Thank you, Lord, for the sacrifice of yourself. Bless us with boldness and courage to stand on the WORD in Jesus 'name. Amen! God bless you.

AUGUST 26

THE POINT OF TOUCH!

Touching the anointed one is a necessary step to receive your miracle. Your current flows to the point of touch for the light to turn on. The power of electricity is spread everywhere through work at the main junction. In order to be healed, The Lady had to make physical contact with Jesus 'clothing. People were throwing themselves at Jesus to touch him. The power of healing and deliverance flows through those touched by shadow. It is crucial that we locate the point of contact.

Witness the force when contact is made.

Mark 5:30 And Jesus, immediately knowing in himself that virtue had gone out of him, turned him about in the press, and said, Who touched my clothes?

When you possess the anointing of God, your cloth and shadow serve as the touchpoint. Once you make contact with the point and feel healed or delivered, you'll realize a transformation has occurred. Don't interfere with God's role as God. It's important to touch Him, not anyone else. When you enter into prayer, locate the spot where you can sense the presence of the throne room. Your body experienced something. The word of God affirms that touching is essential. Anointing with oil involves a physical point of touch.

Mark 6:13 And they cast out many devils, and anointed with oil many that were sick, and healed them.

To heal, one must be touched by Holy oil. It is the point of contact with the sick, and the ill recover from sins.

James 5:14 Is any sick among you? Let him call for the elders of the church; and let them pray over him, anointing him with oil in the name of the Lord: 15 And the prayer of faith shall save the sick, and the Lord shall raise him up; and if he has committed sins, they shall be forgiven him.

To achieve the desired outcome, we must abide by the word of God. My friend and I attended a church in Mesquite, Texas today. A few bottles of olive oil were brought by my friend, who told me to pray over them. The congregation needs this oil from me. Practicing the word is necessary if we want to please God. He has the highest level of authority. Both of us placed our hands on the oil, prayed, and blessed it. She follows my teachings.

AUGUST 26

Today, the lady pastor at church revealed to my friend that I am her teacher. She informed me that you have a wide reach as a teacher and minister. We met her the first time, at least I met her the first time. However, she utilized the gift of the Word of knowledge and brought joy to both of us through her ministry. If you do not touch the throne room, His clothes, and His Word by acting as it says in the formula, it won't act. The objective is to touch in order to be anointed, thereby breaking the yoke and nothing more. Your failure to abide by God's instructions has trapped you in a repetitive pattern. It makes life harder when we choose to follow someone who is unaware of what they're doing. Why do people rush towards Jesus and fall in order to touch him? Our life is not whole without this missing component. We prioritize pleasing others over pleasing God.

Matthew 14:35 And when the men of that place knew of him, they sent out into all that country round about, and brought unto him all that were diseased; 36 And besought him that they might only touch the hem of his garment: and as many as touched were made perfectly whole.

We need the flow of the Holy Spirit, where all come to the wireless connection or Wi-Fi and get healed. It's the place where you can experience the presence of the Spirit of God and establish a connection. Everything is fine then. We place greater confidence in technology than in our God. Our God's influence makes it simple for others to have faith. Our problem is we have done away with God, and the point of touch is foreign. Starting from the beginning, we need to depend solely on the word. Do not diminish the word through a powerless form of religion. This is the moment of touch and receiving.

At lunchtime, one of my friends mentioned she goes to a specific park and prays beneath a specific tree. She mentioned that she always encounters God in that place. The specific spot where Moses touched the Burning Bush. Wherever you make contact with Him, God will grant your desires. It is Jesus, not any organization or religion, who provides wealth, health, healing, and deliverance. Particularly individuals who lack the Holy Spirit. How can you be certain that they do not possess the Holy Spirit? Because they will not speak in tongues. Miracles, healings, words of knowledge, prophecies, and deliverance from demons are impossible without the Spirit of God. Would you mind opening the Bible and immersing yourself in the Word of God? A truth-seeking Indian brother asked the pastor why people weren't being baptized in Jesus' name. What is the reason behind our churches not accepting the Bible's teaching on receiving the Holy Spirit? According to the pastor, our duties include baptizing, officiating your wedding, and conducting your funeral. Have you considered the state of your soul? It is required to have a point of contact. The woman, possessing alabaster oil, paid no attention to the judgmental Jews driven by greed. She had reached the point where she could make contact with the Lord. Why should we worry about the critics?

Luke 7:37 And, behold, a woman in the city, which was a sinner, when she knew that Jesus sat at meat in the Pharisee's house, brought an alabaster box of ointment, 38 And stood at his feet behind him weeping, and began to wash his feet with tears, and did wipe them with the hairs of her head, and kissed his feet, and anointed them with the ointment. 47 Wherefore I say unto thee, Her sins, which are many, are forgiven; for she loved much: but to whom little is forgiven, the same loveth little.

Get to that point and connect with His Garment, His throne room. Experience the power of God and receive all that you desire. May the Lord assist you in discovering the point of connection where you encounter Him and achieve wholeness. People frequently question how these churches, which are described as sick, can possibly heal anyone. May the Lord give you courage, wisdom, and boldness to find that place where you have a meeting point with your maker. We worship a good God. He will help you. Wait on God; He will give you strength, renew, and bless you. Just wait! Don't rush, as the waiting time can be unpredictable.

Take it easy and be patient. Hopeless, horrible, and harmful churches are the result of compromise. Our success depends on waiting patiently. If you're going through a problem or need help to make a decision, don't forget to give God a chance. Keep your misguiders out; many do not know about what's happening.

The woman made physical contact with Jesus, kissed his feet, and used her tears to wipe them. The spectator inquired about why Jesus permitted her to touch. She has transgressed morally. The religious authority is somewhat inaccurate. Send me the word; the word touched the servant and was healed. A point of touch is essential for healing. I had a pain in my shoulder; I touched and prayed. I experienced a powerful healing when the Holy Spirit touched me with intense heat. My hand made contact with the painful area of my shoulder, which was the touchpoint. The touch of any hand can bring us the Holy Spirit's touch. It will achieve remarkable performances. Evil spirits will come to kill, steal, and destroy. Touchpoints can be dangerous. Don't rush and make sure to have a spiritual encounter with God before departing, in Jesus' name. Amen.

LET US PRAY

Lord, our experience starts as we touch you. The touch of our word to our situation, our heart, and our life brings mighty change. God can change, revive, and recreate man if they know how to touch, so teach us, Lord. Help us find the touching point where our God can show up and show off. Help us have patience and faith that He comes and touches us. Lord, help us find the point of touch. We learn and teach others to seek the point of touch. It is not in any place but on my knee and anywhere I can touch you for my needs. I know you will do what you did to many who came at that point of touch. I need the point of touch, and all will and can change. Jesus is at that touchpoint. Please touch Him today; your problems, sickness, confusion, and need will meet in Jesus 'name. Amen! God bless you.

AUGUST 27

CONNECTION WITH THE CREATOR IS A MUST!

Our connection with God is necessary to gain His attention. Prayer serves as the link between humans and God. By understanding the plan of crucifixion, Jesus accomplished His goal. Take a moment to reflect on the final hours leading up to Jesus 'Crucifixion. Act fast, or you'll be left without assistance.

Luke 22:41 And he was withdrawn from them about a stone's cast, and kneeled down, and prayed, 42 Saying, Father, if thou be willing, remove this cup from me: nevertheless not my will, but thine, be done. 43 And there appeared an angel unto him from heaven, strengthening him. 44 And being in agony, he prayed more earnestly: and his sweat was as it were great drops of blood falling down to the ground.

Take control of your situation like a boss. Maintain control over situations before confronting them. There's no necessity for someone to remind you to pray. Before facing the storm, trial, and test, pray. When temptation arises, seek help from heaven. Connect and receive support by entering your prayer closet. We must comply with God's plan. The purpose of Jesus 'earthly presence was to show us how to establish a connection with God through kneeling in prayer. Do not think help will come without you crying out for it. Don't wait until you're in trouble to cry out. Do it beforehand. God will dispatch angels to give you the strength you need. It's a key component for overcoming obstacles; without it, failure is likely. How Daniel was getting connected three times a day gave Angel the power to take charge.

Daniel 6:10c he kneeled upon his knees three times a day and prayed,

If you believe that God created angels to assist or serve you, remember that they will only respond if you specifically request their presence.

Hebrews 1:13 But to which of the angels said he at any time, Sit on my right hand, until I make thine enemies thy footstool? 14 Are they, not all ministering spirits, sent forth to minister for them who shall be heirs of salvation?

One thing I always do is stress the value of prayer to the new converts I bring to the Lord. It is essential for all Christians to pray, cry out, and seek God. Knowing how and when to connect is crucial for them. If you don't pray, you'll be disconnected. Without connection, you are left alone, unprotected, and unsupported. Do you have a claim you'd like to make without formally filing a petition? When searching for a new job or legal assistance, the process of filing petitions, known as applications, connects you. Heaven goes through the same process. It's important to submit petitions, requests, and applications.

The only way to receive your assistance is through prayer. Zero communication and zero assistance! What happened to the disciples? Although they were walking with Jesus, they failed to establish a connection with God through prayer.

Matthew 26:40 And he cometh unto the disciples, and findeth them asleep, and saith unto Peter, What, could ye not watch with me one hour?

No strength. Fear took over.

Mark 14:50 And they all forsook him and fled.

Avoid placing your trust in denominations, organizations, or positions when the power of darkness is in play. Seek a connection with God by praying. The heavenly host is working to fulfill your request. List your desired or required qualifications in your applications. I know one lady; she is full of jealousy and lies. Regularly attend a building known as a church, but filled with demons. She has a kind-hearted husband. I wonder what happened there. How did she find a gentleman? God used her mouth to testify. When she was unmarried, she recalled that their denomination would collectively choose a name to pray for. A couple selected her name to pray for her future spouse. Every Wednesday, they prayed for one hour, hoping she would find a good husband.

My Lord, please show mercy to that husband. Although this girl was, and perhaps still is, a mess, her husband is a good man who will face future trials, provisions, and protection based on your filed petitions with faith. By assuming the guise of an angel of light, many religious group organizations fulfill the role of Satan. Attempting to undermine others.

I dreamt of facing adversaries with dog and tiger demons in a self-proclaimed Christian region. It was a challenging location for Jesus to enter. Church buildings can be seen everywhere. Sick churches and organizations that are powerless and anti-Christ. Their lost young generation is alcoholics; they lie and cheat. Those without prayer in their denominations and organizations are unaware of Jesus 'mission. Remember, devils come with a counterfeit plan for the counter-attack. By connecting you with his deceitful plan, the devil knows how to destroy you. How many people go to churches and associate the devil with false agendas? Your role is to engage in dialogue with God and not be misled by hypocritical, false authorities designated by Satan. Seek guidance from the Lord for the answer. Not everything that appears good or claims to be holy or righteous is genuine. What is the implication of having a role, Bible expertise, numerous accolades, and a reputation in the spiritual realm? Nothing! Like Daniel, Moses, and Joshua, it's important for you to have a connection with God. Choosing to connect with God leads to victory, not relying on other sources. Consider David's survival through various afflictions.

Psalm 34:19 Many are the afflictions of the righteous: but the LORD delivereth him out of them all.

Not some afflictions, but believers from all. The sole solution to trouble is to establish a connection with God. Call out to God when you are in need. A divine army will be dispatched to provide assistance.

AUGUST 27

Psalm 63:1 O God, thou art my God; early will I seek thee: my soul thirsteth for thee, my flesh longeth for thee in a dry and thirsty land, where no water is

Prayer to the Lord Jesus is our prime example of achieving victory.

Victory and deliverance are achieved through the power of God's operation. Angels can only fulfill their purpose by establishing a connection with God. Instead of claiming to know God, make it a priority to talk to Him every day. Imagine if your house were engulfed in flames. Is it your expectation that a fire truck will be dispatched to provide help? Contact the fire department and notify them of a fire at the house. In order to send a firetruck, they need the address. Learning how to connect with God is essential for receiving help. The plan of God can be destroyed if you have false, counterfeit teachers, prophets, and denominations. To succeed, you must possess perception, discernment, and wisdom. Don't forget, WORD never undergoes any changes. The Word is God and God is the Word. Continue in truth; Word is truth if you know how to rightly divide the word of truth. Find out which formula is applicable to the doctrine. Instead of listening to Satan's agents, open the word and study. Love your soul. It was His own people, not the Romans, that Jesus fought against. The most dangerous threats come from within, not from external sources. Obey the word and help yourself. Stop seeking validation from people, denominations, pastors, and organizations. Reconnect with your spirituality and God. If you ask for His help, He will provide you with much assistance. In times of trouble, find peace, joy, and strength by connecting with the Lord, in Jesus 'name! Amen!

LET US PRAY

Heavenly Father, in this busy life, we forgot to search for the truth. Following misguiding religion, we failed to follow you. We are everything else but Christian. Jesus, we are not like you. We do not follow your example. Help us follow your model to see the word of God in operation like it was earlier. The numerous doctrines and teachings we have are confusing because they don't establish a connection with you, but with everything else. Our God is the same forever. It is our job to seek, ask, and knock. Help us pray without ceasing; seek your face early. Thank you for the faithfulness of your word. It is the word we need and not the false teaching. Your love is beyond. We are privileged to have all since nothing is impossible. Show us the way since you are that correct way in Jesus 'name. Amen! God bless you!

AUGUST 28

MAY THE LORD HAVE HIS WAY!

The Lord is knocking and seeking permission to implement His plan in your life. May I come and sup with you? I am going to share success strategies with you. Can I assist you as your guide, mentor, and support? Many individuals acknowledge the Lord as their savior. The term "savior" refers to someone who delivers, heals, and saves. Adversity reveals true dependability. God proclaims that you must submit to Him in order for Him to release you from your entanglements. In 2012, my brother passed away. He experienced intermittent sickness. He faced numerous trials and challenges. As his sister, I always prayed for him without fail. Both my mom and many others who were close to me offered prayers. Sister Karen went without food or water for seven days and nights multiple times, praying and fasting for my brother. I followed God's guidance and participated in fasting, but I could only do it for three days and nights. Whenever we prayed, God rescued him from Satan's plan to harm, steal, and ruin his life. The Lord displayed immense mercy towards him. He had a good heart and a deep love for the Lord. My brother provided support for missionaries, prophets, and pastors who were doing good work. He never turned them away and always served them with genuine care. Giving God's servants a glass of water is how you receive their blessings. We are blessed when we provide others with what they require. May the Lord enlighten you about the blessings that come from giving.

Matthew 10:42 And whosoever shall give to drink unto one of these little ones a cup of cold water only in the name of a disciple, verily I say unto you, he shall never lose his reward.

Matthew 25:40 And the King shall answer and say unto them, Verily I say unto you, since ye have done it unto one of the least of these my brethren, ye have done it unto me.

The Lord helped me recall my brother's kind actions on his birthday today. I was confident that my prayers would have healed him when he was sick. Sister Karen and I engaged in fasting and prayer. My brother was deeply loved by Sister Karen's husband. They received a message from the Lord assuring them that my brother would recover and survive. She shared it with me. I experienced a state of contentment. The Lord communicated with me in a dream at a later time. In my dream, God showed my brother and said if I take him now, he will live forever, but if not, there will be no chance of entering the kingdom. Lord, let me feel the same level of numbness where nothing can reach his heart or soul. He won't find any solution or route to enter the kingdom of God. His departure from earth this time guarantees his salvation from death. If you permit me to take Him home, He will have a chance to enter the kingdom. In my dream, I witnessed the way He would transform. I expressed, Lord, may Your plan prevail regardless of any obstacles. My constant prayer to the Lord has been for the salvation of my family's souls. I hope for them to reside

AUGUST 28

eternally in heaven. I was aware of his intention to leave the earth. Prior to seeing him, I had a dream while I was in Texas. I kept this dream to myself and didn't tell anyone.

I traveled to California during this period to assist him. As I was driving to the hospital to see him, I heard a message from God telling me to bring flowers for my brother. I handpicked beautiful roses just for him. Without a doubt, they were truly beautiful. There have been a lot of comments about flower arrangements. While this period lasts, Karen and her husband will go to the hospital and insist that he will not die, but instead survive. God spoke to sister Karen and her husband, assuring them that George would live. The pain of George's passing was too much for Karen's husband to handle. He wondered why God didn't fulfill His promise. I had a conversation with sister Karen a few days later. She informed me that her husband is in bed, upset upon hearing George's news. She stated that we were both aware of God's promise to keep him. Sister Karen sounded very sad, and her husband stopped talking because of sadness. He was grieving over George's loss. Upon sharing my dream, they were both rejuvenated and grasped the Lord's intended significance of living. They both attended the funeral and were happy. Lord, let your will be done. I placed my brother on the sacred altar of God. I attended the prayer services that morning when I had his dream. I went to the altar of God. I prayed until I removed all emotion and attachment. I stated that I was not willing to gamble with his soul. I pleaded for Lord's assistance. I desire to have him by my side for all eternity.

Death is not the end, but the beginning of eternal life. Winning means making it to heaven. Worth living if we make it to heaven. Allow God to have His way. Salvation leads us to eternity through the door of death. When leaving Earth, make sure to find salvation. Let us understand that God's best plan for our lives needs our cooperation, approval, and permission.

In the book of Acts, God has revealed the most perfect plan for salvation. Unless this happens, your sins won't be pardoned. God said, here is my blood; I will wash away your sins if you go in the water in MY NAME, WHICH IS JESUS. NAME ABOVE EVERY NAME, EVERY KNEE SHALL BOW TO THIS NAME, CONFESSING THAT JESUS IS THE JEHOVAH SAVIOR, HEALER, AND DELIVERER.

Lord, let your will be done. The Lord has written in the books; the Lord never spoke in your mind or through prophets or any other way. By surrendering to the Lord, we can access the heavenly treasure. You can choose the treasure of heaven by surrendering to the Lord. With your consent, the invitation is open for you to accept. With your permission, I will do whatever is required for the betterment of my soul.

Revelation 3:20 Behold, I stand at the door and knock: if any man hears my voice, and open the door, I will come into him and will sup with him, and he with me.

We are the dwelling place of God. Nevertheless, we have the freedom to make choices according to God's gift. If our love for Him is real, let your heart's door open.

John 14:23 Jesus answered and said unto him, If a man loves me, he will keep my words: and my Father will love him, and we will come unto him and make our abode with him.

Express love towards your maker, creator, and God. You will be blessed by him and receive a life that is more abundant. He will protect you from enemies who devour, steal, kill, and destroy. When something is destroyed, it cannot be reassembled. Lord, please assist us in loving you with our entire being, in Jesus' name. Lord, I surrender myself, my family, and my country to your will, in Jesus' name. Amen! God Bless you!

LET US PRAY

Heavenly Father, thank you for giving us the free will to choose. We want to know you more by keeping your laws, commandments, and statutes.

Your Word says that if we hold your commandment, then we will be blessed. All you want is to bless us. We want you to bless and keep us. We need your ways in our life. You are the way to the truth and eternal life. No one enters heaven without you. You have shown us the good way. You have given an example to follow. We follow you to find an abundant life. Lord, you know from the beginning to the end of our life, so we surrender, knowing you have a place for eternal rest and peace. We give you all have your way. In Jesus 'Name! Amen! God bless you!

AUGUST 29
YOUR LOVE FOR GOD BRINGS REVELATION!

Your love for Him will be put to the test. You should provide evidence and proof to support your statements. If you pass, the achievement is the blessing; if you fail, you will lose the blessings.

John 14:15 If you love me, keep my commandments.

The first commandment is to hear O Israel, the Lord, thy God is One, and to love the Lord with all your heart, mind, soul, and strength. It was tested in many people's lives. Once you firmly believe in God, a unique test will come your way. Passing will result in God's blessings.

John 14:21 He that hath my commandments, and keepeth them, he it is that loveth me: and he that loveth me shall be loved of my Father, and I will love him and will manifest myself to him.

Since it only comes by revelation, they did not understand Jesus at that time and even today. There is a condition attached to the revelation. Show your love for God by dedicating your heart, mind, soul, and strength to Him, while obeying His commandments. Peter's knowledge of Jesus is derived exclusively from the Spirit of God. God is Spirit. Jesus is the physical manifestation of the Spirit God. By shedding His blood, God incarnate paid the price for the sins of His creation. His life was sacrificed due to the sins of humanity. Life is in the blood. To recognize Jesus needs revelation, which comes from the Spirit. If you need help, don't rely on theologians. Jesus was in the midst of the Israelites, who were unaware of His presence. Our God has kept His identity under His power.

There was this one time when I came across a Korean brother. He is blessed with a variety of spiritual gifts. I had never seen multiple gifts in action at such an advanced level. I yearn to have all these spiritual gifts. He inquired later, "Sister, do you have knowledge of who Jesus is?" Since I had His revelation, I knew who Jesus was." I declared that Jesus is Jehovah manifested in human form. He confirmed with the word "exactly". I mentioned that I had a divine revelation through the scripture.

Isaiah 43:10 Ye are my witnesses, saith the LORD, and my servant whom I have chosen: that ye may know and believe me, and understand that I am he: before me, there was no God formed, neither shall there be after me. 11 I, even I, am the LORD; and beside me, there is no savior.

Jesus is referred to as the savior in the New Testament, while Jehovah God proclaimed Himself as a savior in the Old Testament. According to this, the servant would be God in human form.

1 Timothy 3:16 God manifested in the flesh.

The Devil took out God and replaced Him in the scripture above. The Devil plays the game.

Philippians 2:6 Who, being in the form of God, thought it not robbery to be equal with God: 7 But made himself of no reputation, and took upon him the form of a servant, and was made in the likeness of men:

Through the Word and the Spirit of God, I received a revelation from God. God is Spirit and since Word is God, Word is also Spirit. Not having a revelation of Jesus, people start all kinds of churches.
Jesus, Himself said.

Matthew 16:17 And Jesus answered and said unto him, Blessed art thou, Simon Barjona: for flesh and blood hath not revealed it unto thee, but my Father which is in heaven.

Keeping God's commandment is a way to demonstrate your love for Him. By following His commandment, God's revelation will be bestowed upon you. Paul stated that I knew there is only One God. Paul inquired about the person known as Jesus. Many people were converting to Jesus, so he started killing believers of Jesus. Despite the commandment against killing, his love for God demonstrated his passion for his one God. Paul was completely dedicated to the Lord and loved Him wholeheartedly. He wasn't taught the lesson of One God or Jesus name baptism, but the Spirit God appeared on the Road to Damascus and spoke to him.

Acts 9:5 And he said, Who art thou, Lord? And the Lord said, I am Jesus whom thou 397ersecutes: it is hard for thee to kick against the pricks. 6 And he trembling and astonished, said, Lord, what wilt thou have me to do? And the Lord said unto him, Arise, go into the city, and it shall be told thee what thou must do.

This conversation was in Hebrew according to *Acts 26:14, And when we were all fallen to the earth, I heard a voice speaking unto me, and saying in the Hebrew tongue, Saul, Saul, why persecutes thou me? It is hard for thee to kick against the pricks.*

The absence of Jesus 'revelation to Paul resulted in widespread turmoil. Paul loved the Lord, that is why he killed the believer of Jesus, but when he heard the name Jesus in Hebrew 2424 Iēsoús–Jesus, the transliteration of the Hebrew term, which means "Yahweh saves" (or "Yahweh is salvation"). Now he had no problem with the name. Saves come from Greek Sozo meant healer delivers and savior. All old testament names of Jehovah fall in this one name: JESUS=, Jehovah saves or Jehovah's savior.

He understood that the anticipated Jehovah mentioned by Isaiah was none other than Jesus incarnate. The highest name of Jehovah God revealed to them who love the Lord with all heart, mind, soul, and strength. "Saves" originates from the Greek term "Sozo" which signifies healer, deliverer, and savior. All old testament names of Jehovah are engulfed in one name JESUS= Jehovah saves or Jehovah's savior.

Failing to recognize Jesus as the One God Jehovah means you'll be left behind, even in the 21st century. You can start a new denomination, non-denominations, or organization and still lose. If you reject the name of Jesus, God won't forgive your sins. Every knee shall bow, and the tongue confesses Jesus as God's

AUGUST 29

savior. The mention of that name alone can bring forgiveness for your sins, provided you have faith in Jesus.

Acts 10:43 To him give all the prophets witness that through his name (Jesus) whosoever believeth in him shall receive remission of sins.

The purpose of baptism is to receive forgiveness for sins. Sinners receive the payment of eternal death in hell. Forgiveness can only be obtained through the blood of Jesus. If you're still unaware of who Jesus is, have you ever wondered why? You have no revelation because you do not love God with all your heart, mind, soul, and strength. False teachers, prophets, churches, denominations, and organizations are agents of Satan, blinding your mind with false teaching.

2 Corinthians 4:3 But if our gospel be hid, it is hidden to them that are lost:4 In whom the God of this world hath blinded the minds of them which believe not, lest the light of the glorious gospel of Christ, who is the image of God, should shine unto them.

The revelation of Jesus requires love and obedience to God. The Lord is looking for a bride who will obediently love and do whatever it takes to glorify the name of Jesus. You are unable to comprehend, as you did not receive the same revelation as others during His time. My baptism was performed in the name of Jesus. I experienced a different kind of interaction with God. Recognizing my love for Him, Jesus personally invited me to be baptized in His name. After being baptized in the name of Jesus, I felt as light as a feather. I have been freed from the heavy mountain of sin by God. I had my first encounter with the power of God. Obey His commandments if you have love for Him. This is the taste for all. Amen!

LET US PRAY

Heavenly Father, the test for your bride is to keep the commandment and not to deviate from it.

Your bride must obey the commandment. Your bride's test is the revelation of Jesus. We cannot enter heaven if we do not have a revelation. Thanks for the revelation of One God's manifestation in Jesus. Lord, we thank you. You have revealed to us your identity. All who love you are called chosen and faithful. Help us be faithful till the end. The disciple followed as you instructed in the book of Acts. We continue the book of Acts by keeping you as the chief cornerstone. Thank you for choosing our body as your church and not the building. You are the Jehovah's Spirit, God in the flesh, Jesus. Amen! God bless you!

AUGUST 30

WHAT CHRISTIANS MUST KNOW!

What is the definition of Christians? Christians are Christ-like, repentant, baptized in Jesus 'name to wash away their sins, and have received the Holy Spirit by speaking in tongue. According to the Book of Acts, this is how Christians are defined by the Bible. If you identify as a Baptist, Methodist, Alliance member, or any other doctrine that leads you away from following Christ. If you want to follow Christ, you have to follow the instructions laid out in the Bible. Remember, going to church won't save you, but living by the word will. Your body represents a sanctuary, not a mere structure. God in flesh is Christ, also referred to as the Word. In the Bible, he was the word you read.

Psalms 138:2b, for thou hast, magnified thy word above all thy name.

Luke 21:33 Heaven and earth shall pass away: but my words shall not pass away.

Who should be believed? Put your belief in the Word of the Lord.

As a teacher, I consistently ask each individual to open their Bible. I keep silent about what I know or believe. Although I am not authorized to make changes, there were some who dared to do so and ended up causing trouble. An Antichrist religion has been initiated by them. The word holds the greatest authority. Let's say you're driving and going faster than the speed limit, the cop won't get upset but will politely request your license, insurance, and registration and then issue a ticket. He will advise you to drive carefully. If you commit a crime, the police officer won't scream but instead hand you a ticket. Same with God,

John 12:47 And if any man hears my words, and believe not, I judge him not: for I came not to judge the world, but to save the world. 48 He that rejecteth me, and receiveth, not my words, hath one that judgeth him: the word that I have spoken, the same shall judge him in the last day.

All the books containing your activities will be opened by Jesus. You will be held accountable by the Lord for doing this and that. How do you feel about it? Are you still going to give your personal interpretation? Don't allow anyone to exploit your soul for profit. Open the Bible and discover the truth within.

Acts 17:10 And the brethren immediately sent away Paul and Silas by night unto Berea: who coming thither went into the synagogue of the Jews. 11 These were more noble than those in Thessalonica, in that they received the word with all readiness of mind, and searched the scriptures daily, whether those things were so.

AUGUST 30

The people of Berea eagerly searched scripture with an open mind. Keep an open mind and consider exploring different religions, denominations, or organizations. God is the source of the words "light" and "lamp," not denominations. Ensure that what you hear from others 'teaching and preaching is the Word of God. I repeatedly confirmed its accordance with the Word of God. Jesus spoke with clarity following his resurrection.

Luke 24:45 Then opened he their understanding, that they might understand the scriptures.

The day we enter heaven is the day we are saved. We have to keep going with the truth until that point. Nobody can declare that they are saved. The day of our baptism in Jesus 'name and receiving the Holy Spirit signifies the beginning of our journey to heaven. Joining the army of God was the true meaning of being born again. Our training is kicking off right now. Our training teaches us to become proficient soldiers. Everyone says I am saved since I attend worship services. There are people who act and think like a devil, yet identify themselves as Christians. Make sure that you study the book called the Bible, where you find the truth.

John 8:31 Then said Jesus to those Jews which believed on him, If ye continue in my word, then are ye my disciples indeed; 32 And ye shall know the truth, and the truth shall make you accessible.

This is what the Lord said. You must continue in the word. Attend a house of prayer that focuses on teaching and preaching the truth, rather than religion or tradition. The order of the Word of God must be maintained exactly as written. The story will transform if we embrace the Holy Spirit as our teacher, leader, and guide in discovering all truth. Christians must follow the instructions given by Jesus Christ in the Bible without deviation. Do you observe blind eyes being opened, deaf ears being unstopped, demons being expelled, the sick being healed, and the lame walking? Shadows and clothing were once used for healing people. Listen to the disciple speaking in tongues or prophesying. The power of wisdom and knowledge in action. Gifts of miracles in operation. Do you hear the message coming as one of the nine gifts bringing the interpretation? If not, then it falls into the category of a religious cult. The church mentioned in the book of Acts is not what we are referring to. Your physical form has transformed into a holy sanctuary for God.

Mark 16:17 And these signs shall follow them that believe; In my name shall they cast out devils; they shall speak with new tongues; 18 They shall take up serpents; and if they drink any deadly thing, it shall not hurt them; they shall lay hands on the sick, and they shall recover.

Jesus operates through His disciples.

Mark 16:20 And they went forth and preached everywhere, the Lord working with them, and confirming the word with signs following. Amen!

Through His works, the Lord is showing that His word is effective and trustworthy. God seeks five individuals who are wise and have clean garments. Maintain your garment in that manner.

Ephesians 5:27 That he might present it to himself a glorious church, not having spot, or wrinkle, or any such thing; but that it should be holy and without blemish.

Put aside any worries about churches, people, organizations, or your traditions. Begin reading the word of God and continue in accordance with it. If you're searching for the plan of salvation, focus solely on the book of Acts. By understanding Jesus as the manifestation of God, Jehovah's savior, all problems can be resolved. Christianity is identified by the fruit of love. It's not all about love and doing what feels good. The importance lies not in your present claims, but in what you will hear on the day of judgment. On judgment day, a multitude of books, including the books of life, will be opened for all to see.

Revelation 20:10 And the devil that deceived them was cast into the lake of fire and brimstone, where the beast and the false prophet are, and shall be tormented day and night forever and ever. 11 And I saw a great white throne, and him that sat on it, from whose face the earth and the heaven fled away; and there was found no place for them.

Are you prepared to focus on achieving salvation? Work hard in order to attain salvation. It is a job.

Philippians 2:12 Wherefore, my beloved, as ye have always obeyed, not as in my presence only, but now much more in my absence, work out your own salvation with fear and trembling.

Amen! God Bless you!

LET US PRAY

Our heavenly father, this is the race, and we have enrolled in it by choice. Our God has made a provision so anyone who desires to enroll can.

Do not let us get stuck by compromising with any so- called church facility. Salvation is not group therapy but individual therapy. Lord, help us follow as your word instructs us in the book of Acts for salvation. We thank you for the Bible as a whole. We are told to continue on this journey by your word. It is full of wealth and help for our salvation. It is your love for us to write the word so we do not miss it. Lord, help us know the word of truth to be free. Remove every hindrance, blockage, and stopper of religion in Jesus 'name. Amen! God bless you!

AUGUST 31

WHO BEWITCHED YOU?

Definitions of Bewitch: Someone has control over you by any means. Cast a spell and gain control over someone. Beguile. Miriam Webster says to influence or affect especially injuriously by witchcraft. Fascinated. It is meant to captivate you. It is the way Satan gets control of you.

At my house, during a prayer meeting, a prophetess prayed for one of my family members. Prophetess said her mother bewitched one woman of your family who came by marriage. She performed witchcraft to harm you all. It came to my attention that she inflicted a great deal of damage, division, and hurt in our family. Watch out for the daughters of the witch. Whenever her mother came around, everything turned into chaos.

There was a time when I dreamt about someone I was acquainted with. According to God, she is prideful, jealous, and envious of you. Let's call her Elli to keep her identity confidential. Ellie's behavior underwent a change as soon as her friend moved in. Ellie's actions are shaped by her friend Ava (Satan can appear as a friend, spouse, or anyone). Ava was constantly whispering in Ellie's ear. Although she was religious, Ava had a reputation for being a liar, thief, and manipulator. This particular religious demon goes by the name of Jezebel's spirit. Elli's friend was constantly whispering in her ear. Ava's visit had a profound impact on Elli's personality. I sought guidance from God. What transpired? He demonstrated that her friend had enchanted her. People with these characteristics will always be around, constantly talking in your ear. They have the ability to cast a spell on people no matter where they are. It jeopardizes families, marriages, and society. Ava's mother was dishonest and manipulative. The mother and daughter were identical. Keep them away from the door as they are like Jezebel and Athaliah, a threat to anyone until God removes them.

Paul was the one who established the church in Galatian. The Galatians grasped, approved, and practiced Paul's teachings. However, in time, false teachers arrived and modified them with misleading teachings. The teachings of Paul were not followed by the Galatians. Paul ensured he always visited the work he established, which was focused on the truth. The truth is that repenting, being baptized in Jesus 'name, and receiving the Spirit of God washes away sin and empowers you. Paul made it a habit to oversee the advancement of the work he had set in motion. Some false teachers and prophets came and taught wrong, and Galatians went away from the truth. False teaching poisons one's ear. It is commonly referred to as bewitching. Their objective is to mislead you by delivering different speeches, teachings, or prophecies, all for their personal gain. People who were previously part of Judaism were becoming new believers. Yet, there are those who lack understanding of the New Testament Church. The New Testament Church represents your body. They continued to practice both the Law and Torah. If you are practicing different so-called religious doctrines to join a denomination, non-denomination, or organization, then you need deliverance. That's my personal experience. I was only familiar with the Methodist and Trinity. Changing was hard because I was deceived by false teachings.

Galatians 3:1 O foolish Galatians, who hath bewitched you, that ye should not obey the truth, before whose eyes Jesus Christ hath been evidently set forth, crucified among you?

The act of someone teaching or speaking into your ear has the potential to influence your life. You'll be under their control without being aware of it. You will experience the emotions, thoughts, and behaviors that they desire. A person's transformation is influenced by a spirit. If the spirit is evil, it has the power to enchant you. If it's a good Spirit, it will guide you towards complete truth. We have received the Holy Spirit from our God. God grants the Holy Spirit to instruct and direct you towards complete truth. It's up to you, if you're willing. Spirit is involved when your behavior changes.

Acts 8:9 But there was a certain man, called Simon, which before time in the same city used sorcery, and bewitched the people of Samaria, giving out that himself was some great one: 10 To whom they all gave heed, from the least to the greatest, saying, This man is the great power of God. 11 And to him they had regard because that of a long time he had bewitched them with sorceries.

People have the ability to cast a spell on you without your awareness. Once the person moves away from your ear, you can think clearly. The motive of bewitching is not always good! When someone, whether a friend, mother, preacher, false teacher, false prophet, or anyone else, influences you with evil teachings, make a quick escape. They are capable of taking away your joy, life, and salvation. Women must be mindful, as it has a stronger influence on them compared to men. We must be cautious about who we lend our ears to. I have a great love for the truth. Once you have the truth, then you have freedom. Safety is found in following the Holy Spirit's leading, guiding, and teaching. You can be charmed by someone who is very close to you. Just because someone shows up at your door or contacts you don't guarantee their intentions are good. If someone is wicked, perceive them and make sure to keep your distance. My mom possessed a discerning spirit and cautioned us about whom to avoid. It has rescued me from a multitude of difficulties. Although I didn't comprehend it back then, I consistently valued her counseling and discernment.

Ephesians 4:11 And he gave some, apostles; and some, prophets; and some, evangelists; and some, pastors and teachers; 12 For the perfecting of the saints, for the work of the ministry, for the edifying of the body of Christ: 13 Till we all come in the unity of the faith, and of the knowledge of the Son of God, unto a perfect man, unto the measure of the stature of the ministry, for the edifying of the body of Christ: 15 But speaking the truth in love, may grow up into him in all things, which is the head, even Christ: 16 From whom the whole body fitly joined together and compacted by that which every joint supplieth, according to the effectual working in the measure of every part, maketh increase of the body unto the edifying of itself in love.

If God had sent the apostles, evangelists, pastors, teachers, and prophets, we wouldn't be facing any issues. We will stay safe from being bewitched. The reason for being controlled is a lack of knowledge. If your emotions are engaged or you lack experience or are gullible, you can easily be charmed. It is dangerous for your life if you did not have a perception of right from wrong.

It is common for individuals to seek personal advantages. It's difficult to believe that pastors, teachers, mothers, brothers, fathers, or friends would ever do anything wrong. It is the fact that they could be the most dangerous. Yes, they are those who can do the most harm for personal advantages. Paul was sent by

AUGUST 31

God to assist in the construction of numerous congregations. His motivation did not involve seeking personal gain. He was winning them to heaven. In a different part of the world, he desired to enter The Kingdom and claim the soul he was winning. False teachers lacked the understanding of Jesus Christ's earthly arrival as our savior when approaching new believers. False prophets and teachers began ensnaring his holy followers. Today, there are many organizations, denominations, and non-denominations that have been built on false doctrine.

In order to establish a doctrine, evidence from two or three scriptures is necessary. Lord has a prescribed format to follow. There was a principle that Jesus was unable to violate. Failure to follow the principle results in being bewitched. Be mindful of not falling under the spell of false teachers and prophets. Amen God bless you!

LET US PRAY

Lord, we thank you for the Word of God. We thank you for all that is written and taught in the Word. We must follow as your word says. Follow the prophet's apostle's teaching. We love your ways since it is true. The truth sets us free. No hustle or tussle if we have the truth. Our God is good and knows how to take care of us. Lore, you are a true shepherd who knows how to take care of the sheep. Lord, send us the true shepherd since many are hireling. They see drugs, alcohol, lies, cigars, and many others tormenting the sheep, but can't help because they are not the hirelings or hire laborers. Help us love the truth, so no wicked person has the power to bewitch us. We love the truth and let your truth set us free in Jesus 'name. Amen! God bless you!

ABOUT THE AUTHOR

Hello, I am Elizabeth Das Author of the Book Daily Spiritual Diet a devotional for each day and I did it His Way. As I mentioned I am not the author

but I obeyed the voice of the Lord to write.

Daily Spiritual Diet is a series of 12 months in English, Hindi, and Gujarati, Italian, French, and coming soon 26 languages

My books are published in different languages. The English name is, I did it 'His Way'.

The French name is : Je l'ai fait à "sa manière" The Spanish name is 'Lo hice a " a Su manera "

Gujarati name is 'me te temni rite karyu'.... '☐☐☐ ☐☐

☐☐☐☐☐ ☐☐☐☐ ☐☐☐☐☐☐'

Hindi name is 'Maine uske tarike se kiya'…'☐☐☐☐☐

☐☐☐☐ ☐☐☐☐☐ ☐☐ ☐☐☐☐'

It is also narrated in different languages. Praying to see you saved and most important you find hope.

May Lord Bless you.

ELIZABETH DAS

nimmidas@gmail.com, nimmidas1952@gmail.com